T0319896

Judgment and Leadership

NEW HORIZONS IN LEADERSHIP STUDIES

Series Editor: Joanne B. Ciulla, *Academic Director, Institute for Ethical Leadership and Professor of Leadership Ethics, Department of Management and Global Business, Rutgers Business School, USA*

This important series is designed to make a significant contribution to the development of leadership studies. This field has expanded dramatically in recent years and the series provides an invaluable forum for the publication of high quality works of scholarship and shows the diversity of leadership issues and practices around the world.

The main emphasis of the series is on the development and application of new and original ideas in leadership studies. It pays particular attention to leadership in business, economics and public policy and incorporates the wide range of disciplines which are now part of the field. Global in its approach, it includes some of the best theoretical and empirical work with contributions to fundamental principles, rigorous evaluations of existing concepts and competing theories, historical surveys and future visions.

Titles in the series include:

Judgment and Leadership

A Multidisciplinary Approach to Concepts, Practice, and Development

Edited by

Anna B. Kayes

Professor of Management, Department of Business Administration, Brown School of Business and Leadership, Stevenson University, USA

D. Christopher Kayes

Professor of Management, Department of Management, School of Business, The George Washington University, USA

NEW HORIZONS IN LEADERSHIP STUDIES

Edward Elgar
PUBLISHING

Cheltenham, UK • Northampton, MA, USA

Published by
Edward Elgar Publishing Limited
The Lypiatts
15 Lansdown Road
Cheltenham
Glos GL50 2JA
UK

Edward Elgar Publishing, Inc.
William Pratt House
9 Dewey Court
Northampton
Massachusetts 01060
USA

A catalogue record for this book
is available from the British Library

Library of Congress Control Number: 2021944952

This book is available electronically in the **Elgar**online
Business subject collection
http://dx.doi.org/10.4337/9781839104107

ISBN 978 1 83910 409 1 (cased)
ISBN 978 1 83910 410 7 (eBook)

Printed and bound by CPI Group (UK) Ltd, Croydon, CR0 4YY

To Ben and Braden

Contents

Contributors

Soon Ang, Nanyang Technological University, Singapore

Georgios Christopoulos, Nanyang Technological University, Singapore

Mary Crossan, Western University, Canada

Matthew Eriksen, Providence College, USA

Roseanne J. Foti, Virginia Tech, USA

Katy Fulfer, University of Waterloo, Canada

Rita A. Gardiner, Western University, Canada

Anna B. Kayes, Stevenson University, USA

D. Christopher Kayes, The George Washington University, USA

Markus Kornprobst, Vienna School of International Studies, Austria

Matthijs Moorkamp, Radboud University Nijmegen, the Netherlands

Michael D. Mumford, University of Oklahoma, USA

Vignesh R. Murugavel, University of Nebraska, USA

Tanner Newbold, University of Oklahoma, USA

Brenda Nguyen, University of Lethbridge, Canada

Kari A. O'Grady, Brigham Young University, USA

J. Douglas Orton, Center for Trauma Studies and Resilience Leadership, USA

Andrea Pittarello, Virginia Tech, USA

Terry L. Price, University of Richmond, USA

Roni Reiter-Palmon, University of Nebraska, USA

Thomas Rockstuhl, Nanyang Technological University, Singapore

Eugene Sadler-Smith, University of Surrey, UK

Chris Saunders, Lancaster University, UK

John P. Sullivan, The Brain Always Wins Consultancy, USA

E. Michelle Todd, Louisiana State University, USA

René Torenvlied, University of Twente, the Netherlands

1. Introduction to judgment and leadership

Anna B. Kayes and D. Christopher Kayes

Judgment and Leadership: A Multidisciplinary Approach to Concepts, Practice, and Development presents original thinking and addresses age-old concerns regarding the relationship between judgment and leadership. Judgment and leadership are inseparable. Judgment guides every action that a leader takes and underlies every thought, emotion, or justification that leaders form. This volume extends the study of judgment and leadership across disciplinary and conceptual boundaries.

For the first time, the most original and influential thinkers on judgment and leadership contribute to a single volume. The contributors represent a diverse set of disciplines, including critical studies, psychology, political theory, international policy, adult learning theory, management and organizational studies, philosophy, cross-cultural studies, and neuroscience. The result is an engaging look at one of the most important issues facing organizations, politics, and society: leaders and their judgment. The belief that judgment is important in leadership has been discussed (Shotter and Tsoukas, 2014; Tichy and Bennis, 2007a, 2007b) and has long been associated with how leaders solve problems and take action in the face of challenging situations (Dewey, 1933; Simon, 1973). Building on these ideas, the book offers a working definition of judgment that centers on the application of multiple sources of knowledge, including evidence, experience, and expertise, to solve practical problems. This definition sets the groundwork for the book. The book is organized around three questions:

- What is judgment and how is it formed and practiced by leaders?
- What barriers, blind spots, and other factors can lead to bad judgment?
- How do leaders learn to develop judgment?

Part I: Conceptualization and Processes of Leadership Judgment considers what it means to practice judgment by leaders. Judgment is discussed as it relates to cognition, neuroscience, character, political aspirations, and other factors.

Part II: Leadership Judgment Barriers, Blind Spots, and Bad Judgment looks primarily at factors that challenge leaders as they seek to make good judgments. Hubris, the inability to feel regret, lack of awareness of self-interests, situational variables, and context are among the factors that conspire to limit judgment.

Part III: Developing and Learning Leadership Judgment describes how leaders can cultivate better judgment and provides examples of how they learn and develop better judgment. Development and learning have particular relevance in these chapters that discuss a cross-cultural, interpersonal, crisis, and academic context.

WHY A BOOK ON JUDGMENT AND LEADERSHIP

Despite differences in views on how to cultivate judgment, there is growing consensus around the fact that judgment is an essential component of leadership (see Akinci and Sadler-Smith, 2019; Graduate Management Admissions Council, 2016; Mintzberg, 2004; Vickers, 1984). Yet the role of judgment in the practice and development of leadership is not well understood. This book offers insights into how judgment is enacted in contemporary leadership studies in at least two important ways.

First, the book helps both integrate judgment with and differentiate judgment from similar concepts and ideas. Judgment is often confused with topics such as decision-making, critical thinking (Errington and Bubna-Litic, 2015), practical wisdom (Wittmer and Fukami, 2017), and procedural knowledge. Further, there are a number of similar concepts associated with, but distinct from, judgment. Klein's (2015) naturalistic decision-making, Schon's (1983) reflective practice, and Sternberg's (Sternberg et al., 2000; Sternberg and Hedlund, 2002) practical intelligence all overlap with but also inform our understanding of judgment. From a developmental perspective, judgment also overlaps with discussions of expertise and its development (see Carter, 2013; Ericsson and Lehmann, 1996; Franklin, 2013) as well as learning from experience (Kolb and Kolb, 2005) and integrative thinking (Tetlock, 1994). This book provides a promising forum for making elements of judgment explicit in leadership and providing a basis for the development of judgment in leaders, especially when they face difficult and complex problems.

Further, leadership studies have tended to focus on techniques and outline essential competencies. A quick review of the research yields a list of competencies and techniques: negotiation, perception management, communication, motivation, and others. But, while leadership techniques are important, exercising judgment—which includes combining experience, knowledge, understanding of when to use techniques, and discernment of the right context for the techniques—becomes even more critical for understanding how leaders respond when faced with problems. This book, therefore, not only addresses how to demonstrate judgment, but also deals with questions regarding under what conditions judgment is most vulnerable and under what situations leaders are most likely to be in conflict about what is considered the "right" judgment.

Leadership scholars answer questions about the how, when, and where of judgment from significantly different viewpoints. In this edited volume, we showcase the diversity of thought on judgment and leadership to extend existing understanding and offer new insights. The volume will appeal to scholars, instructors, and others who focus on leadership, including organizational behavior, management, human resource management, higher education, and organizational development. Anyone interested in how leaders form, practice, and develop judgments will find the book an invaluable collection of the latest thinking on the topic.

THEMES ON JUDGMENT AND LEADERSHIP COVERED IN THE BOOK

The volume highlights concepts that are novel to many readers. For example, judgment involves deciphering "seeds versus weeds" (Chapter 6), invokes "dirty hands" (Chapter 9), and requires navigating "disjunctures" (Chapter 13). Judgment can be illustrated through a leader's response to "cosmology episodes" (Chapter 11), monitored through subtle eye tracking (in controlled settings) (Chapter 10), and captured in justification circuits (Chapter 5). The insights are often provocative, such as the idea that a better understanding of judgment comes through an analysis of leadership in the context of totalitarianism (Chapter 4).

Familiar ideas are reinterpreted. For example, Aristotle's notion of *phronesis*, often translated as practical wisdom, is a theme that appears in multiple chapters of the book as a way to understand how leaders exercise judgment. This book reinforces the contemporary relevance of terms like *phronesis*. Cognitive skills play a key role in our understanding of judgment (Chapter 2) as leaders navigate the complexity associated with ill-structured problems (Chapter 15). Even with the tools at leaders' disposal, judgment remains a "best guess" in a complex world (Chapter 7).

Other themes suggest that judgment requires an understanding of a leader's metacognitive processes (e.g., judgments about judgments). Judgment requires leaders to exercise both self-knowledge (Chapter 12) and knowledge of others. Character is key to judgment (Chapter 3). Leaders build judgment through experience as well as through formal education (Chapter 14). At the same time, leadership requires understanding that too much experience, or the wrong experience, can breed hubris (Chapter 8) and degrade judgment.

What is not found in this book is also noteworthy. The academic study of judgment has been dominated by quantitative approaches to judgment, often captured under the heading of judgment and decision-making (see, for example, Bazerman, 2002). While quantitative approaches deserve recognition, we believe this is well-covered territory. Even quantitative data are open to interpretation, representation, and rationalization. This volume, therefore, takes the deliberate position that discernment of data is more important than computation. This does not suggest the book is devoid of systematic study grounded in the behavioral and social sciences. In fact, several authors introduce studies and recommend future directions for the study of judgment and leadership based on systematic studies. Indeed, laboratory studies from psychology or neuroscience, qualitative readings, and content analysis, as well as cross-sectional studies conducted in organizations, all provide foundational insights. Yet we focus here on how systematic study informs our overall understanding of the relationship between judgment and leadership.

In discussions of judgment, everything is open for deliberation. Even the spelling of the term meets with disagreement. We have chosen the more common usage in the United States, "judgment," for the title. The alternative spelling "judgement," also a widely accepted term in British English, is used within some of the chapters. This illustrates a larger theme of the book, understanding judgment as a multidisciplinary study.

Definitions of judgment vary throughout the book as well. More than half a century ago, Herb Simon recognized the challenges of coming up with a unified approach to judgment. In organizations, multiple individuals formulate problems, which leaves evaluation and implementation of problems and their solutions open to interpretation from multiple perspectives (March and Simon, 1958). Negotiation and power dynamics within the organization shape what constitutes a "right decision," and the right interpretation of evidence shifts over time (Trank, 2014). Definitions of judgment vary greatly, from focusing on epistemological concerns (Shotter and Tsoukas, 2014) or moral uncertainty (Kohlberg, 1969) to more decidedly rationalist perspectives (Rousseau, 2012).

We also acknowledge the difficult times during which this volume was composed. Many if not all of the authors wrote their chapters during the COVID-related lockdown and subsequent containment. These events played an obvious role in the minds of several authors, and they view judgment through the shadow of the COVID epidemic.

In addition to the necessary focus on COVID-related examples, the chapters rely on a host of examples that inform our understanding of judgment and leadership. The book features political leaders, U.S. federal law enforcement officers, business leaders, and university administrators, among others. Multiple references to current and historical events serve as cautious reminders that a leader's judgment can come with real consequences. Examples of leaders exercising (good and bad) judgment include George Floyd's death, a CNN news crew being arrested, seven people shot in Louisville protesting George Floyd's death, accusations of espionage and violation of Hong Kong's freedom, terminating relations with the World Health Organization, Enron and the financial crisis of 2008, the lead up to and continuation of the war in Iraq, the shootdown of Malaysian Air Flight MH17, the politics of aid bills to address the economic consequences of the COVID-19 pandemic, and climate change denial.

CONTRIBUTIONS TO THE BOOK

Todd, Newbold, and Mumford, in the chapter "Cognition Counts: Cognitive Skills Contributing to Leader Judgment," emphasize leaders as master problem-solvers, those who are willing to take on and solve problems that others cannot. They emphasize cognitive skills and their influence on performance outcomes. Judgment means judging "the adequacy of the given problem solution." Nine skills are offered: (1) problem definition, (2) cause/goal analysis, (3) constraint analysis, (4) planning, (5) forecasting, (6) creative thinking, (7) idea evaluation, (8) wisdom, and (9) sensemaking.

These cognitive factors can be measured and, thus, leaders find a ready set of tools to help them develop these skills. The authors also mention that the list of nine cognitive skills is not exhaustive and take the position that an emphasis on individual leadership rather than social skills may be the most valuable in discussions of judgment. The chapter provides an engaging set of variables that help frame the overall discussions of judgment that follow in later chapters.

Nguyen and Crossan, in their chapter "Character-Infused Judgment and Decision Making," make the case for including virtue ethics and character in discussions of judgment. The extensive research on judgment and decision-making provides deep insights into judgment and leaders, but research that relies on rational decision-making in the form of probabilities, measurements, and other quantitatively driven processes is inferior to character-driven judgment given the answers leaders need when facing real-life situations. Judgment and decision-making is like a blunt instrument that can be used to achieve a goal. It says little about what goals the leader should be achieving, nor does it address the role of ethics in pursuit of the goal. Character is important because it helps guide leaders in both the development and practice of judgment.

Nguyen and Crossan describe a variety of character-based habits associated with the character-infused leader, including transcendence, drive, collaboration, humanity, humility, integrity, temperance, justice, accountability, and courage. The leader can learn to cultivate character, but the leader needs to be aware of the need to learn and must be intentional about developing these character-based habits.

Gardiner and Fulfer's chapter, "The Judgment of Arendt," shows how the philosophy of Hannah Arendt can help us understand judgment and leadership in the context of mandated use of masks as a preventive measure for the spread of COVID. Arendt's concerns were primarily about the rise and acceptance of totalitarianism in Europe. Yet, in the chapter, themes emerge that relate to current times: Former president Donald Trump was reported to have considered instituting martial law in order to remain in power.

Gardiner and Fulfer's reading of Arendt sheds light on our thinking about judgment and leadership. Lack of judgment is not the result of evil but banality, a lack of empathy for others. Judgment results from courage and the ability to consider the viewpoint of others. Leaders are representative of a "collective political experience." Judgment is born through years of experience, which is held up for judgment by followers, as such judgment results when a leader tries to understand the perspective of others. Thus, leadership judgment results from thinking about process (rather than simply about outcomes), considering diverse viewpoints, and engaging in reflective practice. This chapter highlights how philosophy can help us understand the basic assumptions associated with how we view a leader's judgment and evaluate its value.

Kornprobst, in "Judgments and Justifications," considers COVID and leadership in terms of the consequences of leaders' judgments. He frames the chapter in terms of judgment in international political leadership and its role in consequential policy and political decisions. Leaders, like all humans, work within various limitations. Leaders have free will, but that free will is caught up in "circuits" that are capped by prejudgments, taken-for-granted assumptions, and justifications of actions. Kornprobst argues against discipline-specific reasoning, explaining that judgment involves identifying "repertoires" of possible judgments that are social in nature and not discipline specific, "justifying" or communicating those judgments to others and one's self, and developing structures that support those justifications.

Kornprobst argues that because of the complexity associated with leadership, both leader and follower remain in flux about the right judgment. To be a leader (or a follower, for that matter) requires accepting the constant shifting interpretations of judgments and justifications. We might find that our judgments of leaders appear inconsistent, especially if we apply a rationalist lens. However, our search for consistency will be futile if we don't consider the vast influences and ever-changing nature of what we evaluate as good judgment.

Murugavel and Reiter-Palmon, in "How Leaders Judge Creativity: A Look into the Idea Evaluation Process," describe judgment as a creative process tied to innovation. At its core, judgment is understood by distinguishing "seeds versus weeds." Seeds are those innovative ideas that can flourish in an organization, and weeds are those ideas that are less likely to foster real long-term sustainable innovation. Judgment involves being able to distinguish between the two and is demonstrated in a process called "idea evaluation," which in turn is a subprocess of creative problem-solving.

Murugavel and Reiter-Palmon emphasize evaluating the outcome of leadership judgment by considering judgment as a dependent variable. This chapter provides an example of how we might evaluate outcomes that are associated with judgment in leaders through forecasts. Forecasts involve several dimensions; creativity, thinking, accuracy, and implementation are a few of the potential outcomes we might use to evaluate leaders on their judgment. Leaders, managers, and others exercise judgments that can be evaluated primarily by the future outcomes of their judgments. A partial list of variables to consider when evaluating judgment includes individual characteristics, individual states, and situational influences.

Sullivan, in the chapter "Judgment and Decision Making: A 'Brain-First' Perspective," provides a practice-inspired research agenda on judgment from a brain perspective. Despite the growing influence of neuroscience research in judgment, the extensive findings in this area have been slow to influence our understanding of leadership and judgment. Sullivan provides a path forward. Of particular help in integrating brain science with judgment is his focus on dynamic systems. The benefit of using a dynamic systems perspective is that it offers an alternative to the reductionism that plagues much of the neuroscience field. The brain is primary, according to Sullivan's brain-first approach, but it operates within a complex system. Importantly, it is how we make judgments in a team context that offers the most insight into judgment. Through the eyes of neuroscience, judgment needs to be understood in light of the emotional content of judgment, not just rational thinking.

His chapter brings up a fascinating yet simple question: What effect do physical factors and the status of various bodily functions have on judgment? He ultimately suggests that stress, focus, self-regulation, heart rate variability, and even hydration can help us understand the connection between judgment and leadership.

In his chapter, "Hubris, Bad Judgement, and Practical Wisdom in Politics and Business," Sadler-Smith is concerned with hubris, simply stated as leaders' overconfidence in their own ability to exercise judgment. Hubris is important for judgment because judgment, as a form of decision-making and action-taking in the face of ambiguity, often leads to disastrous consequences: the market crash of 2008, the invasion of Iraq, the handling of COVID-19, and multiple business examples. The thing about hubris is that it is acquired over time. As they acquire more and more power, leaders may be at particular risk. What might start as desirable traits, such as ambition and a desire for influence, become excessive over time. Ultimately, lapses in judgment ensue. In this way, hubris is viewed as an excess of leadership, where desirable qualities may go too far, resulting in impaired judgment.

Leaders overcome hubris by balancing excess and deficiency. Too much of the stuff that makes up good leadership (e.g., the desire for change, the need for power, and confidence and striving) can lead to bad judgments. But failure to have enough of the good stuff means being ineffective and perhaps even failing to achieve status as a leader at all. When leaders get the formula right, they are more likely to move in the direction of good judgment.

Price, in "Feeling and Dirty Hands: The Role of Regret Experienced by Responsible Agents," addresses justification of past actions in light of a leader's own sense of responsibility for the consequences of those actions. He invokes the notion of "dirty hands," the situation where a leader makes the "right" or desirable judgment, but the judgment is morally wrong at the same time. Price makes a promising proposition that requires some paradoxical thinking. The dirty hands phenomenon occurs when leaders contemplate a past judgment. Dirty hands leave leaders feeling regret that they had to take the action. But they also remain convinced that the action was necessary. Thus, dirty hands suggest that a judgment can be both morally wrong and defensible at the same time. Adding to the paradox, leaders often fail to experience regret. They find it easier to convince themselves that they were justified in their action than to struggle with the consequences. When leaders include in their process of making judgments "defense of others and the consent of followers," they come closer to exercising exemplary judgment.

As with other chapters, Price makes note of the importance of context in making judgments. Committing an immoral act such as murder is different than the moral transgression associated with making a business or political deal that you never intend to fulfill. Leaders must learn to navigate the moral ambiguity inherent in the power and politics associated with leadership. Thus, leadership requires making judgments in light of multiple competing (moral) commitments. Further, the role one plays in an organization (e.g., a faculty member versus an administrator, employee versus CEO) may bind the leader in some way to different moral obligations (e.g., the welfare of individual students versus the welfare of an institution).

Pittarello and Foti, in "Context Corrupts: What Makes Leaders Fail to See Their (Mis) behaviors," also consider the ethical elements associated with leaders and their judgments. They show connections between judgment and leadership and behavioral ethics, the study of closely observed behaviors associated with making ethical choices. Here, judgment is a social-cognitive balancing act, say between maintaining a positive self-concept of oneself as honest while simultaneously engaging in activity that is dishonest.

Pittarello and Foti reveal data about how and when leaders justify judgments. They present the results of a number of laboratory studies that provide an excellent example of how methods such as eye tracking can enhance understanding of judgment. In one study, they identify the information that leaders pay attention to and what they ignore when making judgments. This captures not just how leaders reach judgments, but how they justify these judgments retroactively.

In their chapter, "Resilience Leadership Judgment: Findings from a Cosmology Episode Study of the Shootdown of Flight MH17," O'Grady, Moorkamp, Torenvlied, and Orton conduct a detailed analysis of the shootdown of Malaysian Air Flight MH17 and the subsequent government response. The study shows how variants of sensemaking are associated with judgment and the importance of judgment in extreme situations. They discuss "cosmology episodes," situations that become senseless, in the sense that sense is no longer a given. But even when sense no longer exists, leaders must still sensibly find ways to exercise judgment. The words are important. The word *cosmology* provides the sense that the universe as the leader knows it no longer seems to exist. At the same time, the word *episode* suggests that the situation offers a comfortable range of possible sensible judgments in which the world can be made meaningful. This also implies that the range of meaning is limited, or bracketed, by a leader's capacity for judgment.

The study shows that crises are not always easily detected in pre-crisis events and that judgments are as much about retrospective consideration as future anticipation. Discipline-specific knowledge seldom provides enough background to make sense of crisis. These are just a few of the counterintuitive insights found in the chapter.

Ang, Rockstuhl, and Christopoulos, in "Cultural Intelligence and Leadership Judgment & Decision Making: Ethnology and Capabilities," propose a model of leadership judgment based on cultural intelligence. Leaders do not just shape culture; a leader's judgment is shaped by culture as well. They outline four capabilities for improving judgment in leadership— motivational, cognitive, metacognitive, and behavioral—which in turn comprise six leadership processes that are tied to judgment: formulating a vision, communicating the vision, planning and budgeting, designing the organizational structure, influencing and motivating, and monitoring and controlling.

While Ang, Rockstuhl, and Christopoulos emphasize the generalizability of their model, they take important steps to show the cultural element associated with each process. The model contributes to understanding leadership judgment by suggesting clear competencies that leaders can develop to exercise better judgment. This moves the discussion of leadership, culture, and judgment from discussions of "cultural comparison" to "intercultural capabilities."

In "Disjuncture and Development: A Learning Theory Approach to Leadership Judgement," Saunders sharpens our focus on how a leader's "guiding principles" impact judgment. The problem (although Saunders does not really state this as a problem to overcome) is that leaders are often unconscious of their own guiding principles, unaware of the values driving their judgment. Only with intervention or deep reflection do these guiding principles become explicit in the minds of the leaders. The underlying guiding principles of judgment, therefore, are unconscious and tacit, and only by making them explicit can a leader improve judgment.

Writing from the perspective of adult learning, Saunders reviews the various contributions that adult learning theory makes to our understanding of judgment. The emphasis is on the development of judgment, or as Saunders asks, "How do leaders learn to lead?" Experiences, especially those of "disjuncture," when leaders realize they don't know something, form the basis of our judgment.

Eriksen, in "On Facilitating the Development of Leaders' Ability to Exercise Good Judgment," sees relationships as essential for judgment. In one study he conducted, he quotes a federal worker who discussed exercising judgment in the context of relationships and in concert with others in a constantly changing situation or circumstance. Eriksen emphasizes not only the developmental nature of judgment (judgment is something leaders are continually learning), but also the existential nature of judgment (judgment is something that is inseparable from who the leader *is*). Eriksen describes how his approach to judgment informs his teaching and provides a narrative account of how he helps students realize their own capacity for judgment.

Kayes and Kayes, in "Improving Leader Judgment through Experiential Learning," also offer a look at how judgment is learned from experience. Their approach is prescriptive and suggests a model to bridge the academic/practice divide when it comes to learning judgment. They describe a four-process model (with several subprocesses) that helps students learn to exercise judgment in a classroom setting, but that can also be applied in more practical settings, such as the workplace. As in Saunders's chapter, the perspective is adult learning theory, but Kayes and Kayes embed their approach more specifically in Kolb's experiential learning theory and the learning cycle. One of their goals is practical: to provide a model to guide students as they exercise judgment, mainly to improve it as they face more complex problems. Another goal is theoretical: to advance ideas associated with teaching and learning judgment.

In summary, these chapters capture the diversity of perspectives that make up the multidisciplinary study of judgment and leadership. Readers will be rewarded with new insights into how judgment is conceived, how leaders exercise judgment, what prevents judgment, and how leaders learn judgment. Taken as a whole, these chapters show that leaders need to reach beyond their disciplinary training and limited experience to improve judgment. By viewing judgment from multiple perspectives, the contributors reveal the significance of judgment as a leadership process, which will further invigorate the study of judgment and leadership.

REFERENCES

Akinci, C., and Sadler-Smith, E. (2019). Collective intuition: Implications for improved decision making and organizational learning. *British Journal of Management*, *30*(3), 558–577. https://doi.org/10.1111/1467-8551.12269.

Bazerman, M. (2002). *Judgment in managerial decision making* (5th ed.). Wiley.

Carter, L., II. (2013). Developing expertise in management decision making. *Academy of Strategic Management Journal, 12*(1), 21–37.

Dewey, J. (1933). *How we think: A restatement of the relations of reflective thinking to the educative process.* Heath.

Ericsson, K. A., and Lehmann, A. C. (1996). Expert and exceptional performance: Evidence of maximal adaptation to task constraints. *Annual Review of Psychology, 47*(1), 273–305. https://doi.org/10.1146/annurev.psych.47.1.273.

Errington, A., and Bubna-Litic, D. (2015). Management by textbook: The role of textbooks in developing critical thinking. *Journal of Management Education, 39*, 774–800. https://doi.org/10.1177/1052562915594839.

Franklin, C. L., II. (2013). Developing expertise in management decision-making. *Academy of Strategic Management Journal, 12*(1), 21–37.

Graduate Management Admissions Council. (2016). *Integrated reasoning: Critical skills for today's business environment.* http://www.gmac.com/market-intelligence-and-research/research-insights/curriculum-and-delivery/integrated-reasoning.aspx.

Klein, G. (2015). A naturalistic decision making perspective on studying intuitive decision making. *Journal of Applied Research in Memory and Cognition, 4*, 164–168. https://doi.org/10.1016/j.jarmac.2015.07.001.

Kohlberg, L. (1969). Stages and sequences: The cognitive-developmental approach to socialization. In D. A. Goslin (Ed.), *Handbook of socialization theory and research* (pp. 347–380). Rand McNally.

Kolb, A., and Kolb, D. (2005). Learning styles and learning spaces: Enhancing experiential learning in higher education. *Academy of Management Learning and Education, 4*, 193–212. https://doi.org/10.5465/amle.2005.17268566.

March, J. G., and Simon, H. A. (1958). *Organizations.* John Wiley & Sons.

Mintzberg, H. (2004). *Managers, not MBAs.* Pearson Education.

Rousseau, D. M. (Ed.). (2012). *The Oxford handbook of evidence-based management.* Oxford University Press. https://doi.org/10.1093/oxfordhb/9780199763986.001.0001.

Schon, D. A. (1983). *The reflective practitioner: How professionals think in action.* Basic Books.

Shotter, J., and Tsoukas, H. (2014). In search of *phronesis*: Leadership and the art of judgment. *Academy of Management Learning and Education, 13*, 224–243. https://doi.org/10.5465/amle.2013.0201.

Simon, H. (1973). The structure of ill-structured problems. *Artificial Intelligence, 4*, 181–201. https://doi.org/10.1016/0004-3702(73)90011-8.

Sternberg, R. J., Forsythe, G. B., Hedlund, J., Horvath, J. A., Wagner, R. K., and Williams, W. M. (2000). *Practical intelligence in everyday life.* Cambridge University Press.

Sternberg, R. J., and Hedlund, J. (2002). Practical intelligence, g, and work psychology. *Human Performance, 15*(1–2), 143–160. https://doi.org/10.1207/S15327043HUP1501&02_09.

Tetlock, P. E. (1994). Integrative complexity. In M. Hewstone and A. S. R. Manstead (Eds.), *Dictionary of social psychology* (pp. 326–328). Blackwell.

Tichy, N. M., and Bennis, W. G. (2007a). *Judgment: How winning leaders make great calls.* Penguin.

Tichy, N. M., and Bennis, W. G. (2007b). Making judgment calls. The ultimate act of leadership. *Harvard Business Review, 85*(10), 94–102, 165.

Trank, C. Q. (2014). "Reading" evidence-based management: The possibilities of interpretation. *Academy of Management Learning and Education, 13*, 381–395. https://doi.org/10.5465/amle.2013.0244.

Vickers, G. (1984). Judgment. In G. Vickers and The Open Systems Group (Eds.), *The Vickers papers* (pp. 230–245). Harper & Row.

Wittmer, D. W., and Fukami, C. V. (2017). Educating future business leaders to be practically wise: Designing an MBA curriculum to strengthen good decision-making. In O. Gunnlaugson and W. Kupers (Eds.), *Wisdom learning: Perspectives on wising up in management education* (pp. 229–247). Routledge.

PART I

Conceptualization and processes of leadership judgment

2. Cognition counts: cognitive skills contributing to leader judgment

E. Michelle Todd, Tanner Newbold and Michael D. Mumford

Over the past few decades, an abundance of literature has been devoted to examining leader performance. Multiple models of leadership have been proposed, with models emphasizing the leader as a teacher (e.g., transformational leadership), the leader as a politician (e.g., charismatic leadership), the leader as a warrior (e.g., ethical leadership), and the leader as a problem-solver (e.g., leader initiating structure) (Zaccaro, 2014; Mumford et al., 2017). Recently, the approach to understanding leadership from a problem-solving perspective has garnered great support, with its proponents emphasizing that we may better understand leaders from the ways in which they solve the complex problems that they face (Mumford et al., 2017; Mumford and Higgs, 2020a). In fact, the importance of the leadership role is highlighted by the need for someone—the leader—to solve problems when others cannot. More specifically, when people are presented with a highly complex problem, they bring the problem to the leader for guidance, discretion, and/or a solution (Mumford and Higgs, 2020b). Thus, leaders require the capacity to solve complex problems in a distinctly social context (e.g., the team or firm). This kind of social problem-solving is a form of complex cognition, requiring the application of certain cognitive skills to bolster leader performance.

Indeed, it has been argued that the cognitive skills leaders apply are "perhaps the most powerful" predictor of successful performance (Mumford and Higgs, 2020b, p. 3). This argument has received strong support, with evidence demonstrating the significance of a variety of complex cognitive skills to effective leadership (e.g., Marcy and Mumford, 2007; Marta et al., 2005; Martin et al., 2019; Watts et al., 2019). For example, a study assessing the performance of 1,807 Army leaders found that cognitive skills, such as creative thinking and social judgment, were strongly positively related to leader performance (Connelly et al., 2000). Notably, a follow-up study examined how these skills predicted continuance in the Army 20 years later, with continuance serving as a marker of good performance (Zaccaro et al., 2015). Findings were that these skills significantly predicted continuance over a 20-year period, suggesting that cognitive skills are reliable predictors of leader performance. Moreover, models seeking to explain how leaders make decisions and solve problems have focused on cognition, with cognitive skills such as forecasting and planning being emphasized as particularly important to effective leadership (Mumford et al., 2007, 2017). Therefore, the cognitive skills predictive of performance should be a key concern of leaders and researchers alike.

Subsequently, the question becomes: Which cognitive skills are predictive of leader performance? In a model developed by Mumford et al. (2017), they argued that there are nine critical skills that leaders may apply to improve their performance. Leaders should be skilled at (1) problem definition, (2) cause/goal analysis, (3) constraint analysis, (4) planning, (5) forecasting, (6) creative thinking, (7) idea evaluation, (8) wisdom, and (9) sensemaking. Theoretical and empirical support for the pertinence of these skills to leader performance has been provided across a number of studies, with studies suggesting that controlled and conscious cognitive analysis enables leaders to make better decisions and may even improve their judgment (e.g., Antes and Mumford, 2012; Marcy and Mumford, 2010; Shipman et al., 2010; Strange and Mumford, 2005; Todd et al., 2019). However, when scanning the research on these skills, it becomes apparent that research has largely focused on general leader performance and problem-solving. It has been suggested that these skills are also predictive of leader judgment, but the distinct relationship between cognitive skills and leader judgment is unclear. Thus, this chapter examines leader judgment relative to cognitive skills and expands upon the cognitive skills that may best serve leader judgment.

LEADER JUDGMENT

In order to ascertain which cognitive skills are relevant to leader judgment, we must consider the definition of "judgment." Countless definitions and conceptualizations of judgment have been provided, with judgment being defined as a context-dependent decision-making process (Tichy and Bennis, 2007), a cognitive process which includes making critical distinctions and drawing conclusions through assessment and deliberation (Kirkebøen, 2009), or the process of using past experience and knowledge to analyze the potential consequences of a decision (Priest, 1988). Notably, in some of the most referenced scholarly articles on judgment, judgment is not explicitly defined or is used interchangeably with "decision making" (e.g., Einhorn and Hogarth, 1981; Tversky and Kahneman, 1974). However, in other research, judgment and decision making are distinctly and separately defined (e.g., Priest, 1988), with decisions and decision making typically being described as relevant to choice, and judgment referring to evaluation. Based on this multitude of definitions, it can be unclear what is meant when judgment is referenced. Cumulatively, our understanding of judgment is that it is the process of evaluating and deliberating a potential choice or solution. With this understanding, we then may ask: How does this definition of judgment apply to leadership? What is *leader judgment*?

In defining leader judgment, we must consider the actual role of the leader and when and how judgment is required. Leaders exercise social influence (Bass and Bass, 2009; Yukl, 2011). More specifically, leaders operate within a social context, where leaders must take into account social information and must understand that their actions will have consequences for the group, organization, stakeholders, or a broader social context (Mumford et al., 2000b; Tam et al., 2020). Importantly, a distinguishing factor of leader judgment from judgment in general is the evaluation of solutions presented by subordinates. For example, an R&D project manager may delegate a problem for a team to work on. Subsequently, the team will generate a solution to that problem and then present the solution to the manager to be judged. Then, the leader's task is to judge the adequacy of the given problem solution. Thus, leader judgment is evaluating presented problem solutions. This type of judgment is unique to leaders and has received little attention in the context of the literature on judgment in general. Therefore, we use this definition of leader judgment henceforth to examine how leaders may best execute this type of judgment vis-à-vis the application of cognitive skills.

COGNITIVE SKILLS AND LEADER JUDGMENT

The nine cognitive skills deemed critical to leader performance (listed earlier in this chapter) may also generally represent cognitive skills relevant to leader judgment. Though it is likely that all the cognitive skills contribute to leader judgment in some capacity, in this chapter we highlight the significance of four of these skills—goal analysis, constraint analysis, forecasting, and idea evaluation—as pertinent to effective leader judgment. When presented with a problem solution, leaders should analyze that solution with regard to its meeting of requisite goals (i.e., goal analysis) (Vessey et al., 2011; Caughron et al., 2020). Leaders need to be able to understand the goals operating within the team, organization, and society and ascertain which are relevant to the given problem solution. Then, they should judge the extent to which the problem solution meets those goals, while considering how goals may change over time. In addition to analyzing goals, leaders should engage in constraint analysis to make adequate judgments of problem solutions (Medeiros et al., 2017). A key facet of constraints is that they are malleable and may change over time (Acar et al., 2019). Therefore, the constraints bearing on the problem may change, new constraints may have been added, or old constraints may have been removed. As such, leaders should judge the adequacy of the problem solution vis-à-vis the state of current relevant constraints, while also considering that those constraints may change.

When judging problem solutions, leaders should also apply forecasting and idea evaluation skills (Mumford et al., 2015). With respect to forecasting, leaders should identify the downstream consequences and implications of the solution if it were implemented. What impact will the application of this solution have on the firm, customers, and relevant stakeholders? Adequately asking and answering this type of question should enable leaders to more deeply evaluate the solution presented and form a sound judgment. Relatedly, skill in idea evaluation allows leaders to determine the standards by which the solution should be judged and consider revisions that may be made to improve the solution (Watts et al., 2017).

Although there are limited studies explicitly examining the impact of goal analysis, constraint analysis, forecasting, and idea evaluation skills on leader judgment, research and theory regarding overall leader performance support the utility of these particular skills for leader judgment (Antes and Mumford, 2012; Mumford et al., 2017; Shipman and Mumford, 2011). Using this research as a guide, the following paragraphs examine these skills in greater depth and how they may contribute to leader judgment. These skills and their potential contributions to leader judgment are then summarized in Table 2.1.

Goal analysis. Goal analysis refers to the identification of potentially viable goals to be pursued from a larger set of objectives (Mumford et al., 2017). Goal analysis should not be confused with goal setting, which is an outcome of applying various leadership skills such as forecasting. During goal analysis, leaders must appraise the significance of goals, the merits of pursuing a goal in relation to other objectives, and system readiness for the pursuit of particular goals. Leaders can make sense of problems by appraising them with respect to goals (Berson and Avolio, 2004). Leaders should also consider the goals of subordinates, the team, the organization, stakeholders, and other relevant parties (Mumford et al., 2020).

Some support has been provided for the importance of goal analysis to leader performance. In a study conducted by Strange and Mumford (2005), undergraduate participants assumed the role of a leader of an experimental secondary school tasked with creating a plan for the school.

Prior to plan development, participants were given cases illustrating other educational interventions, with the cases being of either good or bad quality. Participants were then instructed to analyze these cases with respect to causes, goals, both, or neither. The strongest leader plans were obtained from participants who analyzed good cases with respect to causes, and bad cases with respect to goals. Thus, goal analysis supports leader performance, especially when prior events have gone poorly.

In another study, Shipman et al. (2010) asked undergraduate participants to assume the role of the leader of a high school and write a vision statement of their plans for the school. Prior to developing their vision statements, participants were provided with cases delineating other successful schools. Within these cases, a manipulation was embedded, such that the information provided encouraged participants to focus on isolated facts or implications of the case material. Participants were also asked to focus their vision statements on either their goals for the school, or on the causes of school performance. It was found that both goals and causes were useful in vision formation, with facts proving most useful when people think about goals. Thus, goal analysis also has positive implications for the development of effective leader visions.

In addition to improving overall leader performance and vision formation, goal analysis may be important to leader judgment. Goal analysis prompts the appraisal of goal attainment and the stability of goals (Mumford et al., 2017). In the context of leader judgment, this analysis is particularly useful. When a problem solution is presented to a leader, the leader should assess the solution based on its alignment to current and future goals, as well as stable and unstable goals. With greater skill in goal analysis, leaders are better able to analyze the extent to which a solution aligns with all relevant goals that have a meaningful impact, including project goals, organizational goals, and team goals. Thus, goal analysis should enable leaders to ascertain the impact a solution will have on key goals and promote more sound judgment.

Additionally, goal analysis is especially useful during crises or highly ambiguous situations—times in which effective leader judgment is critical. During crises or ambiguous situations, leaders are concerned with making sense of conflicting information and identifying which goals are most important (Caughron et al., 2020; Mumford et al., 2007; Weick, 1995). This can prove quite difficult, as different stakeholders are likely to have competing goals, and they may push leaders to prioritize variables they deem important (Bundy et al., 2013; Maitlis, 2005; Meer et al., 2017). In these situations, more extensive goal analysis is necessary to identify and assess the goals operating across multiple levels and multiple groups, in order to make an informed judgment.

Constraint analysis. A constraint is defined as a restriction or limitation in a given situation (Medeiros et al., 2014). Thus, many factors may serve as constraints, such as time (Byron et al., 2010) and financial resources (Lavie et al., 2010; Posen et al., 2018). For example, the financial resources one has to generate a solution act as a limitation with regard to the feasibility of its implementation. Researchers have also formed taxonomies of constraints, with constraints being labeled as input, output, or process constraints (Acar et al., 2019) or fundamental, thematic, information, and resource constraints (Medeiros et al., 2014). The development of these taxonomies points to a growing interest in identifying and understanding the impact that constraints have on complex performance, such as creative problem-solving and leader judgment. Some previous research suggests that constraints may negatively impact complex performance (e.g., Amabile, 1983; Amabile and Gryskiewicz, 1989; Friedman,

2009), whereas other research suggests that constraints may positively impact complex performance (e.g., Medeiros et al., 2014, 2018; Onarheim, 2012; Stokes, 2007). These conflicting results suggest that beyond the type of constraints, the way people handle constraints may be just as—if not more—important. Given that all problems are constrained in some manner (Medeiros et al., 2017), leaders must appropriately identify and analyze the constraints bearing on any problem.

Support for the impact of constraint analysis on leader performance has been provided in recent studies. In one study, Peterson et al. (2013) asked participants to work on Strange and Mumford's (2005) vision formation task. Prior to developing their visions, participants were provided training in constraint management. Participants were asked to manage and assess resource constraints, worker skill constraints, goal constraints, and system capability constraints. It was found that leader visions significantly improved following the constraint management training, suggesting that leaders may improve their visions when they adequately analyze constraints. In another study, Medeiros et al. (2014) asked 318 undergraduate participants to assume the role of a leader of an advertising firm and devise an advertising campaign for the firm. Prior to developing their campaigns, participants received an email from their supervisor which established certain constraints bearing on the situation. Results demonstrated that better campaigns were produced when the constraints presented were malleable and participants actually assessed and managed constraints, suggesting that leaders should analyze constraints in order to improve their performance.

An important facet of constraints is that they are not fixed—they are malleable and may change over time. Old constraints may be adjusted or removed, and new constraints may be added. To examine the impact of changing constraints, Medeiros et al. (2018) conducted an experiment manipulating when constraints were added during the creative problem-solving process. Specifically, participants assumed the role of a restaurant manager and were tasked with designing a new restaurant. Manipulations were embedded within the study, such that constraints were added at different stages of the creative problem-solving process. It was found that constraints introduced early in the process did not hinder creative problem-solving; however, constraints introduced during mid- and late-stage processes negatively impacted creative problem-solving. Thus, it is critical for leaders to monitor and analyze constraints during later stages and consider how the presence of different constraints influences both previous and future processes (Medeiros et al., 2020).

The malleability of constraints points to the importance of constraint analysis for leader judgment. As constraints can change over time, it may be particularly important for a leader to analyze constraints when engaging in judgment. When presented with a problem solution, the leader should assess if the solution adequately accounts for relevant constraints. Indeed, it has been argued that problem solutions should be evaluated within the boundaries set forth by constraints (Medeiros et al., 2020). Thus, leaders should ask: What are the current constraints bearing on the problem? Have constraints changed? Does the solution fit within the current constraints of the problem? Asking these types of questions and identifying any issues with solutions based on changes in constraints should help leaders better evaluate problem solutions. Thus, constraint analysis should improve leader judgment.

Forecasting. Another important cognitive skill is forecasting, which is the envisioning of potential outcomes resulting from actions that may be taken (Todd et al., 2019). As the mental simulation of the potential outcomes of future actions, it is not surprising that forecasting is critical to the evaluation of problem solutions and the planning of actions to be taken (Mumford and Higgs, 2020b). Indeed, studies have shown that forecasting skill helps leaders more successfully evaluate the implications of ideas and formulate viable plans for the implementation of ideas (Byrne et al., 2010; Shipman et al., 2010). Additionally, it has been found that people may forecast using different strategies to improve their forecasting skill and ultimately positively impact their performance on complex tasks (Osburn and Mumford, 2006; Todd et al., 2019).

Recent studies examining forecasting skill have emphasized its importance for leaders. For example, Shipman et al. (2010) evaluated the strategies that leaders use when they forecast, and how strategies impact leader visions. In this study, participants completed the Strange and Mumford (2005) task, which asked them to take on the role of a leader and then develop a vision statement. As participants developed their vision, they were asked to provide written forecasts of the outcomes of their vision. Participants' forecasts were content analyzed and then factored to yield four strategies that were applied during forecasting: (1) extensiveness of forecasting, (2) timeframe of forecasting, (3) forecasting negative outcomes, and (4) forecasting resources. It was found that both forecasting extensiveness and forecasting timeframe were significantly positively correlated with leader vision statements. These results suggest that forecasting, especially forecasting using certain strategies, improves leader performance. Moreover, these findings were confirmed in studies by Byrne et al. (2010) and McIntosh et al. (2021). It is also noteworthy that forecasting skill was found to be a stronger predictor of leader performance than traditional ability measures, such as intelligence and divergent thinking.

Another recent study found that forecasting skill may be trained to improve leader performance. Todd et al. (2019) provided self-paced forecasting skill training programs to participants, where participants were trained on strategies related to forecasting extensiveness, forecasting timeframe, or both forecasting extensiveness and timeframe. A final group of participants received no training. It was found that participants who received forecasting training—regardless of which type of training—provided higher-quality solutions to a leader problem-solving task. Not only do these results emphasize the utility of forecasting skill, but they also support that forecasting may be developed and trained.

Although forecasting skill appears to be critical, it is also quite difficult (Medeiros et al., 2020). Especially in highly complex situations, it is difficult to determine the potential impact of a particular action (Fleming, 2002). This inherent difficulty involved in forecasting illuminates why forecasting skill is key to leader judgment. Compared to their subordinates, leaders should have more relevant expertise, case-based knowledge, and elegant mental models, which allow leaders to more effectively forecast (Rouse and Morris, 1986; Mumford et al., 2000b). Effective leader forecasting enables leaders to more accurately identify the potential consequences of actions. When leaders judge problem solutions, this effective forecasting should help leaders to more accurately identify the consequences of solution implementation, which should improve leader judgment. Moreover, people tend to be biased and overestimate the potential success of their ideas when they forecast (Runco and Smith, 1992; Berg, 2016). Thus, forecasting during leader judgment is necessary to provide external evaluation removed from the developer of the solution.

Idea evaluation. Skill in idea evaluation refers to the cognitive appraisal of ideas with respect to some set of standards (Watts et al., 2017). Leaders must evaluate ideas in order to improve upon solutions and perform well (Tam et al., 2020). In fact, it has been argued that leader performance is often contingent on a leader's skill in idea evaluation (Watts et al., 2017). Idea evaluation is of critical importance because it is not feasible for leaders to act on all generated solutions. Rather, leaders must evaluate solutions to determine which solutions should be pursued (Mumford et al., 2017). In order to effectively evaluate solutions, leaders should select the appropriate standards by which solutions will be judged, consider revisions that may be made, and compensate for weaknesses in ideas (Kuipers et al., 1988; Todd, 2020; Watts et al., 2017). The standards leaders commonly apply to assess a solution relate to appropriateness, relevance, and originality (Runco et al., 1987), which may prompt leaders to consider implementation cost, congruence of the solution with the current system and environment, and solution novelty (Bink and Marsh, 2000). When leaders revise ideas, they address identified limitations of ideas, which enables leaders to target the aspects of ideas that should be refined and revised (Mumford et al., 2002). Then, leaders may apply certain strategies to compensate for weaknesses in ideas (Todd, 2020). Runco and Smith (1992) and Lonergan et al. (2004) have provided additional empirical support for the importance of idea appraisal and revision to complex problem-solving and leader performance.

The importance of idea evaluation skill to leader performance has been demonstrated in recent research. Mumford et al. (2000a) assessed the cognitive skills of Army officers at different leadership ranks ranging from second lieutenant to full colonel. In comparison to junior and mid-level officers, it was found that senior-level officers demonstrated stronger idea evaluation skills. In another study, Marshall-Mies et al. (2000) found that leader idea evaluation skills predicted performance among 250 officers attending the Industrial College of the Armed Forces. Together, these results suggest that effective idea evaluation skills are necessary for leadership.

Evidence has also been provided to support that idea evaluation is a highly complex skill that requires more than surface-level assessment. Lonergan et al. (2004) asked undergraduate participants to take on the role of a leader in charge of designing advertising campaigns. Prior to developing their advertising campaigns, participants were shown ideas of varying quality and originality. Instructions were given to encourage participants to apply either innovative or operative standards in idea evaluation and idea revision of the given ideas, after which participants developed their advertising campaigns. It was found that the strongest campaigns were developed by leaders when they were given highly innovative ideas and appraised those ideas using operative standards, and when they were given ideas high in operating efficiency and appraised those ideas using innovative standards. Thus, effective leaders actively assess ideas and compensate for idea weaknesses. Moreover, this study has direct implications for leader judgment. The findings of this study suggest that when evaluating given problem solutions, or when making leader judgments, leaders should apply idea evaluation skill by identifying standards by which solutions will be judged, identifying weaknesses in solutions, and compensating for those weaknesses.

Given that idea evaluation involves appraising ideas, its applicability to judgment is unequivocal. The components of effective idea evaluation—selecting appropriate idea judgment standards, addressing limitations in ideas, and compensating for weaknesses in ideas—point to the ways in which skilled idea evaluation may improve leader judgment (Lonergan et al., 2004; Watts et al., 2017). Skill in idea evaluation is also critical to leader judgment because of the nature of situations that call for leader judgment. In highly complex situations, idea evaluation is substantially more difficult, making it critical that leaders provide judgment

Table 2.1   Contribution of cognitive skills to leader judgment

Cognitive skill	Definition	Contribution to leader judgment
Goal analysis	The process of analyzing and identifying potentially viable goals to be pursued from a larger set of objectives	Allows for the identification of optimal goals based on significance, relative merit, and system readiness Allows for the appraisal of goal attainment and goal stability relative to problem solutions presented
Constraint analysis	The process of identifying and analyzing constraints bearing on a problem or problem solution	Allows for the appraisal of solution fit with respect to boundaries set forth by constraints Allows for the awareness and adaptation to dynamic environmental restrictions and requirements
Forecasting	The process of envisioning potential outcomes associated with the implementation of various problem solutions	Allows for the identification of the potential short- and long-term consequences of contemplated solutions Allows for the utilization of expertise to provide an external assessment of solution consequences
Idea evaluation	The process of giving a cognitive appraisal of problem solutions with respect to a set of standards	Allows for the appraisal of solutions according to critically relevant standards Allows for the identification of solution aspects that require refinement or revision and strategies for compensating for solution weaknesses

(Licuanan et al., 2007). Indeed, a study asking participants to critique given ideas found that effective criticism of ideas was inhibited by problem complexity (Gibson and Mumford, 2013). However, effective criticisms were provided by participants who were skilled at idea evaluation and actively analyzed given ideas and provided a limited number of deep criticisms. Therefore, the application of strong idea evaluation skills appears to help reduce the complexity of the problems and improve leader judgment. Moreover, as leaders develop and acquire greater expertise, better-organized case-based knowledge, and stronger mental models, problem complexity decreases, resulting in more effective idea evaluation and subsequent leader judgment (Mumford et al., 2000a, 2017). Additionally, the stronger mental models held by leaders enable leaders to handle pressing constraints, such as time pressure and external stressors, better than subordinates, which allows leaders to better evaluate solutions and make more successful judgments (De Dreu, 2003; Suri and Monroe, 2003). Thus, it is critical for leaders to be skilled in idea evaluation in order to effectively evaluate solutions and make appropriate judgments.

SKILL DEVELOPMENT AND ASSESSMENT

When given a problem solution, leaders should apply goal analysis, constraint analysis, forecasting, and idea evaluation skills in order to make effective judgments. Although the preceding discussion examines each skill individually, it is important to recognize that situations requiring leader judgment are highly complex, and thus may necessitate the application of multiple skills simultaneously. Furthermore, depending on the situation, some skills may be more or less important to apply. Thus, it is apparent that the application of these skills is not simple. It is also noteworthy that these complex cognitive skills require great effort that may be cognitively depleting (Mumford et al., 2017). Subsequently, the next question becomes:

How can leaders best develop and apply these skills in order to make effective judgments? The following discussion seeks to examine this question.

Cognitive skills may not only be a powerful predictor of leader judgment, but also serve as an effective basis for the development of leader judgment. Research has suggested that leader decision making, problem-solving, and social judgment may be developed (Judge et al., 2004, Mumford et al., 2017; Scott et al., 2004), and research has shown that cognitive skills may be developed and trained (e.g., Osburn and Mumford, 2006; Ellspermann et al., 2007; Peterson et al., 2013; Basadur et al., 1982). For example, Todd et al. (2019) developed a forecasting training intervention that was significantly related to improvements in leader performance. When people were trained on strategies intended to encourage more extensive forecasting and forecasting across broader timeframes, leader performance improved. The strategies trained to improve extensiveness of forecasting included (1) consider a variety of stakeholder groups, (2) consider how various stakeholder groups might react to different outcomes, (3) consider how potential actions might benefit or harm others, (4) consider what alternative actions might be required due to emergent contingencies, and (5) consider alternative situations comparable to the situation at hand. The strategies trained to improve the timeframe of forecasting included (1) consider how long it took for events to unfold in past efforts, (2) consider when it was opportune to take action in past efforts, (3) consider how alternative actions might connect or unfold over time, (4) consider how constraints might emerge or unfold over time, and (5) consider gaps in one's knowledge relevant to the timing of actions. In order to develop forecasting skill, leaders may also apply these strategies to practice problems, thoughtfully applying each strategy to the given problem and then reflecting on the information provided by applying each strategy and how that information informs their judgment on the problem.

In another study, Runco and Basadur (1993) provided evidence that skill in idea evaluation may be trained, and they suggested that this training improves leader judgment. More specifically, leaders who were given training provided more original solutions to problems and judged the originality of ideas more accurately after training. This training focused on experiential problem-solving, where people were asked to solve and evaluate multiple different problems. Specifically, participants were given real-world problems and then asked to engage in a two-step problem-solving process. First, focus on generating ideas to solve the problem. Then, at a separate and distinct time, evaluate those ideas. In order to develop idea evaluation skill, a similar approach may be used: Practice generating ideas to solve realistic problems that you may face on your own. Then, at a distinct time separate from idea generation, evaluate the utility of those ideas. To encourage deeper idea evaluation, establish the set of standards by which the idea should be judged, and then evaluate based on those standards.

It has also been argued that goal analysis may be trained to improve leader performance (Mumford et al., 2000a). Specific suggestions for goal analysis training include instructing leaders in appraising the stability of goals, the value of goal attainment, stakeholder payoffs, goal synergies, and tradeoffs in goal attainment (Mumford et al., 2017). Similar to the exercises discussed above, leaders may practice developing goal analysis skill by examining job-relevant previous or fictitious problem solutions and reflecting on these strategies.

Formal training interventions, however, are not the only method for developing cognitive skills. For example, self-reflection, systematic peer feedback, and structuring task demands to require leaders to actively analyze constraints may all support the development of cognitive skills relevant to leader judgment (Strange and Mumford, 2005; McIntosh et al., 2021;

Caughron and Mumford, 2008). For example, leaders may request feedback from peers specific to the identification of constraints relevant to a given problem solution.

Additionally, it has been argued that, given the strong predictive power of cognitive skills, leader performance should be assessed based on these skills (Mumford et al., 2017; Mumford and Higgs, 2020b). It stands to reason that leader judgment may also be effectively assessed by cognitive skills. For example, it is not difficult to develop example situations that require leader judgment, and then ask leaders to analyze goals and constraints, as well as forecast consequences and evaluate sample solutions. Utilizing situational judgment measures, for example, and evaluating them for these skills may serve as an avenue for leader judgment assessment. Although this example is speculative, it clearly shows that skill evaluation may be a promising outlet for the assessment of leader judgment.

LIMITATIONS

Before turning to conclusions, certain limitations should be considered. Perhaps most notably, research on leader cognitive skills and leader judgment is relatively limited when compared to the attention often devoted to more socially grounded models of leadership (Mumford et al., 2017; Zaccaro and Klimoski, 2001). Therefore, observations, such as the importance of goal analysis to leader judgment, are necessarily speculative. However, the evidence of the strong relationship between cognitive skills and leader performance, combined with the nature of leader judgment, provides a grounded basis to make informed assessments about the relationship between cognitive skills and leader judgment. An additional limitation is that it is possible that there may be other cognitive skills that are strong predictors of leader judgment beyond the skills discussed in this chapter. Indeed, as previously mentioned, cognitive skills such as wisdom may be important and deserve further attention in relation to research on leader judgment. Relatedly, the relative importance of various cognitive skills is unknown. It is possible that certain cognitive skills may be more important when providing judgments of solutions from different domains. These limitations point to the need for more research investigating cognitive skills and leader judgment. For example, studies are needed investigating the impact of cognitive skills on leader judgment, the dependencies and interactions among skills applied in leader judgment, and the impact environmental context and problem solution domain has on the relationship between cognitive skills and leader judgment.

It is also important to note that although this chapter has focused on cognitive skills that may improve leader judgment, that does not belittle the importance of other variables that may improve leader judgment. These variables include mastery motives, learning goals, types of case-based knowledge, expertise, and certain personality characteristics such as extraversion and openness (Goodall et al., 2014; Ligon et al., 2008; Vessey et al., 2011; Watts et al., 2019; Zaccaro et al., 2018). Work on complex problem-solving and decision making suggests that the aforementioned variables may have a positive impact on leader judgment, but more research is needed to examine these relationships and their interaction with cognitive skills.

CONCLUSION

In this chapter, a new conceptualization of leader judgment has been provided, emphasizing the importance of certain cognitive skills during leader judgment. In particular, skill in goal analysis should improve leader judgment by enabling leaders to determine the impact a solution will have on key goals. Constraint analysis should improve leader judgment by encouraging leaders to assess the extent to which a solution adequately accounts for relevant constraints. Forecasting skill should improve leader judgment by allowing leaders to better anticipate the consequences of solution implementation. Idea evaluation should improve leader judgment by enabling leaders to better select standards by which solutions should be judged, identify and compensate for weaknesses in solutions, and offer solution revisions. The implications of these findings to the assessment and development of leaders are substantial. Early research on cognitive skill development for leaders is promising and suggests that the skills that may improve leader judgment may be trained. However, more research is needed targeting the impact of cognitive skills on leader judgment and examining tools for assessment and development. We hope this chapter will serve as an impetus for research examining the relationship between cognitive skills and leader judgment.

REFERENCES

Acar, O. A., Tarakci, M., and van Knippenberg, D. (2019). Creativity and innovation under constraints: A cross-disciplinary integrative review. *Journal of Management, 45*, 96–121.

Amabile, T. M. (1983). The social psychology of creativity: A componential conceptualization. *Journal of Personality and Social Psychology, 45*, 357–376.

Amabile, T. M., and Gryskiewicz, N. D. (1989). The creative environment scales: Work environment inventory. *Creativity Research Journal, 2*, 231–253.

Antes, A. L., and Mumford, M. D. (2012). Strategies for leader cognition: Viewing the glass "half full" and "half empty". *The Leadership Quarterly, 23*, 425–442.

Basadur, M., Graen, G. B., and Green, S. G. (1982). Training in creative problem solving: Effects on ideation and problem finding and solving in an industrial research organization. *Organizational Behavior and Human Performance, 30*, 41–70.

Bass, B. M., and Bass, R. (2009). *The Bass handbook of leadership: Theory, research, and managerial applications*. New York, NY: Simon & Schuster.

Berg, J. M. (2016). Balancing on the creative highwire: Forecasting and success of novel ideas in organizations. *Administrative Science Quarterly, 61*, 433–468.

Berson, Y., and Avolio, B. J. (2004). Transformational leadership and the dissemination of organizational goals: A case study of a telecommunication firm. *The Leadership Quarterly, 15*, 625–646.

Bink, M. L., and Marsh, R. L. (2000). Cognitive regularities in creative activity. *Review of General Psychology, 4*, 59–78.

Bundy, J., Shropshire, C., and Buchholtz, A. (2013). Strategic cognition and issue salience: Toward an explanation of firm responsiveness to stakeholder concerns. *Academy of Management Review, 38*, 352–376.

Byrne, C. L., Shipman, A. S., and Mumford, M. D. (2010). The effects of forecasting on creative problem-solving: An experimental study. *Creativity Research Journal, 22*, 119–138.

Byron, K., Khazanchi, S., and Nazarian, D. (2010). The relationship between stressors and creativity: A meta-analysis examining competing theoretical models. *Journal of Applied Psychology, 95*, 201–212.

Caughron, J. J., and Mumford, M. D. (2008). Project planning: The effects of using formal planning techniques on creative problem-solving. *Creativity and Innovation Management, 17*, 204–215.

Caughron, J., Ristow, T., and Antes, A. (2020). Uncertainty and problem solving: The role of leader information-gathering strategies. In M. Mumford and C. Higgs (Eds.), *Leader thinking skills: Capacities for contemporary leadership* (pp. 71–97). New York, NY: Routledge.

Connelly, M. S., Gilbert, J. A., Zaccaro, S. J., Threlfall, K. V., Marks, M. A., and Mumford, M. D. (2000). Exploring the relationship of leadership skills and knowledge to leader performance. *The Leadership Quarterly, 11*, 65–86.

De Dreu, C. K. (2003). Time pressure and closing of the mind in negotiation. *Organizational Behavior and Human Decision Processes*, *91*, 280–295.

Einhorn, H. J., and Hogarth, R. M. (1981). Behavioral decision theory: Processes of judgement and choice. *Annual Review of Psychology*, *32*, 53–88.

Ellspermann, S. J., Evans, G. W., and Basadur, M. (2007). The impact of training on the formulation of ill-structured problems. *Omega*, *35*, 221–236.

Fleming, L. (2002). Finding the organizational sources of technological breakthroughs: The story of Hewlett-Packard's thermal ink-jet. *Industrial and Corporate Change*, *11*, 1059–1084.

Friedman, R. S. (2009). Reinvestigating the effects of promised reward on creativity. *Creativity Research Journal*, *21*, 258–264.

Gibson, C., and Mumford, M. D. (2013). Evaluation, criticism, and creativity: Criticism content and effects on creative problem solving. *Psychology of Aesthetics, Creativity, and the Arts*, *7*, 314–331.

Goodall, A. H., McDowell, J. M., and Singell, L. D. (2014). Leadership and the research productivity of university departments. *IZA Discussion Paper Series*.

Judge, T. A., Colbert, A. E., and Ilies, R. (2004). Intelligence and leadership: A quantitative review and test of theoretical propositions. *Journal of Applied Psychology*, *89*, 542–552.

Kirkebøen, G. (2009). Decision behaviour-improving expert judgement. In T. M. Williams, K. Samset, and K. J. Sunnevåg (Eds.), *Making essential choices with scant information* (pp. 169–194). London: Palgrave Macmillan.

Kuipers, B., Moskowitz, A. J., and Kassirer, J. P. (1988). Critical decisions under uncertainty: Representation and structure. *Cognitive Science*, *12*, 177–210.

Lavie, D., Stettner, U., and Tushman, M. L. (2010). Exploration and exploitation within and across organizations. *Academy of Management Annals*, *4*, 109–155.

Licuanan, B. F., Dailey, L. R., and Mumford, M. D. (2007). Idea evaluation: Error in evaluating highly original ideas. *Journal of Creative Behavior*, *41*, 1–27.

Ligon, G. S., Hunter, S. T., and Mumford, M. D. (2008). Development of outstanding leadership: A life narrative approach. *The Leadership Quarterly*, *19*, 312–334.

Lonergan, D. C., Scott, G. M., and Mumford, M. D. (2004). Evaluative aspects of creative thought: Effects of appraisal and revision standards. *Creativity Research Journal*, *16*, 231–246.

Maitlis, S. (2005). The social processes of organizational sensemaking. *Academy of Management Journal*, *48*, 21–49.

Marcy, R. T., and Mumford, M. D. (2007). Social innovation: Enhancing creative performance through causal analysis. *Creativity Research Journal*, *19*, 123–140.

Marcy, R. T., and Mumford, M. D. (2010). Leader cognition: Improving leader performance through causal analysis. *The Leadership Quarterly*, *21*, 1–19.

Marshall-Mies, J. C., Fleishman, E. A., Martin, J. A., Zaccaro, S. J., Baughman, W. A., and McGee, M. L. (2000). Development and evaluation of cognitive and metacognitive measures for predicting leadership potential. *The Leadership Quarterly*, *11*, 135–153.

Marta, S., Leritz, L. E., and Mumford, M. D. (2005). Leadership skills and the group performance: Situational demands, behavioral requirements, and planning. *The Leadership Quarterly*, *16*, 97–120.

Martin, R. W., Elliott, S., and Mumford, M. D. (2019). Errors in creative problem-solving: Identify, deliberate, and remediate. *Creativity Research Journal*, *31*, 248–260.

McIntosh, T., Mulhearn, T. J., and Mumford, M. D. (2021). Taking the good with the bad: The impact of forecasting timing and valence on idea evaluation and creativity. *Psychology of Aesthetics, Creativity, and the Arts*, *15*, 111–124.

Medeiros, K. E., Partlow, P. J., and Mumford, M. D. (2014). Not too much, not too little: The influence of constraints on creative problem solving. *Psychology of Aesthetics, Creativity, and the Arts*, *8*, 198–210.

Medeiros, K., Steele, L., Watts, L., and Mumford, M. (2018). Timing is everything: Examining the role of constraints throughout the creative process. *Psychology of Aesthetics, Creativity, and the Arts*, *12*, 471–488.

Medeiros, K. E., Watts, L. L., and Mumford, M. D. (2017). Thinking inside the box: Educating leaders to manage constraints. In C. Zhou (Ed.), *Handbook of research on creative problem-solving skill development in higher education* (pp. 25–50). Hershey, PA: IGI Global.

Medeiros, K., Williams, B., and Damadzic, A. (2020). Creative problem solving: Processes, strategies, and considerations for leaders. In M. Mumford and C. Higgs (Eds.), *Leader thinking skills: Capacities for contemporary leadership* (pp. 176–204). New York, NY: Routledge.

Meer, T., Verhoeven, P., Beentjes, H., and Vliegenhart, R. (2017). Communication in times of crisis: The stakeholder relationship under pressure. *Public Relations Review, 43*, 426–440.

Mumford, M. D., Friedrich, T. L., Caughron, J. J., and Byrne, C. L. (2007). Leader cognition in real-world settings: How do leaders think about crises? *The Leadership Quarterly, 18*, 515–543.

Mumford, M. D., and Higgs, C. (2020a). *Leader thinking skills: Capacities for contemporary leadership.* New York, NY: Routledge.

Mumford, M. D., and Higgs, C. (2020b). Leader thinking skills. In M. Mumford and C. Higgs (Eds.), *Leader thinking skills: Capacities for contemporary leadership* (pp. 1–13). New York, NY: Routledge.

Mumford, M. D., Higgs, C., Todd, E. M., and Elliott, S. (2020). Thinking about causes: How leaders identify the critical variables to act on. In M. Mumford and C. Higgs (Eds.), *Leader thinking skills: Capacities for contemporary leadership* (pp. 122–147). New York, NY: Routledge.

Mumford, M. D., Lonergan, D. C., and Scott, G. (2002). Evaluating creative ideas: Processes, standards, and context. *Inquiry: Critical Thinking across the Disciplines, 22*, 21–30.

Mumford, M. D., Marks, M. A., Connelly, M. S., Zaccaro, S. J., and Reiter-Palmon, R. (2000a). Development of leadership skills: Experience and timing. *The Leadership Quarterly, 11*, 87–114.

Mumford, M. D., Steele, L., McIntosh, T., and Mulhearn, T. (2015). Forecasting and leader performance: Objective cognition in a socio-organizational context. *The Leadership Quarterly, 26*, 359–369.

Mumford, M. D., Todd, E. M., Higgs, C., and McIntosh, T. (2017). Cognitive skills and leadership performance: The nine critical skills. *The Leadership Quarterly, 28*, 24–39.

Mumford, M. D., Zaccaro, S. J., Harding, F. D., Jacobs, T. O., and Fleishman, E. A. (2000b). Leadership skills for a changing world: Solving complex social problems. *The Leadership Quarterly, 11*, 11–35.

Onarheim, B. (2012). Creativity from constraints in engineering design: Lessons learned at Coloplast. *Journal of Engineering Design, 23*, 323–336.

Osburn, H. K., and Mumford, M. D. (2006). Creativity and planning: Training interventions to develop creative problem-solving skills. *Creativity Research Journal, 18*, 173–190.

Peterson, D. R., Barrett, J. D., Hester, K. S., Robledo, I. C., Hougen, D. F., Day, E. A., and Mumford, M. D. (2013). Teaching people to manage constraints: Effects on creative problem-solving. *Creativity Research Journal, 25*, 335–347.

Posen, H. E., Keil, T., Kim, S., and Meissner, F. D. (2018). Renewing research on problemistic search—a review and research agenda. *Academy of Management Annals, 12*, 208–251.

Priest, S. (1988). The role of judgment, decision making, and problem solving for outdoor leaders. *Journal of Experiential Education, 11*, 19–26.

Rouse, W. B., and Morris, N. M. (1986). On looking into the black box: Prospects and limits in the search for mental models. *Psychological Bulletin, 100*, 349–363.

Runco, M. A., and Basadur, M. (1993). Assessing ideational and evaluative skills and creative styles and attitudes. *Creativity and Innovation Management, 2*, 166–173.

Runco, M. A., Okuda, S. M., and Thurston, B. J. (1987). The psychometric properties of four systems for scoring divergent thinking tests. *Journal of Psychoeducational Assessment, 5*, 149–156.

Runco, M. A., and Smith, W. R. (1992). Interpersonal and intrapersonal evaluations of creative ideas. *Personality and Individual Differences, 13*, 295–302.

Scott, G., Leritz, L. E., and Mumford, M. D. (2004). The effectiveness of creativity training: A quantitative review. *Creativity Research Journal, 16*, 361–388.

Shipman, A. S., Byrne, C. L., and Mumford, M. D. (2010). Leader vision formation and forecasting: The effects of forecasting extent, resources, and timeframe. *The Leadership Quarterly, 21*, 439–456.

Shipman, A. S., and Mumford, M. D. (2011). When confidence is detrimental: Influence of overconfidence on leadership effectiveness. *The Leadership Quarterly, 22*, 649–665.

Stokes, P. D. (2007). Using constraints to generate and sustain novelty. *Psychology of Aesthetics, Creativity, and the Arts, 1*, 107–113.

Strange, J. M., and Mumford, M. D. (2005). The origins of vision: Effects of reflection, models, and analysis. *The Leadership Quarterly, 16*, 121–148.

Suri, R., and Monroe, K. B. (2003). The effects of time constraints on consumers' judgments of prices and products. *Journal of Consumer Research*, *30*, 92–104.

Tam, S. K., Eubanks, D., and Friedrich, T. (2020). Leader decision making capacity: An information processing perspective. In M. Mumford and C. Higgs (Eds.), *Leader thinking skills: Capacities for contemporary leadership* (pp. 227–259). New York, NY: Routledge.

Tichy, N. M., and Bennis, W. G. (2007). *Judgment: How winning leaders make great calls*. New York, NY: Penguin Group.

Todd, E. M. (2020). Effective strategies for creative idea evaluation: The customer's always right. Doctoral dissertation, University of Oklahoma. ShareOK.

Todd, E. M., Higgs, C. A., and Mumford, M. D. (2019). Bias and bias remediation in creative problem-solving: Managing biases through forecasting. *Creativity Research Journal*, *31*, 1–14.

Tversky, A., and Kahneman, D. (1974). Judgment under uncertainty: Heuristics and biases. *Science*, *185*, 1124–1131.

Vessey, W. B., Barrett, J., and Mumford, M. D. (2011). Leader cognition under threat: "Just the facts". *The Leadership Quarterly*, *22*, 710–728.

Watts, L. L., Mulhearn, T. J., Todd, E. M., and Mumford, M. D. (2017). Leader idea evaluation and follower creativity: Challenges, constraints, and capabilities. In M. D. Mumford and S. Hemlin (Eds.), *Handbook of research on creativity and leadership* (pp. 82–99). Cheltenham, UK and Northampton, MA, USA: Edward Elgar Publishing.

Watts, L. L., Steele, L. M., and Mumford, M. D. (2019). Making sense of pragmatic and charismatic leadership stories: Effects on vision formation. *The Leadership Quarterly*, *30*, 243–259.

Weick, K. E. (1995). *Sensemaking in organizations*. Thousand Oaks, CA: SAGE Publications.

Yukl, G. (2011). Contingency theories of effective leadership. In A. Bryman, B. Jackson, K. Grint, and M. Uhl-Bien (Eds.), *The SAGE handbook of leadership* (pp. 284–296). London: SAGE Publications.

Zaccaro, S. J. (2014). Leadership memes: From ancient history and literature to twenty-first-century theory and research. In D. Day (Ed.), *The Oxford handbook of leadership and organizations* (pp. 13–38). Oxford: Oxford University Press.

Zaccaro, S. J., Connelly, S., Repchick, K. M., Daza, A. I., Young, M. C., Kilcullen, R. N., … and Bartholomew, L. N. (2015). The influence of higher order cognitive capacities on leader organizational continuance and retention: The mediating role of developmental experiences. *The Leadership Quarterly*, *26*, 342–358.

Zaccaro, S. J., Green, J. P., Dubrow, S., and Kolze, M. (2018). Leader individual differences, situational parameters, and leadership outcomes: A comprehensive review and integration. *The Leadership Quarterly*, *29*, 2–43.

Zaccaro, S. J., and Klimoski, R. J. (2001). The nature of organizational leadership. An introduction. In S. J. Zaccaro and R. J. Klimoski (Eds.), *The nature of organizational leadership: Understanding the performance imperatives confronting today's leaders* (pp. 3–41). San Francisco, CA: Jossey-Bass.

3. Character-infused judgment and decision making

Brenda Nguyen and Mary Crossan

CHARACTER-INFUSED JUDGMENT

Judgment concerning medical problems, business opportunities, military maneuvers, and ethical and political issues is often characterized by deep complexity, problems with diverse variables that are intricate and deeply connected such that deductive calculations of reactions and outcomes are insufficient to capture the phenomenon (Thiele, 2006). The basic components of good judgment – such as situational awareness, cognitive complexity, analytically minded, decisive, critical thinking, intuitive, insightful, pragmatic, and adaptable – prove to be beneficial regardless of whether one is embroiled in an ethical dilemma, a business negotiation, navigating office politics, or resolving personal conflict. However, the judgment and decision making (JDM) field has mainly focused on a descriptive view of decision making and has offered little in terms of a prescriptive perspective (Mantere and Ketokivi, 2013).

This chapter therefore offers a prescriptive view of JDM that incorporates character into it, revealing three important insights. First, it shifts the focus of decision making towards the role of the individual; in particular, we propose that who the agent is will provide insights into the quality of JDM. Second, a character-infused perspective to JDM addresses the development of the individual agent to provide thoughts on how to make more quality decisions. Third, we explicate how character-infused JDM accounts for the duality of the individual and the context in which the agent is situated. We examine how the agent may be constrained by the situation but also how they can exert influence over the context. We organize the above elements into three sections, describing why a character-infused perspective is needed, providing an overview of character, and discussing the what, who, when, where, and how of character-infused judgment.

WHY: OVERVIEW OF JDM AND THE CHARACTER-INFUSED VIEW

The JDM literature is vast, with major advancements in the understanding of decision making unearthing knowledge of human rationality such as human cognitive limitations around bounded rationality and biases (e.g., Bazerman and Moore, 2012; Bell et al., 1988; Eisenhardt and Zbaracki, 1992; Kahneman et al., 1982; March, 1994; Simon, 2013; Stanovich, 1999). Furthermore, the literature on leadership reasoning has found that leaders continue to make decisions that veer away from rational reasoning, revealing the need to understand how to make better decisions (e.g., Green, 2004; Green et al., 2009). Yet the vast majority of ped-agogical, methodological, and scientific research continues to draw upon rational models of decision making (Mantere and Ketokivi, 2013). Other areas of JDM have focused on intuitive or affective models, but with a descriptive focus. Therefore, character also offers insights into intuitive and affective decision making through the virtue-based view of what to cultivate in terms of habits and affect to complement the judgment and behavior of the individual decision maker. Thus, we provide an overview of the JDM literature and offer character as a supple-mental lens to the rational, intuitive, and affect models.

Scholars have often sought to model good decisions after those with high cognitive capacity (Stanovich, 1999) or an expert decision maker (Reyna, 2004). Models that use intelligence as a point of reference contend that decision making triggers system I automatic processes but that high-effort deliberative reasoning, system II, can inhibit the biased response of system I. This "default-interventionist" process labeled by Evans (2008) describes how individuals can make better decisions in overcoming the biases of human decision making by the intervention of the logical system. In particular, those with higher intelligence have a greater ability to employ logical reasoning over belief-bias reasoning (Kokis et al., 2002). Highly intelligent individuals are therefore more apt to inhibit belief-bias reasoning (Stanovich, 1999), and under the assumption that logical reasoning rules good decision making, this supports the dominant power of system II. Based on the assumptions of the dual-process theory, allowing system II to maintain executive control while suppressing system I is believed to produce superior deci-sions (more rational). Thus, slowing down the process of decision making to activate system II, the more effortful and conscious process, will result in better decision making. However, it is interesting to point out that the dual-process model often depicts a conflict between these two systems and that logic and belief (i.e., values) are competing influences within a person. The view is such that there is value in logical reasoning but other values beyond that such as belief reasoning constitute the inferior choice.

There are however a number of issues with these assumptions. While system I and II are described as two independent components in the brain, there has not been evidence that they work independently. Some researchers suggest that these two systems operate and develop in parallel (Klaczynski, 2000, 2001). Another important consideration is that when individ-uals have considerable experience, the conscious process may inhibit good decision making (Wilson and Schooler, 1991). In naturalistic studies of decision making for occupations such as firefighting and for other emergency response workers, the non-conscious process domi-nates. The expert recognizes the situation as one that has already been encountered and then proceeds to recall a mental model to help solve the problem (Klein, 1999). Thus, some scholars have claimed that the unconscious reasoning leads to superior decision making (Dijksterhuis and van Olden, 2006).

Furthering the poor decision behaviors of humans, scholars have explained that there is an ego-driven component to evaluations and judgment that contributes to our poor decision making. These ego-driven decisions and processes are motivated by a need to protect our self-concept and beliefs about the world around us. For example, post-hoc rationalizations of decisions are motivated by a need to explain why our decisions were right. As such, the rational and the intuitive/affective are partners in crime: the intuitive and emotional side controls the desire while the rational creates ways to justify the decision to ourselves and to others (Haidt, 2001). The self-confirmation effect describes a process of evaluation and decision making that leads individuals to remember selective information that reaffirms who they believe they are rather than using all information to evaluate themselves against possible alternative selves (Andrews, 1991; Epley et al., 2004; Epstein, 1994).

Early decision scientists (Savage, 1954; Simon, 1979) have indicated that the classic model of rationality requires knowledge of all the relevant alternatives, their consequences and ties, with all measurable and predictable parameters and without surprises. These conditions are rarely met if ever in real-life situations. Furthermore, decision models based on rationality have taken evidence from studies operating with these assumptions and parameters, but real-life situations cannot assume that rational models will provide the correct answers. Stiglitz (2010) noted that doing so can lead to disastrous consequences, like the financial crash of 2008. Some scholars have thus criticized the assumptions of the rational model and suggest that JDM scholars should consider other forms of decision making once thought of as inferior. In particular, Kruglanski and Gigerenzer (2011) stated that "the argument[s] that heuristics are aligned with error-prone judgments, and complex statistical rules are not aligned with rational judgments ... miss the ecological nature of judgment and run the risk of misinterpreting the adaptive use of less effortful rules as signs of limited capacities or even irrationality" (p. 106). Moreover, other scholars propose that while rationality is useful for strategic decision making, it would be strengthened through other decision-making mechanisms like experience, learning, and intuitive processes (Khatri and Ng, 2000). For decision making that is more complex such as strategic decision making, because of the ill-structured nature of the problem, it cannot be programmed (Mintzberg et al., 1976).

Another line of scholars who have also critiqued the JDM perspective believe that the principles underlying rational reasoning and statistical theory are not easy to grasp and that they are often not compatible with natural human intuitions (Lewis and Keren, 1999). Moreover, research has shown that when decision-making tasks more closely mimic complex human decisions, the conscious and rational process produces less consistency (Levine et al., 1996) and less post-choice satisfaction (Dijksterhuis and van Olden, 2006; Wilson et al., 1993). For example, empirical studies have been successful in demonstrating JDM principles in simple decision-making problems but less successful in applying these mathematical principles to more complex decision-making cases (Dijksterhuis et al., 2006). Further, while the JDM literature has described how humans make decisions, it has yet to discuss how the agent *should* make decisions. For example, while there is much discussion on how to achieve desired goals, less work has addressed what those goals should entail. As Simon (1983) articulated: "Reason is wholly instrumental. It cannot tell us where to go; at best it can tell us how to get there. It is a gun for hire that can be employed in the service of any goals we have, good or bad" (pp. 7–8).

To address this gap, however, requires a dive into a prescriptive lens of decision making to complement the dominant descriptive views. Indeed, we are not the first to suggest how character may unlock the unanswered questions in JDM. Haidt and Joseph (2007) also proposed that there is a growing consilience between the two literatures, suggesting that "virtue theory may yield deep insights into the architecture of human social and moral cognition" (p. 368). As such, a character perspective offers an important lens through which to view the JDM literature, as it can serve to enhance decision making by not just offering the decision maker guidance on the appropriate process in decision making, but also offering a compelling perspective on the "right way of being." Many scholars have long believed that good judgment requires the consideration of both the goal pursued and the means to achieve such an end, particularly from the perspective of the human good (Fowers, 2003; Melé, 2010; Roca, 2008). By expanding the focus beyond rules of self-regulation, character can help to recast JDM to introduce other considerations needed by the decision maker to enhance the quality of the decision. Furthermore, as we show in later sections, our reactions and the outcomes they produce are often a product of learned behavior that has resulted from underdeveloped skills or habituated practice. Thus, an examination of how to make better decisions needs to incorporate learning, which we discuss in the *how* section.

Through the character approach, we offer a complementary model to the traditional JDM model as we begin to answer other important critical questions concerning judgment. While JDM offers a substantial amount of knowledge concerning how one can achieve a particular decision, "character-infused" judgment focuses on the quality of that decision, what goals one should pursue, and what factors should be considered in the decision making. The term "infused" implies that character and judgment are intricately connected and that any theory on judgment that does not consider character results in an insufficient account of JDM. We propose that character strength has been missing from much of the discussion in the JDM literature, and thus we seek to examine how character-infused decision making deviates from JDM by taking a developmental stance on judgment. To achieve this, we draw upon the character model (see Figure 3.1) developed by Crossan and colleagues (2017), who based their work on classic Aristotelian virtue theory, as well as more recent extensions by Peterson and Seligman (2004) in their virtues in action (VIA) model. We discuss the details of this particular model in the below section on character overview.

The character lens offers an alternative paradigm of the decision maker to offer one that is more holistic, virtue based, developmental, experiential, and reflective. It takes the perspective that judgment requires both the analytical component advocated by current JDM scholars and the intuitive and developmental aspects of the brain that have been given less scientific space. As stated by Thiele, "Whole brain judgment is a product of bi-hemispheric activity that is linguistic and imaginative, symbolic and concrete, habituated and inventive, calculative and intuitive, explicit and tacit" (2006, p. 160). The complexity of judgment thus requires an equally complex, multifaceted and multilayered model to begin to unravel the nature of human judgment. The character-infused view therefore provides insights into the development of JDM, particularly the intuitive and affective processes, that has been treated as a separate component from the rational parts of JDM. Character offers a way to address this disparate treatment of JDM through the process of habits and virtue-based orientation. Haidt and Joseph (2007) advocated character in supplementing our understanding of ethical decision making (EDM), stating that "an important feature of this approach [virtues] is that moral education is accomplished by shaping emotions and intuitions, rather than by dictating explicit rationales or principles ... [It] emphasizes practice and habit rather than propositional knowledge and reasoning" (p. 368). We extend this view beyond applications to EDM to the broader application of JDM. We shift the attention of JDM from one that is concerned with actions – what individuals should be doing – to one giving priority and importance to character by asking what kind of person we should become. To begin, we outline the character model and then introduce character into the current JDM paradigm through a series of questions around judgment.

Source: Crossan et al. (2017).

Figure 3.1   Character framework

CHARACTER OVERVIEW

The importance of virtue and character has been documented in the early work of Plato and Aristotle, and more recent invigorations of the topic have been discussed by Anscombe (1958), MacIntyre (2007), Solomon (1992), Kupperman (1995), and Hursthouse (2001) among others. As such, a large body of philosophical theory on character exists (Hursthouse, 2001; MacIntyre, 2007) as well as more recent psychological theory on character (Peterson and Seligman, 2004). Despite this body of work, comparatively little actionable research has been applied to judgment and decision making (Crossan et al., 2013b). Research on character has only recently been emerging within the management field. Character scholars (e.g., Hannah and Avolio, 2011; Hannah et al., 2011; Wright and Quick, 2011) have established that character is something that occurs within the person, has a moral component that is related to but separate from values and personality, and that while it is acquired during an individual's development, it continues to develop as the individual ages.

Recently, Crossan and colleagues (2017) sought to refine the definition and understanding of character. They define character as the amalgam of virtues, traits, and values that enable human excellence and social betterment (Cameron et al., 2004; Moore, 2005). "Virtue is a deep property of a person that defines the human goodness of the individual. The virtue ethicist sees virtue as rooted in human character – habituated patterns of thought, emotion, motivation or volition, and action that are consistently morally excellent and develop well-being" (Bright et al., 2014, p. 447). Some of these virtues are personality traits, such as conscientiousness and openness, which are relatively stable dispositional variables (Bono and Judge, 2004). These traits predispose individuals to behave in certain ways, if not overridden by other forces such as culture/norms, reward systems, or peer pressure. As such, our view of traits is that while they represent a predisposition to certain things, this does not mean they cannot be changed or transformed but rather they exist as one version, or what Marcus (2004) terms one "draft," of the individual. Experience, specifically character-infused EDM, provides certain types of exposure that leads to learning and growth, or "edits."

Crossan et al. (2017) identified and validated ten dimensions of character (aka virtues): accountability; collaboration; courage; drive; humanity; humility; integrity; judgment; justice; temperance; and transcendence. These dimensions of character are interdependent, with judgment (aka practical wisdom) directing the behavioral manifestation of the other character dimensions across situations (Arjoon, 2010; MacIntyre, 2007; Sison and Fontrodona, 2013). Consistent with Aristotle's notion of virtue and vice, with virtue conceptualized as a desirable mean state between the vice of excess and the vice of deficiency, each character dimension draws on the others in order to be exercised appropriately. As such, the mean state is not a middle way between strength and weakness but rather a depth of the character dimension that resists excess/deficiency because of its connectivity to other character dimensions. For example, courage is a virtue that relies on other virtues to avoid the trappings of becoming reckless (e.g., having low temperance). Thus, cowardliness is a vice of courage deficiency and recklessness is a vice of excess courage (Aristotle, 1999, Nicomachean Ethics, 1106a26–b28). The interconnectivity between the virtues and the possible explanation for why some behaviors that appear to be virtuous are vices has been neglected in the management and decision-making literature.

In the theory of leader character, judgment holds an important role in achieving the virtuous mean state. Individuals need the capacity to exercise the dimensions as needed in any context (Melé, 2010; Roca, 2008). Practical wisdom, therefore, requires situational appreciation – the capacity to recognize, in any particular situation, the features that are salient for decision making and subsequent action (Price, 2000; Rest, 1986; Rest and Narvez, 1994). Importantly, this implies that individuals are able to exercise the required character dimension when needed. As such, if a character dimension is not appropriately developed, it will hinder the exercise of other dimensions. For example, if courage is weak, an individual may not be able to exercise justice in a situation (i.e., speak up against an unfairness). Thus, all of the character dimensions are important in order to exercise appropriate judgment.

While values are an important aspect of character, not all values are character-infused. Wright and Huang (2008) stated that character is not simply a set of any deeply held personal values. Character encompasses only values that are virtuous. Furthermore, some aspects of character are trait-like in nature, such as conscientiousness (goal-oriented consistent with the dimension of drive); however, virtuous traits as defined by MacIntyre (2007) are a "set of dispositions to behave systematically in one way or another, to lead one particular kind of life" (p. 38). Thus, traits that have been nurtured and practiced for the production of the common good can be thought of as character-infused traits. Unlike personality, the theory of character distinguishes that character can be good or bad and that "good" character is distinguished by a combination of character strengths that enable the individual to achieve the common good. Furthermore, the underpinning of character is the ability to nurture and develop character, which implies that a character-infused trait can be strengthened and developed. Personality theory, however, views traits as relatively stable throughout an individual's adulthood (e.g., introversion/extroversion).

THE WHAT, WHO, WHERE, WHY, AND HOW OF CHARACTER-INFUSED JUDGMENT

What Is a Good Decision: Anchoring in Character

Scholars have long debated on what makes a good decision. Some JDM scholars focus on the mathematics, logics, and probability of decision making (Kahneman, 2003; Simon, 1955), others choose to examine the facts of the problem without the burden of the associated values, also known as the "separation thesis" lens (Freeman, 1994), and for many, good judgment means being "rational," which exclusively includes "economic rationality" (Melé, 2010). Pitz and Sachs (1984) believed that good decisions can be thought of as those with a mathematical or logical structure imposed on the decision task to generate a set of consistent responses. As such, this involves a process and outcome that is based on accurate (or probabilistic) assessments of the cause and effect (from formal probability theory), that is, an analysis of taking a particular action and knowing the respective outcome: option A will lead to outcome A while option B will lead to outcome B. The appropriate choice from those assessments results from weighing a cost/benefit analysis (expected utility theory). As such, the worth of a decision is determined by the probability of the events and their associated utilities (utility is based on what one personally values) (see Von Neumann and Morgenstern's early work (1944) for further details). Individuals make decisions that maximize utility, which is believed to lead to a good life. Poor decisions therefore are those that depart from this prescribed logic (Kahneman et al., 1982; Slovic, 1999) and will lead to poor work and life outcomes. In this description of a good decision, the focus is on the process of achieving or not achieving the intended goal. In other words, JDM is concerned with instrumental rationality which guides productive actions towards particular ends. The issue of concern is whether the practice leads to the desired intended outcome. In other words, the technical expertise and knowledge determines the quality of the outcomes and whether this technical knowledge can serve the objective pursuit of unbiased knowledge and goals of the decision maker.

Critiques of the rational model of decision theory, such as that by David Hume (1955), questioned whether there is a set of reasons behind the judgment, such as which factors to choose when determining what is important, what factors can be dismissed, when to stop collecting information, that in the end justify the judgment. Bounded rationality was therefore a response to this problem in order to factor in concerns such as information constraints, time limitations, and uncertain environments (Simon, 1990). Simon asserted that humans do not make optimal decisions but rather they engage in satisficing – that is, resolving to a decision that is acceptable rather than ideal. In this vein, humans use shortcuts or heuristics to help them come to an acceptable decision. The literature on heuristics has flourished to include a two-system view of the cognitive framework (see Kahneman, 2011), with emotions (Elster, 1999) and intuition (Gilovich et al., 2002) having a distinct influence on the cognitive system. JDM scholars today have largely modeled decision making through this cognitive lens, with some offering alternative views (intuitive decision making, social-intuitionist model, etc.).

The field of JDM has made great strides in understanding the decision-making process; however, the line of inquiry has largely been a descriptive process of decision making. The prescriptive endeavor has aimed at avoiding the pitfalls of human error and judgment with ideals directed towards the rational. Borrowing from Melé (2010), rationality leads one to make an efficient weapon, but it does not question whether this weapon should be made, nor does it say under what conditions. While other prescriptive views of what is good have been examined through a deontological and consequentialist approach, the virtue-based view has received less attention (Craft, 2013; Ford and Richardson, 2013). The virtue-based view focuses less on what is right; rather, it states that an analysis of what is right depends on the character of the agent within a particular context. As applied to what is a good decision, virtue-based decision making is not based on learning the rules (laws, norms, etc.) and ensuring adherence to those rules; nor is it based on maximizing any particular outcome (e.g., happiness). Virtue-based decision making is a matter of trying to determine the kind of people we should be and of attending to the development of character within our communities and ourselves. As such, examining who that agent is, and is becoming, is critical to understanding good judgment. In examining the agent, and understanding who the agent is, we come to also describe the virtues the agent possesses that lead to a good decision.

To capture the aforementioned issues concerning judgment, we prefer to focus on quality judgment, as quality captures the good and the bad along with the spectrum in between. Moreover, knowing what is a good judgment may not be apparent immediately and can only be known over time. As such, we argue that the aim should be to exercise quality judgment – ensuring that the exercise of character does not undermine judgment. We therefore define quality judgment as character-infused judgment, with the aim of judging from strength of character.

Who: The Character of the Agent

Virtue resides within the individual. To say that someone possesses a certain character means that the individual has the appropriate beliefs, awareness, desires, motivations, emotions, and behavioral tendencies. Aristotle indicated that contained within a virtue is the intellectual, emotional, motivational, and behavioral components (Alzola, 2015). Thus, a person of virtue will have developed and continues to seek the appropriate knowledge, the appropriate emotions/desires/attitudes, and the appropriate virtue-based motivation (see Crossan et al., 2013a, on the virtue-based orientation), and ensures that virtuous actions follow from the knowledge, emotions, and motivations. According to Aristotle, judgment is the ultimate virtue, and to be a person who possesses good judgment means to have all of the virtues. In other words, judgment requires all of the other virtues to be present and better or worse judgment depends on the strength of the other virtues. A virtue therefore can become a vice when there are weaknesses in other virtues. A person who possesses the virtue of integrity might develop the behaviors associated with integrity (being candid, authentic, transparent, principled, and consistent) and ensure that the other dimensions of character are developed so that integrity does not act as a vice. For example, without supporting strength in humility and humanity, integrity would manifest as being dogmatic, rigid, and arrogant. We clarify here that our account of a virtuous person is not a reductive one of virtues which examines mainly the behavioral manifestations of character. Rather, our stance is that virtuous behavior is anchored in the virtuous inner states (awareness, intentions, deliberations, emotions, etc.) of the individual (see Nguyen and Crossan, 2021, for a comprehensive account of virtue-based EDM). As such, a full account of a virtuous person requires the examination of the person in their wholeness, because a particular virtuous behavior is only one aspect of virtuousness. We cannot say that a person is courageous because they spoke up against a corrupt institution or that they are not courageous because they did not speak up. To ascribe a person as courageous requires the examination of the cultivated qualities of the person – whether they have, for instance, a habit of acting, feeling, valuing, and developing courage.

Therefore, a full understanding of character-infused judgment requires examining the character of the person at the center of the judgment process. A behavior may appear virtuous, such as a humane act of helping another person. But if that person does it because it is the cultural norm, or because someone else is observing the act, then the quality of the humane act cannot be the same as that in which the individual has acquired the awareness for humanity, formed intentions to act humanely, decided to act humanely, and has reflected on how to exercise humanity. In other words, a person possesses the virtue of humanity when that person becomes a person who is humane. We therefore argue that the quality of judgment from the former and the latter descriptions will be different and this spotlight on who is the agent is a missing perspective in JDM. We also argue that the difference is revealed in the individual when taking into account time, context, and the character development of the individual. We address the time and context in the following sections, and discuss the unique aspect of character development next.

A character-infused judgment approach assumes that individuals have the ability to be cognitively complex, situationally aware, analytical, decisive, a critical thinker, intuitive, insightful, pragmatic, and adaptable (as depicted in Figure 3.1). As an example, to be cognitively complex means that an individual is able to perceive and interpret a multitude of stimuli and information while applying various classification schemes to describe phenomena (Yasai-Ardekani, 1986). Additionally, cognitive complexity allows one to operate in environments of uncertainty because of a higher tolerance for uncertainty and environmental complexity (Streufert et al., 1968). The cognitively complex individual continually takes in more information, spends more time processing the information (Dollinger, 1984; Sieber and Lanzetta, 1964), and assesses competing arguments and hypotheses (Bartunek et al., 1983; Chang and McDaniel, 1995). Character-infused judgment is continually developed as the decision maker learns from new experiences. However, it is not just experience that leads to development but a focused learning, one that is defined by the dimensions of good character. While there are time constraints that bound one to make decisions, because an endless search of information is not pragmatic, character-infused judgment would privilege virtuous motivations, values, and actions above other factors and provide the decision maker with the appropriate character-infused tools (situational awareness, intuitions, cognitive complexity, etc.) to make certain types of quality judgments.

The ability to make good judgment, defined as character-infused judgment, comes from the exercise of character daily. As such, strength of character, as shown through one's decisions, is the exercise of character that starts from the daily habits of being. Expressing character in daily habits comes in the form of character awareness, activation, practice, and reflection of thoughts, words, and action and integrity as a wholeness of the person. It is both the conscious decision making and subconscious brought into human consciousness through this cycle of "living" character. Character therefore is in part the continual striving for excellence in which the decision maker can navigate the elements of biological, learned, processes and the contextual forces that may derail the decision maker towards non-virtuous development.

Character-infused decision making therefore takes the perspective that the individual is at the crux of the decision making while having certain predetermined limitations, but has the ability to set the course of their destiny in the practice of character through striving for daily excellence. As a developmental model, the character model can help to identify areas of strength and, in particular, areas of weakness that can be further developed to support the areas of strength. The JDM literature therefore serves to inform the decision maker of the nature of human biases and fallacies. The decision maker – who desires to judge well – needs, however, to understand the interplay of motivations and calculations, aversions and desires, passions and prejudices, beliefs and misbeliefs that inform human thought and action.

Where: The Role of Context in the Decision-Making Process

Numerous studies have shown the detrimental effect of performance pressures, a common contextual force, on cognitively arduous tasks (Baumeister, 1984; Beilock and Carr, 2001; Lewis and Linder, 1997) such as EDM (Mumford et al., 2006). In particular, Goldberg and Greenberg (1994) demonstrated that competition with peers, pressure due to professional implication, and on-the-job pressure were the most important predictors of unethical behaviors such as overstating positive and understating negative results. Research has found competitive pressures to cause business students to make questionable ethical choices when analyzing cases (Nill et al., 2004). An account of these forces has provided evidence for the all-encompassing effect of situational forces on behavior and judgment. Contextual forces provide the boundary conditions for salient information (e.g., gain/loss frame in prospect theory) and also act as an overwhelming source of pressure and govern the decision outcome that robs the decision maker of choice. For example, in group settings, humans go along with the perceived norms of the group while secretly holding counter beliefs (i.e., group think, group norms) (Janis, 1982) and it is more difficult to account for the contributions of each individual member, resulting in lower output than the sum of its members (i.e., social loafing) (Postmes et al., 2001). Other numerous biases associated with context have been well documented, including contrast effects, primacy/recency effects, and halo effects. Thus, most of the research in JDM has focused on explaining how humans make universal judgment errors and that given the same context/conditions all humans will act similarly. Furthermore, while personality scholars maintain that some traits such as honesty or humility may predict ethical choices (Ashton et al., 2014), these ethic-related traits are subject to contextual conditions as outlined by trait activation theory (Tett and Burnett, 2003; Tett and Guterman, 2000). Specifically, when a situation presents strong cues to act unethically, the trait will remain dormant, while in situations that are more ambiguous, when the cues are weaker, the individual's trait will predict behavior. The assumption therefore is that in social settings, there is a deterioration of the decision maker in their attitudes, beliefs, values, and actions such that the norms of the group are dictated by the context and the behaviors of others. As such these social pressures direct and guide the decision maker (Janis, 1982).

Aristotle (1999) states that "matters concerned with conduct and questions of what is good for us have no fixity … the agents themselves must in each case consider what is appropriate to the occasion" and "such things depend on particular facts and the decision rests with perception" (p. 47). What it means to act well is thus always conditioned by the specific circumstances and how our pursuit of worthy aims can be adapted to the situation. This does not imply that we change on a whim or aimlessly walk through a situation allowing the forces to channel our behaviors. In fact, it is the opposite: in the face of strong situational pressures, such as stress, time, money priming, performance pressures, and power, character allows the individual to not only recognize the pressures at play, but also weigh that information to inform the decision-making process without permitting its consumption of the individual in the decision. In other words, the agentic individual – the self-regulatory and self-reflective person – has the ability to dictate their own behavior. Much of the work on environmental or contextual forces in the JDM literature, however, reveals them to be an overwhelming power that is nearly impossible to overcome and reigns over predetermined biological processes. While the strength of these pressures is not to be taken lightly, we reject the proposition that agency has less importance in the judgment process compared to other factors. Indeed, much of the JDM literature attempts to understand human judgment by examining and describing the common responses rather than the behaviors from outliers, and thus only recognizes a restricted range of possible behaviors that humans are capable of. In taking the range-restricted approach, scholars have come to conclude that much of judgment is predetermined without the role of the individual as a decider.

A quintessential example of situational pressures that cause an individual to act in unethical ways has been provided by the Milgram studies on obedience. A number of studies using the Milgram (1965) paradigm have demonstrated that people are willing to engage in questionable behavior towards others, including physically harming them, simply because an authority figure asked them to do so (Blass, 1999). One explanation for this finding is that individuals may actually use a person of higher authority as an excuse for engaging in a questionable behavior. The individuals engaging in the behavior are able to place the responsibility for the consequences of their own actions on the authority figure. Other explanations for this behavior have focused on the power held by the authority figure (Blass, 1999). Specifically, the perception of the authority figure as an expert has been suggested as the reason for the followers' obedience. Furthermore, Mumford et al. (1993) found that individuals were more likely to make unethical decisions when such decisions appear to be supported by organizational authorities. However, what is less discussed among scholars is, while 65 percent obeyed the experimenter, who were the 35 percent that did not (some recent investigations have found that the study contained serious reporting flaws; Perry, 2013) and why did those individuals resist pressures from a legitimate authority figure?

Aristotle believed that experience is key to the formation of good judgment and that this experience develops over time and space. Because of the nature of experience, strong judgment is rarely found in young adults. Neuroscience has supported this as the corpus callosum, which connects the two hemispheres of the brain and allows for the integrated thought, is not fully developed until individuals reach their mid to late twenties (Tanaka-Arakawa et al., 2015). Character develops amid the conflicts and trials of life; as such, good judgment is formed through the errors and mishaps. Studies in judgment, however, generally focus on one-time discrete decisions made by individuals. As such, a one-time decision does not provide an opportunity for feedback and learning, an essential component of developing good judgment.

Learning from experience, however, involves making future decisions that reflect the learning. It is not merely the perception and recognition of the errors in judgment, but it needs to be followed by a correction in action directed towards character. Aristotle spoke of habits as the pivotal pillar in building character, for it is the actions of a person that defines their character. Recognition of exemplary individuals who embody character can inspire one to activate one's own character. Character, once activated with an intention to follow through, can begin a process of the right habit formation. Indeed, there is a line of research that suggests habits need not be completely consciously decided. Work in the area of strategic automaticity or "instant habits" indicates that these behaviors originate from conscious acts of will. Such habits control one's action by putting unconscious capacities of the mind to work (Gollwitzer and Schall, 1998), speak to the ability of the individual to consciously choose particular goals, and use implementation strategies (e.g., "when x happens I will do y") to aid in goal initiation, attainment, and termination. In one study where the participants performed preventative health examinations, it was found that implementation intentions led to automated or habitual action initiation (Orbell et al., 1997). Further, while old habits predicted the health behaviors for those who did not form implementation intentions, prior habits had no predictive power for those that formed the intentions. This suggests that implementation intentions created new habits. Strategic automaticity with the use of implementation intentions has been suggested to enhance perceptual and motor abilities, facilitate effective operation during distractions, reduce stereotyped responses, attenuate the negative effects of emotions and moods, help to avoid temptations, and even offset disruptive priming effects (Gollwitzer et al., 2012). Thus, these findings support a number of important implications for character-infused judgment: that the individual can consciously choose their goals, that they can form habits both automatically and consciously to support those goals, and that, in turn, those habits will provide a strength against contextual/situational forces that may shift the individual's intentions.

While character research acknowledges the strong situational forces that are at play in daily life and extraneous situations, the role of the decision maker and their agency can help navigate the contextual forces. Various contexts will activate the different character dimensions in what could be moment-to-moment experience (e.g., accountability in group work) but each dimension also requires the support of other dimensions (e.g., humanity in group work). For example, in team decision making, character-based judgment might activate accountability to ensure that the person is accountable for their contribution and also that they take ownership for each decision of the team even if at the time of the decision making they disagreed with the team. At the same time, judgment might also activate the dimension of humanity to be able to empathize and relate to the needs of others in the team in order to motivate them effectively, an ability that is highly valued in leaders. Character-based judgment therefore acts like a central control by assessing the context and determining which appropriate character dimension is needed even before the decision-making process. It is needed in the perception and interpretation of the context, the people, and the self. Post decision making, assessment and reflection of the event contributes to the learning and further development of character. Judgment requires experience with different situations; the more judgment is informed by experiences and the stronger the reflex becomes. As such, character itself is a deliberate process that requires attention and practice. Thus, it is the pursuit of character, and the choice to enact it, in the decision-making process (through perception, interpretation, belief system, intent, etc.) that defines the decision as good.

Finally, while we espouse the role of character in counteracting situational forces, the distinction of character and context is artificial. Rather, there is an entwinement of the individual and the context where the individual operates. Furthermore, the socio-political context (including power differentials and social/cultural norms) is a real constraint to individual agency. However, while individual agency may be constrained, it is never fully lost (Giddens, 1984). The goal of character-infused judgment is to seek and explore how the individual can foster and strengthen agency so that this agency can guide the individual through strong situational pressures. The agency of the individual, however, is strengthened through the development of character. The awareness that the individual can act as both the supporter and the disruptor of context through their own agency is forged through the character of the individual. As such, the recursive nature of the individual and context is created and re-created by the character of the agent. In this view, strength of character allows for the possibility of the individual to exist within the context and to endogenously disrupt the context (Nielsen, 2006; Weaver, 2006). Therefore, the unique qualities of character establish new insights for the field of JDM.

Why: Why Do We Choose One Decision over Another?

The problem with the way decision making has been studied is that it often assumes that the good decision maker has unlimited time, cognitive resources, and energy, and is unbiased and error free. In taking this position, scientists have come to explain the decision process and its structural components in terms of functional and instrumental understandings, with a focus on its errors. For example, heuristics and biases (some have made references to system I) have been described as adaptive mechanisms for coping with complex, dynamic environments (Hogarth, 1981), but they are thought of as unrefined, and thus error-prone decision-making tools. Moreover, as discussed in detail earlier, the stable biological limitations imposed on the decision maker generate particular explanations for the choices made. Satisficing, for example, emerged from a view of limited human cognitive capacity to analyze information (Simon, 1955). In turn, these assumptions of the human decision maker place constraints that limit their possibilities for action. In particular, the boundaries of satisficing do not permit the possibility of excellence in judgment, exemplary judgment, and reflection in judgment. It fails to describe anomalies, individuals and behaviors that do not fit the pattern, resulting in an inadequate account of human judgment. As such, the ability of the current perspective to understand the entire spectrum of human judgment is limited and therefore this perspective constitutes a restrictive view. Such a perspective can, however, be useful in describing common and average decision making, but movement beyond this range restriction is prohibited.

The architecture of the decision-making process has also been applied to the understanding of individual differences. In particular, the same higher mental processes that have traditionally served as prototypical examples of choice and free will – such as goal pursuit and judgment – have been argued to occur without conscious choice and free will (Bargh and Ferguson, 2000). Because system II is believed to be the analytical and reasoning part of the brain, scholars have claimed that there is a link between this system and general intelligence (Reber, 1989; Stanovich, 2010). This proposition has led to an increasing use of individual differences methodology within the dual-process research. Under this work, some researchers have sought to support this perspective by linking intelligence with working memory, associating working memory with system II processes, and showing a lack of relationship between intelligence and automatic processes or system I. Scientists, therefore, have accumulated evidence in support of a deterministic process, ungoverned by an agentic being, by designing studies narrowly to demonstrate that the deliberate and analytical process is prophesied by biological factors such as intelligence or contextual factors such as priming and mood (Bargh and Chartrand, 2013; Bargh and Ferguson, 2000), and that the automatic mental and behavioral processes can proceed without the intervention of conscious deliberation and choice (see, e.g., Chaiken and Trope, 1999; Cohen et al., 1990; Posner and Snyder, 2004).

The quest for creating inventories and documenting the processes of judgment does not sufficiently address the complexity of human judgment. To study judgment in isolation of time, reflection, and motivation is to generate an incomplete account of judgment. To accept that free will is absent from human judgment is to deny the possibility of human growth, learning, and development. We thus reject the thesis of deterministic and other causal forces outside of the individual as the primary account of the variability in judgment. Instead, we embrace the thesis that it is the lack of character development in judgment that directs individuals towards less thoughtful behaviors. It is the lack of character-driven goals (i.e., vision, which is an element of transcendence) that results in inaccurate perceptions of the forces that constrain the situation and the individual decision maker. For example, an underdeveloped humanity, resulting in an inability to relate to others, can lead an individual to make inaccurate judgments about the extent to which situational and/or individual forces bring about a particular outcome (i.e., attribution error; Fiske and Taylor, 2013). Or similarly, strength of character, through temperance, can lead one to refrain from judgment of the situation by remaining patient in order to gather more information (perhaps seeking more information through multiple observations). Decision scientists have assumed that biases are universal human attributes, but they may not be. For example, the attribution bias, sometimes named the fundamental attribution bias for its universal nature, has not been directly tested empirically. These cognitive errors we make as adults are not present in young children (e.g., children do not exhibit the bystander intervention effect), suggesting our decision process is largely based on our learned experiences (Latané and Nida, 1981).

A character-infused judgment approach takes the perspective that character is something that can be activated and developed within the individual such that it can become infused in the entire decision-making process – from what we choose to pay attention to, to how we assess the situation, and how we thus choose to act from our perception and assessment. Good character is therefore assumed to be present in human beings but has yet to be fully realized and practiced in judgment. Because character is based on the individual, poor decision making is thought to be a sign of underdeveloped character. Humans are responsible for their judgment and decisions because they come from the individual's intentions and free choice to deliberately act with strong/weak character. While the situation poses a great force that channels a person towards a certain decision, it is the strength and depth of character that can steer the individual through situational pressures. As such, one must first have a commitment to developing character (an essence of virtue; Alzola, 2015) and thus tie the pursuit of character to who they want to become. This pursuit of character excellence is practiced and developed through everyday decision making. Each decision one makes should reference character, and one must ask whether each decision is one of good character.

How: Towards Developing Better Judgment via the Character Lens

Good judgment is the ultimate virtue, one that we demand of our leaders and seek personally to improve our life. Good judgment means to make prudent and wise decisions in political, business, and life affairs. Ever since Plato explored the virtue of phronesis (i.e., practical wisdom), and Aristotle raised it to ethical and political prominence, theorists have been fascinated with the capability of judgment. We have outlined how individuals can harness the full potential of phronesis by examining Aristotle's original conceptualization, in which strength of character is essential for optimal judgment. Strength of character will provide an understanding of how emotions and intuition can contribute and enhance the rational mind and how it can inform the individual to handle complex situations. The view of character as a guide to judgment provides an alternative perspective to the belief that good judgment is to mirror the rational ideal of bias reduction or greater executive control. Some research however has delved into alternative forms of reasoning, advocating for strengthening intuition (Lipshitz et al., 2001). For example, in studying decision making in naturalistic settings, scholars have revealed that individuals in this context have well-formed mental models that allow them to react in the most appropriate ways in situations of crisis. Research with firefighters indicates that their decisions are based on the ability to perform reasonable actions without a prolonged need for deliberation or analysis (Phillips et al., 2004). Still, we ascertain that the missing element in reasoning, whether it be rational models or intuitive models, is a prescriptive lens to which development can be aimed.

Emotions research has focused on a parallel perspective speaking to the errors of emotional judgment, and of tempering emotions. The vast majority of researchers in the field of decision science adhere to what is called the "influence-on-metaphor," in which emotions are portrayed as an external force that influences a non-emotional process. "It is assumed that the domain of emotion is qualitatively different and functionally separate from the domain of cognition" (Pfister and Bohm, 2008, p. 6). Decision making is then seen as an essentially cognitive process, which does not necessarily entail emotions. As such, emotions may have an influence on decision making but decision making per se might also proceed without emotion. Furthermore, Fredrickson's (2004) broaden-and-build theory examines the bias in decision-making frameworks to show that positive emotions – and not just negative ones – play an activating role in the decision-making process, such as discovery and creativity. This is the premise of traditional approaches of behavioral decision making (Slovic et al., 1988) but is also reflected in current dual-system theories (Kahneman, 2003; Sloman, 1996). This antagonism between emotion and decision making is commonly accompanied by further dichotomies: "irrational emotions disturb rational cognitions, intuitive feelings outsmart deliberate thinking, and hot affect overwhelms cold logic" (Pfister and Bohm, 2008, p. 6).

Emotions should not, however, be viewed as a threat to rationality but rather the rationality of decision making might actually depend on an individual's capacity to form appropriate emotions (De Sousa, 1987). Aristotle believed that reason is useless on its own and must be combined with emotion to induce action: "knowledge becomes understanding when it is coupled with feeling. Only a deep understanding, charged with strong feelings, is capable of modifying structured patterns of behavior" (Lowen, 1975, p. 62). Emotions research shows that both positive and negative emotions can serve to enhance judgment by focusing our attention towards relevant information (Forgas, 1995). Recent research shows that strong emotions can serve to enhance performance if they elicit a high and steady heart rate rather than a variable and inconsistent heart rate which leads to inferior performance (Lehrer et al., 2020). Crossan and colleagues (2021) describe the physiological, affect, behavior, and cognitive underpinnings of character development, reinforcing the point that all dimensions of character require regulation of these systems. A character-infused view of emotional development seeks to first strengthen emotions that have a virtuous purpose. For example, excitement that enables drive to achieve lofty goals, pain linked to empathy and compassion to strengthen humanity, anger fueled by injustice, or calmness to deepen temperance in the face of fear.

The JDM literature attempts to address how one can make good judgment, with an emphasis on "what is the right thing to do in a given situation"; using a character lens gives greater value to "what is the right way of being" (Hannah and Jennings, 2013). As stated earlier in this chapter, judgment is instrumental: it can be used for any goal or any aim (Simon, 1983). Character-infused judgment, however, provides the orientation needed. Crossan and colleagues (2013a) used the virtue-based orientation to describe how Rest's EDM model can be reinvigorated to explicate what Rest (1986) likely intended when he developed his descriptive framework. What is clear is that our decision making can be developed, but how it should be developed, what aspects should be the focus, and towards what goal are questions that a character-infused view can address.

The preceding discussion about the importance of character in JDM leads to the question about how it can be developed. We contend that understanding how it can be developed reinforces an understanding of what character is and how it functions. Scholars have provided broad guidance on this question and have addressed the issue using several approaches, including the leader-as-learner approach to help leaders learn how to navigate a world of complexity and uncertainty (Antonacopoulou and Bento, 2018), incorporating somatic learning to develop critical reflection (Rigg, 2018), art-based methods of learning such as the use of music to develop character (Crossan et al., 2019), sensuous learning methods to help break difficult habits and address vulnerabilities (Antonacopoulou, 2008), and the 4R GNOSIS approach to critical action learning (Antonacopoulou, 2018). Some of these learning perspectives have been applied to character development, such as the 4R GNOSIS approach to the development of phronesis (character-infused judgment) by way of strengthening reflexivity (Antonacopoulou, 2018), or the role of critical moments in the shaping and development of character (Byrne et al., 2018).

We emphasize here that while individuals can engage in learning and development, not all learning is equal. An individual can learn the wrong things, learn to model in the wrong way, or learn approaches that can lead to more harm than good. For example, a large amount of resources in organizations are being placed into unconscious bias training, but it has shown little effect on the actual biased behavior of those who have participated in the learning (Hagiwara et al., 2020). Furthermore, there is evidence to suggest that it may have the opposite effect and create resentment and anger among those with higher status (Dover et al., 2016).

As such, we emphasize and advocate for character-infused learning that spans from the individual to the group level and the community/organization level learning through the activation, embedding, and sustaining of character (Crossan et al., n.d.). Crossan and colleagues (n.d.) describe that character activation refers to the awareness and intentionality needed to exercise character. Individuals can choose to begin learning and practicing character and develop character-infused habits. The contagion level is associated with how easily character activated in one person leads to character being activated in others. Influence from an individual's social network can help with the learning and practice of character. Also, the individual becomes a character influence on others. Finally, character embedding captures the idea that behaviors associated with character can be institutionalized in an organizational setting or in a community in the form of repositories, traditions, rituals, symbols, and so on. The environment therefore has the potential to become a source of character reinforcement.

It would be incomplete to discuss development without touching on the practice of reflecting. In the most reductive view, reflection is consciously thinking about and analyzing our past (Mintz, 2006). However, most people intend reflection to be a means of learning from experience (Boyd and Fales, 1983). The practice of reflecting is activated by an event, usually when something did not result in the outcome that was desired. For virtue ethics, reflection is not just the practice of problem solving, but also an essential component of becoming a virtuous person (Merritt, 2000). A virtue-based reflection means to encourage a person to do the right thing for the right reason (Mintz, 2006). Some have critiqued that reflection itself cannot improve character (Doris, 2002; Merritt, 2000). We agree that a simplistic view of reflection – to examine errors – does not mean reflecting well. Character-infused reflection goes beyond thinking about the errors of the past; it needs to be done with the purpose of living a virtuous life. The reflector has to make judgments about what to reflect on, how to reflect, when to reflect, and when to stop reflecting (Tiberius, 2008). The reflector hence must account for the quality of reflection, and to do this requires a character-infused orientation to the practice (Nguyen and Crossan, 2021). For example, an individual can reflect on whether character was exercised in past events (e.g., did I act judiciously, with humanity and integrity?).

To engage in character-infused reflection means to evaluate our judgment alongside all of the character dimensions. Character-infused reflection provides a compass for the reflector on what to reflect about and how to continually engage in reflection towards the virtuous ideal. An individual might ask themselves if they behaved with humility or whether their intentions were humble or ego driven. Further, they might ask themselves if they assessed the situation with character or with self-interest. Or, how they could have exercised their past action with more humility. Character-infused reflection therefore is a bridge to developing character by learning from the past and applying the learning to new experiences. It creates a continual path forward towards what Aristotle meant by eudaimonia – the good life.

CONCLUSION

Character-infused judgment requires the fundamental examination of the individual – who is the person at the center of the decision. Understanding of the individual, however, requires favoring the particulars – that is, the character – of the individual over the abstract. The particulars include the emotions, intuition, and the development of the individual and the socio-political context in which the individual operates. This examination has been largely ignored or drowned out by the dominant descriptive theories focusing on reasoning, logic, and the rational treatment of judgment. To judge well means to also examine the process of coming into judgment, which forces the acknowledgment of the individual who is both situated in context and has agency to affect the context. Thus, judging within one circumstance is never the same as judging in another, demanding that the individual must engage in the circumstance differently each time. Factors may need to be weighed differently and the rules may need to be enforced differently. Therefore, it is in these spaces of "differences" that character is revealed, exercised, and developed, to allow for good judgment to exist when the nature of the problem is undetermined and uncertain.

REFERENCES

Alzola, M. (2015). Virtuous persons and virtuous actions in business ethics and organizational research. *Business Ethics Quarterly*, *25*(3), 287–318. https://doi.org/10.1017/beq.2015.24.

Andrews, J. D. W. (1991). Integrative psychotherapy of depression: A self-confirmation approach. *Psychotherapy: Theory, Research, Practice, Training*, *28*(2), 232–250.

Anscombe, G. E. M. (1958). Modern moral philosophy. *Philosophy*, *33*(124), 1–19. Retrieved from https://www.jstor.org/stable/3749051.

Antonacopoulou, E. P. (2008). Mastering business action: Implications for management learning in business schools. In M. Bild, P. Märtesson, and K. Nilsson (Eds.), *Teaching and learning at business schools* (pp. 279–293). Aldershot, UK: Gower Publishing Limited.

Antonacopoulou, E. (2018). Energising critique in action and in learning: The GNOSIS 4R Framework. *Action Learning: Research and Practice*, *15*(2), 102–125. https://doi.org/10.1080/14767333.2018.1460580.

Antonacopoulou, E., and Bento, R. F. (2018). From laurels to learners: Leadership with virtue. *Journal of Management Development*, *37*(8), 624–633. https://doi.org/10.1108/JMD-12-2016-0269.

Aristotle. (1999). *The Nicomachean ethics* (Rev.). Cambridge, MA: Harvard University Press.

Arjoon, S. (2010). Aristotelian-thomistic virtue ethics, emotional intelligence and decision-making. *Advances in Management*, *3*(4), 7–13.

Ashton, M. C., Lee, K., and de Vries, R. E. (2014). The HEXACO honesty-humility, agreeableness, and emotionality factors: A review of research and theory. *Personality and Social Psychology Review*, *18*(2), 139–152. https://doi.org/10.1177/1088868314523838.

Bargh, J. A., and Chartrand, T. L. (2013). *Handbook of research methods in social and personality psychology*. New York: Cambridge University Press. https://doi.org/10.1017/cbo9780511996481.

Bargh, J. A., and Ferguson, M. J. (2000). Beyond behaviorism: On the automaticity of higher mental processes. *Psychological Bulletin*, *126*(6), 925–945. https://doi.org/10.1037/0033-2909.126.6.925.

Bartunek, J. M., Gordon, J. R., and Weathersby, R. P. (1983). Developing "complicated" understanding in administrators. *Academy of Management Review*, *8*(2), 273–284.

Baumeister, R. F. (1984). Choking under pressure: Self-consciousness and paradoxical effects of incentives on skillful performance. *Journal of Personality and Social Psychology*, *46*(3), 610–620.

Bazerman, M. H., and Moore, D. A. (2012). *Judgment in managerial decision making*. Hoboken, NJ: John Wiley & Sons.

Beilock, S. L., and Carr, T. H. (2001). On the fragility of skilled performance: What governs choking under pressure? *Journal of Experimental Psychology: General*, *130*(4), 701–725.

Bell, D. E., Raiffa, H., and Tversky, A. (Eds.). (1988). *Decision making: Descriptive, normative, and prescriptive interactions*. Cambridge: Cambridge University Press.

Blass, T. (1999). The Milgram paradigm after 35 years: Some things we now know about obedience to authority. *Journal of Applied Social Psychology*, *29*(5), 955–978. https://doi.org/10.1111/j.1559-1816.1999.tb00134.x.

Bono, J. E., and Judge, T. A. (2004). Personality and transformational and transactional leadership: A meta-analysis. *Journal of Applied Psychology*, *89*(5), 901–910.

Boyd, E. M., and Fales, A. W. (1983). Reflective learning: Key to learning from experience. *Journal of Humanistic Psychology*, *23*(2), 99–117. https://doi.org/10.1177/0022167883232011.

Bright, D. S., Winn, B. A., and Kanov, J. (2014). Reconsidering virtue: Differences of perspective in virtue ethics and the positive social sciences. *Journal of Business Ethics*, *119*(4), 445–460. Retrieved from http://www.jstor.org/stable/pdf/42921306.pdf.

Byrne, A., Crossan, M., and Seijts, G. (2018). The development of leader character through crucible moments. *Journal of Management Education*, *42*(2), 265–293. https://doi.org/10.1177/1052562917717292.

Cameron, K. S., Bright, D., and Caza, A. (2004). Exploring the relationships between organizational virtuousness and performance. *American Behavioral Scientist*, *47*(6), 766–790. https://doi.org/10.1177/0002764203260209.

Chaiken, S., and Trope, Y. (1999). *Dual-process theories in social psychology*. New York: Guilford Press.

Chang, C.-K., and McDaniel, E. D. (1995). Information search strategies in loosely structured settings. *Journal of Educational Computing Research*, *12*(1), 95–107.

Cohen, J. D., Dunbar, K., and McClelland, J. L. (1990). On the control of automatic processes: A parallel distributed processing account of the Stroop effect. *Psychological Review*, *97*(3), 332–361.

Craft, J. L. (2013). A review of the empirical ethical decision-making literature: 2004–2011. *Journal of Business Ethics*, *117*, 221–259. https://doi.org/10.1007/s10551-012-1518-9.

Crossan, M. M., Byrne, A., Seijts, G. H., Reno, M., Monzani, L., and Gandz, J. (2017). Toward a framework of leader character in organizations. *Journal of Management Studies*, *54*(7), 986–1018. https://doi.org/10.1111/joms.12254.

Crossan, M., Ellis, C., and Crossan, C. (2019). Using music to activate and develop leader character. In E. Antonacopoulou and S. Taylor (Eds.), *Sensuous learning for practical judgment in professional practice* (pp. 45–69). Cham: Springer International Publishing. https://doi.org/10.1007/978-3-319-98863-4_3.

Crossan, M., Ellis, C., and Crossan, C. (2021). Towards a model of leader character development: Insights from anatomy and music therapy. *Journal of Leadership and Organizational Studies*. https://doi.org/10.1177/15480518211005455.

Crossan, M. M., Mazutis, D., and Seijts, G. H. (2013a). In search of virtue: The role of virtues, values and character strengths in ethical decision making. *Journal of Business Ethics*, *113*(4), 567–581. https://doi.org/10.1007/s10551-013-1680-8.

Crossan, M., Mazutis, D., Seijts, G., and Gandz, J. (2013b). Developing leadership character in organizations. *Management Learning*, *12*(2), 285–305. Retrieved from http://dx.doi.org/10.5465/amle.2011.0024A.

Crossan, M., Nguyen, B., Vera, D., Sturm, R. E., Maurer, C., and Ruiz-Pardo, A. (n.d.). Character infused organizational learning. *Management Learning*.

De Sousa, R. (1987). What are emotions for? A new biological hypothesis. In *The rationality of emotion* (pp. 190–195). Cambridge, MA: MIT Press.

Dijksterhuis, A., Bos, M. W., Nordgren, L. F., and Van Baaren, R. B. (2006). On making the right choice: The deliberation-without-attention effect. *Science*, *311*(5763), 1005–1007. https://doi.org/10.1126/science.1121629.

Dijksterhuis, A., and van Olden, Z. (2006). On the benefits of thinking unconsciously: Unconscious thought can increase post-choice satisfaction. *Journal of Experimental Social Psychology*, *42*(5), 627–631. https://doi.org/10.1016/j.jesp.2005.10.008.

Dollinger, M. J. (1984). Environmental boundary spanning and information processing effects on organizational performance. *Academy of Management Journal*, *27*(2), 351–368.

Doris, J. (2002). *Lack of character: Personality and moral behavior*. New York: Cambridge University Press.

Dover, T. L., Major, B., and Kaiser, C. R. (2016). Members of high-status groups are threatened by pro-diversity organizational messages. *Journal of Experimental Social Psychology*, *62*, 58–67. https://doi.org/10.1016/j.jesp.2015.10.006.

Eisenhardt, K. M., and Zbaracki, M. J. (1992). Strategic decision making. *Strategic Management Journal*, *13*(S2), 17–37. https://doi.org/10.1002/smj.4250130904.

Elster, J. (1999). *Alchemies of the mind: Rationality and the emotions*. Cambridge: Cambridge University Press.

Epley, N., Keysar, B., Van Boven, L., and Gilovich, T. (2004). Perspective taking as egocentric anchoring and adjustment. *Journal of Personality and Social Psychology, 87*(3), 327–339. https://doi.org/10.1037/0022-3514.87.3.327.

Epstein, S. (1994). Integration of the cognitive and the psychodynamic unconscious. *American Psychologist, 49*(8), 709–724. https://doi.org/10.1037/0003-066x.49.8.709.

Evans, J. S. B. T. (2008). Dual-processing accounts of reasoning, judgment, and social cognition. *Annual Review of Psychology, 59*, 255–278. https://doi.org/10.1146/annurev.psych.59.103006.093629.

Fiske, S. T., and Taylor, S. E. (2013). *Social cognition: From brains to culture*. Thousand Oaks, CA: SAGE.

Ford, R. C., and Richardson, W. D. (2013). Ethical decision making: A review of the empirical literature. *Citation Classics from the Journal of Business Ethics, 13*(3), 19–44. https://doi.org/10.1007/978-94-007-4126-3_2.

Forgas, J. P. (1995). Mood and judgment: The Affect Infusion Model (AIM). *Psychological Bulletin, 117*, 39–66. https://doi.org/10.1037/0033-2909.117.1.39.

Fowers, B. J. (2003). Reason and human finitude: In praise of practical wisdom. *American Behavioral Scientist, 47*(4), 415–426. https://doi.org/10.1177/0002764203256947.

Fredrickson, B. L. (2004). The broaden-and-build theory of positive emotions. *Philosophical Transactions of the Royal Society B: Biological Sciences, 359*(1449), 1367–1377. https://doi.org/10.1098/rstb.2004.1512.

Freeman, R. E. (1994). The politics of stakeholder theory: Some future directions. *Business Ethics Quarterly, 4*(4), 409–421. https://doi.org/10.2307/3857340.

Giddens, A. (1984). *The constitution of society*. Cambridge: Polity.

Gilovich, T., Griffin, D., and Kahneman, D. (2002). *Heuristics and biases: The psychology of intuitive judgment*. Cambridge: Cambridge University Press.

Goldberg, L., and Greenberg, M. (1994). A survey of ethical conduct in risk management: Environmental economists. *Ethics and Behavior, 4*(4), 331–343.

Gollwitzer, P. M., Boyer, U. C., and McCulloch, K. C. (2012). The control of the unwanted. In R. R. Hassin, J. S. Uleman, and J. A. Bargh (Eds.), *The new unconscious* (pp. 485–515). Oxford: Oxford University Press. https://doi.org/10.1093/acprof:oso/9780195307696.003.0018.

Gollwitzer, P. M., and Schall, B. (1998). Metacognition in action: The importance of implementation intentions. *Personality and Social Psychology Review, 2*(2), 124–136. https://doi.org/10.1080/08870446.2014.953531.

Green, S. E. (2004). A rhetorical theory of diffusion. *Academy of Management Review, 29*(4), 653–669. https://doi.org/10.5465/AMR.2004.14497653.

Green, S. E., Li, Y., and Nohria, N. (2009). Suspended in self-spun webs of significance: A rhetorical model of institutionalization and institutionally embedded agency. *Academy of Management Journal, 52*(1), 11–36. https://doi.org/10.5465/AMJ.2009.36461725.

Hagiwara, N., Kron, F. W., Scerbo, M. W., and Watson, G. S. (2020). A call for grounding implicit bias training in clinical and translational frameworks. *The Lancet, 395*(10234), 1457–1460. https://doi.org/10.1016/S0140-6736(20)30846-1.

Haidt, J. (2001). The emotional dog and its rational tail: A social intuitionist approach to moral judgment. *Psychological Review, 108*(4), 814–834. https://doi.org/10.1037//0033-295X.

Haidt, J., and Joseph, C. (2007). The moral mind: How five sets of innate intuitions guide the development of many culture-specific virtues, and perhaps even modules. *The Innate Mind, 3*, 367–392.

Hannah, S. T., and Avolio, B. J. (2011). The locus of leader character. *Leadership Quarterly, 22*(5), 979–983. https://doi.org/10.1016/j.leaqua.2011.07.016.

Hannah, S. T., Avolio, B. J., and May, D. R. (2011). Moral maturation and moral conation: A capacity approach to explaining moral thought and action. *Academy of Management Review, 36*(4), 663–685. https://doi.org/10.5465/amr.2010.0128.

Hannah, S. T., and Jennings, P. L. (2013). Leader ethos and Big-C character. *Organizational Dynamics, 42*, 8–12. https://doi.org/10.1016/j.orgdyn.2012.12.002.

Hogarth, R. M. (1981). Beyond discrete biases: Functional and dysfunctional aspects of judgmental heuristics. *Psychological Bulletin*, *90*(2), 197–217. https://doi.org/10.1037/0033-2909.90.2.197.

Hume, D. (1955). *An inquiry concerning human understanding*. New York: Liberal Arts Press.

Hursthouse, R. (2001). *On virtue ethics*. Oxford Scholarship Online. https://doi.org/10.1093/0199247994 .001.0001.

Janis, I. L. (1982). *Groupthink: Psychological studies of policy decisions and fiascoes*. Boston, MA: Houghton Mifflin.

Kahneman, D. (2003). A perspective on judgment and choice: Mapping bounded rationality. *American Psychologist*, *58*(9), 697–720. https://doi.org/10.1037/0003-066X.58.9.697.

Kahneman, D. (2011). *Thinking, fast and slow*. New York: Macmillan.

Kahneman, D., Slovic, P., and Tversky, A. (Eds.) (1982). *Judgment under uncertainty: Heuristics and biases*. Cambridge: Cambridge University Press. Retrieved from https://books.google.com/books?hl =en&lr=&id=_0H8gwj4a1MC&oi=fnd&pg=PR8&dq=kahneman+1982&ots=YFbe9WP7UO&sig= Sa0weqFOztN477JJng8qi-AZeRY.

Khatri, N., and Ng, H. A. (2000). The role of intuition in strategic decision making. *Human Relations*, *53*(1), 57–86. https://doi.org/10.1177/0018726700531004.

Klaczynski, P. A. (2000). Motivated scientific reasoning biases, epistemological beliefs, and theory polarization: A two-process approach to adolescent cognition. *Child Development*, *71*(5), 1347–1366. https://doi.org/10.1111/1467-8624.00232.

Klaczynski, P. A. (2001). Framing effects on adolescent task representations, analytic and heuristic processing, and decision making: Implications for the normative/descriptive gap. *Journal of Applied Developmental Psychology*, *22*(3), 289–309. https://doi.org/10.1016/S0193-3973(01)00085-5.

Klein, G. (1999). Applied decision making. In P. A. Hancock (Ed.), *Human performance and ergonomics* (pp. 87–107). San Diego, CA: Academic Press.

Kokis, J. V., Macpherson, R., Toplak, M. E., West, R. F., and Stanovich, K. E. (2002). Heuristic and analytic processing: Age trends and associations with cognitive ability and cognitive styles. *Journal of Experimental Child Psychology*, *83*(1), 26–52. https://doi.org/10.1016/S0022-0965(02)00121-2.

Kruglanski, A. W., and Gigerenzer, G. (2011). Intuitive and deliberate judgments are based on common principles. *Psychological Review*, *118*(1), 97–109. https://doi.org/10.1037/a0020762.

Kupperman, J. (1995). *Character*. New York: Oxford University Press. Retrieved from https://www .google.com/books/edition/Character/X8QVDAAAQBAJ?hl=en&gbpv=0.

Latané, B., and Nida, S. (1981). Ten years of research on group size and helping. *Psychological Bulletin*, *89*(2), 308–324.

Lehrer, P., Kaur, K., Sharma, A., Shah, K., Huseby, R., Bhavsar, J., and Zhang, Y. (2020). Heart rate variability biofeedback improves emotional and physical health and performance: A systematic review and meta analysis. *Applied Psychophysiology Biofeedback*, *45*(3), 109–129. https://doi.org/10.1007/ s10484-020-09466-z.

Levine, G. M., Halberstadt, J. B., and Goldstone, R. L. (1996). Reasoning and the weighting of attributes in attitude judgments. *Journal of Personality and Social Psychology*, *70*(2), 230–240. https://doi.org/ 10.1037/0022-3514.70.2.230.

Lewis, B. P., and Linder, D. E. (1997). Thinking about choking? Attentional processes and paradoxical performance. *Personality and Social Psychology Bulletin*, *23*(9), 937–944. https://doi.org/10.1177/ 0146167297239003.

Lewis, C., and Keren, G. (1999). On the difficulties underlying Bayesian reasoning: A comment on Gigerenzer and Hoffrage. *Psychological Review*, *106*(2), 411–416. https://doi.org/10.1037/0033 -295X.106.2.411.

Lipshitz, R., Klein, G., Orasanu, J., and Salas, E. (2001). Taking stock of naturalistic decision making. *Journal of Behavioral Decision Making*, *14*(5), 331–352. https://doi.org/10.1002/bdm.381.

Lowen, A. (1975). *Bioenergetics*. New York: Coward, McCann, Geoghegan. Retrieved from https:// scholar.google.com/scholar?hl=en&as_sdt=0%2C33&q=Lowen%2C+A.+%281975%29.+ Bioenergetics.+New+York%3A+Coward%2C+McCann%2C+Geoghegan.&btnG=.

MacIntyre, A. C. (2007). *After virtue: A study in moral theory*. Notre Dame, IN: University of Notre Dame Press.

Mantere, S., and Ketokivi, M. (2013). Reasoning in organization science. *Academy of Management Review*, 38(1), 70–89. https://doi.org/10.5465/amr.2011.0188.

March, J. G. (1994). *Primer on decision making: How decisions happen*. New York: Free Press.

Marcus, G. (2004). *The birth of the mind: How a tiny number of genes creates the complexities of human thought*. New York: Basic Books.

Melé, D. (2010). Practical wisdom in managerial decision making. *Journal of Management Development*, 29(7), 637–645. https://doi.org/10.1108/02621711011059068.

Merritt, M. (2000). Virtue ethics and situationist personality psychology. *Ethical Theory and Moral Practice*, 3(4), 365–383.

Milgram, S. (1965). Some conditions of obedience and disobedience to authority. *Human Relations*, 18(1), 57–76.

Mintz, S. M. (2006). Accounting ethics education: Integrating reflective learning and virtue ethics. *Journal of Accounting Education*, 24(2–3), 97–117. https://doi.org/10.1016/j.jaccedu.2006.07.004.

Mintzberg, H., Raisinghani, D., and Theoret, A. (1976). The structure of "unstructured" decision processes. *Administrative Science Quarterly*, 21(2), 246–275. https://doi.org/10.2307/2392045.

Moore, G. (2005). Corporate character: Modern virtue ethics and the virtuous corporation. *Business Ethics Quarterly*, 15(4), 659–685. https://doi.org/10.5840/beq200515446.

Mumford, M. D., Devenport, L. D., Brown, R. P., Connelly, S., Murphy, S. T., Hill, J. H., and Antes, A. L. (2006). Validation of ethical decision making measures: Evidence for a new set of measures. *Ethics and Behavior*, 16(4), 319–345.

Mumford, M. D., Gessner, T. E., Connelly, M. S., O'Connor, J. A., and Clifton, T. C. (1993). Leadership and destructive acts: Individual and situational influences. *Leadership Quarterly*, 4, 115–148.

Nguyen, B., and Crossan, M. (2021). Character-infused ethical decision making. *Journal of Business Ethics*. https://doi.org/10.1007/s10551-021-04790-8.

Nielsen, R. P. (2006). Introduction to the special issue. In search of organizational virtue: Moral agency in organizations. *Organization Studies*, 27(3), 317–321. https://doi.org/10.1177/0170840606062424.

Nill, A., Schibrowsky, J. A., and Peltier, J. W. (2004). The impact of competitive pressure on students' ethical decision-making in a global setting. *Marketing Education Review*, 14(1), 61–73.

Orbell, S., Hodgkins, S., and Sheeran, P. (1997). Implementation intentions and the theory of planned behavior. *Personality and Social Psychology Bulletin*, 23(9), 945–954. https://doi.org/10.1177/0146167297239004.

Perry, G. (2013). Deception and illusion in Milgram's accounts of the obedience experiments. *Theoretical and Applied Ethics*, 2(2), 79–92. Retrieved from https://muse.jhu.edu/article/536095.

Peterson, C., and Seligman, M. E. (2004). *Character strengths and virtues: A classification and handbook*. Washington, DC: American Psychological Association.

Pfister, H.-R., and Bohm, G. (2008). The multiplicity of emotions: A framework of emotional functions in decision making. *Judgment and Decision Making*, 3(1), 5–17. https://doi.org/10.1111/1467-8721 .00203\r10.1037/0003-066x.58.9.697.\r10.1037/0033-2909.127.2.267\r10.1146/annurev.psych.56 .091103.070234\r10.1037/033-295x.110.1.145.

Phillips, J. K., Klein, G., and Sieck, W. R. (2004). Expertise in judgment and decision making: A case for training intuitive decision skills. In D. K. Koehler and N. Harvey (Eds.), *Blackwell handbook of judgment and decision making* (pp. 297–315). Chichester: Wiley-Blackwell.

Pitz, G. F., and Sachs, N. J. (1984). Judgment and decision: Theory and application. *Annual Review of Psychology*, 35, 139–163. https://doi.org/10.1146/annurev.ps.35.020184.001035.

Posner, M. I., and Snyder, C. R. (2004). Attention and cognitive control. In D. A. Balota and E. J. Marsh (Eds.), *Cognitive psychology: Key readings* (pp. 205–223). New York: Psychology Press.

Postmes, T., Spears, R., and Cihangir, S. (2001). Quality of decision making and group norms. *Journal of Personality and Social Psychology*, 80(6), 918–930. https://doi.org/10.1037/0022-3514.80.6.918.

Price, C. P. (2000). Evidence-based laboratory medicine: Supporting decision-making. *Clinical Chemistry*, 46(8), 1041–1050. https://doi.org/10.1093/clinchem/46.8.1041.

Reber, A. S. (1989). Implicit learning and tacit knowledge. *Journal of Experimental Psychology: General*, 118(3), 219–235. https://doi.org/10.1037/0096-3445.118.3.219.

Rest, J. (1986). *Moral development: Advances in research and theory*. New York: Praeger.

Rest, J., and Narvez, D. (1994). *Moral development in the professions: Psychology and applied ethics.* Hillsdale, NJ: Lawrence Erlbaum Associates.

Reyna, V. F. (2004). How people make decisions that involve risk: A dual-processes approach. *Current Directions in Psychological Science, 13*(2), 60–66. https://doi.org/10.1111/j.0963-7214.2004.00275.x.

Rigg, C. (2018). Somatic learning: Bringing the body into critical reflection. *Management Learning, 49*(2), 150–167. https://doi.org/10.1177/1350507617729973.

Roca, E. (2008). Introducing practical wisdom in business schools. *Journal of Business Ethics, 82*(3), 607–620. https://doi.org/10.1007/s10551-007-9580-4.

Savage, L. (1954). *The foundations of statistics.* New York: John Wiley & Sons. https://doi.org/10.1163/_q3_SIM_00374.

Sieber, J. E., and Lanzetta, J. T. (1964). Conflict and conceptual structure as determinants of decision-making behavior. *Journal of Personality, 32*(4), 622–641.

Simon, D. (2013). *Evolutionary optimization algorithms: Biologically-inspired and population-based approaches to computer intelligence.* Hoboken, NJ: John Wiley & Sons.

Simon, H. A. (1955). A behavioral model of rational choice. *Quarterly Journal of Economics, 69*(1), 99–118. https://doi.org/10.2307/1884852.

Simon, H. A. (1979). Rational decision making in business organizations. *American Economic Review, 69*(4), 493–513. https://doi.org/10.2307/1808698.

Simon, H. (1983). *Reason in human affairs.* Stanford, CA: Stanford University Press. Retrieved from https://philpapers.org/rec/SIMRIH-2.

Simon, H. A. (1990). Bounded rationality. In J. Eatwell, M. Milgate, and P. Newman (Eds.), *Utility and probability* (pp. 15–18). London: Macmillan Press.

Sison, A. J. G., and Fontrodona, J. (2013). Participating in the common good of the firm. *Journal of Business Ethics, 113*(4), 611–625. https://doi.org/10.1007/s10551-013-1684-4.

Sloman, S. A. (1996). The empirical case for two systems of reasoning. *Psychological Bulletin, 119*(1), 3–22. https://doi.org/10.1037/0033-2909.119.1.3.

Slovic, P. (1999). Trust, emotion, sex, politics, and science: Surveying the risk assessment battlefield. *Risk Analysis, 19*(4), 689–701. https://doi.org/10.1023/A:1007041821623.

Slovic, P., Lichtenstein, S., and Fischhoff, B. (1988). *Decision making.* Retrieved from https://scholarsbank.uoregon.edu/xmlui/bitstream/handle/1794/22321/slovic_189.pdf?sequence=1.

Solomon, R. C. (1992). Corporate roles, personal virtues: An Aristotelean approach to business ethics. *Business Ethics Quarterly, 2*(3), 317–339. https://doi.org/10.2307/3857536.

Stanovich, K. E. (1999). *Who is rational? Studies of individual differences in reasoning.* Mahwah, NJ: Lawrence Erlbaum Associates. Retrieved from https://www.researchgate.net/publication/265235988.

Stanovich, K. E. (2010). *Rationality and the reflective mind.* New York: Oxford University Press.

Stiglitz, J. (2010). *Freefall: America, free markets, and the sinking of the world economy.* New York: W. W. Norton.

Streufert, S., Streufert, S. C., and Castore, C. H. (1968). Leadership in negotiations and the complexity of conceptual structure. *Journal of Applied Psychology, 52*(3), 218–223.

Tanaka-Arakawa, M. M., Matsui, M., Tanaka, C., Uematsu, A., Uda, S., Miura, K., Sakai, T., and Noguchi, K. (2015). Developmental changes in the corpus callosum from infancy to early adulthood: A structural magnetic resonance imaging study. *PLoS ONE, 10*(3), e0118760. https://doi.org/10.1371/journal.pone.0118760.

Tett, R. P., and Burnett, D. D. (2003). A personality trait-based interactionist model of job performance. *Journal of Applied Psychology, 88*(3), 500–517. https://doi.org/10.1037/0021-9010.88.3.500.

Tett, R. P., and Guterman, H. A. (2000). Situation trait relevance, trait expression, and cross-situational consistency: Testing a principle of trait activation. *Journal of Research in Personality, 34*(4), 397–423. https://doi.org/10.1006/jrpe.2000.2292.

Thiele, L. P. (2006). *The heart of judgment: Practical wisdom, neuroscience, and narrative.* Cambridge: Cambridge University Press.

Tiberius, V. (2008). *The reflective life: Living wisely with our limits.* Oxford University Press on Demand.

Von Neumann, J., and Morgenstern, O. (1944). *Theory of games and economic behavior*. Princeton, NJ: Princeton University Press.

Weaver, G. R. (2006). Virtue in organizations: Moral identity as a foundation for moral agency. *Organization Studies*, *27*(3), 341–368. https://doi.org/10.1177/0170840606062426.

Wilson, T. D., Lisle, D. J., Schooler, J. W., Hodges, S. D., Klaaren, K. J., and LaFleur, S. J. (1993). Introspecting about reasons can reduce post-choice satisfaction. *Personality and Social Psychology Bulletin*, *19*(3), 331–339. https://doi.org/10.1177/0146167293193010.

Wilson, T. D., and Schooler, J. W. (1991). Thinking too much: Introspection can reduce the quality of preferences and decisions. *Journal of Personality and Social Psychology*, *60*(2), 181–192. https://doi.org/10.1037/0022-3514.60.2.181.

Wright, T. A., and Huang, C.-C. (2008). Character in organizational research: Past directions and future prospects. *Journal of Organizational Behavior*, *29*(7), 981–987. https://doi.org/10.1002/job.521.

Wright, T. A., and Quick, J. C. (2011). The role of character in ethical leadership research. *Leadership Quarterly*, *22*(5), 975–978. https://doi.org/10.1016/j.leaqua.2011.07.015.

Yasai-Ardekani, M. (1986). Structural adaptations to environments. *Academy of Management Review*, *11*(1), 9–21. https://doi.org/10.5465/amr.1986.4282607.

4. The judgment of Arendt

Rita A. Gardiner and Katy Fulfer

THE JUDGMENT OF ARENDT

The political philosopher Hannah Arendt argued that judgment was a vital component of human deliberation, enriching understanding and enhancing decision-making abilities. In this chapter, we explore Arendt's approach to judgment in relation to leadership and politics. After a short introduction of her life and work, we examine how Arendt applies her ideas to leadership and the political realm. Next, we examine how she conceptualizes judgment, connecting her approach with the work of leadership scholars who view judgment as a form of practical wisdom. Then, we explore how an Arendtian approach to judgment offers insight into contemporary political events related to COVID-19. Specifically, we examine the conflicting opinions, and sometimes violent responses, to political orders mandating mask-wearing in public. In the concluding section, we explore how Arendtian judgment provides an additional contribution that may help scholars further understand the interconnections among leadership, judgment, and complex issues.

HANNAH ARENDT – BIOGRAPHICAL SKETCH

Born in 1906 in Hanover, Arendt was a German Jew who studied philosophy with some of the major existential phenomenologists including Martin Heidegger and Edmund Husserl. She fled Nazi Germany in 1933, escaping first to Paris, and later to New York. Like many new immigrants, Arendt had many jobs including au pair, book editor, and part-time professor before turning to writing. Her books, *The Origins of Totalitarianism* and *The Human Condition*, were to bring her fame.

However infamy was to follow Arendt's coverage of the 1961 trial of Adolf Eichmann, who was a senior Nazi official involved in the detailed organization of the Holocaust. First published in the *New Yorker* and later as a book entitled *Eichmann in Jerusalem*, she argues that evil like his is not monstrous, but banal. Eichmann's banality arose from his sheer thoughtlessness and lack of care about the suffering of others, and a refusal to take responsibility for his actions. Such thoughtlessness, Arendt maintains, was due to his inability to judge. For leaders to minimize harm, she argues, they need to develop sound judgment. This judgment not only requires a willingness to consider the viewpoints of others, but it also requires courage. Such courage is not only the purview of individual leaders, but arises from joint leadership action, as we illustrate in the next section.

ARENDT AND LEADERSHIP

Although Arendt held some political leaders in high esteem – Winston Churchill being one – contemporary theories such as authentic leadership or transformational leadership would be unlikely to have found favor with her, since these leadership theories place too much emphasis on the self. A focus on the self can lead to what she (1958) termed a fallacy, that of "the strong man who is powerful because he is alone" (p. 190). No one acts alone, Arendt tells us; rather, we need the support of others to be successful in any enterprise. This is especially true in the political realm where leaders must build strong coalitions among diverse stakeholders if they wish to stay in power. Additionally, Arendt's approach to leadership has similarities with relational approaches (Cunliffe and Eriksen, 2011), but her emphasis is on the fate of the political (Gardiner, 2020).

For Arendt (1958), leadership arises when people come together over a common cause. It is through this coming together in pursuit of a common goal that a small group of activists can strive to overcome injustice(s). Historical examples of this type of leadership action, according to Arendt, include the American town hall gatherings in the 18th century. In these gatherings, people came together to discuss political issues of the day. Today, collective actions of groups such as Black Lives Matter are also indicative of an Arendtian notion of leadership.

Although Arendt focuses on the importance of collective action in her reflections on leadership, this does not mean that individual leaders have nothing to learn from her approach to judgment, as judging is fundamental to a political leader's ability to govern well (Gardiner, 2020). Governing well requires leaders to put others before their own self-interest; in Arendtian terms, it requires leaders to care for the world. This caring for the world of others is enhanced by a willingness to judge. For Arendt, judgment is closely connected to practical wisdom or *phronesis* (Gardiner and Fulfer, 2017). Yet being willing to judge is sometimes regarded pejoratively, since people argue that everyone's opinion is valid, therefore it is wrong to judge others. But this argument confuses the activity of judging with being judgmental. Being judgmental, from an Arendtian perspective, is not judging but pre-judgment, that is, allowing unexamined opinions to dominate our deliberations. Arendt (1961a) also contends that the manner in which someone judges shows "what kind of a person he is" (p. 223). Thus, it is by observing how a leader judges during a particular crisis through attending to their actions and decisions that we can obtain a sense of who they are. And being willing to judge is particularly important for leaders in crisis situations.

In a global pandemic, like COVID-19, it is vital for political leaders to judge, not least because their decisions have huge impacts on people's lives and livelihoods (Grint, 2020). But what might it mean for a political leader to judge a particular situation wisely? To address this question, we first consider how scholars have approached this topic, before turning to consider Arendtian judgment in more depth through examining some disagreements regarding mask-wearing. What we wish to emphasize is that judging is not the same as being judgmental; rather, as we will show, while the latter may be construed as a way of thinking and acting that ignores others, an Arendtian approach to judgment depends upon a multiplicity of viewpoints, so as to enrich one's understanding.

LEADERSHIP, JUDGMENT, AND PRACTICAL WISDOM

According to several leadership scholars, the ability to judge wisely might best be described as a habit or disposition that leaders build over the course of their career (Tichy and Bennis, 2007; Shotter and Tsoukas, 2014a). Shotter and Tsoukas (2014b) note that good judgment and wise decision-making are fundamental to the exercise of leadership. In their view, however, many scholars do not consider the lived embodied experiences that make up leadership judgment in sufficient depth. Instead, there is an over focus on rationality as it pertains to decision-making. The problem with this approach, according to Shotter and Tsoukas (2014b), is that it "fails to bring to our attention the nature of the distinctly felt, bodily awareness and the qualities of the activities involved in the carrying out of judgment" (p. 378).

Phronesis, or practical wisdom, is intricately connected to judging. In connecting the ability to judge with practical wisdom, Shotter and Tsoukas (2014a) engage with Arendt's work, noting that central to judging is the use of one's imagination so as to obtain a "responsive attunement to the situation at hand" (p. 237). It is through this imaginative reflection that we will be able to consider a situation from multiple perspectives and, hopefully, judge a situation more wisely. We add the caveat "hopefully," because Arendt (1958) argues that we can never fully know the outcome of any decision we make, since we cannot know in advance how others will respond to our action. This is why Arendt argues, following Aristotle, that we must develop our capacity for judgment. When we have developed our judgment sufficiently, it will be easier to judge the best course of action. That action will become clearer when leaders examine an issue carefully by bringing different perspectives into account. In their attempt to judge wisely, then, a leader must do more than appeal to their own idiosyncratic beliefs.

Arendt (1992) proposes that a person "enlarge" their thinking by training their imagination "to go visiting" to help ensure that a person's perspective is pluralistic (p. 43). What this means, in practice, is that a leader imagines how someone else, differently situated than they are, might judge a particular situation. For Arendt, it is considering other standpoints, rather than particular feelings, that matters. She defines a standpoint as "the place where they stand, the conditions they are subject to, which always differ from one individual to the next, from one class or group as compared to another" (p. 43). Considering someone's subjective feelings, in her view, would only lead to adopting their particular biases, something Arendt describes as passive or uncritical. Rather than achieving generality through a singular perspective, visiting ensures generality from its multiplicity. A leader has considered a situation from various standpoints, enabling them to have a broader sense that captures more perspectives. Arendt contrasts the generality of a concept, which aims to be universal, with that of visiting, which focuses on particularity. By understanding that the particular perspectives one visits cannot be reduced to each other, a leader avoids collapsing their visiting into a single, homogenous point of view. In this way, a person's thought is sufficiently "general" to form a judgment.

The central political experiences upon which Arendt (1951) based most of her judgments were the events of the Second World War, notably the Holocaust, and the rise of totalitarianism. Specifically, she (1994) contends that many actions of totalitarian leaders "exploded" long-held "categories for political thought and our standards for moral judgment" (p. 310). In the case of some new crisis emerging, Arendt maintains that it is of relatively little use to refer to events from the past. The problem with "the wisdom of the past is that it dies, so to speak, in our hands as soon as we try to apply it honestly to the central political experiences of our time" (Arendt, 1994, p. 309).

Rather than turning to past events for guidance, therefore, leaders need to judge each event in the here and now. This is especially true for political leaders when faced with a crisis for which there is no rule book to follow. In these instances, Arendt (2018) tells us we must "think without bannisters," that is, use our imagination to help us judge what to do in a situation for which there are no guidelines. And, in what follows, we apply Arendtian judgment to think through some concerns relating to COVID-19.

POLITICAL JUDGMENTS DURING THE COVID-19 PANDEMIC

Today, it seems that COVID-19 represents a collective political experience, not least because it is a global pandemic. In such times of crisis, people look to leaders for guidance and understanding, concerning ways to reduce the spread of the virus, save lives, and maintain economic stability. One challenge that political leaders face, however, is that information about COVID-19 changes rapidly. Early in the pandemic, for example, it was not known that COVID-19 was transmitted through aerosol particles, which stay in the air longer, in addition to larger respiratory droplets. Constant change, even when it results from gaining more precise information, makes it difficult for political leaders to judge the wisest course of action.

Additionally, there is the problem of misinformation, or outright lies, sometimes artfully described as "alternative facts." Lying is nothing new in politics. Arendt (1961b) argues that politicians have often manipulated facts and lied about the truth. There can be political advantage in lying to the public, and this may be the reason why some politicians manipulate the truth with gusto. Many of Donald Trump's lies about COVID-19 fall into this latter category. For example, on July 4, 2020 Trump said that "99% of COVID-19 cases [in the United States] are 'totally harmless'" (Paz, 2020), although he had no scientific proof for this assertion. Arendt (1961b) asks us to consider the following question: "Why shouldn't a liar stick to his lies with great courage, especially in politics, where he might be motivated by patriotism or some other kind of legitimate group partiality?" (p. 249). One reason is that a political leader who indulges in this kind of behavior places their own selfish and partisan interests before the good of society. When political leaders seek to enforce a singular perspective, their judgment is not only less than robust, but it may also inhibit the ability for others to speak truthfully. As such, the propensity to fabricate lies not only affects a political leader's ability to act wisely, but it also influences the decision-making ability of citizens to judge what is true or false.

Ideally, the political realm is a dynamic space where people dialogue and debate with others. But this dynamism is curtailed when political leaders, rather than listening to diverse viewpoints, prefer to fabricate their own reality. What concerned Arendt was how this political fabrication on behalf of leaders could lead to a dulling of conscience on behalf of citizens (Gardiner, 2020). To sum up, weighing different opinions is crucial for sound deliberation, since if leaders only trust their gut, their response is likely to be less fulsome than if they had taken the time to consider other viewpoints carefully.

The quickly changing pace of knowledge around COVID-19, as well as misinformation spread online, and responses to injustice are all part of the environment leaders must negotiate in responding to COVID-19. And yet, if we take Arendt seriously, judgment cannot be done quickly. Instead, judging wisely requires a leader to consider pluralistic perspectives and use these deliberations to guide their actions. In what follows, we want to explore how Arendtian judgment works in practice. We examine different responses to mask-wearing that have emerged during these pandemic times to tease out what Arendtian judging looks like in a contemporary situation. What becomes evident is that, in a constantly changing situation, political leaders need to be particularly astute in understanding how to cope with the complexities and ambiguities of this global crisis.

TESTING ARENDTIAN JUDGMENT: TO MASK OR NOT TO MASK?

In this section, the focus is on mask-wearing. This issue has raised innumerable challenges with regard to judging appropriate action for politicians and citizens alike. To some, this issue may seem clear-cut. Yet, in visiting the perspectives of others, which as we have shown is an important aspect in forming wise judgments, we see how a simple idea, in this case the wearing of masks in public places, becomes more complicated when we take into account alternative perspectives. This multi-perspective approach is necessary for practicing the kind of "enlarged mentality" that Arendt saw as critical to the ability to judge wisely and, we would add, fundamental to the practice of trying to lead wisely (Ladkin, 2020).

As we previously outlined, for Arendt (1992), visiting – that is, imagining what it means to be in another person's situation – enables us to be better able to comprehend a particular issue from multiple viewpoints. Thus, if we think from the place of others, as Arendt teaches us, rather than condemning or condoning a person's act of wearing or not wearing a mask, we can enrich our understanding of the diverse standpoints that exist. Rather than seeing this issue in binary terms, we aim to show how thinking through this particular issue through diverse standpoints enhances one's judgment. In so doing, we not only enhance our own ability to judge from the place of another, but also discover some valid reasons why mandatory mask-wearing may be problematic for some people.

Although in early 2020 there was a lack of consensus among medical professionals about the efficacy of mask-wearing, scientific evidence now indicates there is great benefit to it, since mask-wearing helps to prevent COVID-19 from spreading throughout the community (WHO, 2020). Consequently, many municipalities enacted orders to make the wearing of masks mandatory in public spaces. In scientific communities there may well be a growing consensus, but when we look at society and the political realm more generally, this is not the case for a host of different reasons, some of which we identify below.

The experience of wearing a mask can feel a little claustrophobic at first, particularly for those of us unused to a face covering. As a result, some people may experience difficulties breathing when they begin to wear a mask. Spectacle-wearers may find their spectacles fog up from the mask, causing irritation as they pause what they are doing to wipe their spectacles. Conversely, for people with a small nose, they may find the mask slipping off as they move around. In turn, they may need to wiggle their nose to prevent such slippage. In short, mask-wearing can not only feel unnatural, but it can also act as a barrier to a person's sense of well-being and impede communication. And yet the reason most people wear masks appears to be that they judge it wise to do so and, hence, many citizens comply with mandatory orders. That is, people are willing to put up with the inconvenience of masks, because it is something that they can do, along with social distancing and hand-washing, to help prevent the spread of a deadly virus.

However, some citizens refuse to don a mask. Although it would seem to us that the scientific evidence is such that donning a mask makes sense, when we try and think through the standpoint of others, which Arendt suggests is indicative of good judgment, we may find that some individuals have valid reasons for not wearing a mask. People with severe respiratory illnesses, for example, may find wearing a mask impacts their breathing. Indeed, wearing a mask for someone who suffers from acute asthma could prove detrimental to their physical health. The second reason a person might find mask-wearing difficult is if they are hearing impaired. In this instance, mask-wearing by others may impede the former's ability to read lips. Without being able to read lips, some hearing-impaired individuals may find it difficult to understand what another person is saying. Thus, mask-wearing may negatively affect their ability to navigate public spaces, enter into conversations, or understand what the other person is saying. From this viewpoint, one can see why the wearing of masks, unless they are made with see-through material so that a person's mouth is visible, may be a problem.

A third valid reason that has been raised against mask-wearing is by some people who have experienced trauma from a violent encounter. Placing a mask on one's face can cause some rape survivors, for example, to experience memories of their attack, thus aggravating their trauma. For this reason, some survivors maintain that wearing a mask is detrimental to their mental health (Reiger, 2020). Taking this perspective into account, we judge that these trauma victims/survivors have a good case to make in terms of why mask-wearing is problematic for them.

Despite these concerns, for the most part, citizens comply with these mandates to wear masks because they have weighed the advice from medical professionals that mask-wearing is one of the best preventative measures, along with social distancing and frequent hand-washing, to prevent community spread. If most medical professionals are in favor of masks, why then do some political leaders judge it important for mask-wearing orders to be made, and others not? If scientific evidence is clear about the benefits of mask-wearing, why has mask-wearing created a political controversy?

The answer, it appears, is that many people see the wearing of masks as an affront to their personal liberty. They reject the language of mask-wearing as one's civic duty or an act of solidarity, focusing instead on their right to make decisions for themselves (Gardiner and Fulfer, 2021). Across the United States, there have been protests, sometimes violent, where protesters have come together to denounce these public ordinances. Yet, from an Arendtian perspective, there appears a confusion between the right to obey and the need to comply. From an individual perspective, being told to obey an order can seem frustrating. But this approach is indicative of placing self-interest before that of the community. Complying with these political requests is not so much about individual liberty as making a considered judgment related to the health of others.

In this section, we have begun to think through the issue of mask-wearing from different perspectives, as a way of illustrating Arendt's notion of judgment. But the reasons we have outlined for why mask-wearing might be problematic for some groups of people are not the ones that have elicited the most protests or media headlines. Rather, the issue that has been most front and center relates to how government decrees mandating mask-wearing is contrary to individual civil liberty. The issue of mask-wearing does not present an uncomplicated binary where you are either for mask-wearing and preventing the spread of COVID-19, or you are selfish and focused on your own comfort. Moreover, judging can be difficult since, as Arendt (1992) tells us, it may require us "to make the effort to understand those whose point of view we do not share" (p. 100). And this effort-making can be more difficult when people express views we find distasteful. But to judge wisely, political leaders need to be willing to consider diverse viewpoints. In the case of COVID-19, how political leaders have responded to scientific knowledge around mask-wearing, as well as people's uptake of this knowledge, is instructive. We turn now to examine some of the messages from political leaders around mask-wearing, using an Arendtian lens to demonstrate the importance of careful judgment, considering diverse perspectives, and resisting overly simplistic approaches to complex issues.

USING ARENDTIAN JUDGMENT: EXAMINING LEADERS' MESSAGES AROUND MASK-WEARING

The issue of mask-wearing has been somewhat confused by the mixed messages emerging from some political leaders (Smith, 2020). In the United States, for example, former president Trump has flip-flopped on whether or not mask-wearing is a patriotic thing to do. It is no wonder that many people were, and still are, confused. This public confusion is further increased when political leaders argue that wearing a mask is an individual choice, an option rather than a mandate. It is telling that those political leaders who take this approach are often unwilling to wear masks themselves. Those who initially refused to wear masks were often male politicians, many of whom appear to find the wearing of a mask restrictive to their macho image or their political ideology (Glick, 2020). The politicization of mask-wearing has also been apparent in other countries. The Brazilian president Jair Bolsonaro not only refuses to wear a mask, for example, but also refuses to take the COVID-19 pandemic seriously (Glick, 2020). Similarly, the U.K. prime minister Boris Johnson also took a rather cavalier approach to the pandemic at first. Unfortunately, he, Trump, and Bolsonaro became infected with the virus. So, too, did many of their country's citizens. The problem when political leaders fail to take the issue of mask-wearing seriously is that they encourage reckless action on the part of others. This recklessness reveals itself through a refusal to listen to expert medical advice, preferring instead to go with their own gut reactions rather than judging carefully. In turn, such reckless political action on the part of political leaders leads to confusion on the part of the public as to who or what to believe.

Consider, for example, the struggle between Georgia governor Brian Kemp and Atlanta mayor Keisha Lance Bottoms. In summer 2020, Kemp issued an order preventing municipalities from enacting their own public health guidelines, arguing that people do not need laws or policy to follow public health recommendations (Neuman, 2020). However, Bottoms signed an executive order on July 8, 2020 requiring masks to be worn in public places. Other municipalities put similar policies into effect (Neuman, 2020). Before mandating that masks be worn in public, Bottoms asked Kemp to reconsider his stance (Whitehead and Hurt, 2020). In response, Kemp issued an order rescinding municipalities' orders, and then filed a lawsuit against Atlanta's City Council and its mayor for overstepping the proper, in his view, (state-level) authority. What explains this political fracas between two leaders? Is it a lack of judgment, that is, a refusal to think in the place of another, as Arendt argues is vital to good deliberation?[1] It might be tempting to paint the struggle between Kemp and Bottoms as one of privileging the economy (Kemp) versus privileging the health of the community (Bottoms), yet Kemp's attempts to control the message and policy around masks ignores the lived realities of how COVID-19 is affecting many residents of Atlanta, where about half the state's cases have been. By taking a command-and-control style approach to this situation, Kemp may be adopting the wrong leadership approach (Grint, 2020).

This case reveals what is at stake when diverse perspectives, on which Arendt's notion of judgment centers, are not considered. Each municipality in Georgia may not require a mandatory mask order. Enforcing a singular perspective that fails to take into account multiple perspectives and contexts may prove problematic for reasons we have outlined. Further, Kemp's rhetoric around personal liberty invites others to focus on themselves rather than their community. By framing the issue in terms of individual liberty, Kemp fails to acknowledge the myriad of ways in which residents are asked to give up personal liberty to ensure the safety and liberty of others – speed limits being one common example to which most of us consent. In contrast, Bottoms's decisions seemed to be evidence-based. She listened to public health officials and considered how their recommendations will impact residents of Atlanta (Bethea, 2020).

As exhibited by both the image of the macho, mask-free leader and the struggle for authority, it is problematic when leaders refuse to listen to others, such as medical professionals, who may possess more knowledge about a specific issue. This refusal to listen can lead to a lack of judgment and poor decision-making. Such poor decision-making on the part of political leaders has many negative consequences for a society, one of which is that it leads to poorly thought through government policies. In the midst of a crisis, poorly conceived policies are dangerous to the health of the community. What is more, a lack of political judgment can prove devastating to the health of the political realm, especially when violence is allowed to overtake deliberation. When violence emerges in politics, we have not only lost our ability to deliberate with one another, but our democratic institutions are at risk (Arendt, 1969).

ARENDTIAN JUDGMENT, AND LEADERSHIP STUDIES

In this chapter, our aim has been to illustrate the ways in which Arendt's notion of judging has much to offer leadership scholars. As we have seen, her approach to leadership and judgment has affinities with those leadership and management scholars who are influenced by phenomenological considerations of the interconnections between judgment and practical wisdom (Cunliffe, 2016; Cunliffe and Eriksen, 2011; Ladkin, 2000; Shotter and Tsoukas, 2014a; 2014b). The ability to judge wisely is especially important within the context of a global pandemic. Such crisis situations demand a great deal of our political leaders, not least because they represent a novel "situation for which you cannot plan or predict all contingencies" (Kayes et al., 2013, p. 190).

Using Arendt's approach to judging, as we have shown here, can help us understand contemporary issues from diverse aspects. What is more, judging with Arendt enables us to comprehend the integrity, or lack thereof, of political leaders. As we follow her approach, we must take into account other perspectives that differ from our own. Now this does not mean that we just accede to the government's mandate or to another's viewpoint, which would be tantamount to an irresponsible gesture on Arendt's view. Rather, what we need to do is to consider different viewpoints on a particular issue so as to improve our ability to judge wisely.

There are several ways that her work can enrich leadership scholarship on judgment. Given space limitations, our focus is on three aspects: eschewing the dangers of outcomes-based thinking, gaining an appreciation for diverse views and ways of thinking, and the benefits of reflexive practice (Cunliffe, 2016; Yanow and Tsoukas, 2009).

First, seeing leadership solely in terms of outcomes is problematic, since it can narrow a leader's ability to judge an issue from a different perspective. COVID-19 presents a special challenge for leaders, as any public health measure or policy is intended to promote a particular outcome (e.g., preventing as many deaths as possible, stabilizing the economy). The best leaders can hope for is to manage these challenges with care, but this requires a capacity to judge each situation carefully and sensitively. It also requires that leaders do not act in a manner that makes the situation worse (Grint, 2020). Eschewing outcome-based thinking in favor of a richer approach that takes diverse perspectives into account may help leaders sort through the complexities of a crisis situation, allowing them to judge more wisely (Cunliffe and Eriksen, 2011; Shotter and Tsoukas, 2014a; O'Reilly et al., 2015).

Instead of focusing on outcomes-based thinking, leadership learning is best perceived as a process (Kayes and Kayes, 2011). This process is enhanced when leaders take a reflective approach that can enable them to obtain greater understanding of a situation (Cunliffe, 2016). For Arendt (1992), forming judgments requires attention to context and particularity. This attention supports a process-based approach. In addition, forming judgments through a process may yield more impactful responses than outcomes-based thinking. Whereas outcomes-based thinking glosses over an issue with a single brush, a process approach allows for a back-and-forth that captures nuance and the particularity of a situation.

Second, the ability to judge cultivates an appreciation of diverse views. Judgment requires leaders to exercise wisdom, which requires leaders to base their decisions on an understanding of different viewpoints (Ladkin, 2020). Ultimately, however, leaders need to take "a meta-view as to which is most apt in a given situation" (p. 132). Developing a meta-view requires one to bring together multiple perspectives on a particular issue. Using a phenomenological-inspired approach like Arendt's allows us to see that even seemingly straightforward decisions become complex when taking other opinions into account. However, the complexity gleaned from thinking through an issue from multiple perspectives enables leaders to judge an issue more wisely.

Finally, an Arendtian approach to judgment indicates the need for reflexive practice. We agree with Cunliffe (2016) that becoming a reflexive practitioner entails "a willingness to question that which may be taken for granted – what is being said and not said – and examining the impact this has or might have" (p. 741). Such a reflexive practice, according to Cunliffe (2016), operates on two levels. The first level requires leaders to engage in self-reflexivity by examining their beliefs and values. The second level requires leaders to be critically reflexive of organizational practices. In our case, we would take this argument further, and suggest that this critical reflexivity is essential to the well-being of the political realm, requiring leaders to be mindful of how their words and deeds influence others. The health of our democratic institutions is at risk whenever our political leaders fail to judge a situation in a fulsome manner.

Excessive confidence is not what we need from leaders in a situation for which there are no ready-made answers. For a leader to take an all-knowing stance, akin to pretending to be a master of the universe who has all the answers, is not appropriate, especially in crisis situations (Grint, 2020; Knights and McCabe, 2015). Such a God's eye view of the world is not leadership in an Arendtian (1958) sense but mastery (Gardiner, 2020). And yet, as Grint (2020) argues, people turn to charismatic leaders who offer them confidence as a way to assuage their concern and panic at the unknowability of what is occurring now and into the future. From an Arendtian perspective, when people do this, they are not judging wisely. In fact, they are not judging at all, preferring to allow someone else to make the decision for them. And that inability to judge may lead to unwise actions, not just on the part of leaders but also on the part of their loyal followers, such as that we witnessed in the insurrection on Capitol Hill in Washington, DC, on January 6, 2021.

Global challenges from climate breakdown to societal unrest mean that leaders have to come to terms with unexpected events. Arendt might argue that it was ever thus, and we delude ourselves to think otherwise. In any event, what we can be sure of is that crises are a part of our political, social, and organizational lives. Rather than being surprised at this, we need to face up to the challenges that the unexpected brings. One way of doing so is for leaders to cultivate an approach to leading that not only encourages reflexive practice, but is also attentive to the ever-changing nuances of a situation (Cunliffe and Eriksen, 2011). In conclusion, Arendtian judgment may help leaders grapple with some of the complex problems emerging from global and local catastrophes, in what we might call our new (ab)normal.

NOTE

1.　This struggle between the governor and mayor took place amid protests against police brutality in Atlanta, following the killing of Rayshard Brooks on June 12, 2020, and amid growing public disquiet regarding those children who have had to go back into quarantine after outbreaks of COVID-19 in schools that had few precautions in place when they re-opened.

REFERENCES

Arendt, H. (1951). *The origins of totalitarianism*. Harcourt, Brace & Company.
Arendt, H. (1958). *The human condition*. Chicago University Press.
Arendt, H. (1961a). The crisis in culture: Its social and political significance. In *Between past and future* (pp. 197–226). Viking Press.
Arendt, H. (1961b). Truth and politics. In *Between past and future* (pp. 227–265). Viking Press.
Arendt, H. (1969). *On violence*. Harcourt, Brace & Company.
Arendt, H. (1992). *Lectures on Kant's political philosophy*. Ed. R. Beiner. Chicago University Press.
Arendt, H. (1994). Understanding and politics (The difficulties of understanding). In *Essays in Understanding 1930–1954* (pp. 307–328). Harcourt, Brace & Company.
Arendt, H. (2018). *Thinking without a banister: Essays in understanding*. Ed. J. Kohn. Schocken Books.
Bethea, C. (Apr 28, 2020). Scenes from a closed Atlanta, as Georgia reopens. *The New Yorker*. https://www.newyorker.com/news/video-dept/scenes-from-a-closed-atlanta-as-georgia-reopens.
Cunliffe, A. L. (2016). "On becoming a critically reflexive practitioner" redux: What does it mean to be reflexive? *Journal of Management Education*, 40(6): 740–746. https://doi.org/10.1177/1052562916668919.
Cunliffe, A. L., and Eriksen, M. (2011). Relational leadership. *Human Relations*, 64(11): 1425–1449. https://doi.org/10.1177/0018726711418388.
Gardiner, R. A. (2020). How do leaders judge what is a responsible course of action? In D. Ladkin (ed.), *Rethinking leadership: A new look at old questions* (pp. 115–128). Second edition. Edward Elgar Publishing.
Gardiner, R. A., and Fulfer, K. (2017). Family matters: An Arendtian critique of organizational structures. *Gender, Work and Organization*, 24(5): 506–518. https://doi.org/10.1111/gwao.12177.

Gardiner, R. A., and Fulfer, K. (2021). Virus interruptus: An Arendtian exploration of political world-building in pandemic times. *Gender, Work and Organization*, 28(S1): 151–162. https://doi.org/10.1111/gwao.12510.

Glick, P. (Aug 1, 2020). Why some male leaders won't follow COVID-19 safety protocols. *Scientific American*. https://www.scientificamerican.com/article/why-some-male-leaders-wont-follow-covid-19-safety-protocols/.

Grint, K. (2020). Leadership, management and command in the time of the Coronavirus. *Leadership*, 16(3): 314–319. https://doi.org/10.1177/1742715020922445.

Kayes, A., and Kayes, D. C. (2011). *The learning advantage: Six practices of learning-directed leadership*. Palgrave Macmillan.

Kayes, D. C., Allen, C. N., and Self, N. (2013). Integrating learning, leadership, and crisis in management education: Lessons from army officers in Iraq and Afghanistan. *Journal of Management Education*, 37(2): 180–202. https://doi.org/10.1177/1052562912456168.

Knights, D., and McCabe, D. (2015). "Masters of the universe": Demystifying leadership in the context of the 2008 global financial crisis. *British Journal of Management*, 26, 197–210. http://doi:10.1111/1467-8551.

Ladkin, D. (2020). How can individuals take up the leader role wisely? In D. Ladkin (ed.), *Rethinking leadership: A new look at old questions* (pp. 128–151). Second edition. Edward Elgar Publishing.

Neuman, S. (July 16, 2020). Georgia's Governor issues order rescinding local mask mandates. NPR.org. https://www.npr.org/sections/coronavirus-live-updates/2020/07/07/16/891718516/georgias-governor-issues-order-rescinding-local-mask-mandates.

O'Reilly, D., Leitch, C. M., Harrison, R. T., and Lamprou, E. (2015). Leadership, authority and crisis: Reflections and future directions. *Leadership*, 11(4): 489–499. https://doi.org/10.1177/1742715015596633.

Paz, C. (Nov 20, 2020). All the president's lies about the coronavirus. The Atlantic. https://www.theatlantic.com/politics/archive/2020/11/trumps-lies-about-coronavirus/608647/.

Reiger, S. (Aug 3, 2020). Masks provide COVID-19 protection but can surface old traumas for sexual assault survivors. CBC.ca. https://www.cbc.ca/news/canada/calgary/masks-covid-19-sexual-assault-trauma-1.5672079.

Shotter, J., and Tsoukas, H. (2014a). In search of phronesis: Leadership and the art of judgment. *Academy of Management Learning and Education*, 13(2): 224–243. https://doi.org/10.5465/amle.2013.0201.

Shotter, J., and Tsoukas, H. (2014b). Performing phronesis: On the way to engaged judgment. *Management Learning*, 45(4): 377–396. https://doi.org/10.1177/1350507614541196.

Smith, S. (Aug 9, 2020). Unmasked: How Trump's mixed messaging on face-coverings hurt U.S. coronavirus. NBCNews.com. https://www.nbcnews.com/politics/donald-trump/calendar-confusion-february-august-trump-s-mixed-messages-masks-n1236088.

Tichy, N., and Bennis, W. (Oct, 2007). Making judgment calls. *Harvard Business Review*, 94–102. https://hbr.org/2007/10/making-judgment-calls.

Whitehead, S., and Hurt, E. (July 8, 2020). Atlanta mayor orders masks to be worn in public spaces. NPR.org. https://www.npr.org/sections/coronavirus-live-updates/2020/07/08/888904008/atlanta-mayor-to-order-masks-to-be-worn-in-public-spaces.

WHO (Aug 5, 2020). Coronavirus disease (COVID-19) advice for the public: When and how to use masks. https://www.who.int/emergencies/diseases/novel-coronavirus-2019/advice-for-public/when-and-how-to-use-masks.

Yanow, D., and Tsoukas, H. (2009). What is reflection-in-action? A phenomenological account. *Journal of Management Studies*, 46(8): 1339–1362. https://doi.org/10.1111/j.1467-6486.2009.00859.x.

5. Judgments and justifications

Markus Kornprobst

INTRODUCTION

Analyzing the reasoning of political leaders is a very important scholarly endeavor. It is especially in moments of crisis when these judgments make a major difference – for better or for worse. The SARS-CoV-2 (COVID-19) Crisis illustrates this all too well. During the crisis, decision-making authority moved up the executive ladder, entrusting presidents, prime ministers, chancellors, and so on with plenty of decision-making power. How they used it had a profound impact on the states they governed. Following the determination of a public health emergency of international concern (PHEIC) by the World Health Organization (WHO) at the end of January 2020, some leaders waited too long to respond with adequate countermeasures. This way the virus could spread easily, and it was no coincidence that, by May 2020, the United States, Russia, Brazil, and the United Kingdom had experienced the highest absolute numbers of infections in the world even though these states were not among the first ones to be affected by the pandemic.

While it is important to focus on leaders' judgments, we should never forget that they hardly ever make up their minds all by themselves. They are influenced in doing so in various ways. There are closer and more distant advisors. Some leaders anxiously watch out for public opinion surveys or listen carefully to lobbyists. A leader's own political party may assert itself vis-à-vis this leader. Parliament may be able to put pressure on him or her. Experts often matter, too. SARS-CoV-2 illustrates this again very well. Suddenly, leaders felt the need – some more and some less so – to listen to medical doctors, especially epidemiologists (who did not necessarily agree among one another). Some foreign ministers and health ministers also established themselves as important players.

The thrust of my argument is to take leaders and their individual imprints on their reasoning seriously and, at the same time, study carefully the influences on this reasoning exerted by other players. Keeping with George's focus on leaders and developing his analytical restraint further (George, 1991, p. 24), the epistemology underpinning my argument is compositional pragmatism. There is no such thing as point-predicting political decisions. All researchers can do is trace the winding roads through which actors come to figure out what to do in an unfolding situation. I contend that two concepts are of crucial importance for this scholarly endeavor: *judgment* and *justification*. Judging is subsuming particulars under universals, which are taken from repertoires of taken-for-granted ideas. Justifying is about sending reasons for one's own judgments to audiences as well as passing judgments on the justifications given by others. I develop a three-circuit map for the empirical study of how actors relate judgments and justifications. The perimeter circuit produces first hunches (pre-judgments), justifications exchanged in the resonance circuit push and shove (pre-)judgments over and over, and all this judging and justifying feeds back into the constellation of repertoires, whose universals give rise to this judging and justifying in the first place.

All of this amounts to a distinctly eclectic approach to studying judgments and justifications. I borrow insights from cognitive and social psychology, social theory, communication theory, and, most of all, political theory. This eclecticism makes for what appear to me to be two important contributions: Following broad conceptualizations of judgment in political theory, the process of judging that this chapter proposes features individual aspects as well as social ones. Thus, it captures the *multidimensionality of judgment*. Furthermore, linking judgment and justification together, the three-circuit map offers a heuristic tool for studying how communicative encounters – private and public – affect judgments as well as how this interplay of judging and justifying leaves a legacy for future decision-making situations. The map, in short, helps studying the *communicative constitution of judgments*.

This chapter is organized into four main sections. First, I introduce compositional pragmatism. Second, I define judgment and justification. Third, I outline a map for studying the interrelatedness of judging and justifying. Fourth, I describe the methodology of structured, focused communication analysis for doing empirical research. The conclusion that follows summarizes my findings and discusses their implications. Throughout this chapter, I repeatedly draw from my much more detailed study on judgments, justifications, and co-managing international crises (Kornprobst, 2019). I illustrate my (meta-)theoretical points by drawing from my previous empirical research on British, French, and German attempts to co-manage the Bosnian Crisis in the early 1990s. My illustration for a structured, focused communication analysis is taken from my current research on the co-management of the SARS-CoV-2 Crisis.

COPING WITH ANALYTICAL CHALLENGES: COMPOSITIONAL PRAGMATISM

Doing research on reasoning would be easy if all political decision-makers were to make up their minds in the same way all the time. If, say, decisions were objective computational outputs based on the input of objective costs, including risks, and benefits, there would not be much need to delve into practical reasoning. Researchers would have it easy. All they would have to do is punch the input into a computer and they could point-predict the decisions of the actors they study.

The empirical evidence against such over-simplifications, however, is overwhelming. Two key empirical findings of the existing literature are to be taken seriously. First, different leaders make sense of and decide differently in different situations even if these situations are comparable (Lebow, 1981, p. 335; Stern, 2009, p. 191; Saunders, 2017). This heterogeneity has a lot to do with how different leaders draw from different subjective and intersubjective reservoirs to make sense of a situation. In light of different clues they put to use, a situation may appear to be a major threat to one leader but merely an issue of minor concern to another. These variations of sense-making are likely to make decision-making vary as well. With one leader employing risk-prone heuristics and the other one risk-averse ones, for example, even leaders who widely share understandings of a situation as a crisis may not end up making similar decisions.

Second, actors rarely make sense and decisions all by themselves. Even in crisis situations, where decision-making authority – formally and informally – moves towards the upper echelons of the executive, leaders usually communicate with others. There are plenty of domestic and international communicators (Janis and Mann, 1977; Kurizaki, 2007), who communicate in private and public (Janis, 1972; Seymour, 2014), and convey messages ranging from successful crisis responses (Seeger, 2006; Gartner, 2011, p. 545), via one's own just causes (Berinsky, 2007; Goetze, 2008), to demarcations between ingroup and outgroup (Brewer, 2009; Gruffydd-Jones, 2017). Leaders, of course, also seek to make meaning.[1] They seek to "sell" their policies to domestic and, at times, international audiences. Yet even the most successful meaning-makers are also exposed to some meaning-making themselves, some of which shapes their sense- and decision-making. During the Kosovo Crisis, for example, Tony Blair stood tall on the domestic and international stages. The prime minister's messages for humanitarian intervention resonated widely. Yet he, too, was influenced by other communicators, ranging from Robin Cook's ideas of an ethical foreign policy to Alastair Campbell's spin-doctoring. Hence, research on practical reasoning needs to take communication seriously.

Taken together, this makes for a three-fold analytical challenge. Not only is there a need for conceptualizing the heterogeneity of practical reasoning and the many possible flows of communication, but there is also the challenge of inquiring into the linkages of reasoning and communication. There are some hints in the literature about how reasoning and communication are linked to one another. Lasswell (1941), for example, writes about reasoning and mass publics, Hermann et al. (1987, p. 335) about small decision-making units, and Boltanski and Thévenot (2006) about how communicating actors put to use orders of worth (and reproduce them by doing so). These studies are important, not least because they remind us of the breadth of communicative influences on leaders. Yet there is a need to build upon these insights, taking this full breadth seriously.

Coping with these analytical challenges requires switching epistemological gears. Big generalizations (for example, all individuals, facing the same constraints, make the same judgments) and even simple linear causal relationships (say, constraint X causes judgment Y) won't do. These epistemological assumptions about generalizations as well as causality on one hand and the heterogeneity of reasoning as well as complex relationships between reasoning and communication on the other simply do not match. Instead, the subject matter invites what I refer to as *compositionist pragmatism*. This epistemology is close to Latour's "compositionist manifesto" (Latour, 2010) as well as Jackson and Nexon's "configurationalist analysis" (Jackson and Nexon, 1999; Jackson, 2014).

At its core are a conceptual and an explanatory move. Compositional pragmatism is on the lookout for focal concepts (Pavitt, 1981). These are concepts that are widely used across different theoretical schools of thought (within or even across different academic disciplines). The task is then to define these concepts broadly in order to generate conceptual definitions that come as close as possible to capturing the multifaceted nature of a phenomenon instead of limiting it to a few very specific ones. In Blumer's language, researchers should strive for "sensitizing" and not "definite" conceptualizations (Blumer, 1954). Pragmatist writings in international relations theory make a similar point (Friedrichs and Kratochwil, 2009, p. 715; Sil and Katzenstein, 2010, pp. 43–48) and Craig's advocacy for pragmatism in communications theory is not far removed from it either (Craig, 2007).

The explanatory move then puts the focal concepts in relation to one another. The heuristic means for doing so is a map that enables the researcher "to follow the actors," as Latour (2005, p. 12) puts it. The map is the vehicle for doing thorough empirical research. The point is to explain how actors under empirical scrutiny come to reason and act the way they do in an unfolding situation while closely following how they, metaphorically put, move back and forth on the map. This includes watching out for feedback loops and plenty of contingency. While the conceptual move is all about staying away from overly narrow conceptual boxes, the explanatory one revolves around steering clear of all too easy unidirectional causal arrows that, formulated a priori, neatly lead from one scholarly box to the next.

Addressing the question of how to study practical reasoning and how it relates to communication, the following two sections implement these moves. The next section defines practical reasoning as judgments and communication as justification. The section thereafter deals with the question of how to trace the causal relationships between the two concepts.

TWO SENSITIZING CONCEPTUALIZATIONS: JUDGMENTS AND JUSTIFICATIONS

Protagonists of different approaches to reasoning employ the term judgment, often without defining it, to characterize reasoning. This applies to scholars of rational choice (Ostrom, 1998), political psychology (Simon, 1982), appropriateness (Messick, 1999), argumentation (Habermas, 1991), and practice (Bourdieu, 1984). Thus, judgment appears to be a very promising candidate for a focal concept. I inclusively define *political judging as the human faculty to orient oneself substantially and procedurally in an unfolding situation by subsuming – sometimes more intuitively, sometimes more reflectively – the particulars of this situation under selected universals of political life.*

Judging, therefore, is, above all, subsuming particulars under universals (Beiner, 1983). Actors select universals out of a constellation of repertoires of universals[2] that is at their disposal. *Universals* are already established clues that anchor judgments. They encompass what some cognitive and social psychologists refer to as schema (Bartlett, 1932; Anderson, 1978),[3] argumentation research as topoi, loci, or commonplaces (Aristotle, 1975; Kornprobst, 2008), and Bourdieu as well as Bourdieu-inspired scholarship as nomoi and doxa (Bourdieu, 1977; Emirbayer and Johnson, 2008). In other words, universals range from being idiosyncratic, that is, held only by a certain individual, to being widely shared, as well as from being fully reflected to being deeply habitualized. Furthermore, there are not only substantive universals, anchoring judgments about what an unfolding situation is like and what responses by a political entity are to be carried out. There are also procedural ones that provide orientation for agents about how to assert themselves and the political entity on which behalf they act vis-à-vis other actors. Perhaps most importantly, procedural universals provide clues about the political efficacy of actors in a given encounter with others. They provide some actors with more authority than others. The *particulars* are the specific interpretations of a situation that become intelligible in light of the selected universals. This subsuming of particulars under universals provides actors with inklings (intuitive) and thought-through (reflective) orientations about how to make sense of and act in a situation substantially as well as about their political efficacy, the efficacy of others, and ways to assert themselves procedurally.

During the Bosnian War, for example, François Mitterrand drew from a repertoire of universals that he shared with other European leaders, from a repertoire that prevailed in French debates on foreign policy, and from an idiosyncratic one that he had acquired through his very own specific socialization process. The French president selected several universals to make the evolving situation in Bosnia intelligible to himself. There was, to mention just one universal taken from each repertoire, a Europhile universal that made him determined not to let the Bosnian Crisis have adverse effects on critical integration steps (Maastricht Treaty). Applying France's great power universal (*la grande nation*), he was resolved to have his country play a leading role in managing the crisis. Steeped in history since his student years, his reasoning was shaped by historical analogies, especially the alliance patterns of the world wars. Serbia had always been an ally of France.

Justification is a useful focal concept for communication. The founders of the discipline of Communications frequently focused on justification when they conceptualized communicative processes (Lasswell, 1941; Berelson et al., 1954, pp. 15–29), and this focus has stayed in place across different approaches (Taylor, 2002; Pingree, 2006; George, 2016). It is found in other disciplines, such as Sociology and Economics, as well (Boltanski and Thévenot, 2006). I define *political justifying as the communicative process of giving and contesting reasons of assertions that are composed of particulars and universals, and come to succeed or fail to resonate to varying degrees.*[4] Justifications, too, are about particulars and universals. How they are related is, within the confines of imaginability drawn by the constellation of repertoires, up to the agents who assemble the message. They may channel their justifications through private or public encounters, and combine reasons in different ways. They may invoke various types of reasons (or linkages across them), say utilitarian, justice-related, or emotional. Resonance may vary from being fully convinced by a justification (Habermas, 1991) to mere acquiescence (Nölle-Neumann, 1982).

To return to the illustration above, Mitterrand was a sender of justifications. He dejustified coercing the Serbs and justified a humanitarian peace mission – UNPROFOR – instead. At the same time, Mitterrand was exposed to all kinds of justifications for a more interventionist stance in domestic and international politics. His very own prime minister, Alain Juppé, pushed for a much more hard-nosed crisis management. So did a number of vocal intellectuals, known as the New Philosophers (*nouveaux philosophes*). Helmut Kohl, the German chancellor, and increasingly the Clinton administration (and here especially Madeleine Albright) put pressure on Mitterrand.

BRINGING JUDGMENTS AND JUSTIFICATIONS TOGETHER: THE THREE-CIRCUIT MAP

Tracing how actors relate judging and justifying to one another is facilitated by a conceptual map that encompasses three simultaneously operating circuits: perimeter, resonance, and structuration. The perimeter circuit produces what Gadamer (1972, p. 261) referred to as *pre-judgments*. They amount to hunches about how to subsume particulars under universals. The hallmark of pre-judgments is that they are sticky. Agents are very reluctant to throw them out entirely. Yet the perimeter circuit really is a circuit. Situations to be made intelligible do not stand still. This makes it necessary for actors to keep on making pre-judgments.

In the resonance circuit, judgments shape justifications and vice versa. Those actors who, underpinned by active procedural judgments, perform the role of interlocutor, send justifications and defend their judgments while those whose passive procedural judgments endow others with communitive authority are mere receivers. Receivers amend their prior judgments, including their pre-judgments, depending on how close these are to prior judgments and as long as they do not violate any pre-judgments.[5] There are three degrees of amending judgments. First, receivers *harden or soften* prior judgments. The prior judgments remain in place but become stronger or weaker relative to other judgments. Second, they *elaborate on or abridge* prior judgments. Core universals and particulars remain in place but (interpretations) of particulars and universals are added or subtracted. Third, receivers *reconcile* prior judgments. They may harmonize them (no rank-order), subordinate some under others (rank-order), or even exceptionalize some prior judgments. The last qualifies the applicability of *a prior* judgment due to extraordinary circumstances.[6]

Finally, there is the structuration circuit. Judging and justifying, usually without much reflection, feeds back into the constellation of repertoires that gives rise to perimeter and resonance judgments in the first place. This does not leave the constellation untouched. Again, there are three degrees of changes. First, universals used frequently in perimeter and resonance judgments *gain salience* while those not put to use *lose salience*. Second, universals may acquire *new interpretations* in light of the linkages to particulars and other universals invoked in perimeter and resonance judgments. Third, particulars that are strongly emphasized in perimeter and resonance judgments may become *new universals*. None of these three degrees of changes happen from one day to the next. The structuration circuit operates much more slowly than the other two. It takes time for new (interpretations of) universals to sink into the background.

We can now return to Mitterrand. What did all of this justifying against his non-interventionist stance do with his judgments? All the judgments I discussed above already – European-integrationist, great power role, no war against the Serbs – were pre-judgments. He held on to them throughout his management of the crisis. But the domestic and international pressures made him repeatedly reconcile his pre-judgments, pushing him towards adding teeth to his humanitarian approach. Rank-ordering his pro-European judgments and his determination not to fight the Serbs, he agreed to Operation Deny Flight, ensuring that the West European Union became a crisis actor to be reckoned with and insisting on a humanitarian mandate that was confined to protecting civilians in case they were attacked by either conflict party. This kind of pushing and shoving of his prior judgments continued after the First Markale Massacre of Serb forces against civilians in Sarajevo. It is, given his sticky pre-judgments, however, very doubtful whether Mitterrand would ever have agreed to the bombardments of the Serbs that eventually led to the Dayton Agreement. It was his successor, Jacques Chirac, whose pre-judgments put pro-intervention universals to use and made him listen attentively to an interventionist domestic public opinion and public opinion makers, who made sure that France played a leading role in the shift from a humanitarian approach to peace enforcement.

Mitterrand and Bosnia is just a simple illustration of how the map can be used as a heuristic device. A focus on just one leader in this crisis would probably not be enough. Putting a number of other domestic players, and here certainly Juppé, under scrutiny would be analytically rewarding, too. In the international realm, the judgments and justifications of others

– the NATO allies Clinton, Major, and Kohl, Russia's Yeltsin, and the UN secretary-general Boutros-Ghali come to mind immediately – would be well worth analyzing as well.

STRUCTURED, FOCUSED COMMUNICATION ANALYSIS: ILLUSTRATING A METHODOLOGY

The three-circuit map is a vehicle for studying judging and justifying empirically. While there are different ways of conducting such empirical research, a structured, focused communication analysis (Kornprobst, 2019) is especially apt. It balances the needs for studying contexts, judgments, and justifications. I largely borrow the label from George (1979), who used structured, focused comparisons to study the political judgments (but not justifications) of leaders. Carrying out a structured, focused communication analysis encompasses five research tasks: (a) identifying the constellation of repertoires from which actors drew to orient themselves in the evolving situation; tracing the (b) perimeter circuits, (c) resonance circuits, and (d) structuration circuits that they were embedded in; and, finally, (e) discussing alternative explanations.

Writing this chapter a year after the global SARS-CoV-2 outbreak and hoping for plenty of empirical analyses to research this important case, I switch my empirical illustrations to the early stages of the (mis-)management of this crisis. What if we wanted to study why WHO determined a PHEIC only at the end of January 2020 and not earlier? After all, doctors in Wuhan, most notably Li Wenliang, warned already of human-to-human transmission of a new coronavirus in December 2019. PHEICs are important because they put states and medical systems on high alert to get ready to counter the (potential) international spread of disease (Art 1, IHR). Time is of the essence. Delays in determining a PHEIC cause the loss of precious time to respond to an outbreak and curb a disease before it is too late.

Before dealing with the five research tasks, the researcher needs to select to select a time frame to focus on as well as the leaders to be analyzed. When it comes to the former, a time period from 8 December, that is, the time when Chinese doctors started exchanging their experiences about a "mysterious virus" on online platforms (Kim, 2020), to 30 January – this is when the PHEIC was finally determined – would be plausible. Selecting decision-makers is somewhat more difficult. At a minimum, it would have to be the WHO Director-General Tedros Adhanom Ghebreyesus. According to the International Health Regulations (IHR), he was in charge of making the "final determination" (Art. 49(5)) of a PHEIC, having considered the information received from the affected state (Art 12(4e)), the advice by an Emergency Committee (Art 12(4c)), the available scientific evidence (Art. 12(4d)), and weighed the risk of the spread of a disease against the repercussions of travel and trade barriers (Art. 12(4b) and Art. 12(4e)). These legal provisions already suggest adding another group of actors. The affected state was China. Tedros, on several occasions, directly communicated with Xi Jinping. The chairperson of the Emergency Committee was Didier Houssin. It would also be rewarding to analyze his judgments and justifications. Beyond this, another group could even be added, such as the leaders of the United States, Germany, and the United Kingdom, whose assessed and voluntary contributions to the WHO budget provide them with some clout in Geneva.

The first task is to uncover the constellation of repertoires. The following guiding questions are useful to ask: Prior to SARS-CoV-2, how did universals held by WHO actors, medical practitioners, and WHO member states under scrutiny evolve? How did the idiosyncratic ones embraced by the leaders under analysis develop? How do universals converge and diverge across the leaders and the political entities they represent? In all likelihood, such an analysis would underline that there is a great divide between medical and political repertoires (Kickbusch and Liu, 2019). This should make a difference for encounters between Houssin and state leaders, with Tedros (a medical doctor, turned politician, turned international bureaucrat) situated somewhere in the middle. It is equally likely that such an analysis would find out that political repertoires, too, are highly diverse. Xi's increasingly determined foreign policy universals, for example, are very different to Merkel's persistently cautious ones. To add further to the complexity, some of the universals that leaders hold are idiosyncratic, while they share others more widely domestically as well as internationally. Universals prevailing in Germany, for instance, are Europeanized to a certain extent (Kornprobst, 2019).

Second, tracing the perimeter circuit involves identifying the leaders' first inklings. These potentially pertain to the full range of orientations: how to make sense of the crisis, what kinds of decisions are thinkable and unthinkable, who they are to listen to and not, and what techniques are at their disposal to enable themselves to make meaning. Asking the following questions helps to get at these first inklings: What universals did leaders fall back upon by themselves when addressing the crisis? What particulars did these universals make them see? Did the unfolding of the situation prompt them to select new universals by themselves and did this make them see different particulars? Did the perimeter judgments of leaders intersect, and if so, how? While these questions are always fascinating to ask, they are of special salience in the case at hand with regard to the state leaders. Prior to the spread of SARS-CoV-2, most of them routinely played down health issues, focusing on matters of security and economics instead. Pre-judgments subjugating health under such matters may very well be part of the explanation.

Third, in analyzing the resonance circuit, analysts should cast their net widely. Leaders exchange justifications with many different actors in domestic and international locales. The interplay of medical experts and political elites is to be examined carefully. So is media coverage of the spread of disease. The analysis should be structured by the following questions: What competing justifications were leaders exposed to in domestic and international locales and who sent these? Did the leaders' prior judgments make them participate in these justificatory contestations, and if so, how did they defend and send justifications and with what repercussions for their standing and the crisis interpretations of others (congruence test)? Which of these justifications, if any, were sufficiently in sync with the leaders' prior judgments so as to make them amend, that is, harden/soften, elaborate/abridge, reconcile, these judgments (diffusion test)? Did the exchange of justifications make leaders' prior judgments more consonant, and if so, how? Answering these questions would shed light on a number of crucial aspects of the crisis response, including Xi's strategies for how to script a narrative of control during the crisis and suppress dissenting voices (especially some doctors in Wuhan) and make it stick internationally, too (or at least prevent official WHO criticism despite late Chinese reporting of the new coronavirus).

Fourth, there is the inquiry into how judging and justifying leaves marks on the constellation of repertoires. When it comes to structuration, three questions should be asked: How did perimeter judgments feed back into the constellation of repertoires? How do resonance judgments feed back into the constellation of repertoires? Does this feedback re-produce or change repertoires and their overlaps? It is, for example, very likely that SARS-CoV-2 will become itself a universal. How the universal will be interpreted, how these interpretations will link up with other universals to form a program of action, and how widely shared such interpretations will be across nations as well as the medical–political divide will be of crucial importance in whether humankind will be more ready to prevent or control the next pandemic.

Last but not least, alternative explanations should be discussed, too. This includes simple utilitarian accounts that assume exogenously given preferences, psychological approaches that focus on the biases of individual leaders but not their communicative interaction, norms-based contentions about social appropriateness (and, thus, neither judgment nor justification), studies on persuasion and arguing (coming down heavily on justification rather than judgment), and tacit common sense (which is assumed to be ontologically prior to justification).

CONCLUSION

This chapter made a meta-theoretical, theoretical, and methodological case for how to study judgments. I argued for a compositional pragmatism that attempts to trace the winding roads through which actors come to orient themselves rather than superimpose overly narrow scholarly categories upon them. I contended that judgments and justifications are intricately interwoven. Justifications push and shove judgments. Both are enabled by a constellation of repertoires, which, in turn, is made, re-made, and unmade by the interplay of judgments and justifications. I presented a structured, focused communication analysis, illustrating it with a research design to inquire into the process that led to the (much belated) determination of a PHEIC in the case of SARS-CoV-2.

Overall, my contention cautions students of political processes not to withdraw into ever smaller (meta-)theoretical niches of ever more self-referential academic disciplines. Doing justice to the multifaceted processes of judgment requires moving beyond narrow disciplinary boundaries and the even narrower confines of approaches within them. Otherwise we'll simply miss too much when we try to understand how leaders figure out what to do. And understanding their doings is more important than ever. We live in times in which one crisis follows the other, globalization and deglobalization forces clash, contestation about the international order becomes sharper and sharper, and even domestic cleavages become increasingly pronounced. In these times, it is very likely that the judgments and justifications of leaders, for better or for worse, will make a major difference. And, once again, there will be plenty of variation about how leaders come to judge and justify.

NOTES

1. I borrow this distinction between sense-, decision-, and meaning-making from Boin et al. (2016).
2. I borrow the term "constellation" from Bernstein (1991).
3. Note that the notion of schema originates in political theory (Kant, 1956). The same, of course, applies to judgment (Plato, 1925; 1961; Aristotle, 1934; 1975; Kant, 1956: B171–172; 1974; Arendt, 1958; 1964).
4. I developed this definition during my collaboration with Uriel Abulof on making sense of the concept of justification (Abulof and Kornprobst, 2017a; 2017b).
5. Note, however, that the roles of sender and receiver are not always unambiguously distributed. Usually, even the most active procedural judgments are somewhat counter-balanced by at least some passive ones.

6. Exceptionalizing, similar to compromising (Boltanski and Thévenot, 2006), is unstable. Actors seek to return to at least a milder form of reconciling prior judgments as soon as possible.

REFERENCES

Abulof, U., and Kornprobst, M. (2017a). Introduction: The politics of public justification. *Contemporary Politics 23*(1), 1–18.

Abulof, U., and Kornprobst, M. (2017b). Unpacking public justification. *Contemporary Politics 23*(1), 126–133.

Anderson, R. C. (1978). Schema-directed processes in language comprehension. In A. M. Lesgold, P. W. Pellegrino, S. D. Fokkema, and R. Glaser (Eds.), *Cognitive psychology and instruction* (pp. 67–82). Nato Conference Series, vol. 5. Boston, MA: Springer. https://doi.org/10.1007/978-1-4684-2535-2_8.

Arendt, H. (1958). *The human condition*. Chicago: University of Chicago Press.

Arendt, H. (1964). *Eichmann in Jerusalem: A portrait of the banality of evil*. New York: Penguin.

Aristotle. (1934). *Nicomachean ethics*. London: William Heinemann.

Aristotle. (1975). *The art of rhetoric*. Cambridge, MA: Harvard University Press.

Bartlett, F. C. (1932). *Remembering: A study in experimental and social psychology*. Cambridge: Cambridge University Press.

Beiner, R. (1983). *Political judgment*. Chicago: University of Chicago Press.

Berelson, B., Lazarsfeld, P., and McPhee, W. (1954). *Voting: A study of opinion formation in a presidential campaign*. Chicago: University of Chicago Press.

Berinsky, A. J. (2007). Assuming the costs of war: Events, elites, and American public support for military conflict. *Journal of Politics 69*(4), 975–997.

Bernstein, R. J. (1991). *The new constellation: The ethical-political horizons of modernity/postmodernity*. Cambridge: Polity.

Blumer, H. (1954). What is wrong with social theory? *American Sociological Review 19*(1), 3–10.

Boin, A., Stern, E., Sundelius, B., and Hart, P. (2016). *The politics of crisis management: Public leadership under pressure*. Cambridge: Cambridge University Press.

Boltanski, L., and Thévenot, L. (2006). *On justification: Economies of worth*. Princeton, NJ: Princeton University Press.

Bourdieu, P. (1977). *Outline of a theory of practice*. Cambridge: Cambridge University Press.

Bourdieu, P. (1984). *Distinction*. London: Routledge.

Brewer, S. A. (2009). *Why America fights: Patriotism and war propaganda from the Philippines to Iraq*. Oxford: Oxford University Press.

Craig, R. T. (2007). Pragmatism in the field of communication theory. *Communication Theory 17*(2), 125–145.

Emirbayer, M., and Johnson, V. (2008). Bourdieu and organizational analysis. *Theory and Society 37*(1), 1–44.

Friedrichs, J., and Kratochwil, F. (2009). On acting and knowing: How pragmatism can advance international relations research and methodology. *International Organization 63*(4), 701–731.

Gadamer, H. G. (1972). *Wahrheit und Methode*. Tübingen: J. C. B. Mohr.

Gartner, S. S. (2011). On behalf of a grateful nation: Conventionalized images of loss and individual opinion change in war. *International Studies Quarterly 55*(2), 545–561.

George, A. L. (1979). Case studies and theory development: The method of structured, focused comparison. In P. G. Lauren (Ed.), *Diplomacy: New approaches in history, theory, and policy* (pp. 43–68). New York: Free Press.

George, A. L. (1991). A provisional theory of crisis management. In A. L. George (Ed.), *Avoiding war: Problems of crisis management* (pp. 22–27). Boulder, CO: Westview.

George, C. (2016). *Hate spin: The manufacture of religious offense and its threat to democracy*. Cambridge, MA: MIT Press.

Goetze, C. (2008). When democracies go to war: Public debate and the French decision on war in 1999 and 2003. *Global Society 22*(1), 57–77.

Gruffydd-Jones, J. (2017). Dangerous days: The impact of nationalism on interstate conflict. *Security Studies 26*(4), 698–728.

Habermas, J. (1991). *Erläuterungen zur Diskursethik*. Frankfurt am Main: Suhrkamp.

Hermann, M. G., Hermann, C. F., and Hagan, J. D. (1987). How decision units shape foreign policy behavior. In C. F. Hermann, C. W. Kegley Jr., and J. N. Rosenau (Eds.), *New directions in the study of foreign policy* (pp. 309–336). London: Allen & Unwin.

Jackson, P. T. (2014). Making sense of making sense: Configurational analysis and the double hermeneutic. In D. Yanow and P. Schwartz-Shea (Eds.), *Interpretation and method: Empirical research methods and the interpretive turn* (pp. 267–283). London: Routledge.

Jackson, P. T., and Nexon, D. H. (1999). Relations before states: Substance, process and the study of world politics. *European Journal of International Relations 5*(3), 291–332.

Janis, I. L. (1972). *Victims of groupthink: A psychological study of foreign-policy decisions and fiascoes*. Boston, MA: Houghton Mifflin.

Janis, I. L., and Mann, L. (1977). *Decision making: A psychological analysis of conflict, choice, and commitment*. New York: Free Press.

Kant, I. (1956). *Kritik der reinen Vernunft*. Hamburg: Felix Meiner.

Kant, I. (1974). *Kritik der Urteilskraft*. Frankfurt am Main: Suhrkamp.

Kickbusch, I., and Liu, A. (2019). Global health governance. In Hertie School of Governance, *The governance report 2019* (pp. 83–102). Oxford: Clarendon.

Kim, J. (2020). Wuhan coronavirus: China plays the blame game. *The Diplomat*, 27 January. Available at https://thediplomat.com/2020/01/wuhan-coronavirus-china-plays-the-blame-game/. Accessed 5 October 2020.

Kornprobst, M. (2008). *Irredentism in European politics: Argumentation, compromise and norms*. Cambridge: Cambridge University Press.

Kornprobst, M. (2019). *Co-managing international crises: Judgments and justifications*. Cambridge: Cambridge University Press.

Kurizaki, S. (2007). Efficient secrecy: Public versus private threats in crisis diplomacy. *American Political Science Review 101*(3), 543–558.

Lasswell, H. D. (1941). The garrison state. *American Journal of Sociology 46*(4), 455–468.

Latour, B. (2005). *Reassembling the social: An introduction to actor-network-theory*. Oxford: Oxford University Press.

Latour, B. (2010). An attempt at a "compositionist manifesto". *New Literary History 41*(3), 471–490.

Lebow, R. N. (1981). *Between peace and war: The nature of international crisis*. Washington, DC: Johns Hopkins University Press.

Messick, D. M. (1999). Alternative logics for decision making in social settings. *Journal of Economic Behavior and Organization 39*(1), 11–28.

Nölle-Neumann, E. (1982). *Die Schweigespirale*. Frankfurt am Main: Ullstein.

Ostrom, E. (1998). A behavioral approach to the rational choice theory of collective action. *American Political Science Review 92*(1), 1–22.

Pavitt, C. (1981). Preliminaries to a theory of communication: A system for the cognitive representation of person- and object-based information. *Annals of the International Communication Association 5*(1), 211–232.

Pingree, R. J. (2006). Decision structure and the problem of scale in deliberation. *Communication Theory 16*(2), 198–222.

Plato. (1925). *Statesman*. London: William Heinemann.

Plato. (1961). *Meno*. Edited and translated by R. S. Bluck. Cambridge: Cambridge University Press.

Saunders, E. N. (2017). No substitute for experience: Presidents, advisers, and information in group decision making. *International Organization 71*(1), 219–247.

Seeger, M. W. (2006). Best practices in crisis communication: An expert panel process. *Journal of Applied Communication Research 34*(3), 232–244.

Seymour, L. J. M. (2014). Let's bullshit! Arguing, bargaining and dissembling over Darfur. *European Journal of International Relations 20*(3), 571–595.

Sil, R., and Katzenstein, P. J. (2010). *Beyond paradigms: Analytic eclecticism in the study of world politics*. Basingstoke: Palgrave Macmillan.

Simon, H. A. (1982). *Models of bounded rationality*. Cambridge, MA: MIT Press.

Stern, E. K. (2009). Crisis navigation: Lessons from history for the crisis manager in chief. *Governance* 22(2), 189–202.

Taylor, P. (2002). *Global communications, international affairs and the media since 1945.* London: Routledge.

6. How leaders judge creativity: a look into the idea evaluation process

Vignesh R. Murugavel and Roni Reiter-Palmon

INTRODUCTION

The ever-changing world of business implores organizations to adapt and compete to survive and maintain effectiveness. Organizations turn to creative ideas to foster change and grow in fluctuating markets (Amabile, 1996; Shalley et al., 2004; Sharma, 1999). Creative and innovative efforts allow organizations to increase efficiency, develop competitive advantages, and respond to consumer expectations (Mumford et al., 2014). It is of no surprise that many companies turn to the creativity of their employees for innovation and therefore seek to facilitate the process of innovation.

One way researchers have defined innovation is as a process that involves the creation, development, and application of creative products (Mumford et al., 2012; Mumford and Gustafson, 1988). Ultimately, the process of organizational innovation is contingent upon the creative processes of the people (Mumford and Gustafson, 1988). It is this process that organizations seek to leverage. However, the production of novel and useful ideas alone is not sufficient to enact change and growth for an organization as a whole. Woodman and colleagues (1993) describe organizational-level creativity and innovation as a function of the characteristics of the employees, the teams in which the employees operate, and the organization. It is the role of a leader to ensure that these three levels operate in tandem for innovation to result (Mumford et al., 2014). Leaders and how they manage creative efforts are critical to the success of an organization.

Sharma (1999) identified a set of central dilemmas in managing innovation in companies. The primary dilemma that is discussed is the identification of especially productive creative ideas and separating them from nonproductive ones. This central dilemma, referred to as *seeds versus weeds*, will be the focus of this chapter. The following sections will elaborate on the process of distinguishing between seeds and weeds. Later sections of this chapter will describe the qualities in leaders and the situation that best facilitate a process of evaluating and selecting creative ideas.

IDEA EVALUATION

As Sharma (1999) describes, companies are rarely met with a shortage of original ideas. It is the lack of resources for implementation and associated risk to general company functioning from new ideas that restrict a firm's ability to innovate. Only a few ideas from the many that are produced reach a point of implementation. As such, a process of distinguishing between seeds and weeds is needed. This process identifies ideas that are practically viable, cost-effective, and can be developed and applied within the resource constraints of the company. Often, ambiguity and uncertainty pervade many of the points on which ideas are assessed. Distinguishing between seeds and weeds requires balancing the features of the ideas, the context of application, and the organizational goals and standards. This balancing act is complex and difficult. Much of the literature on leadership and innovation asserts that the leader is best positioned to evaluate and select ideas for implementation (e.g., Drazin et al., 1999; Mumford et al., 2014; 2017; Sharma, 1999). The leadership role provides a wide perspective that allows leaders to effectively align creative ideas with application contexts and organizational goals.

Distinguishing between seeds and weeds is formally described in the literature on creativity as the process of idea evaluation. Idea evaluation fits into a larger process of creative problem-solving, which occurs in response to ambiguous and unstructured situations. Creative problem-solving is modeled using a cognitive framework. Creativity researchers have proposed many different models of creative problem-solving, each with varied sets of cognitive mechanisms (e.g., Finke et al., 1992; Guilford, 1967; Mumford et al., 1991; Runco and Chand, 1995; Sternberg, 1988). While models may differ in specific processes, all models include idea evaluation, suggesting that it is a critical aspect of creativity (Reiter-Palmon and Illies, 2004).

The Idea Evaluation Process. For an idea to be creative it must be both novel and useful (Hennessey and Amabile, 2010). As such, an idea's creativity is composed of two dimensions: idea originality and idea quality (Runco and Basadur, 1993). Idea originality relates to the uniqueness and novelty of an idea. Idea quality refers to the feasibility and usefulness of the idea and the appropriateness of an idea in addressing the issues at hand. During the idea evaluation process, ideas are assessed for their originality and quality (Blair and Mumford, 2007).

The effectiveness of the idea evaluation process is a critical determinant of a person's ability to choose the best idea among the weeds. Leaders with more effective idea evaluation processes are more likely to identify ideas worth implementing. In an early study on leadership and innovation, Andrews and Farris (1967) analyzed the influence of leadership practices on the performance of scientific groups. In the study, groups of scientists of similar characteristics (e.g., training, experience, and seniority) but with different supervisors showed different levels of innovative performance. The authors concluded that the practice of critical evaluation by the leader was a key contributor to follower innovation. Later research on leadership echoes the observations made by Andrews and Farris (1967). For example, Marshall-Mies and colleagues (2000) found that implementation planning skills and solution evaluation skills of high-level executives were important cognitive skills that can contribute to predicting leadership performance.

Elsewhere, Mumford and colleagues (2000) also determined that idea evaluation was critical for effective leadership. The authors examined the acquisition of requisite cognitive skills by leaders across various officer grade levels in the U.S. Army. Creative problem-solving skills and idea evaluation skills were found to be especially relevant for senior-level officers compared to lower officer levels. In a similar vein, Mumford and colleagues (2017) identified nine skills that leaders use in addressing complex problems: problem definition, cause/goal analysis, constraint analysis, planning, forecasting, creative thinking, idea evaluation, wisdom, sensemaking/visioning. Among this set of nine, many represent cognitive activities found in models of idea evaluation (i.e., cause/goal analysis, constraint analysis, forecasting). Not to mention, idea evaluation itself, as a more general skill, was identified as being directly related to leadership performance (Watts et al., 2017). The following sections of this chapter describe the cognitive process of leadership evaluation and present empirically identified influences on the process. Figure 6.1 depicts a framework for understanding leadership idea evaluation.

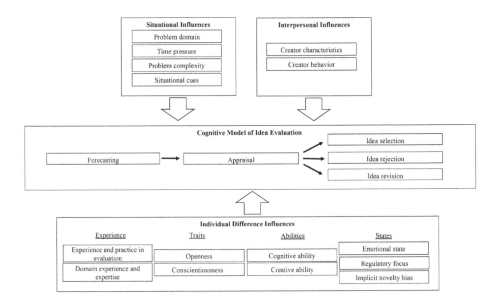

Figure 6.1   A framework of leadership idea evaluation and influences on the process

FORECASTING

Mumford and colleagues (2002) proposed a comprehensive cognitive model of how a person evaluates creative ideas. The model denotes forecasting, appraisal, and final decision choice as key operations. According to the model, idea evaluation begins with forecasting. The process of evaluation inherently requires comparison. An idea cannot be evaluated with respect to only itself. Forecasting, or the process of anticipating the most plausible outcomes of implementation, produces a basis upon which a comparison can take place. The goals and requirements of the problem or situation are factored into forecasting. Due to its cornerstone position in the idea evaluation process, Mumford and colleagues propose that it is especially critical for creative output and successful implementation. The authors' claim is further substantiated by empirical work on forecasting.

Byrne and colleagues (2010) used trained judges to quantify the effectiveness of a participant's forecasting. The authors found that forecasting effectiveness for idea implications and implementation was related to the creativity of ideas, denoting the importance of forecasting in creative thinking and implementation planning. As implied through the quantification of forecasting as an index of effectiveness, forecasting is not always a perfect process. There are instances when forecasting is highly accurate and there are instances when forecasting can be subject to error. Dailey and Mumford (2006) compared participants' forecasting of ideas to the ideas' real outcomes to determine forecasting accuracy. As a general finding, people were able to accurately forecast the requirements and consequences of ideas. Moreover, familiarity with the ideas' content domain resulted in more accurate forecasts.

Berg (2016) extended the literature on creative idea forecasting to managers. Berg examined the circus arts industry and found that creators of creative acts were better than their managers at predicting the success of ideas produced by *other* creators. Creators were not better than managers at predicting the success of their *own* ideas. The author concludes that expertise in a domain may be applied differently during evaluation for leaders than during evaluation for creators. Expertise may produce personal biases that could interfere in evaluating one's own ideas. This study shows that forecasting by leaders can have utility. Further sections of this chapter will explore the role of expertise and differences in evaluating one's own ideas and others' ideas.

APPRAISAL

After forecasting, the next key operation that is discussed in Mumford et al.'s (2002) model is appraisal. In this process, the creativity of an idea is assessed and the viability of the idea is determined. A set of standards derived from the goals and requirements of the creative effort is used to make evaluations of ideas. The implementation context is also considered during appraisal.

Accuracy. A primary concern for idea evaluation researchers is whether people can accurately evaluate ideas. Several studies by Mark Runco and colleagues (Basadur et al., 2000; Runco, 1991; Runco and Basadur, 1993; Runco and Smith, 1992; Runco and Vega, 1990) have suggested that people can be accurate in their evaluations. A few studies have specifically looked at managers evaluating creativity. For example, Basadur and colleagues (2000) and Runco and Basadur (1993) examined the ability of managers to evaluate ideas before and after creative problem-solving training. Both studies showed that managers were significantly better at judging the originality of an idea after training. From these findings, two key points can be made regarding leaders who evaluate creative ideas. One, leaders can accurately appraise creative ideas. Two, the ability to accurately evaluate ideas is fluid and can be trained. The idea evaluation process in leaders can be improved with experience and practice.

Interpersonal Evaluations. Another relatively large stream of research focuses on whether the evaluation of one's own creative ideas is different than the evaluation of others' creative ideas. Although the ability to accurately evaluate self-generated ideas is important for creative outputs (Cropley, 2006; Finke et al., 1992), leaders rarely evaluate their own ideas. The role of the leaders in facilitating creativity in an organization is more focused on evaluating the ideas produced by followers. Interpersonal idea evaluation may be especially relevant for leaders.

Research on interpersonal and intrapersonal differences in the evaluation of creative ideas began with Runco and Smith (1992). The authors examined student evaluation of creative ideas for solving an open-ended problem that they themselves generated (intrapersonal) and that their peers generated (interpersonal). A strong association between interpersonal and intrapersonal evaluations was observed; approximately 36 percent of the variance between the two was shared. The strength of the relationship indicates that the two forms of evaluations are similar to each other; however, the value of the shared variance reveals that there are some differences between interpersonal and intrapersonal evaluations. In general, evaluations were more accurate for intrapersonal evaluations. Later work by Grohman and colleagues (2006) replicated the results of Runco and Smith (1992). Grohman and colleagues (2006) also examined the influence of creative ideation skills on interpersonal evaluations of idea originality and uniqueness. Findings indicated that creative ideation ability may obstruct the accurate evaluation of an idea's features and qualities (i.e., the idea's originality), whereas the ability may bolster the process of discerning the rarity of an idea (i.e., its uniqueness).

Findings from Runco and Smith (1992) and Grohman et al. (2006) directly apply to leaders. Being an observer of a creative idea rather than the producer makes leaders especially vulnerable to issues of evaluation inaccuracies. When evaluating ideas, the leader may not be privy to the history and context of an idea's genesis. An intrapersonal idea evaluation process may have occurred for the follower before presenting an idea to a leader. Idea rejection and idea revision may have occurred to arrive at the final idea. The leader's appraisal of the idea would not consider the alternatives that were rejected or why and how revisions improved an idea. Prudence from the leader is required to not fall victim to inaccuracies specific to interpersonal evaluation. Leaders who participate in the idea generation process or those who seek out understanding an idea's history and development path may be better evaluators of an idea's creative potential. Additionally, leaders can use their ideation skills to identify the most unique ideas from a set of generated ideas. However, leaders should be careful not to misjudge how novel an idea is in a given domain. Leaders are especially useful for evaluating more objective qualities such as appropriateness, feasibility, and relative uniqueness. Moreover, leaders who do not interfere and allow intrapersonal evaluation processes to transpire may better facilitate innovation.

FINAL DECISION CHOICE

Idea selection. The appraisal of ideas is thought to involve convergent forms of thinking as opposed to divergent forms (Basadur et al., 1982; Runco and Chand, 1995). That is, thoughts converge to determine a singular outcome. In the case of idea evaluation, the outcome that results from convergent thinking is the final decision choice or idea selection. The research on idea selection focuses on the creativity or successfulness of a chosen idea from a set as opposed to accuracy in the evaluation of each idea in a set. Although the appraisal of ideas and selection of ideas are distinct concepts, they both fit into a larger process of idea evaluation. The two are intertwined. Successfully choosing an idea is a direct result of accurately assessing its creativity. Research on idea selection incorporates theories and empirical findings from idea evaluation literature. Yet literature on idea selection does not always align with literature on evaluation accuracy.

Studies by Runco and colleagues note that evaluations of creative ideas are largely accurate. In contrast, studies by Rietzschel and colleagues (2006; 2010) find that the selection of creative ideas from a set of generated ideas is no better than chance. Rietzschel et al. (2010) found that people tend to overlook the originality of an idea and focus on the idea's feasibility when choosing a creative idea. Because both the novelty and appropriateness of an idea are not considered, less creative ideas are selected. The authors also found that providing an explicit instruction to select creative ideas tended to alleviate the feasibility preference, improving the idea selection process.

The interpersonal versus intrapersonal theme that exists in evaluation accuracy literature is similarly found in idea selection literature. Faure (2004) did not find differences in the selection of one's own ideas versus others' ideas in terms of the selected idea's originality or practicality, but more effective ideas were chosen by groups that were selecting from their own ideas. Elsewhere, using a similar study design, Zhu et al. (2020) found that both intrapersonal and interpersonal idea selection processes failed in choosing the most creative ideas from a set of generated ideas. Furthermore, no difference in the creativity of the chosen idea was observed for those selecting from their own ideas and those selecting from a list generated by others.

These findings fall in line with the observations of Runco and Smith (1992) and Grohman et al. (2006). Interpersonal and intrapersonal differences in the idea evaluation process are based on the criteria used to appraise ideas. Leaders selecting creative ideas must effectively balance idea feasibility and idea originality when making their decisions. When leaders recognize, explicitly, that their role is to choose creative ideas, they may be able to alleviate a natural tendency to discount the novelty of ideas.

Revision. Idea evaluation is thought to result in three possible outcomes (Mumford et al., 2002). Ideas can be dropped from consideration of implementation, accepted for implementation, or revised. When the evaluation outcome of an idea is revision, it is reworked and then reconsidered in another evaluation cycle. Among the already limited literature on the idea evaluation process (Reiter-Palmon, 2018), the least attention is paid to the revision of ideas. The revision of ideas contrasts much of the operations in the larger idea evaluation process. Idea revision involves generative thinking. As such, much of the existing knowledge on idea revision comes from research on other creative problem-solving besides idea evaluation (e.g., idea generation). Few studies have examined idea revision directly within the framework of the idea evaluation process. A recent study by Watts and colleagues (2019) experimentally examined how ideas are refined. Participants were more likely to engage in idea revision processes on a list of initial ideas when the initial set of ideas were self-generated (versus peer-generated).

Similar to the disadvantages of interpersonal idea evaluations in terms of evaluation accuracy and idea selection, interpersonal idea revision may be disadvantaged by a lack of history and context for an idea that the evaluator had no part in designing. The findings of Watts and colleagues (2017) suggest that leaders who are not involved in the generation of an idea may not be effective in revising the idea. The original creators of the idea, the followers, are generally better suited to revise and refine ideas. Nonetheless, the role of the leader is still critical to this sub-process. Leaders indirectly influence idea revisions by identifying the shortcomings and points of alteration of an idea through forecasting and appraisals (Barlow, 2000; Watts et al., 2017).

INFLUENCES ON IDEA EVALUATION

Although many present the leadership role as being well positioned to evaluate creative ideas (e.g., Drazin et al., 1999; Mumford et al., 2014; 2017; Sharma, 1999), a leader's idea evaluation process does not always result in successfully recognizing and selecting a creative idea (Mueller et al., 2012). Several factors may impair or bias leader idea evaluation. Given the importance of an effective idea evaluation process for innovation, researchers have sought to clarify the factors that are most conducive to the idea evaluation process. Both individual difference factors and contextual factors contribute to the efficacy of idea evaluation. A sizable proportion of research on idea evaluation has revealed that idea evaluation differs between individuals. The recognition of creative ideas is more accurate for some than for others.

EXPERIENCE AND EXPERTISE

Experience and expertise are individual differences that are commonly studied in creativity and decision-making research (Kaufman et al., 2013). Expertise represents a special case of experience whereby experience and knowledge in a field surpasses a specified level and a high level of performance in a domain ensues (Jonassen, 2000; Robertson, 1990). Experience is thought to be a key component of idea evaluation. The model of idea evaluation proposed by Mumford and colleagues (2002) recognizes experience as a critical input into the process. Experience in the evaluation context affects how the context is applied to the forecasting and appraisal operations. Furthermore, experience also influences the application of goals and standards. Empirically, experience has been connected to forecasting (Mumford et al., 2000) and the appraisal of creative ideas.

In a series of studies, James C. Kaufman, with many different colleagues, explored differences between novice and expert evaluators of creativity. Kaufman and colleagues (2008) found that established poets (experts), as compared to students (novices), were more reliable in their evaluations of idea creativity. Later work by Kaufman (e.g., Kaufman and Baer, 2012; Kaufman et al., 2013) took a more nuanced look at expertise, introducing quasi-experts into the study. Kaufman et al. (2013) found that quasi-experts were able to accurately evaluate the creativity of ideas similar to experts. These results imply that a high threshold of experience is not required for effective idea evaluation to occur. Rather, idea evaluation can be accurate if only an adequate level of experience has been gained. Different forms of experience were examined as well. For example, Kaufman and colleagues considered English teachers as well as creativity students as having a form of quasi-expertise in rating short stories. Results were similar across different forms of quasi-expertise. Additionally, the authors tested the agreement of quasi-experts' creativity ratings across two tasks (creative writing and engineering design). Quasi-experts were less reliable raters in the domain of engineering compared to writing, indicating that domain affects the degree to which expertise relates to the process of evaluating creative ideas.

The application of the literature on expertise and idea evaluation to leaders evaluating creative ideas is fairly straightforward. First, leaders with more experience will tend to be better evaluators of creative ideas. For leaders to effectively evaluate creative ideas, they need not be true experts in the field; however, it is apparent that some amount of experience is required. It should be noted that the requisite experience a leader needs to effectively evaluate creative ideas may differ across domains. In addition to experience in a domain, experience with an organization or evaluation experience can also make idea evaluation more effective.

TRAITS AND ABILITIES

Although not as heavily researched as experience and expertise, other individual differences have been connected to idea evaluation. Basadur et al. (2000) and Silvia (2008) found that skill in producing multiple ideas was associated with the effective evaluation of creative ideas. Silvia also found a positive relationship between trait openness and idea evaluation accuracy and a negative relationship between conscientiousness and idea evaluation accuracy. The findings are consistent with literature on personality and creativity. Those who are broad-minded and curious (i.e., openness) tend to more readily absorb and seek out new information (McCrae and Costa, 1997). As a result, more open individuals tend to be more creative (Feist, 1999). The same flexibility with new information likely applies to evaluating creative ideas that largely consist of new connections and combinations. Alternatively, individuals who are excessively meticulous, organized, and possess strong self-control (i.e., conscientious) may be more closed off to new perspectives, resulting in less effective idea evaluation processes.

Benedek and colleagues (2016) added cognitive ability to the list of individual differences that affect the idea evaluation process. Like openness, cognitive ability has been consistently connected to creativity in past research (Jauk et al., 2014; Kim, 2005). Benedek and colleagues (2016) showed that the variables openness, intelligence, and language competence work to reduce the tendency to underestimate the creativity of ideas, resulting in more accurate evaluations. The authors also found a relationship between evaluation skill and creative accomplishment. That is, those who had better evaluation skill also tended to have more creative top lifetime creative achievements. This finding suggests that creative people, those that have stronger creative abilities and have more creative accomplishments, tend to be better evaluators of creative ideas. Indeed, researchers have argued that leaders of creative efforts should possess the qualities of creative people (Mumford et al., 2002; 2014; 2017).

The findings of the traits and abilities that are involved in idea evaluation have particular implications for leaders as evaluators of creative ideas. First, due to the demands of their role, effective leaders tend to already possess a high level of intelligence (Foti and Hauenstein, 2007; Judge et al., 2004). Naturally, these leaders will have some level of accuracy in idea evaluation. Creative leaders and leaders who are more broadminded and open to new situations can be even more accurate than leaders whose evaluations solely stem from their general cognitive ability. Similar to intelligence, conscientiousness also characterizes leaders (Judge et al., 2002). However, the relationship between conscientiousness and idea evaluation was found to be negative (Silvia, 2008); therefore, leaders should be careful that their predisposition to order and fastidiousness does not extend to their idea evaluation process.

STATES

General intelligence and openness are thought to be relatively stable individual differences. More fluid individual differences, or states, have also been connected to the evaluation of creative ideas. Studies have shown that variables related to motivation influence the idea evaluation process. For example, Herman and Reiter-Palmon (2011) examined the effects of regulatory focus on the accuracy of creative idea evaluations in a sample of employees. Regulatory focus refers to different approaches that are employed to achieve a goal (Higgins, 1998). Goal pursuit can either have a promotion focus or a prevention focus. A promotion focus corresponds to growth and improvement resulting in a mindset of achieving gains. In contrast, a prevention focus incites feelings of safety and security. As a result, prevention focus mindsets adhere to preventing losses. Herman and Reiter-Palmon (2011) found that those with more promotion focus had more accurate evaluations of an idea's originality but were less accurate in the evaluation of an idea's quality. Those with more prevention focus were found to have more accurate idea quality evaluations and less accurate idea originality evaluations. The authors' findings suggest that how a person approaches their evaluation goals is important for successful idea evaluation. When the regulatory state matches with the corresponding evaluation criteria (i.e., promotion with originality evaluations and prevention with quality evaluations), more accurate evaluations are expected.

de Buisonjé et al. (2017) extended research on idea evaluation and regulatory focus using an experimental design. Participants in evaluation conditions that induced a promotion focus selected more creative ideas from a pool of ideas than participants in a control condition. Furthermore, de Buisonjé and colleagues' study included an experimental induction of mood and self-affirmation. Similar to the positive effects of promotion focus on idea selection, a positive effect of positive mood was found. A positive effect was also found for those who were reminded of their social and cultural adequacy (self-affirmation). These results show that goal pursuit, emotion, and self-regulation are involved in the idea evaluation process. Together, the findings of de Buisonjé et al. (2017) and Herman and Reiter-Palmon (2011) suggest that leaders should consider how they approach the evaluation of creative ideas. Leaders should factor in their internal states when evaluating ideas. Negative moods or uncertainty with the self may negatively affect a leader's ability to distinguish creative ideas from non-creative ones.

In line with this work on motivation and idea evaluation, Mueller and colleagues (2012) find that people have a natural aversion to novel ideas stemming from a motivation to reduce uncertainty. The authors experimentally manipulated the levels of uncertainty in creative ideas and found that people were less likely to recognize a creative idea under conditions of uncertainty. Leaders may be especially likely to have a desire to reduce uncertainty, as they balance goals of practicality and profitability with novelty. The resulting bias towards creative ideas may be particularly damaging to leader idea evaluation if left unchecked. Leaders should fight against their implicit novelty bias if they want to accurately recognize, appraise, and select creative ideas.

SITUATIONAL INFLUENCES

In addition to the individual difference influences on idea evaluation, the context in which an idea is evaluated influences how ideas are appraised and selected. According to Mumford et al. (2002), idea evaluation is a highly contextualized process. Situational differences result in different evaluations of creative ideas. Licuanan and colleagues (2007) purport that situations that make the attributes of a creative idea most salient are most conducive to accurate evaluation. The authors found that idea evaluation accuracy decreases when problems are more complex and increases when the standards for evaluation emphasize the need for original ideas. In concert with these findings, Lonergan et al. (2004) and Rietzschel et al. (2010) found that providing instruction to evaluators yields more accurate evaluations. Reiter-Palmon et al. (2018) extended the positive effects of instruction to the selection of creative ideas. In another study of standards and idea evaluation, Blair and Mumford (2007) discovered that the previously noted preference for feasibility during idea evaluation was overturned when selection occurred under contexts of high time pressure and when strict standards for evaluation were used. Under these situations, risky ideas become viable choices.

Research has also shown that problem domain affects evaluation. Sullivan and Ford (2005) found that participants were able to distinguish between the quality and originality of an idea in some domains but not in others. In domains that do not explicitly produce creative products (e.g., business), the evaluation of idea quality and idea originality are independent. For example, an idea can be considered highly original but low in quality. When creativity is the marker of performance in a field (e.g., advertising), it is much harder to separate an idea's quality from its originality. In these domains, ideas are considered to fall on a singular contin-uum ranging from low creativity to high creativity. This observation highlights a point made earlier in the chapter: the amount of experience needed to accurately evaluate ideas differs by domain. It may be that different amounts of experience are required because idea evaluation may be more difficult in certain domains. For instance, it may be harder to assess an idea's suitability for implementation if the evaluator cannot discern the idea's quality.

Other situational influences were addressed in Mueller et al. (2018). The authors told partic-ipants that they will either have the final say in choosing a creative idea competition's winning idea or be one among a set of judges in choosing the winning idea. Those who were told that their decisions carried more weight turned to provided information on each idea's favorability when assessing its creativity. The authors proposed that being a sole decision-maker results in a strong need for accurate and objective assessment. In the absence of sufficient knowledge and experience in a domain, situational cues such as favorability seem to be used during eval-uation as a rationale for information-driven assessment. In the case of Mueller et al. (2018), the information that is provided from situational cues speaks little to the creativity of the idea. As a result, idea evaluation is negatively affected.

These findings regarding the contextual influences on idea evaluation pose several implica-tions for leaders that evaluate creative ideas. First, leaders may find themselves in ambiguous situations that obscure the salience of the attributes of creative ideas. As a result, idea evalua-tion may be inaccurate if the leader does not seek out additional details and clarification from idea generators. Second, leaders should be aware that they may be more likely to choose risky ideas under time constraints and when they use rigid criteria for evaluation. Third, research indicates that the idea evaluation process might be different across situations for leaders who evaluate creative ideas from various projects. Leaders may find it easier to evaluate ideas that are generated to solve a problem in one domain compared to another. If leaders fail to adjust their evaluation process accordingly, errors in appraising and selecting the best idea for imple-mentation may occur. Finally, leaders should recognize that in certain situations they may be more prone to use criteria that are not relevant to creativity. For example, when leaders have the final say in what ideas get implemented, they may opt for more popular ideas rather than creative ones. To avoid this tendency, a leader should seek out more information on the idea. For leaders to choose the ideas that will most likely be successful, they must be familiar with and understand what criteria they are using to assess ideas.

INTERPERSONAL INFLUENCES

Beyond the characteristics of the evaluator and the context of evaluation, the source of the idea, an idea's creator, can also influence how it is assessed (Zhou et al., 2019). Often, idea evaluation occurs as an interpersonal process (Elsbach and Kramer, 2003). Creative idea assessment from a leader includes both a cognitive appraisal of an idea's characteristics and a social judgment of the idea's creator: the follower. The influence of the follower may not always be removed from the evaluation of their idea.

Lu and colleagues (2019) identified ways that creators can influence how their creative ideas are judged. First, creators who use idea pitching tactics that make the abstract qualities of novel ideas more concrete receive more positive assessments of their creative ideas. These tactics include using demos, prototypes, and tangible exhibits when pitching their ideas. The authors also find that influence tactics similar to those that leaders use to influence their subordinates can change interpersonal idea evaluation. These tactics include making rational arguments, asking a target for advice, appealing to a target's values, and collaborating with the target (Yukl, 2013). Leaders should be aware that how a creator presents an idea may not be wholly indicative of the idea's creative potential.

Zhou et al. (2019) add that the characteristics of creators contribute to their influence on an evaluator's assessment of their creative ideas. For example, creative and innovative behaviors from men are viewed more favorably than those behaviors from women (Proudfoot et al., 2015; Luksyte et al., 2018). Zhou and colleagues (2019) note that biographical qualities that may affect a creator's ability to exert influence and persuade evaluators (e.g., nonnative accents; Huang et al., 2013; gender stereotypes; Luksyte et al., 2018) would ultimately affect interpersonal idea evaluation. As leaders may supervise a diverse set of followers, they must be aware of how follower characteristics can bias their decision-making regarding creative ideas. Leaders should be careful to not let what they believe to be prototypical of a creator influence how that creator's idea is to be assessed.

CONCLUSION

Much of the empirical work that is presented in this chapter studied evaluation in an organizational leadership context; however, the breadth of idea evaluation research extends across many disciplines and targets different populations (Zhou et al., 2019). The theoretical and practical ideas presented in this chapter apply well to leaders but may not generalize to other populations. This limitation should be recognized when applying the presented concepts in the real world.

This chapter reviews and applies theoretical conclusions and empirical findings to leaders who evaluate creative ideas. Leaders use forecasting, appraising, selecting, and revising operations to sort out the weeds from the seeds. Leader qualities, follower qualities, and situational factors contribute to a leader's evaluation of creative ideas. Research on leader idea evaluation is far from complete. Following this growing body of work will allow for a thorough understanding of the many factors that influence idea evaluation and will allow leaders to best capitalize on their critical position in facilitating innovation.

REFERENCES

Amabile, T. M. (1996). *Creativity in context*. Westview Press.
Andrews, F. M., and Farris, G. F. (1967). Supervisory practices and innovation on scientific teams. *Personnel Psychology, 20*, 497–515. http://dx.doi.org/10.1111/j.1744-6570.1967.tb02446.x.
Barlow, C. M. (2000). Deliberate insight in team creativity. *Journal of Creative Behavior, 34*, 101–117. https://doi.org/10.1002/j.2162-6057.2000.tb01204.x.

Basadur, M., Graen, G. B., and Green, S. G. (1982). Training in creative problem solving: Effects on ideation and problem finding and solving in an industrial research organization. *Organizational Behavior and Human Performance*, *30*(1), 41–70. https://doi.org/10.1016/0030-5073(82)90233-1.

Basadur, M., Runco, M. A., and Vega, L. A. (2000). Understanding how creative thinking skills, attitudes and behaviors work together: A causal process model. *Journal of Creative Behavior*, *34*, 77–100. https://doi.org/10.1002/j.2162-6057.2000.tb01203.x.

Benedek, M., Nordtvedt, N., Jauk, E., Koschmieder, C., Pretsch, J., Krammer, G., and Neubauer, A. C. (2016). Assessment of creativity evaluation skills: A psychometric investigation in prospective teachers. *Thinking Skills and Creativity*, *21*, 75–84. https://doi.org/10.1016/j.tsc.2016.05.007.

Berg, J. M. (2016). Balancing on the creative highwire: Forecasting the success of novel ideas in organizations. *Administrative Science Quarterly*, *61*, 433–468. https://doi.org/10.1177/0001839216642211.

Blair, C. S., and Mumford, M. D. (2007). Errors in idea evaluation: Preference for the unoriginal? *Journal of Creative Behavior*, *41*, 197–222. https://doi.org/10.1002/j.2162-6057.2007.tb01288.x.

Byrne, C. L., Shipman, A. S., and Mumford, M. D. (2010). The effects of forecasting on creative problem-solving: An experimental study. *Creativity Research Journal*, *22*, 119–138. https://doi.org/10.1080/10400419.2010.481482.

Cropley, A. (2006). In praise of convergent thinking. *Creativity Research Journal*, *18*(3), 391–404. https://doi.org/10.1207/s15326934crj1803_13.

Dailey, L., and Mumford, M. D. (2006). Evaluative aspects of creative thought: Errors in appraising the implications of new ideas. *Creativity Research Journal*, *18*, 385–390. https://doi.org/10.1207/s15326934crj1803_11.

de Buisonjé, D. R., Ritter, S. M., de Bruin, S., ter Horst, J. M., and Meeldijk, A. (2017). Facilitating creative idea selection: The combined effects of self-affirmation, promotion focus and positive affect. *Creativity Research Journal*, *29*, 174–181. https://doi.org/10.1080/10400419.2017.1303308.

Drazin, R., Glynn, M. A., and Kazanjian, R. K. (1999). Multilevel theorizing about creativity in organizations: A sensemaking perspective. *Academy of Management Review*, *24*, 286–307. https://doi.org/10.5465/amr.1999.1893937.

Elsbach, K. D., and Kramer, R. M. (2003). Assessing creativity in Hollywood pitch meetings: Evidence for a dual-process model of creativity judgments. *Academy of Management Journal*, *46*, 283–301. https://doi.org/10.2307/30040623.

Faure, C. (2004). Beyond brainstorming: Effects of different group procedures on selection of ideas and satisfaction with the process. *Journal of Creative Behavior*, *38*, 13–34. https://doi.org/10.1002/j.2162-6057.2004.tb01229.x.

Feist, G. J. (1999). *The influence of personality on artistic and scientific creativity*. In R. J. Sternberg (Ed.), *Handbook of creativity* (pp. 273–296). Cambridge University Press.

Finke, R. A., Ward, T. B., and Smith, S. M. (1992). *Creative cognition: Theory, research, and applications*. The MIT Press.

Foti, R. J., and Hauenstein, N. M. A. (2007). Pattern and variable approaches in leadership emergence and effectiveness. *Journal of Applied Psychology*, *92*, 347–355. https://doi.org/10.1037/0021-9010.92.2.347.

Grohman, M., Wodniecka, Z., and Kłusak, M. (2006). Divergent thinking and evaluation skills: Do they always go together? *Journal of Creative Behavior*, *40*, 125–145. https://doi.org/10.1002/j.2162-6057.2006.tb01269.x.

Guilford, J. P. (1967). *The nature of human intelligence*. McGraw-Hill.

Hennessey, B. A., and Amabile, T. M. (2010). Creativity. *Annual Review of Psychology*, *61*, 569–598. https://doi.org/10.1146/annurev.psych.093008.100416.

Herman, A., and Reiter-Palmon, R. (2011). The effect of regulatory focus on idea generation and idea evaluation. *Psychology of Aesthetics, Creativity, and the Arts*, *5*, 13–20. https://doi.org/10.1037/a0018587.

Higgins, E. T. (1998). Promotion and prevention: Regulatory focus as a motivational principle. In M. P. Zanna (Ed.), *Advances in experimental social psychology* (Vol. 30, pp. 1–46). Academic Press.

Huang, L., Frideger, M., and Pearce, J. L. (2013). Political skill: Explaining the effects of nonnative accent on managerial hiring and entrepreneurial investment decisions. *Journal of Applied Psychology*, *98*(6), 1005–1017. https://doi.org/10.1037/a0034125.

Jauk, E., Benedek, M., and Neubauer, A. C. (2014). The road to creative achievement: A latent variable model of ability and personality predictors. *European Journal of Personality, 28,* 95–105. http://dx .doi.org/10.1002/per.1941.

Jonassen, D. H. (2000). Toward a design theory of problem solving. *Educational Technology Research and Development, 48,* 63–85. https://doi.org/10.1007/BF02300500.

Judge, T. A., Bono, J. E., Ilies, R., and Gerhardt, M. W. (2002). Personality and leadership: A qualitative and quantitative review. *Journal of Applied Psychology, 87,* 765–780. https://doi.org/10.1037/0021 -9010.87.4.765.

Judge, T. A., Colbert, A. E., and Ilies, R. (2004). Intelligence and leadership: A quantitative review and test of theoretical propositions. *Journal of Applied Psychology, 89,* 542–552. https://doi.org/10.1037/ 0021-9010.89.3.542.

Kaufman, J. C., and Baer, J. (2012). Beyond new and appropriate: Who decides what is creative? *Creativity Research Journal, 24,* 83–91. https://doi.org/10.1080/10400419.2012.649237.

Kaufman, J. C., Baer, J., Cole, J. C., and Sexton, J. D. (2008). A comparison of expert and nonexpert raters using the consensual assessment technique. *Creativity Research Journal, 20,* 171–178. https:// doi.org/10.1080/10400410802059929.

Kaufman, J. C., Baer, J., Cropley, D. H., Reiter-Palmon, R., and Sinnett, S. (2013). Furious activity vs. understanding: How much expertise is needed to evaluate creative work? *Psychology of Aesthetics, Creativity, and the Arts, 7,* 332–340. https://doi.org/10.1037/a0034809.

Kim, K. H. (2005). Can only intelligent people be creative? A meta-analysis. *Journal of Secondary Gifted Education, 16,* 57–66. https://doi.org/10.4219/jsge-2005-473.

Licuanan, B. F., Dailey, L. R., and Mumford, M. D. (2007). Idea evaluation: Error in evaluating highly original ideas. *Journal of Creative Behavior, 41,* 1–27. https://doi.org/10.1002/j.2162-6057.2007 .tb01279.x.

Lonergan, D. C., Scott, G. M., and Mumford, M. D. (2004). Evaluative aspects of creative thought: Effects of appraisal and revision standards. *Creativity Research Journal, 16,* 231–246. https://doi.org/ 10.1207/s15326934crj1602&3_7.

Lu, S., Bartol, K. M., Venkataramani, V., Zheng, X., and Liu, X. (2019). Pitching novel ideas to the boss: The interactive effects of employees' idea enactment and influence tactics on creativity assessment and implementation. *Academy of Management Journal, 62,* 579–606. https://doi.org/10.5465/amj .2016.0942.

Luksyte, A., Unsworth, K. L., and Avery, D. R. (2018). Innovative work behavior and sex-based stereo-types: Examining sex differences in perceptions and evaluations of innovative work behavior. *Journal of Organizational Behavior, 39,* 292–305. https://doi.org/10.1002/job.2219.

Marshall-Mies, J. C., Fleishman, E. A., Martin, J. A., Zaccaro, S. J., Baughman, W. A., and McGee, M. L. (2000). Development and evaluation of cognitive and metacognitive measures for predict-ing leadership potential. *The Leadership Quarterly, 11,* 135–153. https://doi.org/10.1016/S1048 -9843(99)00046-6.

McCrae, R. R., and Costa, P. T., Jr. (1997). Personality trait structure as a human universal. *American Psychologist, 52,* 509–516. https://doi.org/10.1037/0003-066X.52.5.509

Mueller, J. S., Melwani, S., and Goncalo, J. A. (2012). The bias against creativity: Why people desire but reject creative ideas. *Psychological Science, 23,* 13–17. https://doi.org/10.1177/0956797611421018.

Mueller, J., Melwani, S., Loewenstein, J., and Deal, J. J. (2018). Reframing the decision-makers' dilemma: Towards a social context model of creative idea recognition. *Academy of Management Journal, 61,* 94–110. https://doi.org/10.5465/amj.2013.0887.

Mumford, M. D., and Gustafson, S. B. (1988). Creativity syndrome: Integration, application, and innova-tion. *Psychological Bulletin, 103*(1), 27–43. https://doi.org/10.1037/0033-2909.103.1.27.

Mumford, M. D., Hester, K. S., and Robledo, I. C. (2012). Creativity in organizations: Importance and approaches. In M. D. Mumford (Ed.), *Handbook of organizational creativity* (pp. 3–16). Elsevier.

Mumford, M. D., Lonergan, D. C., and Scott, G. (2002). Evaluating creative ideas: Processes, standards, and context. *Inquiry: Critical Thinking across the Disciplines, 22*(1), 21–30. https://doi.org/10.5840/ inquiryctnews20022213.

Mumford, M. D., Marks, M. A., Connelly, M. S., Zaccaro, S. J., and Reiter-Palmon, R. (2000). Development of leadership skills: Experience and timing. *The Leadership Quarterly, 11*, 87–114. https://doi.org/10.1016/S1048-9843(99)00044-2.

Mumford, M. D., Medeiros, K. E., Steele, L., and Watts, L. L. (2014). Leadership, creativity and innovation: An overview. In M. D. Mumford (Ed.), *Leadership, creativity and innovation* (pp. 1–48). Sage.

Mumford, M. D., Mobley, M. I., Reiter-Palmon, R., Uhlman, C. E., and Doares, L. M. (1991). Process analytic models of creative capacities. *Creativity Research Journal, 4*, 91–122. https://doi.org/10.1080/10400419109534380.

Mumford, M. D., Todd, E. M., Higgs, C., and McIntosh, T. (2017). Cognitive skills and leadership performance: The nine critical skills. *The Leadership Quarterly, 28*, 24–39. https://doi.org/10.1016/j.leaqua.2016.10.012.

Proudfoot, D., Kay, A. C., and Koval, C. Z. (2015). A gender bias in the attribution of creativity: Archival and experimental evidence for the perceived association between masculinity and creative thinking. *Psychological Science, 26*, 1751–1761.

Reiter-Palmon, R. (2018). Creative cognition at the individual and team level: What happens before and after idea generation. In R. Sternberg and J. Kaufman (Eds.), *Nature of creativity* (pp. 184–208). Cambridge University Press.

Reiter-Palmon, R., and Illies, J. J. (2004). Leadership and creativity: Understanding leadership from a creative problem-solving perspective. *The Leadership Quarterly, 15*, 55–77. https://doi.org/10.1016/j.leaqua.2003.12.005.

Reiter-Palmon, R., Kennel, V., de Vreede, T., and de Vreede, G. J. (2018). The role of structure and instruction on creative idea evaluation and selection. In I. Lebuda and V. Glăvenou (Eds.), *Palgrave handbook of social creativity research* (pp. 209–224). Palgrave Macmillan.

Rietzschel, E. F., Nijstad, B. A., and Stroebe, W. (2006). Productivity is not enough: A comparison of interactive and nominal groups in idea generation and selection. *Journal of Experimental Social Psychology, 42*, 244–251. https://doi.org/10.1016/j.jesp.2005.04.005.

Rietzschel, E. F., Nijstad, B. A., and Stroebe, W. (2010). The selection of creative ideas after individual idea generation: Choosing between creativity and impact. *British Journal of Psychology, 101*, 47–68. https://doi.org/10.1348/000712609X414204.

Robertson, W. C. (1990). Detection of cognitive structure with protocol data: Predicting performance on physics transfer problems. *Cognitive Science, 14*, 253–280. https://doi.org/10.1207/s15516709cog1402_3.

Runco, M. A. (1991). The evaluative, valuative, and divergent thinking of children. *Journal of Creative Behavior, 25*, 311–319. https://doi.org/10.1002/j.2162-6057.1991.tb01143.x.

Runco, M. A., and Basadur, M. (1993). Assessing ideational and evaluative skills and creative styles and attitudes. *Creativity and Innovation Management, 2*, 166–173. https://doi.org/10.1111/j.1467-8691.1993.tb00088.x.

Runco, M. A., and Chand, I. (1995). Cognition and creativity. *Educational Psychology Review, 7*, 243–267. https://doi.org/10.1007/BF02213373.

Runco, M. A., and Smith, W. R. (1992). Interpersonal and intrapersonal evaluations of creative ideas. *Personality and Individual Differences, 13*, 295–302. https://doi.org/10.1016/0191-8869(92)90105-X.

Runco, M. A., and Vega, L. (1990). Evaluating the creativity of children's ideas. *Journal of Social Behavior and Personality, 5*(5), 439–452.

Shalley, C. E., Zhou, J., and Oldham, G. R. (2004). The effects of personal and contextual characteristics on creativity: Where should we go from here? *Journal of Management, 30*, 933–958. https://doi.org/10.1016/j.jm.2004.06.007.

Sharma, A. (1999). Central dilemmas of managing innovation in large firms. *California Management Review, 41*, 146–164. https://doi.org/10.2307/41166001.

Silvia, P. J. (2008). Discernment and creativity: How well can people identify their most creative ideas? *Psychology of Aesthetics, Creativity, and the Arts, 2*, 139–146. https://doi.org/10.1037/1931-3896.2.3.139.

Sternberg, R. J. (1988). A three-facet model of creativity. In R. J. Sternberg (Ed.), *The nature of creativity: Contemporary psychological perspectives* (pp. 125–147). Cambridge University Press.

Sullivan, D. M., and Ford, C. M. (2005). The relationship between novelty and value in the assessment of organizational creativity. *Korean Journal of Thinking and Problem Solving, 15*, 117–131.

Watts, L. L., Mulhearn, T. J., Todd, E. M., and Mumford, M. D. (2017). Leader idea evaluation and follower creativity: Challenges, constraints, and capabilities. In M. D. Mumford and S. Hemlin (Eds.), *Handbook of research on leadership and creativity* (pp. 82–99). Edward Elgar Publishing.

Watts, L. L., Steele, L. M., Medeiros, K. E., and Mumford, M. D. (2019). Minding the gap between generation and implementation: Effects of idea source, goals, and climate on selecting and refining creative ideas. *Psychology of Aesthetics, Creativity, and the Arts, 13*, 2–14. https://doi.org/10.1037/aca0000157.

Woodman, R. W., Sawyer, J. E., and Griffin, R. W. (1993). Toward a theory of organizational creativity. *Academy of Management Review, 18*, 293–321. https://doi.org/10.5465/amr.1993.3997517.

Yukl, G. A. (2013). *Leadership in organizations* (8th ed.). Pearson.

Zhou, J., Wang, X. M., Bavato, D., Tasselli, S., and Wu, J. (2019). Understanding the receiving side of creativity: A multidisciplinary review and implications for management research. *Journal of Management, 45*, 2570–2595. https://doi.org/10.1177/0149206319827088.

Zhu, Y., Ritter, S. M., and Dijksterhuis, A. P. (2020). Creativity: Intrapersonal and interpersonal selection of creative ideas. *Journal of Creative Behavior, 54*(3), 626–635. https://doi.org/10.1002/jocb.397.

7. Judgment and decision making: a "brain-first" perspective

John P. Sullivan

Decision making is an ordinary part of our everyday life; everything we engage in from the moment we awaken is part of a complex "brain-first" system, yet we hardly give it any thought. Our ability to make decisions is extraordinary and, in fact, is a part of our neural development that has influenced our ability to evolve, adapt, and survive as a species.

Further, our brain is exceptional at sequencing sensory patterns, affective signals, and cognitive simulations needed to make decisions, even under significant pressure. Decision making is part of our daily and contextual human performance (e.g., sport, tactical/military, medicine, and economic industries) and it cannot be fully understood without both subjective (self-report, *ex post facto* analyses) and objective (neurobiology and psychophysiology) data directly derived from the brain and the 11 other systems it manages.

In this chapter, we will explore several important truths related to the brain-first process of decision making, including: the importance of complex systems analysis; the limits of subjective data in evaluating decision making (Bäckström and Björklund, 2014; Dodou and de Winter, 2014; King and Bruner, 2000); the need to account for individual variation in research and applied interventions (Bock, 1989; Chen et al., 2015; Mielke et al., 2010; Weisz et al., 2014); the importance of a team science approach (Bennett et al., 2018; Hall et al., 2008; Stokols et al., 2008); and the relevant neurobiological/psychophysiological processes – aka, top-down/bottom-up reality of human factors of performance including decision making (Bechara et al., 2000; Cromwell and Panksepp, 2011; Edelman, 1987, 2006; Ferrer et al., 2016; Gold and Shadlen, 2007; Keynan et al., 2019; Panksepp, 2007, 2011, 2017; Rolls, 2015; Rosenbloom et al., 2012). The chapter ends with an exploration of future directions for research and evaluating decision making among teams in real time (Berka and Stikic, 2017; Waldman et al., 2015).

COMPLEX SYSTEMS ANALYSIS OF DECISION MAKING

Decision making cannot be fully understood or appreciated without exploring our neurobiological and psychophysiological processes within a complex systems analysis. Complex systems analysis is based upon chaos theory, which has been the standard for scientific exploration for more than a century within the disciplines of physics, mathematics, computer science, engineering, environmental sciences, and economics, to name a few (Stewart, 1997). Yet the social sciences have been the last to apply chaos theory and our significant understanding of complexity. Complexity and chaotic dynamics describe every known living system and those of the physical world as well. Edward Lorenz (1963) from the Massachusetts Institute of Technology (MIT) is the official modern discoverer of chaos theory. He first observed the phenomenon as early as 1961 and, as a matter of dramatic irony, he discovered it by chance while making calculations in the prediction of weather. From Lorenz's findings, chaos theory has grown to an interdisciplinary theory, stating that, within the apparent randomness of complex systems, there are underlying patterns, interconnected components, constant feedback loops, repetition, self-similarity, and self-organization. The butterfly effect, a principle of chaos, describes how a small change in one state can result in large differences in a later state, meaning there is a sensitive dependence on all elements within complex systems. A metaphor for this behavior is that a butterfly flapping its wings in one part of the world can cause a hurricane in another part of the planet (Lorenz, 1972).

In other words, to reduce decision making and judgment to cognitive aspects alone ignores small differences in our initial internal neurobiological conditions (re: sensory and affective processing) which can impact cognitive responses and yield widely divergent outcomes for such dynamical systems. In turn, this can and does lead to false inferences regarding decision making and render long-term prediction of phenomenon impossible in general. Linearity and closed systems do not adequately describe our nature, as our interpersonal and intrapersonal dynamics are open, nonlinear, and self-organizing (Allen and Varga, 2007). The reductionistic approach, although occasionally relevant and appropriate, is overused and leads us to artificial conclusions regarding the nature of decision making and numerous other phenomena. The important truth and accurate reality is that decision making involves the coordination of sensory, affective/emotional, and cognitive processes in a simultaneous fashion known as a complex system in action (Bechara et al., 2000).

Complex systems analysis serves as a precondition that must be met to fully understand the diversity and depth of decision making and judgment not as a "thing" or "event" but as a dynamic process in context (Fleener and Merritt, 2007; Guastello, 1997, 2007; Guastello et al., 2009). If this precondition is not met from a scientific perspective, any information gathered should be examined with the framework of healthy skepticism and not conflated beyond its limitations. The examination of the process of decision making is a difficult one, and even when a complex systems approach is utilized in experimental design and data collection, an additional precondition should include evaluation of both subjective and objective data in concert.

SUBJECTIVE AND OBJECTIVE DATA IN THE DECISION-MAKING ANALYSIS

Most human factors research solely uses subjective data to gather an understanding about events, and this also often holds true for the assessment of decision making. However, with complex systems such as the decision-making process, this is a misstep that can lead to a great magnitude of error. Although subjective data can be used to good effect in research, by its nature subjective data is *ex post facto* and depends upon subjects' affective, sensory, and cognitive abilities to recall experiences with great accuracy. Unfortunately, we know via robust findings that subjective data and self-report measures are susceptible to bias, the limited capacity of human memory, fatigue and/or inconsistent effort by the responder, and social desirability; however, these factors are often not considered as a part of the post hoc analysis (Choi and Pak, 2014; Gerhard, 2008; Hughes, 2018; van de Mortel, 2008). Hence, if using subjective self-report measures in research, we should be using those measures that have both strong internal and strong external consistency and are also appropriately validated to allow for greater confidence in the responses and data.

An example of this conundrum can be seen in sleep research and/or clinical interventions where subjective evaluations are "best guesses" for our sleep experiences, which comprise approximately one-third of our life for which we have no access. Therefore, in both decision-making and sleep-processing contexts we can use subjective data, but we must be careful to avoid overreaching the findings of such data beyond their actual meaning. In addition, we should proceed with great caution when developing interventions built on subjective data alone, especially when objective data is accessible and can be utilized (Nastasi and Hitchcock, 2015; O'Cathain et al., 2007; Taherdoost, 2016). Furthermore, as the safety of an intervention is reliant upon the most complete assessment possible, it is important to consider effect sizes when interpreting data. In sum, subjective and objective measures assure better outcomes with respect to research and interventions related to decision making as this multimodal approach honors our complex systems and the range of variables critical to decision making and judgment (Creswell and Clark, 2017; Eignor, 2013; Linn, 2015; Shedler et al., 1993).

Objective data that is available to researchers in relation to decision making includes the evaluation of the following systems: central nervous system (CNS), autonomic nervous system (ANS), circulatory system, respiratory system, endocrine system, and the enteric nervous system (ENS). From each of these systems, a detailed understanding of the dynamics of decision making can be contextually explored. Here are some of the data collection opportunities that can be gathered alone or in combination:

Central Nervous System – Brain-First Measures
- DC Potential: Slow cortical potentials measured in millivolts express the level of activation or the arousal level of the central nervous system. An optimal voltage is necessary readiness to respond to internal and external/environmental demands (Bechtereva et al., 1983; Ilyukhina, 2010; Kovac et al., 2018).
- Brainwave (EEG)/AC Brainwave Assessment: Examining brainwaves relates to readiness to read and react processing involved in the informational input; for example:
    - Fronto-central alpha/beta asymmetry (approach motivation) (Hofman and Schutter, 2012; Palmiero and Piccardi, 2017; Allen et al., 2018).
    - Fronto-central alpha/theta power (attention) (Arns et al., 2014; Borghini et al., 2014; Keller et al., 2017; Lau-Zhu et al., 2019).
    - Fronto-central theta/gamma power (memory processing) (Lorist et al., 2009; Schneider et al., 2019; Wójcik et al., 2019).
- Vestibulo-Oculo Reflex Screening: The ability to synchronize visual information with motor and cognitive functions (visual input, optic flow) (Contreras et al., 2011; Lee et al., 2011).
- Complex Reaction Time Measures (See–Feel–Do Measures), including:
    - Multiple Object Tracking (MOT): The scientific study of how our visual system tracks multiple moving objects as a part of informational input and tracking of important data related to executive attention/decisions (Hoke et al., 2017; Parsons et al., 2016; Perico et al., 2017; Romeas et al., 2019).

- Eye Tracking: The process of measuring either the point of gaze (where one is looking) or the environmental context to evaluate fatigue (Al-Moteri et al., 2017; Ashby et al., 2016; Behrend and Dehais, 2020; Brunyé and Gardony, 2017).
  Autonomic Nervous System/Feedback System Measures
- Pupillometry: Pupil reaction reflects the state of sympathetic–parasympathetic balance of the autonomic nervous system and serves as an objective measurement of the brain's readiness (Varchenko et al., 2014).
- Heart Rate Variability (HRV): HRV is linked to the autonomic nervous system (ANS) and the balance between the parasympathetic (rest-and-digest) and sympathetic (fight, flight, or shut-down) branches (De Couck et al., 2019; Sutarto et al., 2010).
  Enteric Nervous System/Gut-Nutritional Health
- Hydration Status: A reduction in hydration status by 1 percent has a negative impact on the brain's ability to process visual input and motor output abilities (Fortes et al., 2018; Hamidi et al., 2016; Houssein et al., 2016; Patsalos and Thoma, 2020; Zaslona et al., 2018).
- Blood Tests: Changes in measurable micronutrients (e.g., Vitamin B12, Vitamin D) impact the brain's ability to perceive and decide (Bagga et al., 2018; Gao et al., 2020).

Since we are a complex system where small changes in one system can impact another, appropriate assessment of this data cannot be understated. Evaluating objective data has evolved to include both laboratory bench science and, equally, applied science via in-field evaluation. In fact, ecological monitoring in real time or by way of a moment-to-moment assessment of biometric data is commonplace in sport, military/tactical, aerospace, and some select industry environments. Objective data that is derived alongside subjective data creates a far greater opportunity to understand decision making and, thus, subsequent judgments from an individual and team perspective than either type of data collection alone. Further, data streams collected in tandem naturally illuminate the individual factors that we understand to be both fact and the reality but are rarely contextualized.

INDIVIDUAL VARIATION IS THE RULE

The notion that individual variation is the rule not the exception has become somewhat of a trite statement – so much so that its incontrovertible truth is almost lost. However, decision making – like many factors of human performance and health – is often forced into a "one-size-fits-all" rubric that is typically not a suitable fit (Brodin and Davis, 2017; Clyde, 2019; Darwin and Kebler, 1859; Downes, 2016; Ecker and Beck, 2017; Edelman, 1987; McCann et al., 2019; Non and Thayer, 2019; Fisher et al., 2018; Kline et al., 2018; Logie, 2018). In fact, when examining decision making in high-performance environments in sport, military/tactical, and aerospace contexts, the individual variations between performers account for significant differences in effectiveness and one's understanding of a performer's strengths, areas for development, and practical/efficacious interventions (Faubert, 2013; Faubert and Sidebottom, 2012; Logie, 2018; Talukdar et al., 2018).

Ultimately, one-size-fits-all approaches do not apply when human variation accounts for such significant differences between persons/performers, and most especially this is true when examining the development of expertise or experts themselves. Also, our brains are clear-cut examples of the concept of human variation. Each brain is inescapably unique and varied (e.g., selective adaptive systems) in both its anatomical structure and its dynamics, even among identical twins (Edelman, 1987, 2006).

When evaluating human factors individual differences may arguably be perceived as an annoyance by some researchers rather than a challenge, much in the same way that physics can and does perceive noise as an annoyance (as misdirected energy) and a part of a total process (indistinguishable from sound). Ultimately, there is a multilayered cost when we do not consider variation in human factors research, including the insufficient examination of decision making. First, and most notably, interventions that are developed from a lack of inclusion of variation can lead to personal and professional harm by not accounting for their effect on development or maintenance of skills and abilities. An overreliance on research that does not account for proper variation/generalization along with significance testing (p-value vs. effect sizes) in applied research has evolved into a faulty standard practice (Colquhoun, 2014; Figueiredo et al., 2013; Grabowski, 2016; Halsey, 2019; Kass et al., 2016; Sullivan and Feinn, 2012; Wasserstein and Lazar, 2016).

Second, by ignoring individual variation, we increase our chances of making errors in research (both Type I and Type II errors) as well as generalizing findings that do not represent a population we are seeking to understand. These missteps often ignore the magnitude of associations, estimations of precision, the consistency and pattern of results, possible bias arising from multiple sources, previous research findings, and foundational knowledge.

Third, research that includes and accounts for human variation opens a new window to carefully considering human factors within health and human performance, but also as an operational improvement method leading to the design of safer and more efficient systems (Albert and Kruglyak, 2015; Fisher et al., 2018; Kline et al., 2018). Decision making and other brain-related abilities need to account for and include individual variation when examining and developing interventions related to decision making to fully safeguard from misleading inferences and or policy/procedure decisions.

Similarly, the examination of decision making, as with all brain-related phenomenon, cannot be fully answered from one scientific discipline, but instead requires a gathering of experts who have differing and shared perspectives and work in a transdisciplinary way. The next section highlights how additional safeguards to human variation needs can be achieved via the application of team science.

THE RISE OF TEAM SCIENCE

Scientific collaboration is more prevalent today than it was decades ago. As we have experienced significant social, technological, and scientific challenges over the past six decades, scientists have increasingly combined efforts with colleagues to engage in research known as team science. In many areas of the physical sciences, technology sector, and biomedical sciences the trend is toward collaborative efforts that bring together researchers with diverse scientific backgrounds (Hall et al., 2008, 2018; Tebes and Thai, 2018). In fact, approximately 90 percent of all published research is authored by at least two or more authors and the trend is largely toward teams of six to ten collaborators (Bozeman and Boardman, 2014; Bozeman and Youtie, 2017).

When we address perplexing questions and solve complex problems that are represented within complex systems – for example, there are significant individual differences, and it is essential to conduct accurate evaluations using multiple subjective and objective data streams – then there is considerable benefit to utilizing an interdisciplinary approach for decision making (Koch and Jones, 2016; Syme, 2008; Tebes et al., 2014). Scientific disciplines are historically siloed and distinctive, at least in part, for historical reasons and reasons of academic/administrative convenience (such as the organization of departments and teaching appointments). However, these classifications and distinctions are unimportant and trivial in many aspects. As scientific experts, we are students of problems or phenomena, and we are taught to apply systematic processes to studying such mysteries. Broadly speaking, the study of scientific phenomena cuts across the borders of categorized subject matter and disciplines in the pursuit of knowledge (Popper, 1963), and this is similarly true for decision making. Although colleges and universities have established and articulated discrete divisions of learning (e.g., distinct departments), this approach inadvertently creates silos that do not mirror those of our society. Thus, it is both the case that team science is essential to fully study and understand decision making and, equally, the case that optimum decision making requires an interdisciplinary framework.

Such cooperative team research has the ability to overcome serious obstacles in the examination of nature's phenomena and of decision making as well. Accurate and reliable brain science research requires not only abstract, theoretical intelligence, but also cooperative efforts to fully unlock relevant internal and external processes (Bozeman and Boardman, 2014; Bozeman and Youtie, 2017). A transdisciplinary team science approach can be successfully utilized in sport, military/tactical, and aerospace environments to examine decision making, and such a team might include professionals such as psychologists, neuroscientists, physiologists, psychophysicists, endocrinologists, and biochemists, to name a few. Of course, the team must be appropriate for the context and research question(s) to be explored, and integration of various disciplines should be considered on an ongoing basis to enhance the research possibilities.

NEUROBIOLOGICAL AND PSYCHOPHYSIOLOGICAL PROCESSES OF DECISION MAKING

To unpackage decision making, we have to explore Neural Darwinism, Gerald Edelman's (1987) neurobiological theory that uses Darwinian natural selection to account for brain development and functioning in terms of selectionist amplification, pruning, and strengthening of neurons, synapses, and dynamic signaling. Edelman's theory uses the known truths regarding our brain development and seeks to understand it from a complex systems perspective as opposed to one system such as cognition alone. During brain development, billions of neurons emerge and send axonal cones to target other neurons and make connective synapses. Both neurons and their synapses are then pruned so that only the most functional cells and connections survive. When neuronal pathways are established, a similar amplification and pruning process occurs among active connections (Chervyakov et al., 2016; Edelman, 1987, 1993, 2006, 2014; Ellis and Toronchuk, 2005; McDowell, 2010; Takahashi et al., 2013).

This evolutionary selection process is the historical truth which indicates that the oldest and most evolved part of our brains as human beings and primates is the lower section of our brains, and the lower section is most involved with emotion, connections to our peripheral nervous system via the vagus nerve, and involuntary functioning (e.g., breathing, salivation, deglutition, defecation, and micturition). Notice that the scientific consensus does not point to our cognitive dominance, either as part of our survival or as part of daily abilities from context to context, but rather our brain has emotional/affective dominance in our daily functioning and survival that works in coordination with our peripheral and enteric nervous systems (Panksepp, 1998, 2000, 2001, 2002, 2003, 2004, 2011, 2017). To highlight this process, it is important to examine the dynamic flow of our decision-making processing from perception to selection.

Decision making is a complex process that involves the coordination of several brain structures. In particular, the amygdala is a lower brain structure involved with emotional processing; and the orbitofrontal cortex (OFC) and lateral prefrontal cortex (LPFC), which comprise part of the pre-frontal cortices, represent a more newly developed part of our brain involved with executive functioning. These brain circuits seem to be essential in human decision making, whereby both emotional and cognitive aspects are taken into consideration when we feel first and then we think. The amygdala and OFC represent the neural correlates of emotion, while the activity of OFC neural populations represents the outcome expectancy of alternatives, and the cognitive aspect of decision making is controlled by the LPFC (Gold and Shadlen, 2007; Nazir and Liljenström, 2016).

Thus, the reality is that the bottom-up of brain functioning negates the cultural myth that decision making is primarily cognitive/rational. Instead, decision making is the result of prediction and an interplay between an intuitive/emotional system (re: lower brain, autonomic, circulatory, respiratory) and a rational/cognitive system (re: pre-frontal, neo-cortical). The amygdala, as a part of the limbic system, has long been associated with emotional processing, and is related to sensory perception, survival, and learning, linking emotional responses and their values (Panksepp et al., 2017; Whalen et al., 2009). The functionality of the amygdala is realized through its connection to the OFC, which receives extensive input to the brain from different sensory inputs. The bidirectional connections between these two structures are supposedly embodied in an affective decision-making process, where the perception and evaluation of environmental context constitute the first phase of evaluation (Schoenbaum et al., 2006). In the second phase, the emotional content is assessed in the amygdala–OFC pathway and is monitored cognitively, and at that point a final decision would be made. The LPFC mainly participates solely in the cognitive evaluation of stimuli. Further, in contrast to the OFC, which pursues short-term evaluations, the LPFC primarily is future oriented. The resultant outcomes are emotional and cognitive evaluations which guide our actions and selections (Gray et al., 2002; Krawczyk, 2002).

The actual value of the selected action is evaluated and compared by the OFC and LPFC and provides the basis for our learning. Through a recurrent pathway from the LPFC to the OFC, a feedback signal is transmitted, and learning occurs in the OFC by changing the neural firing frequencies, depending on the errors/past experiences and emotional/cognitive events. The interconnection between the amygdala and the OFC associates the cue to its emotional value and generates the outcome that induces decision making and any corresponding behavioral change (Anderson and Matessa, 1997; Dixon and Christoff, 2014). The learning of a new pattern and the formation of adaptive behavior are also supported by the OFC, the amygdala, the autonomic nervous system, and the enteric nervous system.

The brain and body are coupled, which is also in contrast to a common cultural myth that these two entities stand alone or are divided. As outlined earlier, the brain and body form a complex system, and our perceptions and feelings change and respond to the state of our body and our gut–brain axis or enteric nervous system.

Affective and cognitive processes are each influenced by both autonomic and enteric responses related to decision making, error detection, memory, and emotions. Decision-making processes can be modulated by stress, and the dynamics that also influence autonomic and enteric responses are crucial factors for determining the direction of the effects on the central nervous system (Gold and Shadlen, 2007; Nazir and Liljenström, 2016).

Decision making and memory are influenced by autonomic responses from the internal state of the organism (e.g., "gut feelings") induced by the outside world. The interactions of circuits involved in emotion with those involved in memory and decision making more accurately describe the complex system of decision making than subjective evaluation alone. The assessment and interpretation of objective data is the reason why we consistently see robust findings with brain-based interventions improving self-regulation, attention, and decision making. Differences in brain wave (EEG) power, heart rate variability (HRV), and respiration have suggested greater involvement of the autonomic nervous system (ANS), suggesting levels of ANS involvement are critical and simultaneously involved with the brain in the "feel-then-action" sequence previously alluded to in the decision-making process.

The sheer nature of decision making and the complex system that it entails requires human performers to not only protect and train the behavioral/physical demands, but also improve the emotional and cognitive functions of their decision making while at work. The resultant judgments that are made by performers are, thus, a product of this nuanced and complex decision-making process.

Neurofeedback and psychophysiological training approaches using brain wave (EEG), heart rate variability (HRV), and respiration rate (and biometric) data, as well as the use of scaffolded training simulations, are well supported in the literature for performance enhancement in multiple environments (e.g., sport, military, aerospace, medicine, and industry). Training is directed to increase awareness of autonomic nervous system responses felt in the body as emotional sensations that correspond to brain response, which in turn promotes enhanced pattern recognition, ideal performance states, and ultimately better accuracy in decision making even under felt pressure. This enhanced awareness and management of associated responses in the brain and body also improves neurophysiological, physiological, and emotional functioning as well as having overall health benefits for performers.

Brain-first interventions such as neurofeedback and HRV training have led to many opportunities to protect and develop talent, with greater sensitivity to human variation as well as the ability to address the truly complex nature of the dynamics that underlie decision making in real-life scenarios. Additionally, due to continued advances within the biomedical technology sector, the technology to train and evaluate the brain and body "interplay" has reduced in size, and the signal quality has also improved to the extent that performance can be evaluated in real time. The use of in-field objective measures with a small footprint/form factors (e.g., wearable devices), and the ability to collect information via an ecological moment-to-moment assessment model, is quite common in many high-performance environments. It is noteworthy that on-the-body technologies have been developed (for training/in-field testing) to evaluate player/war fighter/pilot health, and performance has been submitted to harsh conditions (e.g., collisions, explosions, salt/fresh in/underwater environments). There are significant options available for in-field ecological assessment that can examine both central (brain-based) and peripheral (body) systems in real time, allowing us to more fully understand the various needs to maintain and enhance health and performance of esports performers (as one notably relevant example cohort in this regard).

FUTURE DIRECTIONS

Looking ahead at the landscape, another area that is primed for development includes the use of the abovementioned biomedical advances to examine decision making within the team environment. Although the topic of decision making has gained increasing attention, little is known about this objective process in team settings. However, current studies have examined individual engagement, leadership, and the neuro/psychophysiological dynamics, dealing with complex environmental processes. A feature of these studies is the use of diverse methodologies to measure ecological moment-to-moment assessments. By using subjective psychometrically sound self-ratings and objective measures using electroencephalogram (EEG) technology and measures of the autonomic nervous system (re: heart rate, heat rate variability, and respiration rate), we can gain clear insights to the decision-making process within team contexts. These objective methodological approaches have been applied within military, sport, healthcare, and academic contexts since the early 2000s.

Since teams reflect a part of the complex system of many environments, evaluation of gestures (Schippers et al., 2010), facial expressions (Anders et al., 2011), and other nonverbal communications (Ménoret et al., 2014) can highlight similarities and differences between decision making by way of an individual or group process. Environmental or contextual cueing can be evaluated (Ancona and Chong, 1999), and the way that cues influence team members can be evaluated (Marks et al., 2001; Chung et al., 1999; Salas et al., 2005; von Davier and Halpin, 2013). These observable metrics reflect individual and team dynamics (emotional, cognitive, and behavioral) and outputs of performance. These assessments inform our understanding of operational frameworks related to team coordination/informational flow (Gorman, 2014). Importantly, instead of simplified dichotomous top-down and bottom-up interactions, these methods allow us to see more global social, emotional, cognitive, and event-related perspectives through the lens of complex system analysis (Giere and Moffatt, 2003). Developing more dynamic descriptions and measures of team decision making such as situational awareness, attentional processes, working memory, and team coordination is critical if we are to apply genuinely evidence-based interventions using higher forms of data in comparison to *ex post facto* measures alone (Wiltshire et al., 2018).

Given the fundamental role of emotion, cognition, and communication (nonverbal and verbal), neurophysiological measures can provide additional quantitative measures that link individual, team member, and team processes (Stevens and Galloway, 2017). The apparent importance of complex exchanges of energy in the forms of emotion and communication during teamwork (Gorman et al., 2017) also suggests nonlinear modeling approaches are particularly useful for interpreting the quantitative neurodynamics of a team and its member interactions (Stevens and Galloway, 2017).

SUMMARY POINTS

This chapter proposed that decision making should be approached from a "brain-first" complex systems perspective that allows for comprehensive support and optimization of human performance. To that end, the importance of decision making in relation to human performance across various contexts and environments cannot be understated. This chapter has addressed essential concepts that are necessary to fully and adequately interpret decision making and the role it plays across various industries such as sport, military, aerospace, and medicine. In particular, it is important to utilize mixed methodological research designs as well as a complex systems analysis approach, ensure sufficient attention to human variation variables while also operating from a team science or multidisciplinary platform, and address and understand nuances associated with the neurobiology of decision making.

Decision making has been of interest from the earliest recorded history and continues to be a phenomenon that interests many researchers and practitioners across disciplines and applied contexts, and its importance to humankind should not be underestimated given that the process intimately intersects with the protection of human health, talent, and performance.

REFERENCES

Albert, F. W., and Kruglyak, L. (2015). The role of regulatory variation in complex traits and disease. *Nature Reviews Genetics, 16*(4), 197–212.

Allen, J. J., Keune, P. M., Schönenberg, M., and Nusslock, R. (2018). Frontal EEG alpha asymmetry and emotion: From neural underpinnings and methodological considerations to psychopathology and social cognition. *Psychophysiology, 55*(1), e13028.

Allen, P. M., and Varga, L. (2007). Complexity: The co-evolution of epistemology, axiology and ontology. *Nonlinear Dynamics, Psychology, and Life Sciences, 11*(1), 19–50.

Al-Moteri, M. O., Symmons, M., Plummer, V., and Cooper, S. (2017). Eye tracking to investigate cue processing in medical decision-making: A scoping review. *Computers in Human Behavior, 66*, 52–66.

Ancona, D. G., and Chong, C. L. (1999). Cycles and synchrony: The temporal role of context in team behavior. In R. Wageman (Ed.), *Research on managing groups and teams: Groups in context*, Vol. 2 (pp. 33–48). Elsevier Science/JAI Press.

Anders, S., Heinzie, J., Weiskopf, N., Ethofer, T., and Haynes, J. (2011). Flow of affective information between communicating brains. *Neuroimage, 54*, 439–446.

Anderson, J. R., and Matessa, M. (1997). A production system theory of serial memory. *Psychological Review, 104*(4), 728–748.

Arns, M., Heinrich, H., and Strehl, U. (2014). Evaluation of neurofeedback in ADHD: The long and winding road. *Biological Psychology, 95*, 108–115.

Ashby, N. J. S., Johnson, J. G., Krajbich, I., and Wedel, M. (2016). Applications and innovations of eye-movement research in judgment and decision making [Editorial]. *Journal of Behavioral Decision Making, 29*(2–3), 96–102.

Bäckström, M., and Björklund, F. (2014). Social desirability in personality inventories: The nature of the evaluative factor. *Journal of Individual Differences, 35*(3), 144–157.

Bagga, D., Reichert, J. L., Koschutnig, K., Aigner, C. S., Holzer, P., Koskinen, K., Moissl-Eichinger, C., and Schöpf, V. (2018). Probiotics drive gut microbiome triggering emotional brain signatures. *Gut Microbes, 9*(6), 486–496.

Bechara, A., Damasio, H., and Damasio, A. R. (2000). Emotion, decision making and the orbitofrontal cortex. *Cerebral Cortex, 10*(3), 295–307.

Bechtereva, N. P., Gogolitsin, Y. L., Ilyukhina, V. A., and Pakhomov, S. V. (1983). Dynamic neurophysiological correlates of mental processes. *International Journal of Psychophysiology, 1*(1), 49–63.

Behrend, J., and Dehais, F. (2020). How role assignment impacts decision-making in high-risk environments: Evidence from eye-tracking in aviation. *Safety Science, 127*, 104738.

Bennett, L. M., Gadlin, H., and Marchand, C. (2018). *Collaboration team science: Field guide.* US Department of Health and Human Services, National Institutes of Health, National Cancer Institute.

Berka, C., and Stikic, M. (2017). On the road to autonomy: Evaluating and optimizing hybrid team dynamics. In W. F. Lawless, R. Mittu, D. A. Sofge, and S. Russell (Eds.), *Autonomy and artificial intelligence: A threat or savior?* (pp. 245–262). Springer.

Bock, R. D. (Ed.) (1989). Addendum: Measurement of human variation: A two-stage model. In *Multilevel Analysis of Educational Data* (pp. 319–342). Academic Press.

Borghini, G., Astolfi, L., Vecchiato, G., Mattia, D., and Babiloni, F. (2014). Measuring neurophysiological signals in aircraft pilots and car drivers for the assessment of mental workload, fatigue, and drowsiness. *Neuroscience and Biobehavioral Reviews, 44*, 58–75.

Bozeman, B., and Boardman, C. (2014). *Research collaboration and team science: A state-of-the-art review and agenda.* Springer.

Bozeman, B., and Youtie, J. (2017). *The strength in numbers: The new science of team science.* Princeton University Press.

Brodin, P., and Davis, M. M. (2017). Human immune system variation. *Nature Reviews Immunology, 17*(1), 21–29.

Brunyé, T. T., and Gardony, A. L. (2017). Eye tracking measures of uncertainty during perceptual decision making. *International Journal of Psychophysiology, 120*, 60–68.

Chen, C. M., Yang, J. M., Lai, J. Y., Li, H., Yuan, J. J., and Abbasi, N. U. (2015). Correlating gray matter volume with individual difference in the flanker interference effect. *PLoS ONE, 10*(8), e0136877.

Chervyakov, A. V., Sinitsyn, D. O., and Piradov, M. A. (2016). Variability of neuronal responses: Types and functional significance in neuroplasticity and neural Darwinism. *Frontiers in Human Neuroscience, 10*, 603.

Choi, B. C. K., and Pak, A. W. P. (2014). Bias, overview. *Wiley StatsRef: Statistics Reference Online.*

Chung, G. K. W. K., O'Neil Jr., H. F., and Herl, H. E. (1999). The use of computer-based collaborative knowledge mapping to measure team processes and team outcomes. *Computers in Human Behavior, 15*(3–4), 463–493.

Clyde, D. (2019). Gut microbial structural variation links to human health. *Nature Reviews Genetics, 20*(6), 318–319.

Colquhoun, D. (2014). An investigation of the false discovery rate and the misinterpretation of p-values. *Royal Society Open Science, 1*(3), 140216.

Contreras, R., Ghajar, J., Bahar, S., and Suh, M. (2011). Effect of cognitive load on eye-target synchronization during smooth pursuit eye movement. *Brain Research, 1398*, 55–63.

Creswell, J. W., and Clark, V. L. P. (2017). *Designing and conducting mixed methods research.* SAGE Publications.

Cromwell, H. C., and Panksepp, J. (2011). Rethinking the cognitive revolution from a neural perspective: How overuse/misuse of the term "cognition" and the neglect of affective controls in behavioral neuroscience could be delaying progress in understanding the BrainMind. *Neuroscience and Biobehavioral Reviews, 35*(9), 2026–2035.

Darwin, C., and Kebler, L. (1859). *On the origin of species by means of natural selection.* J. Murray.

De Couck, M., Caers, R., Musch, L., Fliegauf, J., Giangreco, A., and Gidron, Y. (2019). How breathing can help you make better decisions: Two studies on the effects of breathing patterns on heart rate variability and decision-making in business cases. *International Journal of Psychophysiology, 139*, 1–9.

Dixon, M. L., and Christoff, K. (2014). The lateral prefrontal cortex and complex value-based learning and decision making. *Neuroscience and Biobehavioral Reviews, 45*, 9–18.

Dodou, D., and de Winter, J. C. (2014). Social desirability is the same in offline, online, and paper surveys: A meta-analysis. *Computers in Human Behavior, 36*, 487–495.

Downes, S. M. (2016). Confronting variation in the social and behavioral sciences. *Philosophy of Science, 83*(5), 909–920.

Ecker, S., and Beck, S. (2017). Epigenetic variation taking center stage in immunological research. *Epigenomics, 9*(4), 375–378.

Edelman, G. M. (1987). *Neural Darwinism: The theory of neuronal group selection.* Basic Books.

Edelman, G. M. (1993). Neural Darwinism: Selection and reentrant signaling in higher brain function. *Neuron, 10*(2), 115–125.

Edelman, G. M. (2006). *Second nature: Brain science and human knowledge*. Yale University Press.

Edelman, G. (2014). Neural Darwinism. *New Perspectives Quarterly, 31*(1), 25–27.

Eignor, D. R. (2013). The standards for educational and psychological testing. In K. F. Geisinger, B. A. Bracken, J. F. Carlson, J.-I. C. Hansen, N. R. Kuncel, S. P. Reise, and M. C. Rodriguez (Eds.), *APA handbooks in psychology. APA handbook of testing and assessment in psychology, Vol. 1. Test theory and testing and assessment in industrial and organizational psychology* (pp. 245–250). American Psychological Association.

Ellis, G. F., and Toronchuk, I. A. (2005). Neural development: Affective and immune system influences. In R. D. Ellis and N. Newton (Eds.), *Consciousness and emotion: Agency, conscious choice, and selective perception*, Vol. 1 (pp. 81–119). John Benjamins Publishing Company.

Faubert, J. (2013). Professional athletes have extraordinary skills for rapidly learning complex and neutral dynamic visual scenes. *Scientific Reports, 3*, 1154.

Faubert, J., and Sidebottom, L. (2012). Perceptual-cognitive training of athletes. *Journal of Clinical Sport Psychology, 6*(1), 85–102.

Ferrer, R., Klein, W., Lerner, J., Reyna, V., and Keltner, D. (2016). Emotions and health decision making. In C. A. Roberto and I. Kawachi (Eds.), *Behavioral economics and public health* (pp. 101–132). Oxford University Press.

Figueiredo Filho, D. B., Paranhos, R., Rocha, E. C. D., Batista, M., Silva Jr., J. A. D., Santos, M. L. W. D., and Marino, J. G. (2013). When is statistical significance not significant? *Brazilian Political Science Review, 7*(1), 31–55.

Fisher, A. J., Medaglia, J. D., and Jeronimus, B. F. (2018). Lack of group-to-individual generalizability is a threat to human subjects research. *Proceedings of the National Academy of Sciences, 115*(27), E6106–E6115.

Fleener, M. J., and Merritt, M. L. (2007). Paradigms lost? *Nonlinear Dynamics, Psychology, and Life Sciences, 11*(1), 1–18.

Fortes, L. S., Nascimento-Júnior, J. R., Mortatti, A. L., Lima-Júnior, D. R. A. A. D., and Ferreira, M. E. (2018). Effect of dehydration on passing decision making in soccer athletes. *Research Quarterly for Exercise and Sport, 89*(3), 332–339.

Gao, W., Baumgartel, K. L., and Alexander, S. A. (2020). The gut microbiome as a component of the gut–brain axis in cognitive health. *Biological Research for Nursing, 22*(4), 485–494.

Gerhard, T. (2008). Bias: Considerations for research practice. *American Journal of Health-System Pharmacy, 65*(22), 2159–2168.

Giere, R. N., and Moffatt, B. (2003). Distributed cognition: Where the cognitive and the social merge. *Social Studies of Science, 33*(2), 301–310.

Gold, J. I., and Shadlen, M. N. (2007). The neural basis of decision making. *Annual Review of Neuroscience, 30*, 535–574.

Gorman, J. C. (2014). Team coordination and dynamics: Two central issues. *Current Directions in Psychological Science, 23*(5), 355–360.

Gorman, J. C., Dunbar, T. A., Grimm, D., and Gipson, C. L. (2017). Understanding and modeling teams as dynamical systems. *Frontiers in Psychology, 8*, 1053.

Grabowski, B. (2016). "P < 0.05" might not mean what you think: American Statistical Association clarifies p values. *Journal of the National Cancer Institute, 108*(8), djw194.

Gray, J. R., Braver, T. S., and Raichle, M. E. (2002). Integration of emotion and cognition in the lateral prefrontal cortex. *Proceedings of the National Academy of Sciences, 99*(6), 4115–4120.

Guastello, S. J. (1997). Science evolves: An introduction to nonlinear dynamics, psychology, and life sciences. *Nonlinear Dynamics, Psychology, and Life Sciences, 1*(1), 1–6.

Guastello, S. J. (2007). Commentary on paradigms and key word index for NDPLS articles 1997–2006. *Nonlinear Dynamics, Psychology, and Life Sciences, 11*(1), 167–182.

Guastello, S. J., Koopmans, M., and Pincus, D. (Eds.). (2009). *Chaos and complexity in psychology: The theory of nonlinear dynamical systems*. Cambridge University Press.

Hall, K. L., Feng, A. X., Moser, R. P., Stokols, D., and Taylor, B. K. (2008). Moving the science of team science forward: Collaboration and creativity. *American Journal of Preventive Medicine, 35*(2), S243–S249.

Hall, K. L., Vogel, A. L., Huang, G. C., Serrano, K. J., Rice, E. L., Tsakraklides, S. P., and Fiore, S. M. (2018). The science of team science: A review of the empirical evidence and research gaps on collaboration in science. *American Psychologist*, *73*(4), 532–548.

Halsey, L. G. (2019). The reign of the p-value is over: What alternative analyses could we employ to fill the power vacuum? *Biology Letters*, *15*(5), 20190174.

Hamidi, M. S., Boggild, M. K., and Cheung, A. M. (2016). Running on empty: A review of nutrition and physicians' well-being. *Postgraduate Medical Journal*, *92*(1090), 478–481.

Hofman, D., and Schutter, D. J. (2012). Asymmetrical frontal resting-state beta oscillations predict trait aggressive tendencies and behavioral inhibition. *Social Cognitive and Affective Neuroscience*, *7*(7), 850–857.

Hoke, J., Reuter, C., Romeas, T., Montariol, M., Schnell, T., and Faubert, J. (2017). Perceptual-cognitive and physiological assessment of training effectiveness. Paper presented at the Interservice/Industry Training, Simulation, and Education Conference, Orlando, FL.

Houssein, M., Lopes, P., Fagnoni, B., Ahmaidi, S., Yonis, S. M., and Leprêtre, P. M. (2016). Hydration: The new FIFA World Cup's challenge for referee decision making? *Journal of Athletic Training*, *51*(3), 264–266.

Hughes, D. J. (2018). Psychometric validity: Establishing the accuracy and appropriateness of psychometric measures. In P. Irwing, T. Booth, and D. J. Hughes (Eds.), *The Wiley handbook of psychometric testing: A multidisciplinary approach to survey, scale and test development* (pp. 751–779). Wiley.

Ilyukhina, V. A. (2010). Multiform wave organization of neurophysiological processes-universal "language" of human brain in realization of informational-controlling functions. *Journal of Evolutionary Biochemistry and Physiology*, *46*(3), 321–333.

Kass, R. E., Caffo, B. S., Davidian, M., Meng, X.-L., Yu, B., and Reid, N. (2016). Ten simple rules for effective statistical practice. *PLoS Computational Biology*, *12*(6), e1004961.

Keller, A. S., Payne, L., and Sekuler, R. (2017). Characterizing the roles of alpha and theta oscillations in multisensory attention. *Neuropsychologia*, *99*, 48–63.

Keynan, J. N., Cohen, A., Jackont, G., Green, N., Goldway, N., Davidov, A., Meir-Hasson, Y., Raz, G., Intrator, N., Fruchter, E., and Ginat, K. (2019). Electrical fingerprint of the amygdala guides neurofeedback training for stress resilience. *Nature Human Behaviour*, *3*(1), 63–73.

King, M. F., and Bruner, G. C. (2000). Social desirability bias: A neglected aspect of validity testing. *Psychology and Marketing*, *17*(2), 79–103.

Kline, M. A., Shamsudheen, R., and Broesch, T. (2018). Variation is the universal: Making cultural evolution work in developmental psychology. *Philosophical Transactions of the Royal Society B: Biological Sciences*, *373*(1743), 20170059.

Koch, C., and Jones, A. (2016). Big science, team science, and open science for neuroscience. *Neuron*, *92*(3), 612–616.

Kovac, S., Speckmann, E. J., and Gorji, A. (2018). Uncensored EEG: The role of DC potentials in neurobiology of the brain. *Progress in Neurobiology*, *165*, 51–65.

Krawczyk, D. C. (2002). Contributions of the prefrontal cortex to the neural basis of human decision making. *Neuroscience and Biobehavioral Reviews*, *26*(6), 631–664.

Lau-Zhu, A., Fritz, A., and McLoughlin, G. (2019). Overlaps and distinctions between attention deficit/hyperactivity disorder and autism spectrum disorder in young adulthood: Systematic review and guiding framework for EEG-imaging research. *Neuroscience and Biobehavioral Reviews*, *96*, 93–115.

Lee, E. J., Kwon, G., Lee, A., Ghajar, J., and Suh, M. (2011). Individual differences in working memory capacity determine the effects of oculomotor task load on concurrent word recall performance. *Brain Research*, *1399*, 59–65.

Linn, R. L. (2015). The standards for educational and psychological testing: Guidance in test development. In S. Lane, M. R. Raymond, and T. M. Haladyna (Eds.), *Handbook of test development* (pp. 41–52). Routledge.

Logie, R. (2018). Human cognition: Common principles and individual variation. *Journal of Applied Research in Memory and Cognition*, *7*(4), 471–486.

Lorenz, E. N. (1963). Deterministic nonperiodic flow. *Journal of Atmospheric Sciences*, *20*(2), 130–141.

Lorenz, E. (1972). Predictability: Does the flap of a butterfly's wing in Brazil set off a tornado in Texas? Paper presented at the annual meeting of the American Association for the Advancement of Science, Washington, DC.

Lorist, M. M., Bezdan, E., ten Caat, M., Span, M. M., Roerdink, J. B., and Maurits, N. M. (2009). The influence of mental fatigue and motivation on neural network dynamics: An EEG coherence study. *Brain Research, 1270*, 95–106.

Marks, M. A., Mathieu, J. E., and Zaccaro, S. J. (2001). A temporally based framework and taxonomy of team processes. *Academy of Management Review, 26*(3), 356–376.

McCann, H., Pisano, G., and Beltrachini, L. (2019). Variation in reported human head tissue electrical conductivity values. *Brain Topography, 32*(5), 825–858.

McDowell, J. J. (2010). Behavioral and neural Darwinism: Selectionist function and mechanism in adaptive behavior dynamics. *Behavioural Processes, 84*(1), 358–365.

Ménoret, M., Varnet, L., Fargier, R., Cheylus, A., Curie, A., Des Portes, V., Nazir, T. A., and Paulignan, Y. (2014). Neural correlates of non-verbal social interactions: A dual-EEG study. *Neuropsychologia, 55*, 85–97.

Mielke, J. H., Konigsberg, L. W., and Relethford, J. H. (2010). *Human biological variation*. Oxford University Press.

Nastasi, B. K., and Hitchcock, J. H. (2015). *Mixed methods research and culture-specific interventions: Program design and evaluation*, Vol. 2. SAGE Publications.

Nazir, A. H., and Liljenström, H. (2016). Neurodynamics of decision-making – a computational approach. In R. Wang and X. Pan (Eds.), *Advances in cognitive neurodynamics (V)* (pp. 41–47). Springer.

Non, A. L., and Thayer, Z. M. (2019). Epigenetics and human variation. In D. H. O'Rourke (Ed.), *A companion to anthropological genetics* (pp. 293–308). Wiley-Blackwell.

O'Cathain, A., Murphy, E., and Nicholl, J. (2007). Why, and how, mixed methods research is undertaken in health services research in England: A mixed methods study. *BMC Health Services Research, 7*(1), 85.

Palmiero, M., and Piccardi, L. (2017). Frontal EEG asymmetry of mood: A mini-review. *Frontiers in Behavioral Neuroscience, 11*, 224.

Panksepp, J. (1998). *Affective neuroscience: The foundations of human and animal emotions*. Oxford University Press.

Panksepp, J. (2000). Emotions as natural kinds within the mammalian brain. In M. Lewis and J. M. Haviland-Jones (Eds.), *Handbook of emotions*, 2nd edition (pp. 137–156). Guilford Press.

Panksepp, J. (2001). The neuro-evolutionary cusp between emotions and cognitions: Implications for understanding consciousness and the emergence of a unified mind science. *Evolution and Cognition, 7*, 141–149.

Panksepp, J. (2002). On the animalian values of the human spirit: The foundational role of affect in psychotherapy and the evolution of consciousness. *European Journal of Psychotherapy, Counselling and Health, 5*, 225–245.

Panksepp, J. (2003). At the interface of the affective, behavioral, and cognitive neurosciences: Decoding the emotional feelings of the brain. *Brain and Cognition, 52*, 4–14.

Panksepp, J. (2004). *Affective neuroscience: The foundations of human and animal emotions*. Oxford University Press.

Panksepp, J. (2007). The neuroevolutionary and neuroaffective psychobiology of the prosocial brain. In L. Barrett and R. Dunbar (Eds.), *The Oxford handbook of evolutionary psychology* (pp. 145–162). Oxford University Press.

Panksepp, J. (2011). The basic emotional circuits of mammalian brains: Do animals have affective lives? *Neuroscience and Biobehavioral Reviews, 35*(9), 1791–1804.

Panksepp, J. (2017). Instinctual foundations of animal minds: Comparative perspectives on the evolved affective neural substrate of emotions and learned behaviors. In J. Call, G. M. Burghardt, I. M. Pepperberg, C. T. Snowdon, and T. Zentall (Eds.), *APA handbook of comparative psychology: Basic concepts, methods, neural substrate, and behavior*, Vol. 1 (pp. 475–500). American Psychological Association.

Panksepp, J., Lane, R. D., Solms, M., and Smith, R. (2017). Reconciling cognitive and affective neuroscience perspectives on the brain basis of emotional experience. *Neuroscience and Biobehavioral Reviews*, 76, 187–215.

Parsons, B., Magill, T., Boucher, A., Zhang, M., Zogbo, K., Bérubé, S., Scheffer, O., Beauregard, M., and Faubert, J. (2016). Enhancing cognitive function using perceptual-cognitive training. *Clinical EEG and Neuroscience*, 47(1), 37–47.

Patsalos, O. C., and Thoma, V. (2020). Water supplementation after dehydration improves judgment and decision-making performance. *Psychological Research*, 84(5), 1223–1234.

Perico, C., Faubert, J., and Bertone, A. (2017). Three-dimensional MOT task as an assessment tool for attention and working memory: A comparison with traditional measures. *Journal of Vision*, 17(10), 965.

Popper, K. R. (1963). Science as falsification. In *Conjectures and refutations* (pp. 33–39). Routledge.

Rolls, E. T. (2015). Limbic systems for emotion and for memory, but no single limbic system. *Cortex*, 62, 119–157.

Romeas, T., Chaumillon, R., Labbé, D., and Faubert, J. (2019). Combining 3D-MOT with sport decision-making for perceptual-cognitive training in virtual reality. *Perceptual and Motor Skills*, 126(5), 922–948.

Rosenbloom, M. H., Schmahmann, J. D., and Price, B. H. (2012). The functional neuroanatomy of decision-making. *Journal of Neuropsychiatry and Clinical Neurosciences*, 24(3), 266–277.

Salas, E., Sims, D. E., and Burke, C. S. (2005). Is there a "big five" in teamwork? *Small Group Research*, 36(5), 555–599.

Schippers, M. B., Roebroeck, A., Renken, R., Nanetti, L., and Keysers, C. (2010). Mapping the information flow from one brain to another during gestural communication. *Proceedings of the National Academy of Sciences*, 107(20), 9388–9393.

Schneider, D., Göddertz, A., Haase, H., Hickey, C., and Wascher, E. (2019). Hemispheric asymmetries in EEG alpha oscillations indicate active inhibition during attentional orienting within working memory. *Behavioural Brain Research*, 359, 38–46.

Schoenbaum, G., Roesch, M. R., and Stalnaker, T. A. (2006). Orbitofrontal cortex, decision-making and drug addiction. *Trends in Neurosciences*, 29(2), 116–124.

Shedler, J., Mayman, M., and Manis, M. (1993). The illusion of mental health. *American Psychologist*, 48(11), 1117–1131.

Stevens, R. H., and Galloway, T. L. (2017). Are neurodynamic organizations a fundamental property of teamwork? *Frontiers in Psychology*, 8, 644.

Stewart, I. (1997). *Does God play dice?: The new mathematics of chaos*. Penguin UK.

Stokols, D., Hall, K. L., Taylor, B. K., and Moser, R. P. (2008). The science of team science: Overview of the field and introduction to the supplement. *American Journal of Preventive Medicine*, 35(2), S77–S89.

Sullivan, G. M., and Feinn, R. (2012). Using effect size – or why the p value is not enough. *Journal of Graduate Medical Education*, 4(3), 279–282.

Sutarto, A. P., Wahab, M. N. A., and Zin, N. M. (2010). Heart rate variability (HRV) biofeedback: A new training approach for operator's performance enhancement. *Journal of Industrial Engineering and Management*, 3(1), 176–198.

Syme, S. L. (2008). The science of team science: Assessing the value of transdisciplinary research. *American Journal of Preventive Medicine*, 35(2), S94–S95.

Taherdoost, H. (2016). Validity and reliability of the research instrument: How to test the validation of a questionnaire/survey in a research. *SSRN Electronic Journal*, 5(3), 28–36.

Takahashi, H., Yokota, R., and Kanzaki, R. (2013). Response variance in functional maps: Neural Darwinism revisited. *PLoS ONE*, 8(7), e68705.

Talukdar, T., Román, F. J., Operskalski, J. T., Zwilling, C. E., and Barbey, A. K. (2018). Individual differences in decision making competence revealed by multivariate f MRI. *Human Brain Mapping*, 39(6), 2664–2672.

Tebes, J. K., and Thai, N. D. (2018). Interdisciplinary team science and the public: Steps toward a participatory team science. *American Psychologist*, 73(4), 549–562.

Tebes, J. K., Thai, N. D., and Matlin, S. L. (2014). Twenty-first-century science as a relational process: From Eureka! to team science and a place for community psychology. *American Journal of Community Psychology*, *53*(3–4), 475–490.

van de Mortel, T. F. (2008). Faking it: Social desirability response bias in self-report research. *Australian Journal of Advanced Nursing*, *25*(4), 40–48.

Varchenko, N. N., Gankin, K., and Matveev, I. A. (2014, October). Monitoring of the functional state of athletes by pupillometry. In *Proceedings of the 2nd International Congress on Sports Sciences Research and Technology Support (icSPORTS)* (pp. 210–215).

von Davier, A. A., and Halpin, P. F. (2013). *Collaborative problem solving and the assessment of cognitive skills: Psychometric considerations*. ETS Research Report.

Waldman, D. A., Wang, D., Stikic, M., Berka, C., and Korszen, S. (2015). Neuroscience and team processes. In D. A. Waldman and P. A. Balthazard (Eds.), *Organizational neuroscience* (pp. 277–294). Emerald Group Publishing Limited.

Wasserstein, R. L., and Lazar, N. A. (2016). The ASA statement on p-values: Context, process, and purpose. *The American Statistician*, *70*, 129–133.

Weisz, J. R., Ng, M. Y., and Bearman, S. K. (2014). Odd couple? Reenvisioning the relation between science and practice in the dissemination-implementation era. *Clinical Psychological Science*, *2*(1), 58–74.

Whalen, P., Davis, F. C., Oler, J. A., Kim, H., Kim, M. J., and Neta, M. (2009). *Human amygdala responses to facial expressions of emotion*. Guilford Press.

Wiltshire, T. J., Butner, J. E., and Fiore, S. M. (2018). Problem-solving phase transitions during team collaboration. *Cognitive Science*, *42*(1), 129–167.

Wójcik, G. M., Masiak, J., Kawiak, A. T., Kwasniewicz, L. K., Schneider, P., Postepski, F., and Gajos-Balinska, A. (2019). Analysis of decision-making process using methods of quantitative electroencephalography and machine learning tools. *Frontiers in Neuroinformatics*, *13*, 73.

Zaslona, J. L., O'Keeffe, K. M., Signal, T. L., and Gander, P. H. (2018). Shared responsibility for managing fatigue: Hearing the pilots. *PLoS ONE*, *13*(5), e0195530.

PART II

Leadership judgment barriers, blind spots, and bad judgment

8. Hubris, bad judgement and practical wisdom in politics and business

Eugene Sadler-Smith

1. INTRODUCTION

Hubrists overestimate significantly their own abilities and achievements; they believe their performance to be superior to that of others and over-inflate the likelihood of positive outcomes and probabilities of success. As a consequence they take over-confident, over-ambitious and sometimes reckless judgements and decisions. The fact that hubrists tend to be resistant to criticism, and invulnerable to and contemptuous of the advice of others, further compounds the threats they pose both to themselves and to those around them. In ancient Greek mythology, hubris, or *hybris*, was an offence against the gods and associated with divine punishment and retribution in the form of 'nemesis'. Time and again hubristic leaders take decisions that are not in their companies' or countries' best interests.

There are numerous examples in business management, political leadership and civil society which illustrate amply the destructive and sometimes catastrophic consequences that can ensue from hubristically incompetent judgement and decision making. These include the invasion of Iraq in 2003, the financial crash of 2008 and the COVID-19 pandemic of 2020. This should not be taken to imply that destructive consequences ensue automatically from hubris; rather, the proposal is that hubris creates conditions that invite the emergence of unintended negative consequences, especially in volatile, uncertain, complex and ambiguous (VUCA) environments. In business, politics and civil society, hubris is a leadership hazard to the extent that it amplifies the potential for leaders reaching a 'tipping point' and crossing the Rubicon into executive over-reach. In this chapter it is argued that hubris entails a failure of practical wisdom, and on the basis that 'an ounce of prevention is worth a pound of cure' it is argued that hubris should be treated as an important source of risk to be managed and mitigated.

2. HUBRIS

Recent years have witnessed an increase in both popular and scholarly interest in hubris in politics (Owen, 2008, 2018; Owen and Davidson, 2009), economics (Desai, 2015), business (Perman, 2013) and management (Picone et al., 2014). The early work in business management can be traced to behavioural finance researchers' studies of CEO hubris in merger and acquisition decisions. In the 'hubris hypothesis', Richard Roll and his colleagues established that when executives believe over-confidently that they, not the market, know best in valuing proposed mergers and acquisitions (M&As), they end up over-bidding for an acquisition, which results ultimately in a loss-making merger in the combined firm (Roll, 1986). For reviews of the hubris hypothesis see Picone et al. (2014) and Sadler-Smith et al. (2016).

Management researchers have recently extended the study of hubris in business beyond its origins in behavioural finance and behavioural decision theory into mainstream management and organization studies (for example, Hayward, 2007; Petit and Bollaert, 2012; Picone et al., 2014; Tourish, 2020), strategic management (Li and Tang, 2010), business ethics (McManus, 2018), environmental mismanagement (Zhang et al., 2020), collective (organizational) hubris (Ladd, 2012), entrepreneurship (Haynes et al., 2015; Hayward et al., 2006), corporate governance (Park et al., 2018) and leadership studies (Sadler-Smith, 2019; Sadler-Smith et al., 2019; Tourish, 2020). A significant step forward in the study of hubris in political leadership occurred in the early 2000s with the work of David Owen and Jonathan Davidson. Owen and Davidson (2009) established a link between the 'intoxication with power' and bad judgement and leader incompetence. Owen and Davidson argued that hubris is characterized by loss of contact with reality, restlessness, recklessness and impulsiveness and a tendency to allow an over-ambitious 'broad vision' to obviate the need to consider practicalities and realities. The result is hubristic incompetence. Owen and Davidson (2009) characterized these and other behaviours in terms of an 'acquired personality change' that manifests as 'aberrant behaviour' that has a 'whiff of mental instability about it' (they proposed a related 14-symptom psychiatric disorder referred to as 'Hubris Syndrome'). Researchers in other domains, such as business management, have subsequently adapted and applied Owen and Davidson's conceptualization of hubris (for example, Picone et al., 2014; Sadler-Smith, 2019).

A question that often arises is that of the relationship between hubris and narcissism. Narcissism is a stable trait-like phenomenon with pathological dimensions (for example, in Narcissistic Personality Disorder, NPD) linked to factors in childhood or adolescence. Hubris on the other hand has been conceptualized as a state-like 'acquired personality change' (Owen, 2012) triggered by accession to a position of significant power, amplified by overestimations of one's abilities based on a track record of prior success and facilitated by complicit followership and lack of constraints (Asad and Sadler-Smith, 2020). As an 'acquired condition' hubris has both a 'rate of ascent and descent' and has been seen to remit once power is lost (Lovelace et al., 2018; Owen, 2008; Owen and Davidson, 2009; Picone et al., 2014). Hence, unlike narcissism ('intoxication with self'), hubris ('intoxication with power') is a reactive disorder. Nonetheless, it influences leaders' behaviours in maladaptive and unproductive ways. Owen has argued that Hubris Syndrome dogged the political careers of prime ministers Lloyd George, Margaret Thatcher and Tony Blair in the UK and presidents George W Bush and Donald J Trump in the USA (Owen, 2007, 2018; Owen and Davidson, 2009).

These developments, emanating from the foundational work of Roll in business and Owen and Davidson in politics, have built towards a consensus regarding the characteristics and causes of hubris in leadership as follows: when leaders who hold significant power have a track record of recent successes, are the recipients of effusive media praise and the accolades of complicit or compliant followers, and are subject to minimal or ineffective restraints, they are more likely to hold inflated and over-confident self-assessments of their competencies and capabilities and their ability to exercise accurate judgements. As a result they overestimate the probability of accruing further successful outcomes ('what can go right') and underestimate the possibility of inaccurate judgements ('what can go wrong'); they develop contempt towards the advice and criticism of others, and in so doing they create conditions that invite negative unintended consequences. These are the hallmarks of hubris. Ultimately, hubrists in positions of power run the risk of becoming the authors and architects both of their own demise and of wider destructive consequences (Hayward, 2007; Hayward and Hambrick, 1997; Hiller and Hambrick, 2005; Li and Tang, 2010; Malmendier and Tate, 2008; Owen, 2018; Picone et al., 2014; Sadler-Smith, 2019; Sadler-Smith et al., 2016; Taleb et al., 2009; Tourish, 2020).

3.   DESTRUCTIVE LEADERSHIP AND HUBRIS

The term 'destructive leadership' has been used as an overarching conceptual category which encompasses various leader behaviours that are associated with 'harmful consequences for followers and organizations' (Thoroughgood et al., 2018, p. 627). It manifests in a variety of forms ranging from workplace bullying to tyranny (Schyns and Schilling, 2013) and has detrimental effects on various outcomes, including productivity, financial performance, employees' psychological well-being, and morale (Kaiser and Craig, 2014; Krasikova et al., 2013).

In terms of its core characteristics, researchers agree that destructive leadership: (a) involves dominating, coercing and manipulating followers and situations rather than influencing, persuading and gaining followers' commitment; (b) has a selfish orientation which focuses more on the leader's needs than those of the wider social group; and (c) produces outcomes that compromise the quality of life for constituents (Einarsen et al., 2016; Kaiser and Craig, 2014; Krasikova et al., 2013; Padilla et al., 2007; Schyns and Schilling, 2013). Followers and colluders play an important role in fostering hubris, hence it is a relational phenomenon. For example, colluders and conformers may follow destructive leaders in the pursuit of personal gain, acting as 'yes men [sic], engaging in flattery, withholding criticism, and using manipulation to further the leader's goals' (Thoroughgood et al., 2018, p. 642). Also, as Padilla et al. (2007) observed, since there are 'good' and 'bad' results in most leadership situations, there is no requirement that destructive leadership is absolutely, exclusively or entirely destructive or that it is intentionally so (although some destructive leadership behaviours are indisputably intended to produce harmful effects, for example bullying). Padilla and colleagues proposed a 'toxic triangle of destructive leadership' to be used as both a conceptual framework and a template for the analysis of destructive leadership and comprised of: (a) a destructive leader (characterized by traits such as charisma, personalized power, narcissism); (b) susceptible followers (conformers and colluders); and (c) conducive environments (for example, instability, perceived threat, lack of checks and balances).

In the terms set out by Padilla and colleagues, Sadler-Smith (2019) argued that hubristic leadership is destructive because, as noted above: (a) it involves dominance and coercion of followers and manipulation of circumstances to attain leaders' goals and ambitions instead of using influence and persuasion to secure followers' commitment; (b) it focuses on leaders' needs, wants and ambitions through the use of power for self-serving decisions rather than a selfless orientation towards the needs of the wider social group; and (c) it creates the conditions for outcomes to arise, albeit unintentionally, that are detrimental both to the individual and the wider context of which s/he is part. Moreover, followers are complicit in hubristic leadership in that they (over-)empower their leaders through processes such as sycophancy, compliance and connivance. Sadler-Smith (2019) adapted Padilla and colleagues' toxic triangle of destructive leadership as a 'toxic triangle of hubristic leadership'.

The issue of intentionality is significant in framing hubristic leadership as a form of destructive leadership. It is important to note that hubristic leaders do not set out to bring about destructive outcomes (as in the cases discussed below). Hubristic leaders are revealed by events to have behaved *ex ante* in ways that were not intended to cause harm, but their actions nonetheless prepared the way for and resulted in detrimental outcomes *ex post* (Einarsen et al., 2007; Eckhaus and Sheaffer, 2018). In processual terms, volitional actions interacting with environmental circumstances (such as volatility, uncertainty, complexity and ambiguity, and including exogenous shocks) can produce unintended consequences that bring about negative outcomes (MacKay and Chia, 2013; Sadler-Smith, 2019). Hubristic leadership entails 'destructive decision making' (see Kaiser and Craig, 2014) in which poor judgement and ill-advised choices are overtaken by processes that result in unintended negative consequences.

4.   EXAMPLES OF HUBRISTIC LEADERSHIP IN BUSINESS MANAGEMENT AND POLITICS

In business the damaging effects of CEO hubris are manifest in the failures of, amongst others, Richard Fuld at Lehman Brothers (Stein, 2003); Fred Goodwin at Royal Bank of Scotland (RBS) group (Craig and Amernic, 2018); the 2008 financial crisis more generally (Tourish, 2020); Jeffery Skilling and Kenneth Lay at ENRON (Eckhaus and Sheaffer, 2018); John Meriwether at Long-Term Capital Management (Lowenstein, 2000); and Lord John Browne at BP (Deepwater Horizon) (Ladd, 2012). The financial costs of hubristic leadership to businesses, the taxpayer and national economies have been significant; for example, the UK taxpayers' bill for the government bailout of RBS group is estimated to have been of the order of £46 billion.

In politics the damaging effects of presidential or prime ministerial hubris are manifest in the consequences of George W Bush's decision to invade Iraq in March 2003 and in the handling of the COVID-19 pandemic in 2020 by some of those countries that have been worst affected, for example Brazil, the UK and the USA. The cost of the Iraq war has been estimated to be as high as $6 trillion; the costs of COVID-19 to the health, social and economic well-being of Brazil, the UK and the USA in financial terms are, at the time of writing, unknown, but in human terms its costs have been devastating and will reverberate for many years to come.

Iraq Invasion of 2003

In the view of a number of scholars (for example, Beinart, 2010; Owen, 2008) the decision of George W Bush and senior members of his cabinet to invade Iraq in 2003 led to destructive outcomes. The eminent political scientist Jean Edward Smith considers it to be America's worst-ever foreign policy decision (Smith, 2016). A study published under the auspices of the 'Costs of War Project' by the Watson Institute for International Studies at Brown University in 2013 estimated that the cost of the Iraq war could grow to more than $6 trillion over the next four decades (counting benefits to veterans and interest charges) and that it has led to the death of at least 134,000 Iraqi civilians, over 4,000 US military personnel, and may have contributed to the death of as many as four times that number.

The destructive leadership process which led to the 2003 invasion of Iraq has been attributed to the confluence of three factors in the toxic triangle of hubristic leadership (Sadler-Smith,

2019 adapted from Padilla et al., 2007): (a) Bush as a hubristic leader with an over-reliance on instinct and intuition, low openness to experience and low integrative complexity, and appeals to high moral authority (Claxton et al., 2015); (b) a variety of susceptible followers, namely 'active colluders' (Dick Cheney and Donald Rumsfeld), a 'cautious restrainer' (Colin Powell) and an 'anticipatory complier' (Condoleezza Rice); and (c) conducive context of the geopolitical environment pre-9/11 and events of and post-9/11. See Sadler-Smith (2019) for a detailed analysis of hubristic leadership and the Iraq invasion.

Global Financial Crisis of 2007–2008

The global financial crisis of 2007–2008 has been estimated to have cost the US government 'well over $2 trillion' in increased expenditures and decreased revenues, 15 per cent of GDP based on pre-crisis trends ($4.6 trillion), and to 'every single American approximately $70,000' (Mukunda, 2018). The personification of the global financial crisis is to be found in Richard 'Dick' Fuld, the CEO from 1994 to 2008 of the global financial services firm Lehman Brothers, the bankruptcy of which is seen by many both to have helped precipitate and to be emblematic of the crisis. Fuld was said by many to be aloof, distant and intimidating; his leadership style was a 'cocktail of indisputable capability and competence mixed with a hard-edged stiffness and bluntness' (Sadler-Smith, 2019, p. xiii); he was nicknamed 'The Digital Mind Trader', but his hubris was such that his capabilities and self-confidence spilled over into conceit and over-confidence. The Congressional hearing into the fallout from the crisis highlighted a flawed business strategy in which the company under Fuld's leadership was overly aggressive and over-confident in using leverage and debt to finance high-stakes investments as a result of high-risk gambles entered into intentionally and volitionally (Sadler-Smith, 2019, p. xiv).

In the UK, Owen (2011) singled out the then Chief Executive of Royal Bank of Scotland (RBS), Fred Goodwin, as an exemplar of the brash exuberance and excessive self-confidence and contempt for the advice and criticism of others that typifies hubristic leadership. Encouraged by his prior success in the £22 billion hostile takeover of one of the UK's biggest and oldest banks, NatWest, by RBS in 2000, Goodwin 'flew too close to the sun' in the disastrous takeover of ABN Amro in 2007, described by some commentators as one of the worst acquisitions ever. A UK Cabinet Office spokesman, commenting in 2012 on Goodwin's knighthood being annulled by Her Majesty the Queen, said:

> The failure of RBS played an important role in the financial crisis of 2008/9 which, together with other macroeconomic factors, triggered the worst recession in the UK since the Second World War and imposed significant direct costs on British taxpayers and businesses. Fred Goodwin was the dominant decision-maker at RBS at the time. (Sadler-Smith, 2019, p. 62)

There can be little doubt that the judgement and decisions of many senior leaders on Wall Street and in the City of London were instrumental factors that contributed to the global financial crisis of 2008 and the economic and social aftershocks that reverberated for many years afterwards (Owen, 2018).

The Iraq invasion of 2003 and global financial crisis of 2008 demonstrated that preventing or reducing CEOs' hubris constitutes a major priority in politics and business, and a failure to do so could allow the consequences of hubristic leadership to spill over and entangle firms, industries and entire economies and have grave repercussions nationally and internationally (Eckhaus and Sheaffer, 2018; Owen, 2018; Petit and Bollaert, 2012; Sadler-Smith, 2019).

COVID-19

If a reminder was needed for the necessity to manage the risks associated with hubristic leadership we need look no further than the effects of the COVID-19 pandemic in selected countries across the globe in 2020 and 2021. Several of those nations that fared worst in 2020–2021 had the misfortune to be led by prime ministers and presidents who displayed many of the hallmarks of hubris (see above), for example Jair Bolsonaro in Brazil, Boris Johnson in the UK and Donald Trump in the USA. Bolsonaro, Johnson and Trump are hubristic and populistic (Owen, 2018; Pagliarini, 2020; Stebbins, 2017). Moreover, some of these leaders chose to 'weaponize' the pandemic in order to blame others for personal failings (McKee et al., 2020; McKee and Stuckler, 2020). Amongst the nations that fared best in the COVID-19 pandemic were those led by individuals whose leadership styles were the antithesis of hubris and the embodiment of humility, practical wisdom and a respect for expertise, for example Jacinda Ardern (New Zealand), Mette Frederiksen (Denmark) and Angela Merkel (Germany) (Huang, 2020; Ladkin, 2020; Wilson, 2020).

Crayne and Medeiros (2020) provided insights into why three world leaders, Trudeau (Canada), Bolsonaro (Brazil) and Merkel (Germany), varied systematically in their approach to making sense of the COVID-19 crisis. From a sensemaking perspective, Crayne and Medeiros (2020) argued that although there is no objectively 'right' or 'wrong' approach in dealing with an unexpected crisis such as COVID-19, the consequences are potentially devastating when there is a misalignment between the leaders' sensemaking style and the requirements of the situation. In their analysis of President Bolsonaro of Brazil, an ideological right winger who modelled himself on Trump with a 'make Brazil great' populist mantra, Crayne and Medeiros (2020) argued that he used emotions negatively ('some people will die, that's life'), had a past time frame orientation ('we must get back to normal'), adopted a transcendent attitude ('our lives have to go on') and put the locus of causation in situations ('there's no reason not to let [the under 40s] work'). Crayne and Medeiros (2020) singled out Bolsonaro's denial of scientific evidence, advocacy of non-scientific findings and dismissal of information that contravened his narrative. In these respects Bolsonaro evidences the 'epistemic hubris' identified by Sadler-Smith and Cojuharenco (2021). Wilson (2020) noted that a willingness by leaders to be led by expertise reduces the risk of 'dysfunctional and ineffective pandemic leadership' and that the 'lesson from New Zealand [under the leadership of Jacinda Ardern] is that to lead well in a pandemic context, leaders must first themselves be willing to be led by those with relevant expertise' (p. 286). Crayne and Medeiros (2020) contrast Bolsonaro's hubristic approach with the pragmatic approach of Chancellor Angela Merkel of Germany, which used a rational and science-based evidence-based response that is the antithesis of the epistemic hubris of Bolsonaro. There are clear parallels between the approach taken by Bolsonaro and that of Trump, and the pivot away from epistemic hubris in the US response with the election of President Biden.

5.   THE HUBRIS PARADOX AND PRACTICAL WISDOM

One of the paradoxes of hubris is that leader strengths that start out as 'good' (for example, grand ambition and decisiveness in response to uncertainty) can, if taken to excess, turn into weaknesses (such as overweening pride, relentlessness and recklessness). This phenomenon was referred to by Miller (1992) as the 'Icarus paradox' (named after the mythical Greek youth who over-exercised his new-found powers of flight, flew too close to the sun contrary to the wise counsel of his father Daedalus and consequently, but inadvertently, met his demise) and as a 'strengths-into-weaknesses' paradox by Sadler-Smith (2019). For example, the leader strengths of: (a) benign influence becomes the weakness of a narcissistic propensity to see the world as an arena for exercising influence and seeking glory (Owen and Davidson, 2009); (b) positive alignment becomes an over-identification with the organization to the extent that the leader sees themselves as synonymous with the organization (the case of Steve Jobs and Apple is cited, Isaacson, 2012; Sadler-Smith et al., 2016); and (c) sound judgement and proper ambition become excessive confidence and exaggerated self-belief bordering on a sense of omnipotence (Sadler-Smith, 2019, p. 138). These weaknesses represent a significant lapse of leadership judgement.

In recent years scholars from a variety of fields have turned to the Aristotelian concept of practical wisdom to understand judgement and decision making in management and leadership practice (Küpers and Statler, 2008). Bachmann et al. (2018) describe practical wisdom as having enjoyed a remarkable renaissance in management and offering an antidote to the many leadership scandals that have plagued business and transformative paradigm for management theory and practice (p. 147). From the perspective of virtue ethics, effective judgement and decision making is akin to 'practical wisdom' ('prudence' or *phronēsis*) and entails deliberating rationally and rightly about what is good and advantageous; it has the following attributes:

- Practical wisdom creates a 'bridge between the emotive [which has cognitive "weight"] and the rational' (Roca, 2008, p. 612); the emotive is activated by 'experiential' (intuitive) processing, whereas rational (analytical) processing articulates knowing;
- Emotive (experiential) and rational (cognitive) knowing are necessary but not sufficient in themselves, and the interaction of the experiential with the rational system is a 'source of intuitive wisdom and creativity' (Epstein, 1994, p. 715);
- 'Phronetic' (that is 'practically wise') leaders, through both experientiality and rationality, are able to intuitively grasp the important features of ambiguous situations in making choices 'driven by the pursuit of the common good' (Shotter and Tsoukas, 2014, p. 224);
- Practical wisdom (*phronēsis*) is one means by which actors can reconcile the competing demands of the common good and commercial success (Zhu et al., 2016).

In Aristotle's moral philosophy, 'good character' and virtue entails striking a balance by locating the mean between excess and deficiency of a particular behaviour; for example, the virtue of 'courage' is at the mean between the vices of 'recklessness' and 'cowardice'. Hence virtue is 'a state that decides, consisting of a mean, the mean relative to us, which is defined by reason … It is a mean between two vices, one of excess and one of deficiency' (*Nicomachean Ethics*, 1107a1–4) and a 'person of practical wisdom is a paradigm of one having virtue' (Audi, 2012, p. 278). Hence, a 'virtuous state' entails a striving to be 'in balance', and the mean of excess and deficiency is an ethical orientation towards that which is intrinsically 'good' (a virtue, not defined by any polar opposite) and away from that which is intrinsically 'bad' (the vices of excess and deficiency) and that is manifested in action as 'integrity' and wisdom (Audi, 2012, p. 274). Hubris may be seen as an excess of leader virtues such as courage, confidence, ambition, decisiveness and so on, towards recklessness, over-confidence, over-ambition, dogmatism and so on. It therefore entails a failure of good judgement. On the basis that good judgement 'is the most central dimension in the network of leader character' (Crossan et al., 2017, p. 1012), hubris can legitimately be seen to represent a failure of leader character. Moreover, hubris as 'self-aggrandizement' entails an insatiability, smacks of gluttony, and may therefore be considered a 'vice' (see Audi, 2012).

A further distinction in Aristotle's moral psychology and philosophy was between abstract knowledge (an 'entity') and knowledge of how to deal with experiential encounters with particular lived experiences (an 'activity') (Küpers and Statler, 2008). Practical wisdom (see above) – that is, 'knowing how things are and what to do' – entails knowing why (*episteme*), knowing how (*techne*) and knowing what the right choice is (*phronēsis*) (Vandekerckhove, 2019). A practically wise manager is freed from the excesses of over-confidence and the hubris that often flows from it (Bachmann et al., 2018, p. 159). As a 'truthful disposition' to get things 'right' in action (Chappell, 2006), practical wisdom is a component of virtuous character. Virtues as exemplars of good character and 'character strengths' as the 'measurable group of related traits' that reflect universal virtues, and prudence is a leader character strength that is associated with the virtue of temperance that protects against excess (Crossan et al., 2013, p. 287). In Aristotle's moral philosophy, prudence entails the capability of being 'able to deliberate rightly about [judge] what is good and advantageous' (*Nicomachean Ethics*, Book VI, Chapter V).

Hubrists, on the other hand, fail to exhibit prudence; instead, their behaviours exhibit excess, that is, a vice (see above) 'springing from over-valuing ones' achievements' (Stebbins, 2017, p. 1). In terms of the practical matter of judging excesses versus deficiencies, a crucial judgement that an effective leader must be able to exercise is deciding what level of a strength constitutes an undue excess. Under particular circumstances (for example, the toxic combination of hubristic leader, complicit followership and conducive context) the point of excess that circumscribes the boundaries of effective leadership becomes obscured, and a tipping point is reached at which the leader risks crossing the Rubicon between the right amount of a strength and too much of it. As Sadler-Smith (2019) noted:

> It is not possible, unfortunately, to make generalized claims about what 'too much of a good thing' looks like, but self-awareness is a starting point. Leadership is situational, and what constitutes a perilous excess of a given strength in one context may not necessarily be self-defeating in another. Walking the hubris tightrope of excess deficiency is a significant leadership challenge. Whilst it is easy to fall off the leadership tightrope, staying on it can be one of a leader's biggest challenges, especially in turbulent business environments. (p. 143)

The picture is more nuanced and made more complex however because leaders must sometimes incline towards excess (to push the boundaries of possibility) (Bordoni, 2019), whilst at other times they must veer in the opposite direction (to avoid over-reaching themselves); the extent to which they should do so is a matter of the finest practical judgement (prudence or *phronēsis*), and no leader can be expected to make this judgement flawlessly and on all occasions. However, the question has a moral dimension in that achieving the mean between excess and deficiency is an ethical orientation towards that which is intrinsically 'good' (a virtue, not defined by any polar opposite) and away from that which is intrinsically 'bad' (the vices of excess and deficiency) (see Audi, 2012).

Leaders need self-esteem, self-efficacy, locus of control and emotional stability in order to perform effectively (these are important aspects of 'core self-evaluation', or CSE); however, problems arise, as noted by Hiller and Hambrick (2005), when healthy core self-evaluation becomes hyper-core self-evaluation (hCSE). According to Furnham (2004), one of the problems for senior leaders is that whilst it is true that they 'need a great deal of self-esteem to get the job done' they also 'need to lose some of it while on the job' and it is 'those with seemingly limitless self-esteem and concomitant hubris who are the real problem' (Furnham, 2004, p. 143). The world's most successful investor, Warren Buffett, Chairman and CEO of Berkshire Hathaway (his net worth is estimated to be in excess of $70 billion), is reported in his authorized biography (Miller, 2016) as having remarked that:

> Successful investing requires you to do your own thinking and train yourself to be comfortable going against the crowd. You could say that good results come from a properly calibrated balance of hubris and humility – hubris enough to think you can have insights that are superior to the collective wisdom of the market, humility enough to know the limits of your abilities and being willing to change course when errors are recognized. (p. 170)

Buffett articulates a kind of practical wisdom in which an investor evaluates facts and circumstances, applies logic and reason to form a hypothesis, and then acts when the facts 'line up' (Miller, 2016, p. 170). An essential aspect of practical wisdom is being humble in the 'face of one's own achievements' (Bachmann et al., 2018, p. 160), and the wise manager remains cognizant of the fact that knowledge and ignorance are inseparable bedfellows and 'therefore it is knowledge of ignorance that makes for what is wise' (Nonaka et al., 2014, p. 367). Humility is a potential source of mitigation on the basis that leaders of good character are humble in the face of their achievements and are cognizant of the fact that knowledge and ignorance are paradoxical elements (Smith and Lewis, 2011) of practical wisdom (see: the 'paradox of Socratic ignorance', Austin, 1987).

6.   CONCLUSION

One of the most exacting challenges that senior leaders face is determining where to draw the line between excesses and deficiencies of, for example, too much and too little confidence, too much and too little ambition and so on and avoiding going beyond one's limits (Bordoni, 2019). Walking this leadership 'tightrope' between excess and deficiency and exercising good judgement is a significant challenge, especially in response to endogenous shocks emanating from volatile, uncertain, complex and ambiguous environments as in the cases of the Iraq war of 2003, the financial crisis of 2008 and COVID-19.

Hubris has been described as an epidemic that has 'infected' politics and organizations; as such, the following 'immunity factors' have been suggested by Garrard (2018) to protect institutions and organizations against the hubris hazard: (a) cultivating or retaining a personal modesty once a position of significant power has been achieved; (b) staying grounded and eschewing the trappings of power and success; (c) consulting carefully in order to communicate and check, even if it is not to change, their judgements and decisions; (d) accepting that institutional and organizational checks and balances need to be built in to safeguard against the abuse of power; and (e) retaining, or cultivating, a sense of humour and of perspective about themselves, being able to exercise self-criticism and humility. Vigilance and early diagnosis of the emergence of hubristic leadership can thus contribute to the better design of the 'psychological architecture', due diligence and governance structures of firms (Powell et al., 2011; Tang et al., 2015) and thereby militate against the excesses of hubristic leadership.

Ultimately, many of the political and business leaders discussed in this chapter have displayed 'epistemic hubris' manifesting as convictions that one has intellectual authority amounting to an infallibility, an arrogance that one has the right or privilege not to know or not to need to know, and an imperviousness to dissenting voices (Baird and Calvard, 2019). As such, epistemic hubris is a 'learning infirmity' that amplifies the risks of not listening to feedback about one's mistakes and impedes reflexivity (Baird and Calvard, 2019; De Bruin, 2013; Roberts and Wood, 2003). Epistemic hubris is the antithesis of, and therefore contrary to, both practical wisdom and humility. In response to the potentially destructive outcomes that are associated with hubristic leadership, it has been suggested that hubris is a category of risk that needs to be 'managed', and 'hubris risk' could be added to commonly managed business risks such as conduct, credit risk, liquidity risk and market risk.[1] Moreover, the destructive consequences associated with hubristic leadership could be 'prevented' rather than 'cured' by a management learning and education curriculum that warns against the vice of hubris and inculcates the virtue of humility in the leaders and managers of the future (see Sadler-Smith and Cojuharenco, 2021).

NOTE

1. These are the categories of risk identified by the new Governor of the Bank of England, Andrew Bailey. https://www.bankofengland.co.uk/speech/2016/culture-in-financial-services-a-regulators -perspective.

REFERENCES

Asad, S. and Sadler-Smith, E. (2020), 'Differentiating leader hubris and narcissism on the basis of power', *Leadership*, 16(1), 39–61.

Audi, R. (2012), 'Virtue ethics as a resource in business', *Business Ethics Quarterly*, 22(2), 273–291.

Austin, S. (1987), 'The paradox of Socratic ignorance (how to know that you don't know)', *Philosophical Topics*, 15(2), 23–34.

Bachmann, C., Habisch, A. and Dierksmeier, C. (2018), 'Practical wisdom: Management's no longer forgotten virtue', *Journal of Business Ethics*, 153(1), 147–165.

Baird, C. and Calvard, T. S. (2019), 'Epistemic vices in organizations: Knowledge, truth, and unethical conduct', *Journal of Business Ethics*, 160, 236–276.

Beinart, P. (2010), *The Icarus syndrome: A history of American hubris*. New York: Harper.

Bordoni, C. (2019), *Hubris and progress: A future born of presumption*. Abingdon: Routledge.

Chappell, T. (2006), 'The variety of life and the unity of practical wisdom', in T. Chappell (ed.), *Values and virtues: Aristotelianism in contemporary ethics* (pp. 136–157). Oxford: Oxford University Press.

Claxton, G., Owen, D. and Sadler-Smith, E. (2015), 'Hubris in leadership: A peril of unbridled intuition?', *Leadership*, 11, 57–78.

Craig, R. and Amernic, J. (2018), 'Are there language markers of hubris in CEO letters to shareholders?', *Journal of Business Ethics*, 149, 973–986.

Crayne, M. P. and Medeiros, K. E. (2020), 'Making sense of crisis: Charismatic, ideological, and pragmatic leadership in response to COVID-19', *American Psychologist*. https://doi.org/10.1037/amp0000715.

Crossan, M. M., Byrne, A., Seijts, G. H., Reno, M., Monzani, L. and Gandz, J. (2017), 'Toward a framework of leader character in organizations', *Journal of Management Studies*, 54(7), 986–1018.

Crossan, M., Mazutis, D., Seijts, G. and Gandz, J. (2013), 'Developing leadership character in business programs', *Academy of Management Learning and Education*, 12(2), 285–305.

De Bruin, B. (2013), 'Epistemic virtues in business', *Journal of Business Ethics*, 113(4), 583–595.

Desai, M. (2015), *Hubris: Why economists failed to predict the crisis and how to avoid the next one.* New Haven: Yale.

Eckhaus, E. and Sheaffer, Z. (2018), 'Managerial hubris detection: The case of Enron', *Risk Management*, 20(4), 304–325.

Einarsen, S., Aasland, M. S. and Skogstad, A. (2007), 'Destructive leadership behaviour: A definition and conceptual model', *The Leadership Quarterly*, 18, 207–216.

Einarsen, S., Aasland, M. S. and Skogstad, A. (2016), 'The nature and outcomes of destructive leadership behaviour in organizations', in R. J. Burke and C. L. Cooper (eds), *Risky business: Psychological, physical and financial costs of high risk behaviour in organizations* (pp. 323–350). Abingdon: Routledge.

Epstein, S. (1994), 'Integration of the cognitive and the psychodynamic unconscious', *American Psychologist*, 49(8), 709–724.

Furnham, A. (2004), *Management and myths.* Basingstoke: Palgrave Macmillan.

Garrard, P. (2018), *The leadership hubris epidemic.* Basingstoke: Palgrave Macmillan.

Haynes, K. T., Hitt, M. A. and Campbell, J. T. (2015), 'The dark side of leadership: Towards a mid-range theory of hubris and greed in entrepreneurial contexts', *Journal of Management Studies*, 52, 479–505.

Hayward, M. (2007), *Ego check: Why executive hubris is wrecking companies and careers and how to avoid the trap.* Chicago: Kaplan.

Hayward, M. L. and Hambrick, D. C. (1997), 'Explaining the premiums paid for large acquisitions: Evidence of CEO hubris', *Administrative Science Quarterly*, 42, 103–127.

Hayward, M. L., Shepherd, D. A. and Griffin, D. (2006), 'A hubris theory of entrepreneurship', *Management Science*, 52, 160–172.

Hiller, N. J. and Hambrick, D. C. (2005), 'Conceptualizing executive hubris: The role of (hyper) core self-evaluations in strategic decision-making', *Strategic Management Journal*, 26, 297–319.

Huang, P. H. (2020), 'Put more women in charge and other leadership lessons from COVID-19'. http://dx.doi.org/10.2139/ssrn.3604783.

Isaacson, W. (2012), *Steve Jobs.* New York: Simon and Schuster.

Kaiser, R. B. and Craig, S. B. (2014), 'Destructive leadership in and of organizations', in D. V. Day (ed.), *The Oxford handbook of leadership and organizations* (pp. 260–284). Oxford: Oxford University Press.

Krasikova, D. V., Green, S. G. and LeBreton, J. M. (2013), 'Destructive leadership: A theoretical review, integration, and future research agenda', *Journal of Management*, 39(5), 1308–1338.

Küpers, W. and Statler, M. (2008), 'Practically wise leadership: Toward an integral understanding', *Culture and Organization*, 14(4), 379–400.

Ladd, A. E. (2012), 'Pandora's well: Hubris, deregulation, fossil fuels, and the BP oil disaster in the Gulf', *American Behavioral Scientist*, 56, 104–127.

Ladkin, D. (2020), 'What Donald Trump's response to COVID-19 teaches us: It's time for our romance with leaders to end', *Leadership*, 16(3), 273–278.

Li, J. and Tang, Y. I. (2010), 'CEO hubris and firm risk taking in China: The moderating role of managerial discretion', *Academy of Management Journal*, 53(1), 45–68.

Lovelace, J. B., Bundy, J., Hambrick, D. C. and Pollock, T. G. (2018), 'The shackles of CEO celebrity: Socio-cognitive and behavioral role constraints on "star" leaders', *Academy of Management Review*, 43, 419–444.

Lowenstein, R. (2000), *When genius failed: The rise and fall of Long-Term Capital Management.* New York: Random House.

MacKay, R. B. and Chia, R. (2013), 'Choice, chance, and unintended consequences in strategic change: A process understanding of the rise and fall of NorthCo Automotive', *Academy of Management Journal*, 56(1), 208–230.

Malmendier, U. and Tate, G. (2008), 'Who makes acquisitions? CEO overconfidence and the market's reaction', *Journal of Financial Economics*, 89(1), 20–43.

McKee, M., Gugushvili, A., Koltai, J. and Stuckler, D. (2020), 'Are populist leaders creating the conditions for the spread of COVID-19? Comment on "A Scoping Review of Populist Radical Right Parties' Influence on Welfare Policy and its Implications for Population Health in Europe"', *International Journal of Health Policy and Management*. https://www.ijhpm.com/article_3856.html.

McKee, M. and Stuckler, D. (2020), 'If the world fails to protect the economy, COVID-19 will damage health not just now but also in the future', *Nature Medicine*, 26(5), 640–642.

McManus, J. (2018), 'Hubris and unethical decision making: The tragedy of the uncommon', *Journal of Business Ethics*, 149(1), 169–185.

Miller, D. (1992), 'The Icarus paradox: How exceptional companies bring about their own downfall', *Business Horizons*, 35(1), 24–35.

Miller, J. C. (2016), *Ground rules: Words of wisdom from the partnership letters of the world's greatest investor*. New York: HarperCollins.

Mukunda, G. (2018), 'The social and political costs of the financial crisis, 10 years later', *Harvard Business Review*. https://hbr.org/2018/09/the-social-and-political-costs-of-the-financial-crisis-10-years-later.

Nonaka, I., Chia, R., Holt, R. and Peltokorpi, V. (2014), 'Wisdom, management and organization', *Management Learning*, 45(4), 365–376.

Owen, D. (2007), *The hubris syndrome: Bush, Blair and the intoxication of power*. London: Politico's Publishing.

Owen, D. (2008), 'Hubris syndrome', *Clinical Medicine*, 8(4), 428–432.

Owen, D. (2011), 'Psychiatry and politicians – afterword: Commentary on … psychiatry and politicians', *The Psychiatrist*, 35(4), 145–148.

Owen, D. (2012), *The hubris syndrome: Bush, Blair and the intoxication of power*. 2nd Edition. York: Methuen.

Owen, D. (2018), *Hubris: The road to Donald Trump*. York: Methuen.

Owen, D. and Davidson, J. (2009), 'Hubris syndrome: An acquired personality disorder? A study of US presidents and UK prime ministers over the last 100 years', *Brain*, 132, 1396–1406.

Padilla, A., Hogan, R. and Kaiser, R. B. (2007), 'The toxic triangle: Destructive leaders, susceptible followers, and conducive environments', *The Leadership Quarterly*, 18, 176–194.

Pagliarini, A. (2020), 'Facing Bolsonaro's Brazil: A progressive US foreign policy toward Brazil must neither defer to nor confront far-right president Jair Bolsonaro. Instead, it should illuminate his antidemocratic tendencies while centering key global fights against inequality and climate change', *NACLA Report on the Americas*, 52(1), 47–52.

Park, J. H., Kim, C., Chang, Y. K., Lee, D. H. and Sung, Y. D. (2018), 'CEO hubris and firm performance: Exploring the moderating roles of CEO power and board vigilance', *Journal of Business Ethics*, 147(4), 919–933.

Perman, R. (2013), *Hubris: How HBOS wrecked the best bank in Britain*. Edinburgh: Birlinn.

Petit, V. and Bollaert, H. (2012), 'Flying too close to the sun? Hubris among CEOs and how to prevent it', *Journal of Business Ethics*, 108, 265–283.

Picone, P. M., Dagnino, G. B. and Minà, A. (2014), 'The origin of failure: A multidisciplinary appraisal of the hubris hypothesis and proposed research agenda', *Academy of Management Perspectives*, 28(4), 447–468.

Powell, T. C., Lovallo, D. and Fox, C. R. (2011), 'Behavioral strategy', *Strategic Management Journal*, 32, 1369–1386.

Roberts, R. C. and Wood, W. J. (2003), 'Humility and epistemic goods', in M. R. DePaul and L. T. Zagzebski (eds), *Intellectual virtue: Perspectives from ethics and epistemology* (pp. 257–279). Oxford: Oxford University Press.

Roca, E. (2008), 'Introducing practical wisdom in business schools', *Journal of Business Ethics*, 82(3), 607–620.

Roll, R. (1986), 'The hubris hypothesis of corporate takeovers', *Journal of Business*, 59(2, Pt 1), 197–216.

Sadler-Smith, E. (2019), *Hubristic leadership*. London: SAGE.

Sadler-Smith, E., Akstinaite, V., Robinson, G. and Wray, T. C. D. (2016), 'Hubristic leadership: A review', *Leadership*, 13(5), 525–548.

Sadler-Smith, E. and Cojuharenco, I. (2021), 'Business schools and hubris: Cause or cure?', *Academy of Management Learning and Education* (in press). doi.org/10.5465/amle.2019.0289.

Sadler-Smith, E., Robinson, G., Akstinaite, V. and Wray, T. C. D. (2019), 'Hubristic leadership: Understanding the hazard and mitigating the risk', *Organizational Dynamics*, 48(2), 8–18.

Schyns, B. and Schilling, J. (2013), 'How bad are the effects of bad leaders? A meta-analysis of destructive leadership and its outcomes', *The Leadership Quarterly*, 24, 138–158.

Shotter, J. and Tsoukas, H. (2014), 'In search of phronēsis: Leadership and the art of judgment', *Academy of Management Learning and Education*, 13(2), 224–243.

Smith, J. E. (2016), *Bush*. New York: Simon and Schuster.

Smith, W. K. and Lewis, M. W. (2011), 'Toward a theory of paradox: A dynamic equilibrium model of organizing', *Academy of Management Review*, 36(2), 381–403.

Stebbins, R. A. (2017), *From humility to hubris among scholars and politicians: Exploring expressions of self-esteem and achievement*. Bingley: Emerald Group Publishing.

Stein, M. (2003), 'Unbounded irrationality: Risk and organizational narcissism at Long Term Capital Management', *Human Relations*, 56(5), 523–540.

Taleb, N. N., Goldstein, D. G. and Spitznagel, M. W. (2009), 'The six mistakes executives make in risk management', *Harvard Business Review*, 87(10), 78–81.

Tang, Y., Qian, C., Chen, G. and Shen, R. (2015), 'How CEO hubris affects corporate social (ir)responsibility', *Strategic Management Journal*, 36(9), 1338–1357.

Thoroughgood, C. N., Sawyer, K. B., Padilla, A. and Lunsford, L. (2018), 'Destructive leadership: A critique of leader-centric perspectives and toward a more holistic definition', *Journal of Business Ethics*, 151(3), 627–649.

Tourish, D. (2020), 'Towards an organizational theory of hubris: Symptoms, behaviours and social fields within finance and banking', *Organization*, 27(1), 88–109.

Vandekerckhove, W. (2019), 'Practical wisdom, respect and metaphysics: A broad spectrum for philosophy of management', *Philosophy of Management*, 18(3), 211–214.

Wilson, S. (2020), 'Pandemic leadership: Lessons from New Zealand's approach to COVID-19', *Leadership*, 16(3), 279–293.

Zhang, L., Ren, S., Chen, X., Li, D. and Yin, D. (2020), 'CEO hubris and firm pollution: State and market contingencies in a transitional economy', *Journal of Business Ethics*, 161, 459–478.

Zhu, Y., Rooney, D. and Phillips, N. (2016), 'Practice-based wisdom theory for integrating institutional logics: A new model for social entrepreneurship learning and education', *Academy of Management Learning and Education*, 15(3), 607–625.

9. Feeling and dirty hands: the role of regret experienced by responsible agents

Terry L. Price

INTRODUCTION[1]

Leaders often have to make moral judgments in hard cases.[2] In some of these cases, commentators conclude that leaders' decisions ultimately leave them with "dirty hands."[3] According to advocates of this line of argument, their hands are not dirty in the straightforward sense that they simply got things wrong—for example, that they behaved immorally by doing what was easier or simply more conducive to their own interests. That kind of behavior would lend itself to standard moral analysis. Rather, the charge is more nuanced, perhaps "paradoxical": when leaders' hands are dirty, although they did what they had to do—indeed, what (in some real sense) they should have done—the behavior in which they engaged is nevertheless morally wrong or, at least, morally problematic.[4] As we shall see, a lot turns on what it means to call an action "wrong" or "problematic" from a moral perspective. For now, suffice it to say that the problem of dirty hands depends on denying that the requisite behavior was fully justified morally. In the words of philosopher Bernard Williams, such cases "leave [a] moral remainder, [an] uncancelled moral disagreeableness."[5]

What is left over, of course, is the dirt on leaders' hands. How do we (and they) know their hands are dirty? The standard answer is that actors *feel* that their hands are dirty—just as do other wrongdoers, some of whom make literal attempts to clean them. In literature, we find Lady Macbeth's compulsive hand-washing in response to her role in Duncan's murder: "What, will these hands ne'er be clean? ... Here's the smell of the blood still: all the perfumes of Arabia will not sweeten this little hand."[6] Some psychological experiments go so far as to suggest that the nature of the moral wrong committed (lying by email or by telephone) affects the nature of the cleaning that the guilty party will later engage in (accepting hand sanitizer or mouthwash, respectively) from the experimenter.[7] The larger point, though, is that there is a definite "phenomenology" associated with dirty hands.[8] The way it *feels* is evidence that what the leader did was morally wrong or problematic.

My aim in this chapter is to make sense of the phenomenology of so-called dirty hands cases. I say *so-called* because I am skeptical that there are (very many) true dirty hands cases—that is, cases in which leaders do what they should do but there is something left over that escapes moral justification.[9] This is not to deny that the actions in which leaders sometimes engage are ones that, in other circumstances, we would readily deem morally wrong or problematic. Nor is it to deny the feelings themselves that are associated with such cases. Rather, what I will try to show is that the feelings at issue are not decisive when it comes to an assessment of justification. To this end, I will defend an alternative interpretation of the role of feelings that accompany the moral judgments that leaders make. This argument relies on the notion of *responsible-agent regret*.[10] One fact about the phenomenology of leadership is that leaders sometimes have to do things that are regrettable both in the very fact that these actions need to be done and, more important in this context, that they—the leaders—are the ones who morally ought to do them.

I want to be clear at the outset that my analysis of dirty hands does not imply that leaders have free moral reign, that they are fully justified in all such cases after all. To the contrary, the phenomenon of dirty hands and the phenomenology associated with it are just as likely to serve as a resource for rationalization. In other words, dirty hands language sometimes does little more than give leaders a convenient way of talking about why they did what was morally wrong or problematic. These leaders also tell themselves: *Dirty hands are part of the business of leadership and, after all, I feel awful about having to do what I did—necessary though it was.* But all they actually have is a failed justification. So, leaders may sometimes be justified in doing what would be wrong or problematic in other contexts, but not always. What they feel though—the phenomenology of judgment and action—is very much the same across cases. This means that there must be moral limits on leaders' attempts to justify what is potentially morally wrong or problematic. I conclude by offering a way for leaders to check for justification when they are tempted to judge that the situation is one in which they must get their hands dirty.

DIRTY HANDS IN POLITICS AND BEYOND

The problem of dirty hands is most familiar in political contexts. In fact, in his famous article on the topic, Michael Walzer calls it "a central feature of political life" and claims that it "arises not merely as an occasional crisis in the career of this or that unlucky politician but systematically and frequently."[11] One thing, among others, that makes political leadership distinctive is that it countenances the use of violence.[12] Indeed, the very idea of the state assumes a monopoly on the use of force. However, Walzer's prototype for dirty hands cases pushes the limits on what even legitimate agents of the state can justifiably do. One exemplar is the political leader who must authorize torture to prevent a terrorist attack and save innocent lives.[13] Mariam Thalos further expands the list of violent acts "that leaders might be called upon to do in supreme emergencies—murder, torture, rape, slavery, to name only the more despicable of such things …"[14]

Clearly, if anything is morally wrong, such actions are *morally wrong*. Murder is wrong by definition, and it is hard to imagine any situation in which rape or slavery might be fully justified. Contrast these actions, though, with behaviors that strike us as merely *morally problematic*, or might be better described that way. I say *merely* not to diminish their potential seriousness, only to signal that they do not fall within the class of clearly prohibited actions. To call actions such as murder, rape, torture, and slavery *morally problematic* does not capture the gravity of the transgression.[15] It ignores their intrinsic wrongness or what they do to their victims.[16] Some behaviors, though, do not rise to this level but nevertheless leave us thinking—and, when we do them, *feeling*—that things are not quite right. Even if we have not committed a moral wrong, there can nevertheless be something morally problematic about what we have done.

Consider, in this vein, the other main example Walzer uses.[17] A political candidate, in his efforts to get elected, promises a public contract to a "dishonest ward boss" in exchange for the ward boss's support.[18] The candidate does not initiate the deal but, rather, gives in to the request of the ward boss. Although it would be morally wrong for the candidate to offer a bribe in this situation, the moral status of acquiescing to the ward boss's request in this context is less clear. We might think of the candidate's behavior as analogous to giving in to a hostage-taker's demands. Here, my point is that facts about some contexts, cultures, and societies sometimes make it hard (or harder) to say that a particular behavior is morally wrong in the unqualified way that other actions—murder, rape, torture, slavery—are. We may ultimately come to the conclusion that a behavior is too problematic to engage in, but the complexities about the larger system in which we act will be relevant to whether we come down this way. For example, it is at least relevant how (most) others are behaving and whether these behaviors are necessary within this system if we are to have any success at all.

The political candidate's dilemma reflects the fact that leaders often have to work with unsavory characters and operate within less than ideal institutional conditions. Not only, as Machiavelli puts it, do leaders have to deal with "many unscrupulous men," they sometimes find themselves in circumstances characterized by varying levels of corruption.[19] Moreover, the moral rules are not completely clear as to how leaders should respond in these circumstances. Still, if the candidate plays the game in which he finds himself, there is something morally problematic about what he has done. Giving in to the immoral request of a ward boss makes the target of the request something more, or other than, a victim. The candidate is now an involved participant in the activity itself.[20] For one thing, he perpetuates an already corrupt system. Similarly, a very compelling argument against paying ransom is that so doing increases the incentives to take hostages. Those who do so surely know their behavior is morally problematic. The question is whether it is so problematic that it outweighs the potential benefits of giving in to the hostage-taker's demands.

The dirty hands literature, as well as work in leadership ethics, tends to neglect behavior that does not lend itself to moral rules, behavior that I have referred to as *morally problematic* behavior.[21] This is despite the fact that in addition to torture, lying, and cheating—all of which are prohibited by moral rules—Walzer notes that the political actor also gets his hands dirty when he decides to "bargain behind the backs of his supporters, shout absurdities at public meetings, or manipulate other men and women."[22] Manipulation is especially relevant for leadership because leaders draw on all kinds of tactics to get people to do what they—the leaders—believe ought to be done.[23] For example, they sometimes play on followers' desires to avoid conflict or social embarrassment.[24] In many cases, however, leaders exercise influence over followers simply by using behaviors that would ordinarily be perfectly permissible and are morally problematic in the leadership context only because they are used to get followers to do what they would not have done otherwise.[25]

The ubiquity of behaviors that are morally problematic—and, yet, not prohibited outright by morality—gives us one reason to think that the problem of dirty hands extends well beyond political leadership. Another reason is that emergency situations, which might justify rule-breaking behavior, are hardly confined to politics. Here, my concession regarding the potential for extreme cases across leadership contexts contradicts what I have argued elsewhere.[26] There, I claimed that everyday leaders do not face life-or-death circumstances and, accordingly, should strictly follow the moral rules. However, when I drew on this work in leadership training for police officers and medical professionals, they reminded me that they are forced to make decisions about who lives or dies, some of them on a daily basis. We ask them to set aside moral rules against the use of force (in law enforcement) and against hastening death (in the medical context) when these rules are overridden by other, weightier moral concerns such as defense of a third party or respect for a suffering patient's autonomy.[27]

Of course, both kinds of cases raise complexities of their own that merit independent treatment. Police officers sometimes try, but fail, to justify the use of deadly force in cases in which it was unnecessary for self-defense, much less defense of a third party. There are also serious moral questions about what dying patients can consent to and the conditions that would need to hold if we are to protect against both principled and practical threats to the exercise of their autonomy. Suffice it to say, however, that—unless we are pacifists—there are some circumstances in which even killing is justified. And, if an agent can be fully justified in breaking even so important a moral rule, then it would seem that leaders can surely use lesser, merely morally problematic, means without there being anything left over to justify. So, without taking a strong stance on the justification of any particular case of rule breaking, I want to use what we know about justification more generally to make the case for the full justification of some morally problematic behaviors. Before turning to that argument, though, we need to make sense of how it feels to do what is morally wrong or problematic.

FEELING AND RESPONSIBLE-AGENT REGRET

Walzer assumes that there is a very strong link between doing what is morally wrong or problematic, feeling guilty for doing it, and—accordingly—having dirt on one's hands. Recall his political candidate who participates in a corrupt transaction in order to shore up support needed to win the election. Walzer says that the candidate "will feel guilty, that is, he will believe himself to be guilty. That is what it means to have dirty hands."[28] But the connection between behavior and feeling is not as strong as Walzer makes it out to be. First, people sometimes do wrong without experiencing feelings of guilt. Unfortunately, there is no internal detection device that sends reliable emotive signals regarding the moral status of our behavior. Second, our moral emotions do not always track our moral beliefs, let alone morality itself. We all know we can feel irrational unjustified guilt—that is, have the feeling without doing anything wrong or believing that we have.[29] It is the normative ambiguity of our feelings that allows people to use them in their efforts to influence us. Perhaps the best example is when they make us feel guilty in the hope that we will come to believe that we actually are guilty for not doing what they want us to do.[30]

Walzer clearly recognizes that feeling and belief can come apart.[31] The possibility of a truly Machiavellian leader assumes as much. Such a leader's hands are dirty, but he "pretend[s] that they were clean."[32] The Machiavellian leader thus stands out to us as particularly dangerous, because although he knows or believes his behavior to be wrong—otherwise, he would not be *pretending*—he does it without reservation. That is what distinguishes him from "the moral politician": the Machiavellian leader has no "scruples."[33] Leaders rightly worry us when they do not struggle with difficult moral decisions. In this context, it is interesting to note that President Harry Truman's justification for his authorization of the dropping of the atomic bomb on Japan took up only one paragraph in his memoirs.[34] If that brief treatment is any indication of what he felt about having to make that awful decision, we might wonder whether he was as moral as he might have been.[35] The main point, though, is that Truman's feelings were not a decisive indicator of the ultimate moral status of his behavior.

The most we can say, then, is that feeling and behavior go together some of the time. The best leaders, we might assume, feel guilty and so on when they do what they judge to be wrong. That is why Walzer denies that their "guilt feelings can be tricked away."[36] In contrast, leaders who lack such feelings have nothing to be tricked away in the first place. Wrongdoing, then, does not always give rise to feelings of guilt. What about the converse? Is wrongdoing always present when leaders experience guilt feelings? It turns out that this connection does not hold even for good leaders. Walzer admits as much when he claims that "the inhibition against killing another human being is so strong that even if the men believe that what they are doing is right, they will still feel guilty."[37] So, although the best leaders feel guilty when they do what they believe to be wrong, they sometimes have these feelings in the absence of any wrongdoing.

To understand better the indeterminant role of feelings in moral life, it might be helpful to consider some examples from ordinary life. Growing up in rural North Carolina, I once saw my father euthanize a dog that had been hit by a car. The dog's internal organs were exposed, but it was very much still alive and, it seemed me—as a child—very much in pain. My father quickly grabbed a gun from his truck and did what he thought he had to do. Although I never asked him how it affected *him*, I cannot imagine that he did not feel something more than the sadness and disgust that *I* experienced. What I suspect people rightly feel in such cases is a sense of regret—both that what they did had to be done and, most importantly, that it fell on them to have to do it. That is my best description of what I felt when I had to do something similar as an adult, albeit in less extreme circumstances and using less extreme means.

I am also inclined to think that regret, not guilt, best captures what people feel when they do what is in some sense morally problematic but not morally wrong in the sense that the behavior violates some explicit moral rule.[38] Political theorist Nannerl Keohane tells how, while serving as president of Wellesley College, she faced her own dirty hands dilemma. Students protesting the college's financial connection to the apartheid regime in South Africa "ingeniously blocked both of the auto exits from campus by lying in the road and refusing to get up."[39] Keohane justifies her behavior, correctly I would add, this way: "I had a good deal of *personal* sympathy for the students' moral convictions, but … I was responsible for the students and for faculty and staff members who needed to leave the campus to pick up children at day care or make other urgent appointments."[40] It is clear from Keohane's description of the encounter that she felt bad—that she regretted having to be the one to authorize the arrest of the students. Yet it was what she had to do because of her position of leadership.

If Keohane's decision was fully justified, then why would she feel bad? First, her own personal commitments were aligned to some extent or other with the students' cause.[41] Indeed, were she only a faculty member, she might have publicly supported their ends, even if not their means. There is much more room for non-institutional values to loom large when one is not in a position of leadership. However, in her role as president, things were very different. It fell to her to prioritize the interests of campus constituents. That is a large part of the president's job, which—given the actual facts—made it her job. So, it was her responsibility to have the students arrested, a responsibility she could nevertheless regret having to carry out. Second, the actions she took would have been wrong for her to carry out as a faculty member, as it would have been for most other college employees. Given the seriousness of the decision and its potential effects on particular individuals in the college community, only the president would be justified in taking this step to resolve the situation.

Leaders' selves can thus be split by their roles—often in ways that force them to neglect or downplay their own personal commitments. This fact explains why they feel regret when they do what has to be done. As Mariam Thalos puts it, "Dirty hands is the phenomenology of guilt, and not the reality of it."[42] Of course, being in a position of leadership does not mean that leaders' hands are always clean, no matter their behavior. In other words, the leadership position itself cannot fully justify whatever leaders do—albeit regretfully. Thalos's own argument comes close to taking the apologist's line when she puts most of the blame on followers. According to her, it is they who authorize the behavior of leaders.[43] But leaders can be to blame—their hands can really be dirty—even when their behavior is democratically authorized and, moreover, conducive to the ends of democracy.[44] That is because the way leaders get things done matters, in addition to the normative source and outcomes of their behavior. They can be unjustified in what they did not only because there were sufficiently effective (though perhaps inconvenient) alternatives but also because what they did was not actually worth it, given what was ultimately achieved.

The interpretation of dirty hands that I want to defend, then, allows for cases in which leaders are just wrong for acting as they did. However, this concession leaves room for lots of cases in which leaders are fully justified and, yet, feel regret. I am also inclined to think that such behavior is what defines many cases in which we use dirty hands language. Particularly helpful in this context is what Bernard Williams famously refers to as "'agent-regret', which a person can feel only towards … actions in which he regards himself as a participant."[45] Agent-regret is to be distinguished from simply regretting that something happened.[46] It thus gets at the idea that "there is something special about [the agent's] relation to this happening."[47] The regret that leaders feel must be similarly distinguished from followers' regret when something morally problematic has to be done. This is because there is no special relationship between them and the behavior in question.

Williams's original insight is that agents feel a distinctive kind of regret despite the fact that things turned out as they did because of factors beyond their control—for example, as a matter of luck.[48] In other words, we can experience agent-regret even with respect to actions that are unintentional or less than fully voluntary.[49] In dirty hands cases, however, leaders intentionally do what is morally wrong or problematic.[50] That is why we think their hands are dirty. In dirty hands cases, that is, luck is not particularly relevant, even the luck Thomas Nagel refers to as "luck in one's circumstances—the kind of problems and situations one faces."[51] This kind of luck gets at the fact that people do not have complete control over the circumstances in which they find themselves. However, when leaders have to make hard decisions in such circumstances, we know exactly why it fell to them to do so. Because they accepted the responsibilities of leadership, it would be difficult for them to attribute their predicament to bad circumstantial luck. After all, they must face problematic circumstances in the same way all leaders have to face them. They are the ones who had to do and, subsequently, intentionally did what had to be done.

In the leadership context, we can refer to the relevant kind of regret as *responsible-agent regret*. Although it makes sense to include it under the more general category of agent-regret, intention makes the link between agent and behavior much tighter than when agents find themselves connected to a piece of behavior as purely a matter of luck.[52] Other things being equal, we might also think that the regret leaders experience is worse precisely because of the intentionality. The psychological, even moral, costs associated with responsible-agent regret have implications for how we should think about selecting and recruiting leaders. It makes sense that people should have a large say in whether they take on positions of leadership and expose themselves to this kind of moral risk.[53] We cannot always avoid agent-regret, but for the most part, we should be able to avoid responsible-agent regret—unless, that is, we are in a position of leadership.[54]

Indeed, the source of responsible-agent regret can likely be traced to the decision to take on a position of leadership in the first place—that is, by making a choice to bear the additional moral risk.[55] Walzer goes even further: "[P]olitical action necessarily involves taking a risk. But it should be clear," he adds, "that what is risked is not personal goodness—*that was thrown away*—but power and glory."[56] We do not have to accept Walzer's claim that moral loss is irreparable—that personal goodness is "thrown away"—to recognize that genuine ethical choice occurs well before leaders are forced to make moral judgments in hard cases. Responsible-agent regret, as well as the vulnerability to it, is part and parcel of the phenomenology of leadership. Leaders should therefore be unsurprised when they find themselves in situations in which they experience responsible-agent regret, even if their problematic behavior is fully justified from a moral perspective. The only way to avoid this kind of regret is not to take on the responsibilities of leadership in the first place.

DIRTY HANDS AND RATIONALIZATION

This interpretation of the phenomenology associated with dirty hands creates an epistemic problem for leaders. Leaders will be unable to use the feeling of regret to determine the moral status of their behavior. In some cases, leaders will feel responsible-agent regret despite the fact that they are fully justified in doing what may strike us, and them, as morally problematic in some sense or other. In other cases, however, they will feel regret for doing what they should not have done and, indeed, what they ought to feel guilty for doing. Leaders who lack justification should experience guilt because there is real dirt on their hands. They did something morally problematic without sufficient justification for doing it. It is as simple as that. What makes things complicated—the epistemic problem—is that leaders need to figure out how to tell the difference between the two kinds of cases.

Another real-life example might help make the epistemic problem clearer and, potentially, point us—as well as leaders—in the direction of a solution. This one, too, focuses on educational leadership. To please a powerful benefactor, a university president feels compelled to make what will surely be a controversial decision. The decision could be about some new academic, co-curricular, or extra-curricular program. Let us also assume that this decision will negatively impact some members of the university community—thus, the impending controversy. Substantial resources will have to be diverted to support the new program and, worse still, some employees will lose their jobs or some students will lose their scholarships. The president who makes this decision is admittedly sincere about the regret he experiences.[57] In his own mind, he did what had to be done for the sake of the institution. The president might even tell himself that these kinds of decisions come with the responsibilities of leadership. Like leaders who are actually justified in doing what is morally problematic, he experiences the phenomenology of dirty hands. Yet, he has done nothing wrong. Or so he thinks.

But how can the president be sure or, better, reasonably confident in his assessment of the moral status of his behavior? Is mere responsible-agent regret enough, or should he instead feel guilty about what he has done? It turns out that individual agents, because of their tendency to rationalize, are not particularly good at answering this question.[58] That is why leaders who find themselves confronted by hard ethical decisions would be well advised to seek the counsel of followers and others. In the present context, I do not have in mind the creation of "task forces" composed of hand-picked faculty members or individuals who already support the idea of the new program.[59] Task forces generally have little epistemic value. In fact, such consultation can exacerbate the epistemic problem by creating so much momentum for an idea that it is effectively impossible to stop its implementation, even when there is justified opposition from the broader university community. The task force generates its own internal energy by making significant investment behind the scenes and increasing expectations about the success of the proposal.

Under what conditions, then, are leaders right to judge that they would be justified in doing what is morally problematic? The cases I have discussed suggest two promising starting points: defense of others and the consent of followers. Both are in keeping with more general grounds for justifiably doing what one ordinarily ought not to do. The justification for using force to prevent harm to third parties is at least as strong as the justification for self-defense, a very common justification for engaging in behaviors that would be morally wrong in other circumstances. Consent can also protect agents against a claim of immorality. In both kinds of cases, as in purported cases of dirty hands, people who do what is morally problematic may feel regret despite being fully justified in their behavior. The police officer who must use deadly force to save an innocent victim can expect to experience responsible-agent regret. So too the friend, family member, or medical professional who helps a terminally ill patient carry out her wish to die on her own terms.

These moral signposts—defense of third parties and consent—are equally relevant for leaders in so-called dirty hands cases. Recall that Nannerl Keohane's hands were not really dirty after all when she had students arrested for blocking campus exits. She did what she had to do as president of Wellesley College to protect members of the university community. The moral status of the university president in my other example is less clear. Unlike Keohane, this president's behavior was not necessary to protect third parties from harm. Moreover, some members of the university community could rightly point to the negative effects that the president's decision would have on them in terms of lost employment or scholarships. Of course, we cannot expect that leaders—whether in education or other organizations—will get the consent of all, including the members who will be negatively affected by the decision. After all, they must make decisions about what is best for the institution as a whole. We can, however, expect them to get broad-based support from followers—something more than what is available from a "consent-as-shield" task force—especially in contexts of shared governance.[60]

Allow me to conclude by reminding us of where we began and rehearsing how we got to where we are now. Leaders are in the business of making difficult judgments. Without denying the difficulty, I have tried to show that we can very often make sense of it without resorting to a paradoxical notion of justification, in particular the one to which advocates of dirty hands must be committed. On their view, leaders regularly face dilemmas that, when properly addressed, leave leaders less than fully justified even though they have done exactly what they ought to do. Thus the regret. Although I cannot prove that there are no such cases, my argument suggests that they are far fewer than dirty hands advocates would have us believe. Their number is drastically reduced when we identify cases in which leaders are fully justified in their behavior but feel responsible-agent regret. We must also distinguish true dirty hands cases from those situations in which leaders' hands are not only dirty but rightly so—because the leaders in question were wrong to do what they did. Again, the problem for leaders is to discriminate between the two scenarios. The mistake of dirty hands theorists is to conflate the two. They are accordingly left with an abundance of cases in which leaders are justified in doing what has to be done but there is something wrong with doing it all the same.

To address the epistemic problem, I have suggested that leaders need strategies such as appealing to the defense of others and the consent of followers. Unfortunately, by foregoing these strategies, dirty hands theory obscures, rather than clarifies, the problem. The notion of dirty hands, as articulated by its defenders, makes it less likely that leaders will try to distinguish between cases in which a behavior is fully justified and those in which the behavior would be wrong. If leaders do not need—and often cannot get—full justification, there is much less incentive for them to examine the moral reasons behind their judgments. What is the point of appeals to defense of others or follower consent if full justification is ultimately a lost cause? Dirty hands language therefore equips leaders to rationalize their own behavior. It makes it all the easier for them to convince themselves that they had to do what was wrong.

Rationalization does not make the wrongdoing—or even the regret—go away. However, dirty hands theory does give leaders the resources to craft a more comforting explanation for what they did and why they feel as they do. We can think of these leaders as the moral flipside of leaders who also live with responsible-agent regret yet have done nothing wrong. The phenomenology associated with so-called dirty hands cases is thus part of the moral psychology of leadership. Some leaders take it too far and embrace wrongdoing as part of the business of leadership. The best leaders, though, come to terms with responsible-agent regret only when they have good moral reasons to think that it can be separated from wrongdoing. When they are unsure about the moral status of their behavior, the best advice for them is to check morally problematic behavior against the fundamental values of followers—what would be necessary both to protect them and to respect their judgment. That gives leaders a chance to make sure the dirt on their hands is not real or, if it is, that it is not on their hands alone.

NOTES

1. I thank Jessica Flanigan, Javier Hidalgo, Peter Kaufman, and Cassie Price—as well as the volume editors and anonymous reviewers—for their many improvements to this chapter.
2. In this chapter, I take a philosophical approach and focus primarily on individual leaders who are authorized to make decisions based on their judgments and, equally important for my purposes, on how they *feel* as individuals who have made these decisions.
3. See Michael Walzer, "Political Action: The Problem of Dirty Hands," *Philosophy and Public Affairs* 2, no. 2 (Winter 1973): 160–80.
4. Walzer, "Political Action," 168. See Michael Stocker, *Plural and Conflicting Values* (Oxford: Oxford University Press, 1990), 10: "The dirty hands cases I am concerned with are (1) justified, even obligatory, but (2) none the less somehow wrong."
5. Williams, "Politics and Moral Character," in his *Moral Luck: Philosophical Papers 1973–1980* (Cambridge: Cambridge University Press, 1981), 61.
6. Shakespeare, *Macbeth*, in John Dover Wilson (ed.), *The Complete Works of William Shakespeare* (London: Spring Books, 1987), 827–8. Of course, there is no literal blood on Lady Macbeth's hands. She got Macbeth to murder Duncan. Mariam Thalos, "Dirty Hands: The Phenomenology

of Acting as an Authorized Agent," *The Monist* 101, no. 2 (April 2018): 172–3, tries to distinguish between blood and dirt, not entirely successfully to my mind. Interestingly, Pontius Pilate washes his hands to avoid responsibility *before the fact*. It was therefore less a response to the phenomenology of leadership than a tactical attempt to bypass the responsibilities of leadership altogether.

7. Spike W. S. Lee and Norbert Schwarz, "Dirty Hands and Dirty Mouths: Embodiment of the Moral-Purity Metaphor Is Specific to the Motor Modality Involved in Moral Transgression," *Psychological Science* 21, no. 10 (2010): 1423–5.
8. Thalos, "Dirty Hands," 172.
9. For a defense of the stronger conclusion—namely, that there are no such cases—see Kai Nielsen, "There Is No Dilemma of Dirty Hands," *South African Journal of Philosophy* 15, no. 1 (1996): 1–7.
10. For the notion of "agent-regret," see Bernard Williams, "Moral Luck," in his *Moral Luck: Philosophical Papers 1973–1980* (Cambridge: Cambridge University Press, 1981), 27–31.
11. Walzer, "Political Action," 162.
12. Walzer, "Political Action," 174.
13. Walzer, "Political Action," 166–7.
14. Thalos, "Dirty Hands," 171. As an anonymous reviewer notes, these are not mere hypotheticals: psychologists are asked to authorize so-called enhanced interrogation techniques, and rape is sometimes used as a weapon of war.
15. Oddly, Thalos refers to these actions as "distasteful" ("Dirty Hands," 180).
16. There is a definite Kantian framing here, but I do not believe this framing is necessary for the distinction between actions that are morally wrong and those that are merely morally problematic.
17. Walzer, "Political Action," 165–6.
18. Walzer, "Political Action," 165.
19. Niccolò Machiavelli, *The Prince*, ed. Quentin Skinner and Russell Price (Cambridge: Cambridge University Press, 1988), 54.
20. Advocates of dirty hands would suggest he got involved as soon as he entered politics.
21. But see, John M. Parrish, "Benevolent Skulduggery," in Michael A. Genovese and Victoria A. Farrar-Myers (eds.), *Corruption and American Politics* (Amherst, NY: Cambria Press, 2010) for a discussion of Walzer's second, less-well-known example.
22. Walzer, "Political Action," 165.
23. Terry L. Price, *Leadership and the Ethics of Influence* (New York: Routledge, 2020).
24. Marcia Baron, "Manipulativeness," *Proceedings and Addresses of the American Philosophical Association* 77, no. 2 (November 2003): 40.
25. Price, *Leadership and the Ethics of Influence*, 24–8.
26. See, Terry L. Price, *Leadership Ethics: An Introduction* (Cambridge: Cambridge University Press, 2008).
27. See Patrick W. Shaver's 2017 documentary *Officer Involved* for first-hand accounts of how individuals in law enforcement make sense of their behavior in light of the moral—and, for many, religious—prohibition on killing. For life-and-death decisions in the medical context, see Daniel W. Tigard, "Moral Distress as a Symptom of Dirty Hands," *Res Publica* 25 (2019): 355.
28. Walzer, "Political Action," 166.
29. Walzer refers to "superstitious anxiety" ("Political Action," 172).
30. Price, *Leadership and the Ethics of Influence*, 134–8.
31. Walzer, "Political Action," 166–7.
32. Walzer, "Political Action," 168.
33. Walzer, "Political Action," 168, 166. Different still is what we might refer to as *the Kantian leader*, who refuses to get his hands dirty because he is a "moral man and nothing else" (168).
34. Jonathan Glover, *Humanity: A Moral History of the Twentieth Century* (New Haven, CT: Yale University Press, 2000), 104. Walzer writes of the "Machiavellian hero" that he "is unlikely to keep a diary" ("Political Action," 176).
35. That is not to say that Truman's decision was ultimately unjustified, only that Walzer is right that we expect good leaders' feelings to be congruent with the gravity of their behavior.
36. Walzer, "Political Action," 174.

37. Walzer, "Political Action," 173. Walzer has in mind "serving on a firing squad ... [when] the execution is not thought to be (and let us grant this to be the case) an immoral or wrongful act" (173).

38. See Williams's distinction between *regret* and *remorse* ("Moral Luck," 30).

39. Nannerl O. Keohane, *Thinking about Leadership* (Princeton, NJ: Princeton University Press, 2010), 218.

40. Keohane, *Thinking about Leadership*, 218 (emphasis added).

41. Thalos, "Dirty Hands," 183: "[E]xperiences of performing these tasks might conflict with a person's role-independent sense of what they owe others as individual persons—and not as instruments of a larger entity tasked with carrying out the expressed [wishes] of the citizenry."

42. Thalos, "Dirty Hands," 176. Or, better, "[not *necessarily*] the reality of it." Again, I think regret is more fitting than guilt in these cases. One reason is that guilt is not psychologically rich enough to capture the moral experience of engaging in morally wrong or problematic behaviors when we think that we are justified in acting as we do. For example, in a study of police shootings, only 12 percent reported feeling "guilt," whereas 83 percent and 42 percent reported "recurrent thoughts" or "other thoughts and feelings," respectively ("Police Responses to Officer-Involved Shootings," *National Institute of Justice Journal*, National Institute of Justice, January 1, 2006, https://nij.ojp .gov/topics/articles/police-responses-officer-involved-shootings). The inclusion of *thoughts*, in addition to *feelings*, is telling because we ordinarily understand regret as having both cognitive and emotive elements. See "regret," *Dictionary.com*, https://www.dictionary.com/browse/regret, and Melanie Greenberg, "The Psychology of Regret: Should We Really Aim to Live Our Lives with No Regrets?" *Psychology Today* (May 16, 2012), https://www.psychologytoday.com/us/blog/the -mindful-self-express/201205/the-psychology-regret.

43. Thalos, "Dirty Hands," 176. Walzer similarly says they do it "in our name" and "*for us*" ("Political Action," 162–3).

44. Contrary to what Thalos, "Dirty Hands," suggests at 183. Parrish seems to be making a related argument when he appeals to "internally justified corruption" ("Benevolent Skulduggery," 79).

45. Williams, "Moral Luck," 27.

46. Williams, "Moral Luck," 27.

47. Williams, "Moral Luck," 28.

48. Williams, "Moral Luck," 28.

49. Williams, "Moral Luck," 27–8. Thomas Nagel, "Moral Luck," in his *Mortal Questions* (Cambridge: Cambridge University Press, 1979), 29, reserves "moral luck" for cases in which the agent is, at least, negligent.

50. See Williams's allusion to dirty hand problems in "Moral Luck" at 31.

51. Nagel, "Moral Luck," 28.

52. Stephen De Wijze, "Tragic-Remorse—The Anguish of Dirty Hands," *Ethical Theory and Practice* 7, no. 5 (January 2005): 464, denies this point and claims that intentionality is what moves an agent from regret to tragic-remorse in response to the agent's "moral pollution."

53. Walzer, "Political Action," 165.

54. The argument for this claim appeals to Bernard Williams's integrity-based critique of utilitarianism. To require that a person expose himself to responsible-agent regret would be "to alienate him in a real sense from his actions and the source of his action in his own convictions. ... [T]his is to neglect the extent to which *his* actions and *his* decisions have to be seen as the actions and decisions which flow from the projects and attitudes with which he is most closely identified. It is thus, in the most literal sense, an attack on his integrity" (Bernard Williams, "A Critique of Utilitarianism," in J. J. C. Smart and Bernard Williams, *Utilitarianism: For and Against* [Cambridge: Cambridge University Press, 1973], 116–17). So, I am agreeing with Williams that moral agents do not have to take on these responsibilities.

55. Jessica Flanigan has emphasized the importance of this point to me.

56. Walzer, "Political Action," 176.

57. Compare the opening line of rejection letters: "I regret to inform you ..." They are admittedly formulaic, and one wonders whether the writer feels any regret at all. Notice, however, that the language is cleverly ambiguous as to what is regretted—the rejection itself (probably not) or that it

is left to the writer to do the rejecting (more likely). Admittedly, in some cases, it will be a mixture of both.

58. See, Stelios C. Zyglidopoulos, Peter J. Fleming, and Sandra Rothenberg, "Rationalization, Overcompensation, and the Escalation of Corruption in Organizations," *Journal of Business Ethics* 84, Supplement 1 (2009): 68–70; and Vikas Anand, Blake E. Ashforth, and Mahendra Joshi, "Business as Usual: The Acceptance and Perpetuation of Corruption in Organizations," *Academy of Management Executive* 18, no. 2 (2004): 39–53.
59. Even the name suggests that their "task" is to "force" something through.
60. I thank an anonymous reviewer for the distinction between the "consent-as-shield" task force and deeper forms of consent. Javier Hidalgo has rightly pointed out to me the importance of open debate for understanding any substantive consent condition.

REFERENCES

Anand, Vikas, Blake E. Ashforth, and Mahendra Joshi. "Business as Usual: The Acceptance and Perpetuation of Corruption in Organizations." *Academy of Management Executive* 18, no. 2 (2004): 39–53.
Baron, Marcia. "Manipulativeness." *Proceedings and Addresses of the American Philosophical Association* 77, no. 2 (November 2003): 37–54.
De Wijze, Stephen. "Tragic-Remorse—The Anguish of Dirty Hands." *Ethical Theory and Practice* 7, no. 5 (January 2005): 453–71.
Dictionary.com. "Regret." https://www.dictionary.com/browse/regret.
Glover, Jonathan. *Humanity: A Moral History of the Twentieth Century*. New Haven, CT: Yale University Press, 2000.
Greenberg, Melanie. "The Psychology of Regret: Should We Really Aim to Live Our Lives with No Regrets?" *Psychology Today* (May 16, 2012). https://www.psychologytoday.com/us/blog/the-mindful-self-express/201205/the-psychology-regret.
Keohane, Nannerl O. *Thinking about Leadership*. Princeton, NJ: Princeton University Press, 2010.
Lee, Spike W. S. and Norbert Schwarz. "Dirty Hands and Dirty Mouths: Embodiment of the Moral-Purity Metaphor Is Specific to the Motor Modality Involved in Moral Transgression." *Psychological Science* 21, no. 10 (2010): 1423–5.
Machiavelli, Niccolò. *The Prince*. Edited by Quentin Skinner and Russell Price. Cambridge: Cambridge University Press, 1988.
Nagel, Thomas. "Moral Luck." In *Mortal Questions*, 24–38. Cambridge: Cambridge University Press, 1979.
National Institute of Justice. "Police Responses to Officer-Involved Shootings." *National Institute of Justice Journal* (January 1, 2006). https://nij.ojp.gov/topics/articles/police-responses-officer-involved-shootings.
Nielsen, Kai. "There Is No Dilemma of Dirty Hands." *South African Journal of Philosophy* 15, no. 1 (1996): 1–7.
Parrish, John M. "Benevolent Skulduggery." In *Corruption and American Politics*, edited by Michael A. Genovese and Victoria A. Farrar-Myers, 65–98. Amherst, NY: Cambria Press, 2010.
Price, Terry L. *Leadership and the Ethics of Influence*. New York: Routledge, 2020.
Price, Terry L. *Leadership Ethics: An Introduction*. Cambridge: Cambridge University Press, 2008.
Shakespeare, William. *Macbeth*. In *The Complete Works of William Shakespeare*, edited by John Dover Wilson, 809–31. London: Spring Books, 1987.
Shaver, Patrick W. *Officer Involved*. Documentary film. Austin, TX: IndieClever Media, 2017.
Stocker, Michael. *Plural and Conflicting Values*. Oxford: Oxford University Press, 1990.
Thalos, Mariam. "Dirty Hands: The Phenomenology of Acting as an Authorized Agent." *The Monist* 101, no. 2 (April 2018): 170–86.
Tigard, Daniel W. "Moral Distress as a Symptom of Dirty Hands." *Res Publica* 25 (2019): 353–71.
Walzer, Michael. "Political Action: The Problem of Dirty Hands." *Philosophy and Public Affairs* 2, no. 2 (Winter 1973): 160–80.

Williams, Bernard. "A Critique of Utilitarianism." In *Utilitarianism: For and Against*, by J. J. C. Smart and Bernard Williams, 75–150. Cambridge: Cambridge University Press, 1973.

Williams, Bernard. "Moral Luck." In *Moral Luck: Philosophical Papers 1973–1980*, 20–39. Cambridge: Cambridge University Press, 1981.

Williams, Bernard. "Politics and Moral Character." In *Moral Luck: Philosophical Papers 1973–1980*, 54–70. Cambridge: Cambridge University Press, 1981.

Zyglidopoulos, Stelios C., Peter J. Fleming, and Sandra Rothenberg. "Rationalization, Overcompensation, and the Escalation of Corruption in Organizations." *Journal of Business Ethics* 84, Supplement 1 (2009): 65–73.

10. Context corrupts: what makes leaders fail to see their (mis)behaviors

Andrea Pittarello and Roseanne J. Foti

INTRODUCTION

On October 28, 2018, a Boeing 737 Max 8 crashed near Jakarta shortly after take-off. On March 10, 2019, another identical plane crashed near Addis Ababa (Ethiopia). Almost 350 people died in these accidents. Could this tragedy have been prevented? Very much so. Indeed, strikingly, Boeing CEO at the time Dennis Muilenburg *knew* that the planes were dangerous as repeated tests showed that heavier engines placed forward created unsafe flight conditions. Yet Boeing did nothing to prevent those planes from being in service.

Does this story sound familiar to you? It probably does. Almost 50 years ago, Ford launched the subcompact Ford Pinto, a car that suffered severe fuel tank malfunctions causing explosions in several rear-end collisions. As a result, many people died, and hundreds were badly injured. Here too, Ford *knew* about the issues yet decided that the car would stay on American roads. Some 20 years later, Dennis Gioia – Ford's recall coordinator at the time – said: "Why didn't I see the problem and its ethical overtones?" (1992, p. 383). Indeed, how could he fail to see what was going on? What prevented him from acting ethically? Fast forward to 2018 the question remains: Why did Boeing fail to see the gravity of its deadly planes? Both cases present a similar ethical dilemma between focusing on what is the right thing to do (e.g., recalling cars and ground airplanes) and focusing on what was financially self-serving but unethical (profits). The question is: When and what makes leaders and CEOs turn a blind eye to their (mis)behavior?

One possibility is that there are ethical and unethical leaders, and such a distinction can be explained by individual antecedents such as personality, moral development and identity, and follower perception of ethical leadership (cf. Den Hartog, 2015). Accordingly, research suggests that good leaders are defined by cognitive moral development, concern for people, reliability, and responsibility (cf. Bass and Steidlmeier, 1999; Brown et al., 2005; Brown and Treviño, 2006; DeHoogh and Den Hartog, 2008; Turner et al., 2002). Conceptually, Brown and Treviño (2006) suggested links of ethical leadership with three of the big five personality traits: conscientiousness, agreeableness, and emotional stability. Research finds low but significant relations between traits and perceptions of ethical leadership. Conscientiousness and agreeableness were most relevant for overall ethical leader behavior (Kalshoven et al., 2011). Finally, there seems to be mixed evidence on whether dark triads traits such as Machiavellianism and Narcissism negatively correlate with ethical leadership (cf. Den Hartog, 2015; Den Hartog and Belschak, 2012; Hoffman et al., 2013). While promising, this research mostly relies on "follower perception of ethical leader behavior rather than actual behavior or intentions" (Den Hartog, 2015, p. 427). The problem is that perceptions can be biased, making it difficult to understand whether they measure actual unethical behaviors that can ultimately result in major ethical scandals.

Certainly, personality does play an important role, but only a small part of research revealed that unethical behaviors result from traits rather than the situational forces that enable otherwise good people to do wrong (cf. Feldman and Smith, 2013; Tett and Guterman, 2000). Although leadership scholars acknowledge the effect of the context in shaping ethical behaviors, they have mainly focused on ethical cultures and values, industry characteristics, and intraorganizational characteristics (cf. Eisenbeiss and Giessner, 2012). In doing so, they have largely overlooked the influence of more concrete situational forces that affect the *process* through which leaders arrive at (un)ethical conclusions. Squarely fitting this call, psychologists, economists, and behavioral ethicists have recently developed a new field called "behavioral ethics," with the goal of understanding in which situations people make honest (or dishonest) choices. Quoting Bazerman and Gino, "Behavioral ethicists describe the actual behavior of people and how situational and social forces influence it, and they study how decisions can be nudged in a more ethical direction through simple interventions" (2012, p. 89).

As such, behavioral ethics offers another explanation for unethical behavior. One of the core tenets of this approach is that people truly value integrity and see themselves as honest and moral – even more honest than others (cf. Aquino and Reed, 2002; Bazerman and Tenbrunsel, 2011; Greenwald, 1980; Mazar et al., 2008; Sanitioso et al., 1990). Accordingly, researchers consistently found that people are averse to lying, especially when deception hurts others (cf. Gneezy, 2005; López-Pérez and Spiegelman, 2013; Lundquist et al., 2009; Mazar et al., 2008). In other words, dishonesty carries psychological costs (cf. Thielmann and Hilbig, 2019) and spoils our self-concept. Yet people from all walks of life – including respected CEOs and managers – lie, deceive, and cheat (cf. Ayal et al., 2016), posing great threats to society at large. Here is the conundrum: On the one hand, people think they are honest; on the other, they often lie and cheat. How do they balance between doing wrong and feeling honest? In this chapter, we review recent work that merges ethics, behavioral economics, and cognitive psychology to answer the question of what, when, and why good people do bad and what can be done about it. Specifically, we wish to focus on the power of the context and highlight the situational factors that turn otherwise good people into dishonest individuals.

Our goal is to encourage a broader interdisciplinary approach to business ethics and spur novel research to further our understanding of dishonesty and of the possible interventions that could foster the ethical business culture that we all cherish.

COGNITIVE PROCESSES AND DECISIONS

Business ethical decisions – much like any other decisions – result from information processing (Fiedler and Glöckner, 2015). Indeed, people have to scan for and gather information, elaborate it, retrieve from memory prior similar instances, and integrate all these pieces of information before evaluating different alternatives (i.e., judgment) and eventually choosing one.

As such, making a decision requires a series of processing steps of varying complexity (cf. Payne et al., 1988). Because of this complexity, one should carefully attend to and process all the relevant information. However, despite our best intentions, research on bounded rationality (March and Simon, 1958; Simon, 1957) tells us that cognitive capacity is limited, meaning that some information will be filtered out, simplified, or ignored altogether, especially when it interferes with our goals (cf. Simons and Chabris, 1999). But how does such an attention filter play out in shaping unethical decisions[1]?

Building on bounded rationality, Chugh and colleagues (2005) proposed the concept of "bounded ethicality." The idea is that oftentimes people pay little (or no) attention to their (mis)behaviors when doing so is against their self-interest. This phenomenon is called an "ethical blind spot" (Bazerman and Tenbrunsel, 2011). Just like dishonesty is rarely a clear-cut distinction between right or wrong (cf. Shalvi et al., 2011), blind spots vary on the extent to which they are more, or less, intentional. Take for instance conflict of interests: When an auditing company is checking the books of one of its clients, it might fail to see some irregularities. After all, reporting the company would mean losing a profitable client (cf. Bazerman and Sezer, 2016). Similarly, doctors receiving compensations from a pharmaceutical company might fail to notice that their prescriptions favor the companies giving them money. Though no one would agree that these behaviors are moral, it is possible that doctors do not fully realize that their prescriptions are biased. In these examples, blind spots can be unintentional. Conversely, imagine cheating on taxes. In this case, the violation is much clearer, and few would agree (hopefully) that "ignoring" some revenue is unintentional. This setting resembles our opening examples: Clearly, both Boeing and Ford were aware of the ethical issues at stake but ignored them to favor their bottom line. In these situations, what makes it easier for CEOs to overlook such ethical issues? The rest of the chapter focuses on settings in which people – at least to an extent – are aware of their misbehavior, which is frequently the case in many ethical breakdowns. The key questions we address are: What causes blind spots? And most importantly, can blind spots be counteracted?

ATTENTION, JUSTIFICATIONS, AND TEMPTATION

Despite researchers first mentioning blind spots almost a decade ago, only recently have they devoted their time to "objectively" measure them and examine how they determine dishonesty. In taking up such challenge, behavioral economists, management scholars, and cognitive psychologists developed a new line of work that uses eye-tracking methodologies to better understand what makes people ethically blind. Broadly speaking, eye tracking is a non-invasive way to measure attention and information search. Eye movements analyses reveal how long people fixate on certain pieces of information, how often, and how many times they switch between them, providing valuable information on how people arrive at judgments and choices. The main idea is that the more attention that is allocated to certain stimuli, the more important these stimuli are and the more frequently they are chosen (cf. Fiedler and Glöckner, 2015; Fiedler et al., 2013; Orquin and Loose, 2013; Reisen et al., 2008; Weber and Johnson, 2009).

Additionally, measuring eye movements allows us to study preferences in an unbiased manner (cf. Fiedler and Glöckner, 2015), whether people use a deliberate and analytical thinking style or a quick and automatic one (cf. Fiedler and Glöckner, 2012; Horstmann et al., 2009; Kahneman, 2011), and the extent to which a decision is taxing (cf. Laeng et al., 2012). Finally, eye movements are driven by motivations, meaning that attention is also affected by people's desires, goals, and wishes (Balcetis and Dunning, 2006).

For these reasons, eye tracking is a viable tool to assess blind spots. After all, ethical decisions generally entail a choice between two options: an honest (but often less profitable) one and a dishonest (but more profitable) one. For instance, imagine a CEO compiling the end of the year tax return. The CEO realizes that the return does not look as good as he wished. At the same time, he also realizes that he can dishonestly add some expenses that would reduce the taxable income. This would make the numbers look much better. This situation – much more common than we think – poses an ethical dilemma between honesty and fraud. Or consider the earlier Ford Pinto example. Ford compared the cost of recalling and fixing cars to that of paying for lawsuits and settlements. In both cases, a decision maker faces the temptation of adding irrelevant expenses, and that of a more profitable return. Does such tempting information reduce our attention to what's right (but less profitable)?

To answer this question, Pittarello and colleagues (2015) reproduced this dilemma in a controlled laboratory setting. Participants sat in front of a computer screen that recorded their eye movements. The experiment went as follows: Participants saw a cue on the screen followed by six die-roll outcomes. When the rolls disappeared, participants were asked to report the roll appearing closest to the cue. The authors varied the value of the die appearing second-closest to the cue: On some trials, the value was higher than the correct roll, while on other trials it was lower. To incentivize reports, participants were paid based on what they reported, irrespective of whether their response was accurate or not. Reporting higher rolls meant higher payoffs. The authors found that participants made frequent self-serving mistakes (an implicit form of dishonesty, see Leib et al., 2019): On tempting trials, they often reported the tempting higher roll instead of the correct one. Such a roll was tempting because it yielded higher payoffs and was displayed close to the correct but less profitable roll.

Interestingly, they rarely made self-hurting mistakes – that is, reporting non-tempting rolls instead of the correct ones. To find out whether the rate of self-serving mistakes depended on the ability to justify one's misbehavior, the authors further varied the position of the cue. At times, it appeared closer to the correct (but less profitable) die roll and at other times farther away from it. The reasoning was that the closer the cue was to the correct roll, the harder it was for participants to report another number and justify it. In the end, it was a simple perceptual task in which participants were extremely accurate when paid for answering correctly. But the farther the cue was (and hence the closer to the tempting roll), the easier it made it for participants to make an "honest mistake" and earn more money. It turned out that participants lied more the farther the cue was from the truth.

Analyses of eye movements showed two key findings: First, participants spent more time looking at tempting (yet dishonest) rolls at the expense of non-tempting (yet honest) rolls. Second, such a shift of attention predicted the extent to which they lied. Thus, the authors concluded that in ambiguous settings – where ambiguity allows for justifications (cf. Shalvi et al., 2011) – temptation captures attention and shapes the lies we tell. In other words, when cheating pays, people *see what they want to see* and interpret reality in a self-serving way.

Notably, even though participants knew that they were being observed and that their eyes were being tracked, they still lied (~23 percent of the time). This is important because it suggests – contrary to what most would believe – that monitoring does not necessarily reduce dishonesty. Put differently, the more the situation offers room for justifications, the more people do wrong while feeling honest. But one key question remains unanswered: When does temptation capture attention? Could it be that we are immediately drawn to what is wrong? Or could it be that our first impulse is to be honest?

BLIND SPOTS: FAST OR SLOW?

Let's go back to our CEO facing the dilemma of altering the company report. Imagine that he only has little time to think about what to do. Would he lie? Would he be honest? This question is far from trivial. Indeed, one of the thorniest issues in behavioral ethics is whether honesty is a quick or deliberate response. To date, evidence is mixed. Some scholars have found that when people have little time, they tend to lie (cf. Shalvi et al., 2012). Conversely, others have showed that fabricating a lie takes time, and thus dishonesty requires deliberation (cf. Capraro, 2017; Capraro et al., 2019; Zhong, 2011). Since this discussion is outside the scope of this chapter, we refer to the work of Van der Cruyssen and colleagues (2020) and Suchotzki and colleagues (2017) for interested readers.

This notwithstanding, eye tracking can provide some insights into when tempting and dishonest options capture attention. This is because our first fixations are relatively fast and occur outside our volitionary control. To simplify, there are two possibilities. One is that temptation captures attention quickly – suggesting that, to an extent, our first reaction is to be dishonest. Another is that it does so slowly, hinting towards the idea that our first reaction is to be honest.

To test this idea, Pittarello and colleagues (2019) presented participants with a series of digits on the screen. Participants were asked to report the digit indicated by a cue and received money based on the value of the digit they reported (and not for their accuracy). Participants could lie and report a higher value digit appearing close to the correct one and were not penalized for making mistakes. Conceptually replicating the die-roll experiment we saw above, participants frequently cheated. Instead of reporting correctly, they reported tempting digits to earn more money. But when did temptation grab attention?

The authors mapped the eye movements during each of the several decisions over time and space. Put simply, they examined what participants looked at first. Interestingly, it turned out that participants looked first at the dishonest and tempting digits and did so quite rapidly (~700ms). The authors concluded that when presented with a choice between right and wrong, what's wrong captures attention first, meaning that blind spots emerge fairly quickly. Note that this research cannot explain causality. In other words, it is possible that participants' motivation to cheat led them to focus on temptation. At the same time, it is also possible that temptation captured attention first, and then participants decided to lie. That being said, "the first eye movements likely nevertheless reflect the first step in the attentional selection of the stimuli, and – crucially – this first attentional selection is already biased toward the profitable option" (Pittarello et al., 2019, p. 1726).

BLIND SPOTS: AWARENESS OR UNAWARENESS?

Are people aware of their own blind spots? One possibility is that they are truly blind to their own lies and not aware of ignoring what is ethical. This is in line with the bounded-awareness approach (Bazerman and Tenbrunsel, 2011). Another possibility is that people know that they are bending the rules and because doing wrong makes it difficult for people to maintain a positive self-concept (cf. Mazar et al., 2008) they seek out strategies to reduce the tension between doing right or doing wrong (cf. Barkan et al., 2012; Pittarello et al., 2016). If so, biased perception of moral dilemmas would allow people to ease such tension and do wrong without spoiling their idea of being moral.

To tackle this question, Hochman and colleagues (2016) developed a clever experiment that assessed cheating while recording eye movements. Participants took part in a perception study called the "dot task" (Gino et al., 2010). On each trial, participants saw a square divided by a central vertical line. There were 50 dots in each square, some on the right and others on the left side of the square. Participants had to report the side that contained more dots. To incentivize reports, researchers varied the payoff associated with each side, meaning that on some trials participants received more money for reporting more dots on the left [right] even though there were more dots on the right [left]. This setting provided a dilemma because participants could cheat and "incorrectly" report the higher-pay side. To make cheating more (or less) difficult, Hochman and colleagues varied the number of dots appearing on each side of the square. The idea was that when one side contained two more dots than the other (i.e., 24 vs. 26), it was easy for participants to make "mistakes" since the two sides were almost identical. However, when the difference in the number of dots was clear (i.e., 6 dots), cheating would be much harder to justify. As expected, not only did participants cheat but they also showed blind spots: They paid more attention to the high-pay side (even if it contained fewer dots) at the expense of the low-pay (yet correct) side.

But were they aware of these blind spots? Hochman and colleagues further measured pupil size. Simply put, the pupil increases in size when participants are cognitively or emotionally aroused (cf. Hochman and Yechiam, 2011; Janisse, 1973), when they deceive (cf. Wang et al., 2010), and in stressful situations, such as when people experience the tension between doing right or doing wrong (cf. Yamanaka and Kawakami, 2009; Hochman et al., 2010). The reasoning was that if people are not aware of their blind spots, then they should not experience any tension – hence little (or no) pupil size increase. However, if they are, then such tension should be detected by an increase in pupil size.

It turned out that people knew that they were lying. But here is where things get interesting: When cheating was hard to justify, meaning that it was clear that one side had more dots, their pupil size increased. In other words, when there is no "wiggle room" people experience tension resulting from doing something against their good intentions. Crucially, no tension emerged in ambiguous settings: When people can justify their bad behaviors, they do not feel bad about it.

FRAMES, BLIND SPOTS, AND DISHONESTY

Ambiguity is only one of the drivers of dishonesty. Another powerful contextual factor is whether an ethical dilemma is framed as a loss or a gain. Imagine that a CEO on a business trip received an upfront allowance to cover his expenses. Upon returning, the CEO has to give back what he did not spend. Alternatively, imagine another CEO who did not receive any upfront money, and upon returning, has to complete a reimbursement sheet. Clearly, both situations present the opportunity to cheat and claim more than was actually spent. But who is more likely to lie? Research on the endowment effect (cf. Thaler, 1980) showed that when people receive an initial amount (or any object), they feel ownership over it. Because people value what they own, when faced with a situation of returning some of it – because they did not need it to cover their expenses, for instance – people feel as if they are losing it. Because people are generally loss averse (see Chapman et al., 2018 for a discussion on loss aversion; Kahneman and Tverky, 1979), our CEO would experience giving back unused money as a loss (cf. Thaler, 1980), and be more likely to behave dishonestly to keep all or some of it.

For instance, Kern and Chugh (2009) asked participants to play the role of entrepreneurs interested in acquiring a business owned by a competitor. Participants could decide whether to hire a consultant holding private information about the competitor. Doing so would ultimately help complete the acquisition. Half of the participants were told that they had a 75 percent chance of losing the acquisition. The other half, a 25 percent chance of winning. Clearly, both situations are equivalent. Yet it turned out that participants were more likely to hire the consultant when doing so would help them avoid losing.

These results are not limited to hypothetical situations. For instance, Grolleau and colleagues (2016) asked participants to solve 20 math problems consisting of finding two numbers (among many) that added up to ten (cf. Mazar et al., 2008). Participants only had five minutes, which was not enough to solve all the problems. When the time was up, they could shred their work (to ensure that they could not get caught) and would get paid based on how many problems they claimed to have solved, which gave them an incentive to overreport their performance. Resembling the CEO dilemma above, participants in the loss frame were given upfront money and had to return what they did not gain. Those in the gain frame received money based on what they reported solving. Results showed that cheating doubled in the loss compared with the gain frame.

Although there is strong evidence that people cheat more to avoid a loss than secure an equal-sized gain (cf. Reinders Folmer and De Cremer, 2012; Schindler and Pfattheicher, 2017; Van Yperen et al., 2011), it is unclear how framing an ethical dilemma as a loss affects ethical blind spots. In other words, are blind spots amplified when people face a potential loss? Leib and colleagues (2019) offered two competing predictions. One possibility is that tempting and dishonest options that avert a loss would capture more attention than those that secure a gain. After all, losses increase arousal (cf. Hochman and Yechiam, 2011; Löw et al., 2008; Satterthwaite et al., 2007), and make participants more vigilant (cf. Yechiam and Hochman, 2013a, 2013b). Another possibility is that temptation receives the same amount of attention (whether loss preventing or gain securing) but people will be more motivated to cheat to avoid losing.

The authors used the same die-rolling task discussed above and tracked participants' eye movements. In one condition, participants could gain money by dishonestly reporting higher rolls (gain framing). In another condition, participants were initially endowed with an amount of money and reporting higher rolls corresponded to smaller losses (loss framing). Replicating prior work, Leib and colleagues (2019) found evidence for greater cheating in the loss frame than in the gain frame. Interestingly, participants paid equal attention to tempting rolls, irrespective of whether they helped prevent a loss or secure a gain. This means that while loss framing increases dishonesty, it does not increase ethical blind spots. This notwithstanding, the finding has important business applications. As a general warning, leaders should be careful when setting goals for their employees. For instance, one common practice would be offering salesmen an advance and ask them to return what they did not sell at the end of the month. While this could definitely boost performance, it is also possible that some would cut corners and lie to avoid losing what they owned.

Framing is not restricted to how certain outcomes can be (dishonestly) achieved. On a broader level, framing refers to how individuals construe a certain situation, and how they believe that it is appropriate to act in such a situation (cf. Tversky and Kahneman, 1981). These perceptions and decisions are affected by different environmental cues that determine the "right" thing to do. For instance, Tenbrunsel and Messick (1999) found that participants cooperate less when a surveillance system was present (vs. absent). The idea is that such a system turned the situation from an ethical decision to a "business decision." As such, participants adopted a cost–benefit analysis and acted in their best self-interest. Kouchaki and colleagues (2013) applied this idea to dishonesty. Based on prior work by Vohs and colleagues (2008), they found that participants primed with the concept of money (vs. neutral concept) were more likely to engage in unethical behaviors. Although some researchers questioned the robustness of priming effects (cf. Cesario, 2014), it is still interesting to note that situational factors shape how people perceive moral scenarios.

To date, research has yet to study whether a certain decision frame (ethical vs. business) would also change the amount of attention allocated to right and wrong options and thus elicit blind spots. We believe that this is an interesting avenue and encourage future research to explore it further.

WHAT CAN BE DONE ABOUT BLIND SPOTS?

The research above identified what causes blind spots and when they are more, or less, likely to emerge. The question that remains unanswered is: Is there anything that can be done to reduce blind spots and make people pay attention to what is moral? Put differently, what interventions can we devise to increase honesty? One approach would be to implement moral codes and ethics training. While appealing, research showed that they are not always effective (and are actually quite expensive) (cf. Bazerman and Tenbrunsel, 2011). This is because they fail to consider the psychological processes and biases that make us (mis)behave, such as unclear rules, framing, conflict of interests, and time pressure, to name a few. It is imperative to understand the roots of dishonesty and dig deeper into the cognitive mechanisms underlying wrongdoings. By doing so we can tailor specific interventions to fight blind spots and *nudge* (Thaler and Sunstein, 2009) people to be (more) ethical.

Because blind spots are caused by biased attention towards what is wrong (but more profitable) at the expense of what is right (but less profitable), one possibility is to make people focus more on ethical information. A recent laboratory experiment provides initial insights on this approach. Pittarello and colleagues (2019) created an experiment in which participants could cheat by misreporting a more profitable outcome (in this case a digit) instead of a less profitable – but correct – outcome. To make participants pay more attention to the ethical choice, they made such a choice more visually salient than the dishonest choice *before* participants could cheat. The idea is based on extensive research in cognitive psychology showing that people pay attention to and choose more often salient objects over less salient ones (cf. Yantis and Jonides, 1984). Eye movements showed the desired effect: When ethical options were more salient than unethical ones, they received more attention and were chosen more often. While intriguing, manipulating attention in such a bottom-up way does not seem to offer robust evidence (cf. Ghaffari and Fiedler, 2018) and more research is needed in this area.

Shu and colleagues (2012) tested another way to make morality salient and prevent dishonesty. In both laboratory and field settings, the authors presented participants with the opportunity to cheat on several tasks (from simple math problems to insurance forms). Some participants were asked to sign before completing the tasks or the forms, some after. The idea was that signing before would increase self-awareness and attention to the self (cf. Kettle and Häubl, 2011) and make morality accessible, in turn increasing honesty. Although results supported this prediction, a recent replication failed to show the same effects (Kristal et al., 2020).

The idea of reminding people about morality has received quite a bit of attention in the last decade. For instance, Mazar and colleagues (2008) presented participants with simple math problems. Participants were paid per problem solved, and because their performance was not monitored, they could cheat by overreporting their score. Before taking part in the study, half of the participants were asked to recall the "Ten Commandments" – a proxy of morality – and the other half the last ten books they have read. It turned out that participants in the first group did not cheat at all (surprisingly, the number of Commandments recalled did not have any effect). The same effect was found when participants signed an honor code (even when participants' school had no code at all). However, a recent replication by Verschuere and colleagues (2018) failed to produce the same results (but see Amir et al., 2018 for a response).

Dimant and colleagues (2020) tested a different approach based on social norms. Plenty of research showed that what others do (or deem appropriate) powerfully shapes people's behavior in different contexts (cf. Cialdini and Trost, 1998; Cialdini and Goldstein, 2004; Gino et al., 2009). But does this apply to ethical decision making? Dimant and colleagues (2020) asked participants to think about a number between 1 and 6. Next, they would digitally roll a die and observe the outcome. If the outcome matched the number they thought about, they would receive a payoff. If it did not, they would get \$0.

Before making their predictions, participants learned about what others (i.e., a similar sample) did or thought about the same study in the past. Some read that the vast majority of participants were honest, some that the vast minority were dishonest, some that the vast majority said that one should be honest, and some that the vast minority said that one should not be honest. Thus, the norm-nudges were framed positively or negatively (cf. Kahneman and Tversky, 1979) and reported what should/should not be done in the same setting. Surprisingly, none of these messages reduced cheating compared to when no message was given at all. In other words, nudges were ineffective. In a follow-up study, Dimant and colleagues (2020) found that these nudges did not work because they failed "to shift the perception of existing norms" (p. 254). Put differently, social norms did not change how appropriate (or inappropriate) lying behavior was.

From a broader perspective, this result corroborates the idea that subtle interventions are not enough to promote ethical change (cf. Loewenstein and Chater, 2017).

While this research might be disheartening, Zhang and colleagues (2015) found that instilling a vigilant mindset made people pay attention to potential misbehaviors. In their study, participants play the role of financial advisers and recommend one fund to their clients. One of these funds was the fraudulent Madoff's feeder fund – whose trend was far too optimistic and unlikely. Results showed that participants who indicated their suspicions before making a recommendation were more likely to see that the fund was "too good to be true" and, as a result, recommended it less often than those who expressed suspicions after the choice.

CONCLUSIONS

Despite enormous attempts to curb corporate scandals and corruption, questionable leadership decisions continue to dominate the business world. The failure of moral codes and ethics trainings led scholars to step back and examine the cognitive and situational processes underlying unethical behaviors. The research reviewed above showed that context corrupts: Ambiguous situations allow people to justify their misbehaviors and bend the rules while feeling honest. In these settings, people show "ethical blind spots" and fail to pay attention to what is right and moral when doing so is against their self-interest. These "convenient oversights" might lead otherwise good CEOs and managers to focus on the bottom line of the company and downplay (or disregard altogether) the potential harms caused by their wrongdoing. This is more likely to occur when dishonesty allows preventing a loss, for instance when failing to blow the whistle would allow an auditing company not to lose a profitable client. Finally, questionable behaviors become legitimate when framed as "business decisions" – where a cold cost–benefit analysis prevails over moral concerns. Three things are worth discussing. First, we mainly reviewed work using eye tracking to measure attention. While this is certainly apt in controlled settings, it can be difficult to use it in real-life situations. This notwithstanding, it is reasonable to assume that the cognitive processes that eye tracking reflects, such as perception, information processing, and attention, are somewhat universal across populations and potentially shape decisions in similar ways. Second, the majority of the research was conducted on students and not on CEOs or leaders, and the amounts to be gained are small compared to the millions of dollars involved. More research should be conducted with representative samples to increase generalizability. Third, it is important to note that business settings are complex and rarely resemble a clear-cut decision between right or wrong. Complex situations are ripe with ambiguity and possibilities to find loopholes and exploit wiggle room. Ambiguity works on two levels. First, in tempting settings it shifts our attention towards what is more profitable. Second, it makes it easier to us to lie to ourselves and others. Because people want to be moral individuals (cf. Mazar et al., 2008), a brazen lie would be hard to accept and would spoil their self-concept. But a justifiable lie would not (at least, it would do so to a much smaller extent). This is particularly problematic because it allows people to financially benefit (e.g., increase their returns or the bottom line) and at the same time reach the goal (or the illusion of) being moral.

So, what can we do to make people do right? Current research has offered mixed responses to this question. While work on nudges (cf. Thaler and Sunstein, 2009) has gained tremendous traction, gentle pushes are not enough to foster moral decisions and, even if they do, their robustness has been questioned (cf. Kristal et al., 2020). A more promising approach would be to alter the decision context by increasing the transparency of rules and ethical practices and promoting a vigilant mindset (Zhang et al., 2015). By doing so, we should be able to reduce people's ability to justify their wrongdoings or exploit (and look for) loopholes, and make dishonesty more costly and difficult. We hope that this approach would fight our blind spots and increase attention to ethical standards. Finally, another possibility would be making clear that doing wrong would hurt others. Research by Kogut and Ritov (2005a, 2005b) showed that people show more empathy and compassion towards a single person versus a group of many (cf. Slovic, 2010). Accordingly, Amir and colleagues (2016) found that participants cheated less when their actions hurt single individuals than larger groups. Translated to business decisions, it is possible that making salient who will suffer from corporate (mis)behaviors – for example, citizens, specific social groups, investors, customers – would at the very least make our leaders pay more attention to ethics.

To sum, we believe that leadership research would strongly benefit from a multidisciplinary approach that combines research in psychology, behavioral economics, and management to better understand the drivers of misbehaviors. Only by doing so should we be able to craft tailored interventions and make our future leaders focus on what is right and moral.

NOTE

1. Note that here we define unethical behavior following Jones (1991), as behavior that has harmful consequences and is unacceptable to the larger community. We do not discuss morality from a philosophical perspective.

REFERENCES

Amir, A., Kogut, T., and Bereby-Meyer, Y. (2016). Careful cheating: People cheat groups rather than individuals. *Frontiers in Psychology*, *7*, 371.

Amir, O., Mazar, N., and Ariely, D. (2018). Replicating the effect of the accessibility of moral standards on dishonesty: Authors' response to the replication attempt. *Advances in Methods and Practices in Psychological Science*, *1*, 318–320.

Aquino, K., and Reed, I. I. (2002). The self-importance of moral identity. *Journal of Personality and Social Psychology*, *83*, 1423–1440.

Ayal, S., Hochman, G., and Ariely, D. (2016). Dishonest behavior, from theory to practice. *Frontiers in Psychology*, *7*, 1521.

Balcetis, E., and Dunning, D. (2006). See what you want to see: Motivational influences on visual perception. *Journal of Personality and Social Psychology*, *91*, 612–625.

Barkan, R., Ayal, S., Gino, F., and Ariely, D. (2012). The pot calling the kettle black: Distancing response to ethical dissonance. *Journal of Experimental Psychology: General*, *141*, 757–773.

Bass, B. M., and Steidlmeier, P. (1999). Ethics, character and authentic transformational leadership behavior. *The Leadership Quarterly*, *10*, 181–217.

Bazerman, M. H., and Gino, F. (2012). Behavioral ethics: Toward a deeper understanding of moral judgment and dishonesty. *Annual Review of Law and Social Science*, *8*, 85–104.

Bazerman, M. H., and Sezer, O. (2016). Bounded awareness: Implications for ethical decision making. *Organizational Behavior and Human Decision Processes*, *136*, 95–105.

Bazerman, M. H., and Tenbrunsel, A. E. (2011). *Blind spots: Why we fail to do what's right and what to do about it*. Princeton University Press.

Brown, M. E., and Treviño, L. K. (2006). Ethical leadership: A review and future directions. *The Leadership Quarterly*, *17*, 595–616.

Brown, M. E., Treviño, L. K., and Harrison, D. A. (2005). Ethical leadership: A social learning perspective for construct development and testing. *Organizational Behavior and Human Decision Processes*, *97*, 117–134.

Capraro, V. (2017). Does the truth come naturally? Time pressure increases honesty in one-shot deception games. *Economics Letters*, *158*, 54–57.

Capraro, V., Schulz, J., and Rand, D. G. (2019). Time pressure and honesty in a deception game. *Journal of Behavioral and Experimental Economics*, *79*, 93–99.

Cesario, J. (2014). Priming, replication, and the hardest science. *Perspectives on Psychological Science*, *9*, 40–48.

Chapman, J., Snowberg, E., Wang, S., and Camerer, C. (2018). Loss attitudes in the US population: Evidence from dynamically optimized sequential experimentation (DOSE). Working paper no. 25072, National Bureau of Economic Research.

Chugh, D., Bazerman, M. H., and Banaji, M. R. (2005). Bounded ethicality as a psychological barrier to recognizing conflicts of interest. In D. A. Moore, D. M. Cain, G. Loewenstein, and M. H. Bazerman (Eds.), *Conflicts of interest: Challenges and solutions in business, law, medicine, and public policy* (pp. 74–95). Cambridge University Press.

Cialdini, R. B., and Goldstein, N. J. (2004). Social influence: Compliance and conformity. *Annual Review of Psychology, 55*, 591–621.

Cialdini, R. B., and Trost, M. R. (1998). Social influence: Social norms, conformity and compliance. In D. T. Gilbert, S. T. Fiske, and G. Lindzey (Eds.), *The handbook of social psychology* (pp. 151–192). McGraw-Hill.

De Hoogh, A. H. B., and Den Hartog, D. N. (2008). Ethical and despotic leadership, relationships with leader's social responsibility, top management team effectiveness and subordinates' optimism: A multi-method study. *The Leadership Quarterly, 19*, 297–311.

Den Hartog, D. N. (2015). Ethical leadership. *Annual Review of Organizational Psychology and Organizational Behavior, 2*, 409–434.

Den Hartog, D. N., and Belschak, F. D. (2012). Work engagement and Machiavellianism in the ethical leadership process. *Journal of Business Ethics, 107*, 35–47.

Dimant, E., van Kleef, G. A., and Shalvi, S. (2020). Requiem for a nudge: Framing effects in nudging honesty. *Journal of Economic Behavior and Organization, 172*, 247–266.

Eisenbeiss, S. A., and Giessner, S. R. (2012). The emergence and maintenance of ethical leadership in organizations: A question of embeddedness? *Journal of Personality and Social Psychology, 11*, 7–19.

Feldman, Y., and Smith, H. (2013). Law vs. equity: Lessons from behavioral ethics in what makes intervention legitimate? 31st Seminar on New Institutional Economics Journal of Economic Perspectives (symposium volume).

Fiedler, S., and Glöckner, A. (2012). The dynamics of decision making in risky choice: An eye-tracking analysis. *Frontiers in Psychology, 3*, 335.

Fiedler, S., and Glöckner, A. (2015). Attention and moral behavior. *Current Opinion in Psychology, 6*, 139–144.

Fiedler, S., Glöckner, A., Nicklisch, A., and Dickert, S. (2013). Social value orientation and information search in social dilemmas: An eye-tracking analysis. *Organizational Behavior and Human Decision Processes, 120*, 272–284.

Ghaffari, M., and Fiedler, S. (2018). The power of attention: Using eye gaze to predict other-regarding and moral choices. *Psychological Science, 29*, 1878–1889.

Gino, F., Ayal, S., and Ariely, D. (2009). Contagion and differentiation in unethical behavior: The effect of one bad apple on the barrel. *Psychological Science, 20*, 393–398.

Gino, F., Norton, M. I., and Ariely, D. (2010). The counterfeit self: The deceptive costs of faking it. *Psychological Science, 21*, 712–720.

Gioia, D. A. (1992). Pinto fires and personal ethics: A script analysis of missed opportunities. *Journal of Business Ethics,* 11, 379–389.

Gneezy, U. (2005). Deception: The role of consequences. *American Economic Review, 95*, 384–394.

Greenwald, A. G. (1980). The totalitarian ego: Fabrication and revision of personal history. *American Psychologist, 35*, 603–618.

Grolleau, G., Kocher, M. G., and Sutan, A. (2016). Cheating and loss aversion: Do people cheat more to avoid a loss? *Management Science, 62*, 3428–3438.

Hochman, G., Ayal, S., and Glöckner, A. (2010). Physiological arousal in processing recognition information: Ignoring or integrating cognitive cues? *Judgment and Decision Making, 5*, 285–299.

Hochman, G., Glöckner, A., Fiedler, S., and Ayal, S. (2016). "I can see it in your eyes": Biased processing and increased arousal in dishonest responses. *Journal of Behavioral Decision Making, 29*, 322–335.

Hochman, G., and Yechiam, E. (2011). Loss aversion in the eye and in the heart: The autonomic nervous system's responses to losses. *Journal of Behavioral Decision Making, 24*, 140–156.

Hoffman, B. J., Strang, S. E., Kuhnert, K. W., Campbell, W. K., Kennedy, C. L., and LoPilato, A. C. (2013). Leader narcissism and ethical context: Effects on ethical leadership and leader effectiveness. *Journal of Leadership and Organizational Studies, 20*, 25–37.

Horstmann, N., Ahlgrimm, A., and Glöckner, A. (2009). How distinct are intuition and deliberation? An eye-tracking analysis of instruction-induced decision modes. MPI Collective Goods Preprint (2009/10).

Janisse, M. P. (1973). Pupil size and affect: A critical review of the literature since 1960. *Canadian Psychologist*, *14*, 311–329.

Jones, T. M. (1991). Ethical decision making by individuals in organizations: An issue-contingent model. *Academy of Management Review*, *16*(2), 366–395.

Kahneman, D. (2011). *Thinking, fast and slow*. Macmillan.

Kahneman, D., and Tversky, A. (1979). Prospect theory: An analysis of decision under risk. *Econometrica*, *47*, 263–291.

Kalshoven, K., Den Hartog, D. N., and De Hoogh, A. H. B. (2011). Ethical leader behavior and Big Five factors of personality. *Journal of Business Ethics*, *100*, 349–366.

Kern, M. C., and Chugh, D. (2009). Bounded ethicality: The perils of loss framing. *Psychological Science*, *20*, 378–384.

Kettle, K. L., and Häubl, G. (2011). The signature effect: Signing influences consumption-related behavior by priming self-identity. *Journal of Consumer Research*, *38*, 474–489.

Kogut, T., and Ritov, I. (2005a). The singularity effect of identified victims in separate and joint evaluations. *Organizational Behavior and Human Decision Processes*, *97*, 106–116.

Kogut, T., and Ritov, I. (2005b). The "identified victim" effect: An identified group, or just a single individual? *Journal of Behavioral Decision Making*, *18*, 157–167.

Kouchaki, M., Smith-Crowe, K., Brief, A. P., and Sousa, C. (2013). Seeing green: Mere exposure to money triggers a business decision frame and unethical outcomes. *Organizational Behavior and Human Decision Processes*, *121*, 53–61.

Kristal, A. S., Whillans, A. V., Bazerman, M. H., Gino, F., Shu, L. L., Mazar, N., and Ariely, D. (2020). Signing at the beginning versus at the end does not decrease dishonesty. *Proceedings of the National Academy of Sciences*, *117*(13), 7103–7107.

Laeng, B., Sirois, S., and Gredebäck, G. (2012). Pupillometry: A window to the preconscious? *Perspectives on Psychological Science*, *7*, 18–27.

Leib, M., Pittarello, A., Gordon-Hecker, T., Shalvi, S., and Roskes, M. (2019). Loss framing increases self-serving mistakes (but does not alter attention). *Journal of Experimental Social Psychology*, *85*, 103880.

Loewenstein, G., and Chater, N. (2017). Putting nudges in perspective. *Behavioural Public Policy*, *1*, 26–53.

López-Pérez, R., and Spiegelman, E. (2013). Why do people tell the truth? Experimental evidence for pure lie aversion. *Experimental Economics*, *16*, 233–247.

Löw, A., Lang, P. J., Smith, J. C., and Bradley, M. M. (2008). Both predator and prey: Emotional arousal in threat and reward. *Psychological Science*, *19*, 865–873.

Lundquist, T., Ellingsen, T., Gribbe, E., and Johannesson, M. (2009). The aversion to lying. *Journal of Economic Behavior and Organization*, *70*, 81–92.

March, J. G., and Simon, H. A. (1958). *Organizations*. Wiley.

Mazar, N., Amir, O., and Ariely, D. (2008). The dishonesty of honest people: A theory of self-concept maintenance. *Journal of Marketing Research*, *45*, 633–644.

Orquin, J. L., and Loose, S. M. (2013). Attention and choice: A review on eye movements in decision making. *Acta Psychologica*, *144*, 190–206.

Payne, J. W., Bettman, J. R., and Johnson, E. J. (1988). Adaptive strategy selection in decision making. *Journal of Experimental Psychology: Learning, Memory, and Cognition*, *14*, 534–552.

Pittarello, A., Frătescu, M., and Mathôt, S. (2019). Visual saliency influences ethical blind spots and (dis)honesty. *Psychonomic Bulletin and Review*, *26*, 1719–1728.

Pittarello, A., Leib, M., Gordon-Hecker, T., and Shalvi, S. (2015). Justifications shape ethical blind spots. *Psychological Science*, *26*, 794–804.

Pittarello, A., Motro, D., Rubaltelli, E., and Pluchino, P. (2016). The relationship between attention allocation and cheating. *Psychonomic Bulletin and Review*, *23*, 609–616.

Reinders Folmer, C. P., and De Cremer, D. (2012). Bad for me or bad for us? Interpersonal orientations and the impact of losses on unethical behavior. *Personality and Social Psychology Bulletin*, *38*, 760–771.

Reisen, N., Hoffrage, U., and Mast, F. W. (2008). Identifying decision strategies in a consumer choice situation. *Judgment and Decision Making*, *3*, 641–658.

Sanitioso, R., Kunda, Z., and Fong, G. T. (1990). Motivated recruitment of autobiographical memories. *Journal of Personality and Social Psychology*, *59*, 229–241.

Satterthwaite, T. D., Green, L., Myerson, J., Parker, J., Ramaratnam, M., and Buckner, R. L. (2007). Dissociable but inter-related systems of cognitive control and reward during decision making: Evidence from pupillometry and event-related fMRI. *Neuroimage*, *37*, 1017–1031.

Schindler, S., and Pfattheicher, S. (2017). The frame of the game: Loss-framing increases dishonest behavior. *Journal of Experimental Social Psychology*, *69*, 172–177.

Shalvi, S., Dana, J., Handgraaf, M. J., and De Dreu, C. K. (2011). Justified ethicality: Observing desired counterfactuals modifies ethical perceptions and behavior. *Organizational Behavior and Human Decision Processes*, *115*, 181–190.

Shalvi, S., Eldar, O., and Bereby-Meyer, Y. (2012). Honesty requires time (and lack of justifications). *Psychological Science*, *23*, 1264–1270.

Shu, L. L., Mazar, N., Gino, F., Ariely, D., and Bazerman, M. H. (2012). Signing at the beginning makes ethics salient and decreases dishonest self-reports in comparison to signing at the end. *Proceedings of the National Academy of Sciences*, *109*(38), 15197–15200.

Simon, H. A. (1957). *Models of man; social and rational*. Wiley.

Simons, D. J., and Chabris, C. F. (1999). Gorillas in our midst: Sustained inattentional blindness for dynamic events. *Perception*, *28*, 1059–1074.

Slovic, P. (2010). If I look at the mass I will never act: Psychic numbing and genocide. In S. Roeser (Ed.), *Emotions and risky technologies* (pp. 37–59). Springer.

Suchotzki, K., Verschuere, B., Van Bockstaele, B., Ben-Shakhar, G., and Crombez, G. (2017). Lying takes time: A meta-analysis on reaction time measures of deception. *Psychological Bulletin*, *143*, 428–453.

Tenbrunsel, A. E., and Messick, D. M. (1999). Sanctioning systems, decision frames, and cooperation. *Administrative Science Quarterly*, *44*, 684–707.

Tett, R. P., and Guterman, H. A. (2000). Situation trait relevance, trait expression, and cross-situational consistency: Testing a principle of trait activation. *Journal of Research in Personality*, *34*, 397–423.

Thaler, R. (1980). Toward a positive theory of consumer choice. *Journal of Economic Behavior and Organization*, *1*, 39–60.

Thaler, R. H., and Sunstein, C. R. (2009). *Nudge: Improving decisions about health, wealth, and happiness*. Penguin.

Thielmann, I., and Hilbig, B. E. (2019). No gain without pain: The psychological costs of dishonesty. *Journal of Economic Psychology*, *71*, 126–137.

Turner, N., Barling, J., Epitropaki, O., Butcher, V., and Milder, C. (2002). Transformational leadership and moral reasoning. *Journal of Applied Psychology*, *87*, 304–311.

Tversky, A., and Kahneman, D. (1981). The framing of decisions and the psychology of choice. *Science*, *211*(4481), 453–458.

Van der Cruyssen, I., D'hondt, J., Meijer, E., and Verschuere, B. (2020). Does honesty require time? Two preregistered direct replications of experiment 2 of Shalvi, Eldar, and Bereby-Meyer (2012). *Psychological Science*, *31*, 460–467.

Van Yperen, N. W., Hamstra, M. R., and van der Klauw, M. (2011). To win, or not to lose, at any cost: The impact of achievement goals on cheating. *British Journal of Management*, *22*, S5–S15.

Verschuere, B., Meijer, E. H., Jim, A., Hoogesteyn, K., Orthey, R., McCarthy, R. J., … and Barbosa, F. (2018). Registered replication report on Mazar, Amir, and Ariely (2008). *Advances in Methods and Practices in Psychological Science*, *1*, 299–317.

Vohs, K. D., Mead, N. L., and Goode, M. R. (2008). Merely activating the concept of money changes personal and interpersonal behavior. *Current Directions in Psychological Science*, *17*, 208–212.

Wang, J. T., Spezio, M., and Camerer, C. F. (2010). Pinocchio's pupil: Using eye tracking and pupil dilation to understand truth telling and deception in sender–receiver games. *American Economic Review*, *100*, 984–1007.

Weber, E. U., and Johnson, E. J. (2009). Mindful judgment and decision making. *Annual Review of Psychology*, *60*, 53–85.

Yamanaka, K., and Kawakami, M. (2009). Convenient evaluation of mental stress with pupil diameter. *International Journal of Occupational Safety and Ergonomics*, *15*, 447–450.

Yantis, S., and Jonides, J. (1984). Abrupt visual onsets and selective attention: Evidence from visual search. *Journal of Experimental Psychology: Human Perception and Performance*, *10*, 601–621.

Yechiam, E., and Hochman, G. (2013a). Loss-aversion or loss-attention: The impact of losses on cognitive performance. *Cognitive Psychology*, *66*, 212–231.

Yechiam, E., and Hochman, G. (2013b). Losses as modulators of attention: Review and analysis of the unique effects of losses over gains. *Psychological Bulletin*, *139*, 497–518.

Zhang, T., Fletcher, P. O., Gino, F., and Bazerman, M. H. (2015). Reducing bounded ethicality: How to help individuals notice and avoid unethical behavior. *Organizational Dynamics*, *44*(4), 310–317.

Zhong, C. B. (2011). The ethical dangers of deliberative decision making. *Administrative Science Quarterly*, *56*, 1–25.

11. Resilience leadership judgment: findings from a cosmology episode study of the shootdown of Flight MH17

Kari A. O'Grady, Matthijs Moorkamp, René Torenvlied and J. Douglas Orton

The July 17, 2014, shootdown of Malaysian Airlines Flight 17 (MH17) from Amsterdam to Kuala Lumpur (Torenvlied et al., 2015) exemplifies an increasingly frequent occurrence described by researchers through a cluster of complementary research streams as a "normal accident" (Perrow, 1999), an "untoward surprise" (LaPorte, 2007), a "mess" (Roe, 2018), a "complex catastrophe" (De Smet et al., 2012), or a "breakdown" (Boin and McConnell, 2007).[1] Resilience leadership judgment scholars integrate these concepts into the evidence-based concept of a *cosmology episode*, defined here as a perturbation, disruption, crisis, disaster, or catastrophe that challenges – rapidly and deeply – individuals', teams', organizations', communities', and/or nations' beliefs about the nature of the universe and their past, present, and future place in that universe (Weick, 1985, 1993; O'Grady and Orton, 2016; Orton and O'Grady, 2016).

Cosmology episode studies are now comfortably situated as a core specialty area in the emerging discipline of organizational resilience studies (see Kayes, 2015; Lengnick-Hall and Beck, 2005; Meyer, 1982; Orton and Weick, 1990; Staw et al., 1981; Weick, 1985, 1993, 2020a, 2020b; Weick and Orton, 1987; Weick and Sutcliffe, 2001, 2007, 2015). Cosmology episode studies have the potential to extend research on organizing, sensemaking, resilience, and leadership judgment (Shotter and Tsoukas, 2014) into extreme contexts such as firefighting (Weick, 1993), mountaineering (Kayes, 2015), and armed conflict: "Leaders in extreme situations seldom operate with a 'clean slate' …, and thus past training, experience, and knowledge may count for less than judgment" (Kayes et al., 2017, p. 289).

To transform traditional leadership practices (Hitt et al., 2015) into the newer concept of *resilience leadership judgment* (the effective leveraging of diverse management skills to guide a social unit through a perturbation, disruption, crisis, disaster, or catastrophe), we employed a combination of Western European and U.S. research cosmologies to conduct a detailed analysis of the first five days of the MH17 cosmology episode (Torenvlied et al., 2015). In our research methodology, we employed a constructivist research ontology (Berger and Luckmann, 1966), an abductive research epistemology (an evidence-based middle path between the extremes of deductive epistemology and inductive epistemology), and an iterative multi-method research methodology (Lin et al., 2006) that permitted us to create a process model by cycling back and forth between process theory and process data (Orton, 1997). This research methodology is, thus, neither strict theory-testing nor strict theory-generating, but theory-enriching; neither deductive theory exploitation nor inductive theory exploration, but abductive theory elaboration. This style of research, first described by Vaughan (1996) in her study of the 1986 *Challenger* explosion, is a method that has the potential to clarify, advance, and refine the understanding – by executives, scholars, professionals, consultants, and students – of resilience leadership judgment.

In this study of MH17, we elaborate five cosmology episode processes: *anticipating*, *sense-losing*, *improvising*, *sense-remaking*, and *renewing*. The starting point in this elaboration of cosmology episode processes was an earlier cosmology episode study of the 1999 West Nile Virus outbreak (Weick, 2005). Drawing on his earlier studies of the characteristics of organizational sensemaking (Weick, 1988, 1990, 1993, 1995), Weick leveraged the details of the West Nile Virus cosmology episode to suggest an embryonic cosmology episode process model: (1) ongoing streams of events; (2) bracketed cues; (3) temporality, identity, and sociality; (4) plausible stories; and (5) enacted sensible environments. In a subsequent study of the 2010 Haiti earthquake (O'Grady and Orton, 2016; Orton and O'Grady, 2016), two members of the present research team leveraged Weick's early cosmology episode process model to create a more explicit sequence of institutional micro-processes: ongoing streams of events or *anticipating* (Weick and Sutcliffe, 2015); bracketed cues or *sense-losing* (Orton, 1995, 1997, 2000; Fukami, 2002); temporality, identity, and sociality *improvising* (Christianson et al., 2009; Maitlis and Christianson, 2014; Christianson, 2019); plausible stories or *sense-remaking* (Maitlis, 2005; Maitlis and Sonenshein, 2010); and enactive sensible environments or *renewing* (Williams et al., 2017). The purpose of this MH17 cosmology episode study is to elaborate on these five cosmology episode processes in order to improve the resilience leadership judgment of executives, scholars, professionals, consultants, and students.

FIVE INITIAL FINDINGS FROM A COSMOLOGY EPISODE STUDY OF THE MH17 SHOOTDOWN

Numerous leadership researchers in the last 50 years have argued that traditional, heroic, "great man," trait theories of leadership are ill-suited to the successful management of a volatile, uncertain, complex, and ambiguous environment characterized by perturbations, disruptions, crises, disasters, and catastrophes (Lichtenstein et al., 2006). One of the most powerful forces contributing to the rising global sense of insecurity might be a self-inflicted leadership ideology wound:

> People tend to lionize leaders at the top of our organizations, which – unfortunately – creates "non-resilient" leadership. Traditional theories of top-down leadership focused on command, control, and the bottom line do not adequately equip people to manage the complex situations and systems in which they find themselves in today's world. (Aten and O'Grady, 2019)

Consequently, in order to initiate what we hope will be a long-term discussion of an important boundary condition for leadership judgment, in this chapter we attempt to differentiate non-resilience leadership judgment from resilience leadership judgment through a marriage of rich cosmology episode process theories with rich data on the 2014 shootdown of MH17 over Eastern Ukraine.

Table 11.1 displays 60 critical incidents from the first five days of activities by the Dutch government following the July 17, 2014, shootdown of Flight MH17. In the remainder of this chapter, we leverage these critical incidents to present initial findings from our study of MH17. More specifically, we analyze these 60 critical incidents to elaborate on five cosmology episode processes – anticipating, sense-losing, improvising, sense-remaking, and renewing – which are represented as columns in Table 11.1.

FINDING 1 – "ANTICIPATING" AS A RESILIENCE LEADERSHIP JUDGMENT SKILL

Weick's (1995, 2005) discussion of ongoing streams of events emphasizes the *anticipating* period of disasters (Weick and Sutcliffe, 2015), which others have described as an "incubation period" (Turner, 1976) characterized by national cosmologies, enacted environments, and attempted preoccupation with failure. First, effective anticipating requires an awareness that complex human activity takes place around the world within diverse cosmologies at the individual, team, organizational, community, and national levels. Second, effective anticipating requires an awareness of the numerous ways in which humans enact (choose, shape, and construct) the environments to which they must then respond: "The goal is to stay in the action because, once you pull away and adopt a detached atomistic view, you lose context, information, situated cognition, and tools made meaningful by actual use" (Weick, 2005, pp. 60–61). Third, effective anticipating requires a strategy of "preoccupation with failure" (Weick and Sutcliffe, 2015) – a relentless search for weak signals of potential perturbations, disruptions, crises, disasters, and catastrophes: "When you work at the edge of codified knowledge, with an outdated classification system, then you work with vague equivocal cues [that are] weak, mixed, routine" (Weick, 2005, p. 60). An important point to emphasize here, though, is that high awareness of deep received cosmologies, enacted extreme environments, and strategic preoccupation with failure cannot guarantee effective *prediction* of impending catastrophes; instead, *anticipating* increases the likelihood of resilient leadership judgment that reduces the damage caused by catastrophes.

Deep Received Cosmologies as a Component of Effective Anticipating

In the MH17 cosmology episode, the villagers who live at the site of the crash of Flight MH17 find themselves in a disputed area in Eastern Ukraine. Separatists claim this area, which is formally under the authority of the Ukrainian government. On April 14, 2014, three months before the crash, a separatist group declared the area to be the "Donetsk People's Republic." The separatist organization has its own prime minister, Aleksandr Borodai – a Russian citizen who was previously a political adviser to the prime minister of Crimea. The Minister of Defense for the organization is Igor Girkin, who also calls himself Strelkov, a soldier who fought with the Russian army in Chechnya. On July 17, 2014, it has only been three days since the separatists used a surface-to-air missile to shoot down an Antonov-26, which crashed in the village of Izvaryne – only 140 kilometers from the later crash site of MH17.

Organizational cosmologies (Ashforth and Vaidyanath, 2005) are influential determinants of three clusters of resilience leadership judgment: organizing (leadership, structure, culture, and strategy skills), sensemaking (change, decision-making, learning, and sensemaking

Table 11.1   *Sixty critical incidents in the first five days of the shootdown of Flight MH17*

Ongoing events	Bracketed cues	Retrospective, identity-based, and social (RIS) sensemaking	Plausible stories	Enacted organizations
4/14/14: Ukrainian separatist group declares "Donetsk People's Republic."	In the area where MH17 crashed, heavy fighting is taking place.	17:00: Forensic officers of LTFO hear about the crash from the media.	Diplomatic crisis team member meets at airport with Dutch ambassador.	OSCE pushes to continue travel to the first separatists' roadblock.
Donetsk prime minister, Aleksandr Borodai, is a Russian citizen.	Local residents see a partly burning airplane falling to the ground.	At Schiphol … consultation takes place between forensic officers.	Meeting establishes division of tasks and a "to-do" list of first activities in Kyiv.	Team recognizes a lack of protective equipment – helmet or a Kevlar vest.
Donetsk Minister of Defense fought in Chechnya.	Meanwhile, debris, bodies and body parts are falling out of the sky.	Formal request is sent to dispatch three forensic officers.	Activities focus on access to crash site through OSCE and the Red Cross.	Team tells OSCE it is too dangerous to travel to roadblock that night.
7/14/14: Separatists shot down an Antonov-26.	Villagers rush to the places of the crash just after 4:30 p.m.	Team will stay at Schiphol overnight until 1:30 a.m.	They discuss honorary Dutch consul in Donetsk, close to crash site.	Team leader tells Dutch embassy they will not travel any further that evening.
7/17/14: Around 11:30 a.m. boarding starts at gate G3 at Schiphol Airport.	Armed separatists also arrive.	LTFO: Request is made to form an "advance team."	LTFO team leaves for Torez, where Ukraine State Emergency Services have collected bodies.	The forensic team is picked up at 4:00 a.m. by Ukrainian OSCE officials.
Video footage and photos from the plane, sent to family and friends.	Separatists try to shield the area from the approaching villagers.	DSB: Exact names of the team members told to the LTFO.	MOD sends special officer to Charkiv to plan and manage the repatriation process.	Members of the forensic team notice that they are driving in a war zone.
12:31 takeoff: 283 passengers and 15 crew members. 196 Dutch nationality.	16:50: Igor Girkin reports shootdown of Antonov-26 transport plane.	Three employees of diplomacy emergency team, police security guards.	En route, team members agree to accept request to enter unsafe zone.	Members of the forensic team notice many destroyed buildings.
12:52: Cruising altitude of 31,000 feet over German city of Bielefeld.	Girkin removes his message within a few minutes after posting.	16:00: Minister of Foreign Affairs and personal secretary join the team.	In Charkiv, team receives phone number of OSCE's central representative.	At border of separatist territory, another OSCE team awaits them.
15:03: Aircraft crosses the border between Poland and Ukraine.	17:00: First film footage of a plume of smoke is reported on social media.	Three options: (1) crash site, (2) safe space in Ukraine, (3) Netherlands.	7/20/14: Two people may form the team: one LTFO and one military police officer.	The forensic team is awaited by two cars manned by heavily armed separatists.
16:07: MH17 is transferred to air traffic control in East Ukraine.	17:00: Reuters reports passenger airplane has crashed in Ukraine.	Foreign minister must meet with Ukrainians before selecting option.	Two extra officers from the forensic team can join in the team.	Separatists make a very professional impression on the forensic team.
16:19: Air traffic control center has contact with the crew.	17:10: Russian Interfax says plane crashed in the Donetsk region.	No detailed plan developed; what will actually happen next is a void.	Team reasons trip is safe, otherwise they would not have permission to go.	Team traveled to Donetsk, under close supervision of the separatists.
16:20: The two black boxes stopped their recording.	17:13: NOS and RTL-News report that the crash concerns MH17.	First crisis response team arrives in Kyiv on Dutch government plane.	The trip to Izyum is made in the car of the interpreter of the Dutch embassy.	Team successfully repatriates the remains from Flight MH17.

Source: Based on Torenvlied et al. (2015).

skills), and resilience (collaboration, strategizing, improvisation, and resilience skills). Organizational cosmologies, though, are nested in community (Bierly and Spender, 1995), national (Gombault, 2020), societal (Bartunek and Necochea, 2000), and global cosmologies (Gosling and Case, 2013). National-level cosmologies, such as those in place in Haiti on January 12, 2010, are "spiritual-cultural-sociohistorical-macrolevel humanistic" orienting systems (Roysircar et al., 2019, p. 1191, citing O'Grady and Orton, 2016). The MH17 cosmology episode requires an understanding of ongoing streams of events taking place primarily in a Dutch national cosmology; secondly in Malaysian, Australian, Ukrainian, and Russian national cosmologies; and thirdly in the community cosmology of the separatist Donetsk People's Republic.

Enacted Extreme Environments as a Component of Effective Anticipating

In the MH17 cosmology episode, July 17, 2014, is a busy day in Departure Hall 3 of Schiphol Airport. Travelers begin arriving at the check-in desk of MH17, from Amsterdam to Kuala Lumpur. Families with children check in for a holiday flight to destinations in Asia. Business travelers join in, such as several scientists attending an important AIDS conference in Australia. Boarding starts at gate G3 around 11:30 a.m. Video footage and photos from the plane, sent to family and friends or posted on Facebook just before takeoff, show passengers settling in for the long flight. Shortly after 12:00 p.m., the Boeing 777-200 ER is released from the gate. It taxies to the runway and takes off in a northerly direction at 12:31 p.m. On board are 15 crew members and 283 passengers; 196 of the passengers are Dutch nationals. Slowly the aircraft bends to the southeast, leaves Dutch airspace, and reaches a cruising altitude of 31,000 feet, above the German city of Bielefeld, at 12:52 p.m.

The MH17 case reminds us, first, that many normal human activities in the 21st century, such as routinized air travel, are complex social accomplishments made possible by complex leadership, strategy, organizational, and management systems (Hitt et al., 2015). These enacted extreme environments are increasingly referred to by resilience leadership practitioners as a mash-up of volatile, uncertain, complex, and ambiguous environments into a "VUCA" environment (Huber and Glick, 1993; Barton et al., 2015). As Perrow and Weick warned us long ago, technological and digital advances, in the absence of countervailing social and managerial wisdom, have the potential to enact increasingly noxious normal accidents (Perrow, 1999) and cosmology episodes (Weick, 1985).

Strategic Preoccupation with Failure as a Component of Anticipating

In the MH17 cosmology episode, the crew contacts Ukrainian air traffic control about a desired flight altitude change from 35,000 feet to 33,000 feet. Permission is received and at 3:01 p.m., the aircraft starts its descent. At 3:03 p.m., the aircraft crosses the border between Poland and Ukraine. At 4:00 p.m., the crew requests a course change because of weather conditions. At 4:07 p.m., Flight MH17 is transferred to air traffic control Dnipropetrovsk in East Ukraine, which contacts the crew at 4:19:53 because the plane has deviated a few nautical miles from its flight path due to other air traffic. Shortly after 4:20 p.m., the airplane disappears from both Ukrainian and Russian air traffic control radars. The two black boxes – the flight data recorder and the cockpit voice recorder – stopped recording at 4:20 p.m.

The MH17 data remind us of the existence of hybrid spaces between arenas. As Weick and Sutcliffe (2015) have long argued, effective anticipating requires a vigilant stance toward weak signals of potential catastrophe, which is facilitated by a high familiarity not only with one's own industry recipe (Bierly and Spender, 1995), but the ability to cross-pollinate lessons learned from other arenas, such as structure collapses, fatal fires, train wrecks, naval capsizings, aviation crashes, nuclear accidents, chemical leaks, medical errors, disease outbreaks, public shootings, and institutional abuses (Perrow, 1999; Bierly and Spender, 1995; Hällgren et al., 2018; Ramanujam and Roberts, 2018; Gephart et al., 2018).

In summary, resilience leadership judgment can be enhanced by significant investments in the understanding of a wide variety of deep received cosmologies (e.g. national cosmologies), a diverse portfolio of arenas in which cosmology episodes have been studied (e.g. industry recipes), and an expanded number of enacted extreme environments (e.g. volatile, uncertain, complex, and ambiguous environments).

FINDING 2 – "SENSE-LOSING" AS A RESILIENCE LEADERSHIP JUDGMENT SKILL

The familiar Enactment–Selection–Retention sequence of the organizing and sensemaking models (Weick, 1979, 1995) can be run in reverse as a Retention–Selection–Enactment sequence (Weick, 2001), which serves as the foundation of a sense-losing model (Fukami, 2002; Kim, in press; O'Grady and Orton, 2016; Orton, 1995, 1997, 2000; Orton and O'Grady, 2016; Pratt, 2000). In the same way that learning processes are preceded by unlearning processes, sense-remaking processes (Christianson, 2019) are preceded by sense-losing (Orton, 1995, 2000; Fukami, 2002), sense-breaking (Pratt, 2000), and frame restructuration (Kim, in press) processes. The MH17 cosmology episode helps clarify three components of sense-losing: triggering events, vicious cycles, and brutal audits. First, to mark the transition from pre-catastrophe to catastrophe, scholars routinely employ a jagged-edged shape, which they label as a *bracketed triggering event* (or jolt, shock, surprise, disruption, or adversity); the ubiquitous jagged-edged shape implies that the pivot from anticipating to sense-losing is an instantaneous one from a stable situation to a chaotic situation. Second, sense-losing in cosmology episodes is routinely characterized by *vicious cycles*. "Errors are less likely to enlarge if they are understood more fully, more quickly … By understanding triggering events and the ways in which small sensemaking actions can grow into large senseless disasters, we hope to develop a better understanding of how crises can be isolated and contained" (Weick, 1988, p. 308; see also Staw et al., 1981; Weick and Orton, 1987). Third, *brutal honest appraisals*, a fusion of Lagadec's brutal audits (1993) and Coutu's honest appraisals (2002), can be responded to with enactive sense-losing, as seen in the Apollo 13 deliberations described by Stein (2004).

Bracketed Triggering Events as a Component of Effective Sense-Losing

In the MH17 cosmology episode, villagers in Hrabove, in Eastern Ukraine, hear a heavy bang on the afternoon of July 17, 2014. They see bodies, body parts, personal belongings, and debris fall out of the sky. A large part of the airplane (the wings, both engines, the main landing gear, and part of the hull), engulfed by a heavy fire, barely misses the village of Hrabove. The remains of the airplane, its passengers, and its cargo scatter across an area five by ten kilometers near the villages of Hrabove, Petropavlivka, and Rozsypne, with some body parts landing in backyards and on houses. Just after 4:30 p.m., villagers rush to the crash sites, where they see debris, bodies, body parts, and personal belongings in the fields. The villagers in Hrabove come to a gradual understanding that the crash involves a commercial airplane with Western and Asian passengers, including children.

The simplistic presumption of a clearly visible "hinge" from pre-crisis to post-crisis (Roux-Dufort, 2007) – such as the one experienced by the Hrabove villagers – is challenged by concepts such as enacted catastrophes (Allison and Zelikow, 1999), pre-aware whistleblowers (Vaughan, 1996; Starbuck and Farjoun, 2005), the slow deconstruction of reality (Brown, 2000), transition difficulties (Schakel et al., 2016), and constraints on re-evaluation and redirection (Kahn et al., 2018). The MH17 case provides a striking example of how on-the-ground villagers experienced a rapid, but still non-instantaneous, realization that they were part of a pivot from pre-catastrophe operations to post-catastrophe operations. Other social units in the case, such as the Dutch government, experienced the catastrophe in a less sharp, more creeping, and more gradual way. Sense-losing is initiated by triggering events that come in a portfolio of diverse paths – enacted, pre-aware, fast, slow, difficult, and constrained – through which diverse social units become aware that a cosmology episode is taking place.

Deference-to-Expertise Leadership as a Component of Effective Sense-Losing

In the MH17 cosmology episode, soon after the village residents arrive at the crash site, armed separatists also arrive. The separatists try to shield the area from the approaching villagers. Just like the villagers, the separatists try to make sense of what has happened. Around 4:50 p.m. the first message on the fate of MH17 is shown on social media. At that time, Igor Girkin reports on Russian social media that separatists have shot down an Antonov-26 transport plane of the Ukrainian government army near the village of Torez. Because there are no other plane crashes on July 17 and because the wreckage of MH17 lands in an area just north of Torez, it is reasonable to assume Girkin is referring to MH17. (Girkin removes his message within a few minutes after posting.)

Naïve, heroic, overconfident, and over-centralized leaders (Janis, 1972; Aten and O'Grady, 2019) often exacerbate the negative effects of cosmology episodes through iatrogenic, or human-influenced, vicious cycles. "Pre-aware" whistleblowing engineers in the 1986 *Challenger* explosion and the 2003 *Columbia* disintegration objected to the framing of unacceptable "out-of-family" risks as acceptable "in-family" risks (Vaughan, 1996; Starbuck and Farjoun, 2005). Similarly, Girkin likely was pre-aware that an airplane might be crashing in Eastern Ukraine on July 17, 2014. Continuing on this expected trajectory, Girkin seems to have misinterpreted a bracketed triggering event – the shootdown of a plane located in Ukrainian airspace near the location of a recent successful downing of a Ukrainian Antonov – as a desired "in-family issue" rather than an undesired "out-of-family issue." Posting and then un-posting his misinterpretation of the bracketed triggering event on social media is an example of an iatrogenic footprint in which heroic leaders make problems worse. An important remedy for heroic-leadership high-iatrogenic-footprint vicious cycles is deference-to-expertise leadership, which migrates problems to cross-functional teams with the collective expertise necessary to generate effective solutions (Weick and Sutcliffe, 2015; Moorkamp et al., 2020).

Brutal Honest Appraisals as a Component of Effective Sense-Losing

In the MH17 cosmology episode, at 5:00 p.m. on July 17, 2014, Reuters reports that a passenger airplane has crashed in Ukraine. Ten minutes later, the Russian news agency Interfax reports that the plane departed from Amsterdam and crashed in the Donetsk region. Rapidly, media coverage develops along three lines: eyewitness reports, information about the aircraft and passengers, and international political reactions. Eyewitness reports about the crash site emerge as photos on social media posted immediately after the crash, written messages on social media platforms, and broadcasts of quickly arriving journalist teams. Information about the aircraft and passengers is reported away from the crash site; at 5:13 p.m., Dutch nation-wide news channels NOS and RTL-News report, on their websites, that the crash is MH17 – with possibly 295 people on board. International political reactions introduce biased information about the crash from parties in the Eastern Ukrainian conflict – from the Ukrainian side and from the separatists' side.

A significant challenge for the reduction of human suffering in the years ahead will be the discovery of remedies for a post-truth world enacted by self-interested actors leveraging traditional media and social media for their personal benefit (Chace et al., 2021). Especially in highly politicized contexts such as the downing of MH17, the sought-for flattening of vicious cycles can be delayed by overzealous misperception of reality, ends-justify-the-means-driven misinformation, and self-serving fake news – complicating the movement from retentive to selective to enactive sense-losing. The complementary concepts of "brutal audits" (Lagadec, 1993) and "honest appraisals" (Coutu, 2002) suggest a tension between "brutal honest appraisals" and "brutal dishonest appraisals," which can create the flattening of vicious downward cycles enough for social units to identify calmly some of the significant details of their changed circumstances.

In summary, resilient leadership judgment can be increased significantly by investment in understanding the dark side of the sensemaking moon, in which Retention gives way to Selection which gives way to Enactment (Weick, 1979). More specifically, the systematic study of sense-losing in cosmology episodes provides a valuable familiarity with the ways in which bracketed triggering jolts (Meyer, 1982), separations (Jones Christensen et al., 2020), and nightmares (Travadel and Guarnieri, 2020) are eventually transformed – through sense-losing cycles (Patriotta and Gruber, 2015), unfolding processes (McCluney et al., 2020), and resilience trajectories (Walker et al., 2020) – into brutal audits (Lagadec, 1993), sudden realizations (Quinn and Worline, 2008), and honest appraisals (Coutu, 2002).

FINDING 3 – "IMPROVISING" AS A COMPONENT OF RESILIENCE LEADERSHIP JUDGMENT

After the terrorist attacks of September 11, 2001, high-reliability organizing (Weick and Sutcliffe, 2001) evolved into high-resilience organizing (Weick and Sutcliffe, 2007) and it became necessary to reframe the now overly generic high-reliability organizing principle, "commitment to resilience," as the more-precise high-resilience organizing principle of *commitment to improvisation* (O'Grady and Orton, 2016; Orton and O'Grady, 2016). A growing literature citing Weick's (1993) Mann Gulch cosmology episode research has created a vibrant research community studying improvisation during catastrophes. This MH17 study leverages research focused on the temporality, identity, and sociality (Weick, 1995) of bricolage and other forms of improvisation (Weick, 1993). First, MH17 clarifies an evolution from retrospective sensemaking to a more complete portfolio of rolling hindsight, rolling insight, and rolling foresight (Weick, 1995). Second, MH17 emphasizes the nested interplay among individual, team, organizational, community, and national identities (Weick, 1996). Third, MH17 demonstrates the high degree of sociality present in sensemaking's action-interpretation cycles (Maitlis and Christianson, 2014) and updating processes (Christianson, 2019).

Temporality as a Component of Effective Improvising

In the MH17 cosmology episode, forensics officers in the LTFO or National Team of Forensic Investigations ("the team"), part of the Dutch National Police, hear about the crash of MH17 from the media at around 5:00 p.m. on July 17, 2014. A forensics specialist on duty immediately understands that the reported disaster will require the team's involvement and soon receives a call from the team's back office instructing him to head immediately to Schiphol Airport. At the airport, conversations occur among various forensic officers similarly sent to Schiphol. Little is known about MH17, and there is not yet a formal request from the Dutch Ministry of Foreign Affairs to send a forensics dispatch team to Ukraine. On their own authority, the forensics officers decide to wait at Schiphol Airport. During the evening of July 17, a formal request arrives from the Dutch National Police to dispatch three officers. The team members stay at Schiphol until approximately 1:30 a.m.

Temporality improvising has always been a core concern in cosmology episode studies. Weick's early discussions of the constraints of retrospection (1979) reappeared in Weick's "enacted sensemaking" reanalysis of the Bhopal chemical leak: "The explorer cannot know what he is facing until he faces it, and then looks back over the episode to sort out what happened" (1988, pp. 305–306). Similarly, others have highlighted the institutional barriers to organizational resilience imposed by structural inertia, competitive inertia, and organizational momentum (Lengnick-Hall and Wolff, 1999). Later, evidence-based studies of sensemaking, such as a comparison of presence-based sensemaking in the Three Mile Island nuclear accident and the Apollo 13 space exploration explosion, showed some organizations are overly constrained by past actions, cognitions, and emotions, while other organizations are able to leverage retrospective, presence-based, and prospective sensemaking (Stein, 2004). The accumulating studies on temporal sensemaking processes showed up in Weick's post-2001 writings, which emphasize a more complete portfolio of temporal sensemaking, explaining interactions among retrospective, presence-based, and prospective sensemaking (Weick et al., 2005). The Dutch forensics team, for example, seems to have been quite effective in their temporal sensemaking practices during MH17, moving easily between retrospective, present-based, and prospective points of view. The team appears to have exhibited simultaneous "rolling hindsight," rolling insight, and rolling foresight (Weick, 2020b, p. 92).

Identity as a Component of Effective Improvising

In the MH17 cosmology episode, during the morning of July 18, 2014, members of the larger Dutch forensics team continue to assume they will be called upon to respond, much as they have responded to previous crises. The forensics officer on duty decides to go to Driebergen, where the National Unit of the National Police is located. In the first briefing it is clear many Dutch people were on board on Flight MH17. That morning a formal request from the Ministry of Foreign Affairs is made to form an "advance team" of forensics officers. Ultimately, a team of eight people is assembled, including employees who specialize in logistics, in safety research, and in post-mortem research. Two members of the Dutch Safety Board (DSB) also join the team. Around noon, the names of the dispatch team members are specified. Immediately afterwards, the team receives the message that it is expected at Schiphol Airport at 4:00 p.m. that afternoon, to be transported to Ukraine on a Dutch government aircraft. The team rushes, under police escort, to Schiphol Airport, arriving just in time for the flight to Kyiv. The Dutch Minister of Foreign Affairs joins the team at Schiphol Airport for the flight to Ukraine. On board are the Minister of Foreign Affairs, with his personal secretary, three employees of the diplomatic services crisis team, security guards of the special forces, six forensic officers, and two employees of the Dutch Safety Board.

As demonstrated by the gradual assembly process of the team that eventually boards the aircraft, a central question during a cosmology episode, in addition to the questions of "what is going on?" and "how should we respond?," is perhaps the more important question of "who are we in this situation?" *Identity improvising* (Kamoche et al., 2003) – at the national, community, organizational, team, and individual levels – is composed of a diverse array of closely related concepts researchers are using to explain what happens in the identity-infused improvisational space between sense-losing and sense-remaking: adaptation (Levinthal, 1997), bricolage (Paolino, 2020), embodiment (Cunliffe and Coupland, 2012), immanence (Sandberg and Tsoukas, 2020), intuition (Meziani and Cabantous, 2020), self-identity (Brown, 2020), and updating (Christianson, 2019).

Sociality as a Component of Effective Improvising

In the MH17 cosmology episode, after departure from Schiphol, the passengers aboard the Dutch government aircraft start to discuss what should be done on arrival. The forensic team leader has a one-on-one consultation with the Minister of Foreign Affairs. During the flight, they develop three scenarios for deploying the forensic team in Ukraine: (1) investigate everything found on the crash site; (2) carry out the identification of remains of passengers on-site in Ukraine at a safe place; or (3) transport all remains of the passengers to the Netherlands and carry out the identification there. The last scenario is preferred by the forensics team because of doubts about the technical capacity for identification in Ukraine and doubts about whether the work can be conducted safely there. The minister communicates understanding of the forensic team's preference, but he alone cannot decide because the scenarios must be discussed with Ukraine representatives first. No detailed plans for the forensic team are developed during the flight. What will actually happen next is a void.

The "courageous conversations" (Quinn and Worline, 2008) that take place on the flight to Kyiv demonstrate the social nature of sensemaking (Weick, 1995). The team experiments with different action repertoires that can only be developed in a general nature, but help guide subsequent action-interpretation cycles (Maitlis and Christianson, 2014). In *sociality improvising*, one generation of a social unit makes partial sense, acts on that sense, and is then morphed into a second generation of a social unit that updates the previous sensemaking and acts on that revised estimation of events through sense-losing, improvising, and sense-remaking.

In summary, the central institutional micro-process in cosmology episodes is the improvisational liminal space between sense-losing and sense-remaking. Despite enormous pressures during cosmology episodes for rapid decisive action, resilience leadership judgment skills in temporality, identity, and sociality can create the space for effective improvising (Weick, 1995). Numerous cosmology episode studies, such as the present study of MH17, demonstrate the value of a swarm of small win improvisations (Weick, 1984) in making visible a viable survival path through catastrophic circumstances.

FINDING 4 – "SENSE-REMAKING" AS A COMPONENT OF RESILIENCE LEADERSHIP JUDGMENT

Weick's Enactment–Selection–Retention organizing model (1979) proceeds from chaos to order – enactive sense-remaking to selective sense-remaking to retentive sense-remaking (Weick, 1985, 1993; O'Grady and Orton, 2016; Orton and O'Grady, 2016). First, distributed cross-functional teams pivot from the improvising process to the enactive sense-remaking process by generating an embryonic plausible story, sometimes referred to simplistically as a decision: "If people fixate on their first plausible story and stop there, then they do have a sense of sorts, but one that holds together only if newer cues and consequences are ignored" (Weick, 2005, p. 61). Second, selective sense-remaking in extreme contexts is enhanced by a "reluctance to simplify interpretations" (Weick and Sutcliffe, 2015), leading to an embryonic plausible story that is "[redrafted] … so that it becomes more comprehensive, incorporates more of the observed data, and is more resilient in the face of criticism" (Weick et al., 2005, p. 415). Third, retentive sense-remaking leads to a growing confidence that a catastrophe is nearing its end and a collective new normal in the form of a "refinement of sensemaking already underway" (Christianson, 2019, p. 49).

Team Decision-Remaking as a Component of Effective Sense-Remaking

In the MH17 cosmology episode, on arrival at the airport in Kyiv, a meeting takes place between an employee of the diplomatic crisis team and the ambassador of the Netherlands to Ukraine to discuss an initial division of tasks between the diplomatic crisis team and embassy personnel. They also develop a "to-do" list of first activities in Kyiv designed to explore which parties could help the forensic team obtain access to the crash site, such as employees of the Organization for Security and Co-operation in Europe (OSCE) and the Red Cross. The diplomats and ambassador also discuss contacts with other embassies in Kyiv and the honorary consul of the Netherlands in Donetsk, the region close to the crash site of MH17.

The extreme team decision-losing aspects of enactive sense-losing are precursors to the extreme team decision-remaking aspects of enactive sense-remaking (Ancona and Bresman, 2007; Edmondson, 1999; Moingeon and Edmondson, 1997). Extreme-teaming researchers, in a study of Human Terrain Teams deployed by the U.S. military in Afghanistan from 2007 to 2013, identified ten team variables that have been linked to effective team performance within extreme contexts (Lamb et al., 2013a, 2013b; Orton and Lamb, 2011). The Dutch government's ability, in the days after the MH17 shootdown, to generate an effective cross-functional team on short notice under chaotic circumstances is striking. The airport discussions between the newly expanded and newly arrived forensics team and the on-the-ground experts from the

Dutch embassy clarify the ways in which story-telling and narrative rationality can facilitate team effectiveness. *Extreme Team Decision-Remaking* is assumed to produce a sophisticated capacity to monitor embryonic plausible stories generated by numerous empowered cross-functional teams distributed throughout the organization.

Reluctance-to-Simplify Reorganizing as a Component of Effective Sense-Remaking

In the MH17 cosmology episode, the forensics team continues its sense-remaking as it moves from Kyiv to Charkiv, closer to the crash site. The Dutch Ministry of Defense sends a special officer to Charkiv to plan and manage the actual repatriation process of passengers' remains to the Netherlands. En route to Charkiv, members of the team discuss extensively what to do when they are requested to travel into the crash zone; they determine that they will respond positively. Upon arrival in Charkiv, the leader of the team receives the phone number of the central representative of the OSCE.

Two dark images from two complementary studies of the *Challenger* explosion – Starbuck and Milliken's concept of "pushing the envelope until something breaks" (1988) and Vaughan's concept of "the normalization of deviance" (1996) – highlight the importance of *reluctance-to-simplify reorganizing* (Weick and Sutcliffe, 2015). (Numerous studies from researchers in the "Montréal School of Sensemaking" have made the case that sensemaking is inseparable from organizing, leading us to alter Weick and Sutcliffe's initial concept of "reluctance to simplify interpretations" to "reluctance-to-simplify reorganizing" in order to pull the large discipline of structure-focused organization theorists more fully into the conversation about cosmology episodes.) In MH17, while traveling from Kiev to Charkiv, the Dutch forensics dispatch team works through a variety of scenarios envisioning what they might encounter and how they might respond when they meet up with the separatists, move into contested territory, and encounter the train of collected bodies and body parts. Weick described the importance of remaining open to multiple inputs from emerging environments: "The environment continues to change, and action based on the [initial] diagnosis stirs up new puzzles … A fuller story needs to be crafted" (Weick, 2005, p. 58). The ongoing multivocal narration of extreme events – as possible paths forward (Christianson et al., 2009), courageous conversations (Quinn and Worline, 2008), explanations for tragedies (Chikudate, 2009), and healing opportunities (Powley, 2009) – creates a valuable openness to multiple interpretations of still-emerging extreme events.

Re-equilibrium Tipping Points as a Component of Effective Sense-Remaking

In the MH17 cosmology episode, on Sunday, July 20, around 9:00 a.m., the Dutch National Police asks the Dutch forensics dispatch team to travel from Charkiv to the crash site near Torez, this time without safety guarantees. The assignment the team receives is vague: see what they can do about salvaging victims' remains, and also see – if possible – what happened to the plane. Initially, the team is notified that only two people will deploy to the crash site, one team member and one security guard from the Dutch Military Police, both traveling in forensics team clothing, because the OSCE had agreed with the separatists that only forensic experts would have access to the separatist territory. Shortly afterwards, it becomes clear that two extra officers from the team can deploy to the crash site. The leader of the team chooses to add a salvage expert to the deploying group. By telephone, the OSCE agrees the team will go to the village of Izyum to meet members of an OSCE team. On the advice of the Ministry of Defense, members of the newly formed dispatch team decide to call home to say goodbye in case the trip into separatist territories goes poorly. The trip to Izyum is made in the car of the interpreter of the Dutch embassy.

The socially constructed pivot from pre-crisis operations to crisis operations (Schakel et al., 2016) has been overstudied, while the socially constructed pivot from crisis operations to post-crisis operations has been understudied. The Dutch government's actions during the team's movement from Charkiv to Izyum demonstrate that high-reliability organizing is not the absence of risk-taking, but the creation of multiple layers of safeguards against additional catastrophe (Weick and Sutcliffe, 2015). The team comes to terms with the danger they are moving into through artful rationalizations ("it must be safe out there or they wouldn't let me go") and communicates their acceptance of the risks with loved ones back home. In cosmology episodes, numerous cycles of sense-remaking eventually lead to a socially reconstructed *re-equilibrium tipping point* – the enactment, selection, and retention of sufficiently complex organizational actions to move a social unit into a post-catastrophe new normal.

In summary, we see little value – for the scholarly community studying sensemaking – in the rapid proliferation of distinctive new brands of sensemaking (e.g. ecological sensemaking, embodied sensemaking, and prospective sensemaking). Adding a modifier before the word sensemaking prematurely presumes that sensemaking theory is settled social science, which we assert it is not. Alternatively, a cosmology episode studies lens on sensemaking theory illuminates (1) a need to divide sensemaking into the constitutive institutional micro-processes of sense-losing and sense-remaking; (2) a need for disciplined development of Weick's original concepts of enactive, selection, and retention as enactive sense-remaking, selective sense-remaking, and retentive sense-remaking; and (3) a need to extrapolate from the three types of sense-remaking to create a complementary inverse sequence of retentive sense-losing, selective sense-losing, and enactive sense-losing.

FINDING 5 – "RENEWING" AS A COMPONENT OF RESILIENCE LEADERSHIP JUDGMENT

Cosmology episode studies reverse the currently dominant presumed sequence of sensemaking followed by sense-giving (Gioia and Chittipeddi, 1991) into an evidence-based narrative of sense-losing followed by sense-remaking. One way to reconcile these competing sequences is by focusing attention on *renewing*, organizational actions that take place after the socially constructed re-equilibrium tipping point, a sense-giving component of sensemaking cycles that Weick described as "enactive of sensible environments" (1995). First, post-catastrophe learning is manifested in a culture of deep sensitivity to operations (Weick and Sutcliffe, 2015), rather than in a culture of shallow sensitivity to operations characterized not by lessons learned, but by lessons ignored or merely noted or, even worse, lessons mis-learned. Second, rather than leaning on psychological variable-based theories of individual resilience (e.g. Raetze, 2020), organizational resilience researchers (e.g. Alliger et al., 2015) study how organizations enact resilience leadership judgment at the national, community, organizational, team, and individual levels. Third, through a constant cycle of sense-losing (Fukami, 2002; Kim, in press; Meyer, 1982; Pratt, 2000; Staw et al., 1981; Stein, 2004; Weick, 1985, 1993; Weick and

Orton, 1987) and sense-remaking (Christianson et al., 2009; Maitlis and Christianson, 2014; Christianson, 2019), social units enact new belief systems about the nature of the universes they inhabit, their position in those universes, and their beliefs about how to transmit those belief systems to others.

Cultural Sensitivity to Operations as a Component of Effective Renewing

In the MH17 cosmology episode, the OSCE agrees to aid the Dutch forensics dispatch team to continue travel to the crash zone on July 20 until reaching the separatists' first roadblock, where representatives of the OSCE will meet the team. The OSCE proposal appears, from the perspective of the team, to be a bridge too far. The team tells the OSCE that it is too dangerous to travel into separatist territory that night, because the forensic dispatch team does not have an armored car, helmets, or Kevlar vests. The team leader contacts the Dutch embassy to inform the embassy they will not travel any further that evening.

Weick and Sutcliffe described accumulated high-reliability organizing processes as "sensitivity to operations" (2015). Most cosmology episode studies of airplane crashes focus attention on the need for increased sensitivity to operations through a search for uncorrected technological flaws (March et al., 1991), a focus on flawed flight crew sensemaking dynamics (Weick, 1990), and an emphasis on the complex interactions of technological flaws and flight crew updating (Berthod and Müller-Seitz, 2018; Oliver et al., 2017). A smaller number of airplane crash cosmology episodes focus attention on sensitivity to operations outside the airplane: for example, the U.S. Navy's 1988 accidental shootdown of an Iranian airliner (Rudolph and Repenning, 2002) and the U.S. Air Force's 1994 accidental shootdown of two Black Hawk helicopters over Iraq (Snook, 2000; Weick, 2001). For example, the Dutch team's *cultural sensitivity to operations* leads them to create a "relational pause" (Barton and Kahn, 2019) in the potentially dangerous forward momentum.[2]

Enacted Extreme Organizations as a Component of Effective Renewing

In the MH17 cosmology episode, the forensic team leader is called during the night by a representative of the OSCE. The representative informs him that the team will be picked up by OSCE personnel on July 21 around 4:00 a.m. to travel into separatist territory. On the way to the border of separatist territory, members of the forensic team notice they are driving in a war zone, with destroyed buildings. At the border, the team is handed over to Ukrainian representatives from the OSCE.

Configurations of organizational characteristics (e.g. agile, decisive, learning, or high-reliability organizations) are a significant determinant of an organization's capacity to survive cosmology episodes, because "people act within the context of these bracketed elements, under the guidance of preconceptions, and often shape these elements in the direction of preconceptions" (Weick, 1988, p. 307). The ultimately safe travel of the Dutch team through a war-zone environment clarifies the Dutch team's embeddedness within an effective configuration of organizational characteristics. It is important to emphasize, though, that the team was composed of police officers with no war-zone experience, which required the improvisational, fluid enactment of a new organizational form with new organizational characteristics. Enacted organizational characteristics change shape in many ways in extreme contexts in order to create unique new practices that fit the new contexts. *Enacted extreme organizations* are the diverse characteristics – for example, sense of confidence, retained memory, and improved practices – gained by social units after they go through cosmology episodes.

Deep Transmitted Cosmologies as a Component of Effective Renewing

Finally, in the MH17 cosmology episode, the Dutch forensics dispatch team arrives at the border of separatist territory – the front line of the war zone between the Ukrainian army and the separatists – where they are met by Ukrainian representatives to the OSCE and two cars manned by heavily armed separatists. The separatists make a professional impression on the forensic team. After this encounter, the team members travel further to Donetsk, under the close supervision of the separatists, and proceed to successfully repatriate the remains from MH17.

The beginnings and endings of disaster narratives (Seeger and Sellnow, 2016), high-risk narratives (Manning, 1999), and cosmology episode narratives (Maclean, 1993; Weick, 1993) are social constructions. In a dangerous, evolving, "reactive world, a highly refined planning system is less crucial than the capability to make sense out of an emerging pattern" (Weick, 2005, p. 58). Cosmologies and disasters are both malleable – shaped by how people notice and make sense of cues, how they act or do not act upon those cues, how they reengage the disaster with continuous improvising and updating of sense, how they remake sense, and how they shape the refined cosmology. The chaotic condition of "thrownness" characterizes both the beginnings and the endings of cosmology episode narratives. Social units that have survived and learned from one cosmology episode are not immune from similar crises in the future; for example, the 1986 *Challenger* explosion (Vaughan, 1996) was followed by the 2003 *Columbia* disintegration (Beck and Plowman, 2009, 2014) and the 1949 Mann Gulch fire was followed by the 1994 South Canyon fire (Weick, 1996) which was in turn followed by the 2013 Yarnell Hill fire (Parrish et al., 2020). The present critical incident of the crossing of the Dutch forensics dispatch team into separatist-held territory is thus, simultaneously, a socially constructed, chaotic, and cliff-hanging end of one cosmology episode narrative and the socially constructed, chaotic, and continuing beginning of a future cosmology episode narrative. The *deep transmitted cosmology* in place at the end of a cosmology episode is the deep received cosmology for the next cosmology episode.

In summary, the development of resilience leadership judgment is less likely to occur in the up-tempo space in between the noticing of a bracketed triggering event marking the beginning of a catastrophe and the manufacturing of a re-equilibrium tipping point marking the end of a catastrophe, but is more likely to occur in the down-tempo spaces before and after a catastrophe. Furthermore, the anticipating phase of a cosmology episode is a less likely environment for the development of resilience leadership judgment than is the renewing phase of a cosmology episode, during which the emotion-infused memories of a recent catastrophe create powerful motivations, resources, and energy to prevent similar future catastrophes.

CONCLUSION

Resilience leadership judgment – defined in this chapter as the effective leveraging of diverse management skills to guide a social unit through a perturbation, disruption, crisis, disaster, or catastrophe – is a high-priority investment for the executives, scholars, professionals, consultants, and students who currently face increasingly intractable grand challenges (van der Vegt et al., 2015). This chapter is one of many necessary efforts to address the theory, research, education, and practice of resilience leadership judgment.

For resilience leadership judgment theorists, this chapter pulls together numerous efforts to conceptualize the diverse constitutive institutional micro-processes of resilience into an evidence-based model of anticipating, sense-losing, improvising, sense-remaking, and renewing. The chapter is thus an integration of three generations of theorizing by Karl Weick on organizing (Weick, 1979), sensemaking (Weick, 1995), and resilience (Weick and Sutcliffe, 2001, 2007, 2015).

For resilience leadership judgment researchers, this chapter leverages a study of the July 17, 2014, shootdown by separatists in Ukraine of Malaysian Airlines Flight 17 (Moorkamp, 2019; Moorkamp et al., 2020; Torenvlied et al., 2015) to elaborate the original sensemaking-based model of cosmology episodes (Weick, 1993) into a more resilience-based model of cosmology episodes that identifies a fundamental process schism embedded in sensemaking research between sense-losing and sense-remaking (O'Grady and Orton, 2016; Orton and O'Grady, 2016).

For resilience leadership judgment educators, this chapter chronicles an emerging shared vocabulary crafted by scholars who have built on Weick's (1988, 1990, 1993, 2005, 2006) five landmark cosmology episode studies (Bhopal, Tenerife, Mann Gulch, West Nile Virus, Battered Child Syndrome): (1) anticipating (deep received cosmologies, enacted extreme environment, strategic preoccupation with failure); (2) sense-losing (bracketed triggering events, deference-to-expertise leadership, brutal honest appraisals); (3) improvising (temporality, identity, sociality); (4) sense-remaking (team decision-remaking, reluctance-to-simplify reorganizing, re-equilibrium tipping points); and (5) renewing (cultural sensitivity to operations, enacted extreme organizations, deep transmitted cosmologies). The vocabulary of resilience leadership judgment provides a palette for current students to develop their own unique working theories of resilience leadership judgment.

Finally, for resilience leadership judgment practitioners, this chapter provides a tool for internalizing lessons learned from past cosmology episodes, analyzing current unsolved cosmology episodes, and internalizing skills for future cosmology episodes. Poignantly, the MH17 cosmology episode is far from over. The geopolitical sensitivities surrounding the case are increasing as multiple nations' governments wrestle with a contested narrative of what happened on July 17, 2014. As Christianson noted, "once sensemaking is initiated, it is an ongoing process in which provisional understandings are constantly adjusted in response to new information or changing circumstances" (2019, p. 48). As a precursor of what are expected to be numerous future complex catastrophes, the MH17 case has much to offer – especially because the Dutch government seems to have modeled highly effective resilience leadership practices.

We are going to need better theories of organizing, sensemaking, resilience, and cosmology episodes; the MH17 case study can serve as a complex, well-documented, and shared case study in that effort.

NOTES

1. We acknowledge the expert assistance of Karl E. Weick in providing us, during our January 2019 research team kickoff summit, with this helpful framing sentence for this study.
2. In order to better discriminate between "strategy" and "culture" – two large bodies of relevant evidence-based theory, research, education, and practice – we altered Weick and Sutcliffe's closely intertwined concepts of "preoccupation with failure" and "sensitivity to operations" as the forward-looking *strategic preoccupation with failure* described previously and the backward-looking *cultural sensitivity to operations* described here.

REFERENCES

Alliger, G. M., Cerasoli, C. P., Tannenbaum, S. I., and Vessey, W. B. (2015). Team resilience: How teams flourish under pressure. *Organizational Dynamics, 44*, 176–184.

Allison, G. T., and Zelikow, P. (1999). *Essence of decision: Explaining the Cuban Missile Crisis.* Longman.

Ancona, D., and Bresman, H. (2007). *X-teams: How to build teams that lead, innovate, and succeed.* Harvard Business School.

Ashforth, B. E., and Vaidyanath, D. (2005). Work organizations as secular religions. *Journal of Management Inquiry, 22*(4), 359–370.

Aten, J. D., and O'Grady, K. A. (February 2019). Leadership and resilience: An interview with Dr. Kari O'Grady. In Dr. Jamie Aten's "Hope + Resilience" blog in the online version of *Psychology Today*.

Barton, M. A., and Kahn, W. A. (2019). Group resilience: The place and meaning of relational pauses. *Organization Studies, 40*(9), 1409–1429.

Barton, M. A., Sutcliffe, K. M., Vogus, T. J., and DeWitt, T. (2015). Performing under uncertainty: Contextualized engagement in wildland firefighting. *Journal of Contingencies and Crisis Management, 23*(2), 74–83.

Bartunek, J. M., and Necochea, R. A. (2000). Old insights and new times: Kairos, Inca cosmology, and their contributions to contemporary management inquiry. *Journal of Management Inquiry, 9*(2), 103–113.

Beck, T. E., and Plowman, D. A. (2009). Experiencing rare and unusual events richly: The role of middle managers in animating and guiding organizational interpretation. *Organization Science, 20*(5), 909–924.

Beck, T. E., and Plowman, D. A. (2014). Temporary, emergent interorganizational collaboration in unexpected circumstances: A study of the Columbia space shuttle response effort. *Organization Science, 25*(4), 1234–1252.

Berger, P., and Luckmann, T. (1966). *The social construction of reality: A treatise in the sociology of knowledge.* First Anchor.

Berthod, O., and Müller-Seitz, G. (2018). Making sense in pitch darkness: An exploration of the sociomateriality of sensemaking in crises. *Journal of Management Inquiry, 27*(1), 52–68.

Bierly, III, P. E., and Spender, J. C. (1995). Culture and high reliability organizations: The case of the nuclear submarine. *Journal of Management, 21*(4), 639–656.

Boin, A., and McConnell, A. (2007). Preparing for critical infrastructure breakdowns: The limits of crisis management and the need for resilience. *Journal of Contingencies and Crisis Management, 15*(1), 50–59.

Brown, A. D. (2000). Making sense of inquiry sensemaking. *Journal of Management Studies, 37*, 45–75.

Brown, A. D. (Ed.). (2020). *The Oxford handbook of identities in organizations.* Oxford University Press.

Chace, S., Lynerd, B. T., and DeSantis, A. (2021). "A distant mirror": Sensemaking in the era of Trump. *Leadership, 17*(2), 212–229.

Chikudate, N. (2009). If human errors are assumed as crimes in a safety culture: A lifeworld analysis of a rail crash. *Human Relations, 62*(9), 1267–1287.

Christianson, M. K. (2019). More and less effective updating: The role of trajectory management in making sense again. *Administrative Science Quarterly, 64*(1), 45–86.

Christianson, M. K., Farkas, M. T., Sutcliffe, K. M., and Weick, K. E. (2009). Learning through rare events: Significant interruptions at the Baltimore and Ohio Railroad Museum. *Organization Science, 20*(5), 846–860.

Coutu, D. (2002). How resilience works. *Harvard Business Review, 85*(5), 46–56.

Cunliffe, A., and Coupland, C. (2012). From hero to villain to hero: Making experience sensible through embodied narrative sensemaking. *Human Relations, 65*(1), 63–88.

De Smet, H., Lagadec, P., and Leysen, J. (2012). Disasters out of the box: A new ballgame? *Journal of Contingencies and Crisis Management, 20*(3), 138–148.

Edmondson, A. (1999). Psychological safety and learning in work teams. *Administrative Science Quarterly, 44*(2), 350–383.

Fukami, C. V. (2002). 9/11 montage: Professors remember. *Academy of Management Learning and Education, 1*(1), 14–37.

Gephart, Jr., R. P., Miller, C. C., and Helgesson, K. S. (Eds.). (2018). *The Routledge companion to risk, crisis and emergency management.* Routledge.

Gioia, D. A., and Chittipeddi, K. (1991). Sensemaking and sensegiving in strategic change initiation. *Strategic Management Journal, 12*(6), 433–448.

Gombault, A. (2020). Notre-Dame is burning: Learning from the crisis of a superstar religious monument. *International Journal of Arts Management, 22*(2), 83–94.

Gosling, J., and Case, P. (2013). Social dreaming and ecocentric ethics: Sources of non-rational insight in the face of climate change catastrophe. *Organization, 20*(5), 705–721.

Hällgren, M., Rouleau, L., and de Rond, M. (2018). A matter of life and death: How extreme context research matters for management and organization studies. *Academy of Management Annals, 12*(1), 111–153.

Hitt, M., Miller, C. C., and Colella, A. (2015). *Organizational behavior.* Fifth edition. Wiley.

Huber, G. P., and Glick, W. H. (Eds.). (1993). *Organizational change and redesign: Ideas and insights for improving performance.* Oxford University Press.

Janis, I. L. (1972). *Victims of groupthink: A psychological study of foreign-policy decisions.* Houghton Mifflin.

Jones Christensen, L., Hammond, S., and Larsen, M. (2020). Lost person behavior as an antecedent to resilience. In E. H. Powley, B. Caza, and A. Caza (Eds.), *Research Handbook on Organizational Resilience* (pp. 214–231). Edward Elgar Publishing.

Kahn, W. A., Barton, M. A., Fisher, C. M., Heaphy, E. D., Reid, E. M., and Rouse, E. D. (2018). The geography of strain: Organizational resilience as a function of intergroup relations. *Academy of Management Review, 43*(3), 509–529.

Kamoche, K., e Cunha, M. P., and da Cunha, J. V. (2003). Towards a theory of organisational improvisation: Looking beyond the jazz metaphor. *Journal of Management Studies, 40*(8), 2023–2051.

Kayes, D. C. (2015). *Organizational resilience: How learning sustains organizations in crisis, disaster, and breakdowns.* Oxford University Press.

Kayes, D. C., Allen, N., and Self, A. (2017). How leaders learn from experience in extreme situations: The case of the U.S. military in Takur Ghar, Afghanistan. In M. Holenweger, M. K. Jager, and F. Kernic (Eds.), *Leadership in extreme situations* (pp. 277–294). Springer.

Kim, S. (in press). Frame restructuration: The making of an alternative business incubator amid Detroit's crisis. *Administrative Science Quarterly,* 0001839220986464.

Lagadec, P. (1993). *Preventing chaos in a crisis: Strategies for prevention, control and damage limitation.* Translated by Jocelyn M. Phelps. McGraw-Hill.

Lamb, C. J., Orton, J. D., Davies, M. C., and Pikulsky, T. T. (2013a). *Human terrain teams: An organizational innovation for sociocultural knowledge in irregular warfare*. Institute of World Politics Press.

Lamb, C. J., Orton, J. D., Davies, M. C., and Pikulsky, T. T. (2013b). A way ahead for human terrain teams. *Joint Force Quarterly, 70*, 21–29.

LaPorte, T. R. (2007). Critical infrastructure in the face of a predatory future: Preparing for untoward surprise. *Journal of Contingencies and Crisis Management, 15*(1), 60–64.

Lengnick-Hall, C. A., and Beck, T. E. (2005). Adaptive fit versus robust transformation: How organizations respond to environmental change. *Journal of Management, 31*(5), 738–757.

Lengnick-Hall, C. A., and Wolff, J. A. (1999). Similarities and contradictions in the core logic of three strategy research streams. *Strategic Management Journal, 20*(12), 1109–1132.

Levinthal, D. A. (1997). Adaptation on rugged landscapes. *Management Science, 43*(7), 934–950.

Lichtenstein, B. B., Uhl-Bien, M., Marion, R., Seers, A., Orton, J. D., and Schreiber, C. (2006). Complexity leadership theory: An interactive perspective on leading in complex adaptive systems. *Emergence: Complexity and Organizations, 8*(4), 2–12.

Lin, Z., Zhao, X., Ismail, K., and Carley, K. M. (2006). Organizational design and restructuring in response to crises: Lessons from computational modeling and real-world cases. *Organization Science, 17*, 598–618.

Maclean, N. (1993). *Young men and fire*. University of Chicago Press.

Maitlis, S. (2005). The social processes of organizational sensemaking. *Academy of Management Journal, 48*(1), 21–49.

Maitlis, S., and Christianson, M. (2014). Sensemaking in organizations: Taking stock and moving forward. *Academy of Management Annals, 8*(1), 57–125.

Maitlis, S., and Sonenshein, S. (2010). Sensemaking in crisis and change: Inspiration and insights from Weick (1988). *Journal of Management Studies, 47*(3), 551–580.

Manning, P. K. (1999). High risk narratives: Textual adventures. *Qualitative Sociology, 22*(4), 285–299.

March, J. G., Sproull, L. S., and Tamuz, M. (1991). Learning from samples of one or fewer. *Organization Science, 2*(1), 1–13.

McCluney, C. L., Wooten, L. P., and James, E. H. (2020). The unfolding process of organizational resilience in a diversity crisis: A case study of racial incidents at the University of Missouri. In E. H. Powley, B. Caza, and A. Caza (Eds.), *Research handbook on organizational resilience* (pp. 180–201). Edward Elgar Publishing.

Meyer, A. D. (1982). Adapting to environmental jolts. *Administrative Science Quarterly, 27*(4), 515–537.

Meziani, N., and Cabantous, L. (2020). Acting intuition into sense: How film crews make sense with embodied ways of knowing. *Journal of Management Studies, 57*(7), 1384–1419.

Moingeon, B., and Edmondson, A. (Eds.). (1997). *Organizational learning and competitive advantage*. SAGE Publications.

Moorkamp, M. (2019). *Operating under high-risk conditions in temporary organizations: A sociotechnical systems perspective*. Routledge.

Moorkamp, M., Torenvlied, R., and Kramer, E. H. (2020). Organizational synthesis in transboundary crises: Three principles for managing centralization and coordination in the corona virus crisis response. *Journal of Contingencies and Crisis Management, 28*(2), 169–172.

O'Grady, K. A., and Orton, J. D. (2016). Resilience processes during cosmology episodes: Lessons learned from the Haiti earthquake. *Journal of Psychology and Theology, 44*(2), 109–123.

Oliver, N., Calvard, T., and Potočnik, K. (2017). Cognition, technology, and organizational limits: Lessons from the Air France 447 disaster. *Organization Science, 28*(4), 729–743.

Orton, J. D. (1995). *Reorganizing: An analysis of the 1976 reorganization of the U.S. intelligence community*. Doctoral dissertation, University of Michigan.

Orton, J. D. (1997). Iterative grounded theory: Zipping the gap between process theory and process data. *Scandinavian Journal of Management, 13*(4), 419–438.

Orton, J. D. (2000). Enactment, sensemaking and decision making: Redesign processes in the 1976 reorganization of US intelligence. *Journal of Management Studies, 37*(2), 213–234.

Orton, J. D., and Lamb, C. J. (2011). Interagency national security teams: Can social science contribute? *Prism*, *2*(2), 47–64.

Orton, J. D., and O'Grady, K. A. (2016). Cosmology episodes: A reconceptualization. *Journal of Management, Spirituality and Religion*, *13*, 226–245.

Orton, J. D., and Weick, K. E. (1990). Loosely coupled systems: A reconceptualization. *Academy of Management Review*, *15*, 203–223.

Paolino, C. (2020). How to face the unexpected: Identification and leadership in managing bricolage. *Creativity and Innovation Management*, *29*(4), 597–620.

Parrish, D., Clark, T. S., and Holloway, S. S. (2020). The collapse of sensemaking at Yarnell Hill: The effects of endogenous ecological chaos on enactment. *European Journal of Management Studies*, *25*(2), 77–95.

Patriotta, G., and Gruber, D. A. (2015). Newsmaking and sensemaking: Navigating temporal transitions between planned and unexpected events. *Organization Science*, *26*(6), 1574–1592.

Perrow, C. (1999). *Normal accidents: Living with high-risk technologies*. Second edition. Princeton University Press.

Powley, E. H. (2009). Reclaiming resilience and safety: Resilience activation in the critical period of crisis. *Human Relations*, *62*(9), 1289–1326.

Pratt, M. (2000). The good, the bad, and the ambivalent: Managing identification among Amway distributors. *Administrative Science Quarterly*, *45*(3), 456–493.

Quinn, R. W., and Worline, M. C. (2008). Enabling courageous collective action: Conversations from United Airlines Flight 93. *Organization Science*, *19*(4), 497–516.

Raetze, S. (2020). What makes work teams resilient? An overview of resilience processes and cross-level antecedents. In E. H. Powley, B. Caza, and A. Caza (Eds.), *Research handbook on organizational resilience* (pp. 232–247). Edward Elgar Publishing.

Ramanujam, R., and Roberts, K. H. (Eds.). (2018). *Organizing for reliability: A guide for research and practice*. Stanford University Press.

Roe, E. (2018). *Making the most of mess: Reliability and policy in today's management challenges*. Duke University Press.

Roux-Dufort, C. (2007). Is crisis management (only) a management of exceptions? *Journal of Contingencies and Crisis Management*, *15*(2), 105–114.

Roysircar, G., Thompson, A., and Geisinger, K. F. (2019). Trauma coping of mothers and children among poor people in Haiti: Mixed methods study of community-level research. *American Psychologist*, *74*(9), 1189–1206.

Rudolph, J. W., and Repenning, N. P. (2002). Disaster dynamics: Understanding the role of quantity in organizational collapse. *Administrative Science Quarterly*, *47*(1), 1–30.

Sandberg, J., and Tsoukas, H. (2020). Sensemaking reconsidered: Towards a broader understanding through phenomenology. *Organization Theory*, *1*(1), 2631787719879937.

Schakel, J.-K., van Fenema, P. C., and Faraj, S. (2016). Shots fired! Switching between practices in police work. *Organization Science*, *27*(2), 391–410.

Seeger, M., and Sellnow, T. L. (2016). *Narratives of crisis: Telling stories of ruin and renewal*. Stanford University Press.

Shotter, J., and Tsoukas, H. (2014). In search of phronesis: Leadership and the art of judgment. *Academy of Management Learning and Education*, *13*(2), 224–243.

Snook, S. A. (2000). *Friendly fire: The accidental shootdown of US Black Hawk helicopters over northern Iraq*. Princeton University Press.

Starbuck, W. H., and Farjoun, M. (Eds.). (2005). *Organization at the limit: Lessons from the Columbia disaster*. Wiley-Blackwell.

Starbuck, W. H., and Milliken, F. J. (1988). Challenger: Fine-tuning the odds until something breaks. *Journal of Management Studies*, *25*(4), 319–340.

Staw, B. M., Sandelands, L. E., and Dutton, J. E. (1981). Threat-rigidity effects: A multi-level analysis. *Administrative Science Quarterly*, *26*(4), 501–524.

Stein, M. (2004). The critical period of disasters: Insights from sense-making and psychoanalytic theory. *Human Relations*, *57*(10), 1243–1261.

Torenvlied, R., Giebels, E., Wessel, R. A., Gutteling, J. M., Moorkamp, M., and Broekema, W. (2015). *Rapport evaluatie nationale crisisbeheersingsorganisatie vlucht MH17*. Universiteit Twente, Enschede, Netherlands.

Travadel, S., and Guarnieri, F. (2020). Interpreting the nightmare of Fukushima's superintendent: Sensemaking in extreme situations. In E. H. Powley, B. Caza, and A. Caza (Eds.), *Research handbook on organizational resilience* (pp. 275–298). Edward Elgar Publishing.

Turner, B. A. (1976). The organizational and interorganizational development of disasters. *Administrative Science Quarterly, 21*(3), 378–397.

van der Vegt, G. S., Essens, P., Wahlstrom, M., and George, G. (2015). Managing risk and resilience. *Academy of Management Journal, 58*(4), 971–986.

Vaughan, D. (1996). *The Challenger launch decision: Risky technology, culture, and deviance at NASA*. University of Chicago.

Walker, B., Malinen, S., Niswali, K., Nilakant, V., and Kuntz, J. (2020). Organizational resilience in action: A study of a large-scale extended-disaster setting. In E. H. Powley, B. Caza, and A. Caza (Eds.), *Research handbook on organizational resilience* (pp. 320–336). Edward Elgar Publishing.

Weick, K. E. (1979). *The social psychology of organizing*. Second edition. Addison-Wesley.

Weick, K. E. (1984). Small wins: Redefining the scale of social problems. *American Psychologist, 39*(1), 40–49.

Weick, K. E. (1985). Cosmos vs. chaos: Sense and nonsense in electronic contexts. *Organizational Dynamics, 14*(Autumn), 50–64.

Weick, K. E. (1988). Enacted sensemaking in crisis situations. *Journal of Management Studies, 25*(4), 305–317.

Weick, K. E. (1990). The vulnerable systems: An analysis of the Tenerife air disaster. *Journal of Management, 16*, 571–593.

Weick, K. E. (1993). The collapse of sensemaking in organizations: The Mann Gulch disaster. *Administrative Science Quarterly, 38*(4), 628–652.

Weick, K. E. (1995). *Sensemaking in organizations*. SAGE Publications.

Weick, K. E. (1996). Drop your tools: An allegory for organization studies. *Administrative Science Quarterly, 41*, 301–313.

Weick, K. E. (2001). Book review: Scott A. Snook – *Friendly fire: The accidental shootdown of US black hawks over northern Iraq*. *Administrative Science Quarterly, 46*, 147.

Weick, K. E. (2005). Managing the unexpected: Complexity as distributed sensemaking. In R. R. McDaniel and D. Driebe (Eds.), *Uncertainty and surprise in complex systems: Questions on working with the unexpected* (pp. 51–65). Springer-Verlag.

Weick, K. E. (2006). Faith, evidence, and action: Better guesses in an unknowable world. *Organization Studies, 27*, 1723–1736.

Weick, K. E. (2020a). Sensemaking, organizing, and surpassing: A handoff. *Journal of Management Studies, 57*(7), 1420–1431.

Weick, K. E. (2020b). Sensemaking and whistleblowing. In P. J. Svenkerud, J. O. Sørnes, and L. D. Browning (Eds.), *Whistleblowing, communication and consequences: Lessons from the Norwegian National Lottery* (pp. 81–92). Routledge.

Weick, K. E., and Orton, J. D. (1987). Academic journals in the classroom. *Organizational Behavior Teaching Review [now Journal of Management Education], 11*(2), 27–42.

Weick, K. E., and Sutcliffe, K. M. (2001). *Managing the unexpected: Assuring high performance in an age of complexity*. Jossey-Bass.

Weick, K. E., and Sutcliffe, K. M. (2007). *Managing the unexpected: Resilient performance in an age of uncertainty*. Second edition. Jossey-Bass.

Weick, K. E., and Sutcliffe, K. M. (2015). *Managing the unexpected: Sustained performance in a complex world*. Third edition. SAGE Publications.

Weick, K. E., Sutcliffe, K. M., and Obstfeld, D. (2005). Organizing and the process of sensemaking. *Organization Science, 16*(4), 409–421.

Whiteman, G. (2010). Management studies that break your heart. *Journal of Management Inquiry, 19*(4), 328–337.

Williams, T. A., Gruber, D. A., Sutcliffe, K. M., Shepherd, D. A., and Zhao, E. Y. (2017). Organizational response to adversity: Fusing crisis management and resilience research streams. *Academy of Management Annals*, *11*(2), 733–769.

PART III

Developing and learning leadership judgment

12. Cultural intelligence and leadership judgment & decision making: ethnology and capabilities

Soon Ang, Thomas Rockstuhl and Georgios Christopoulos

1.   INTRODUCTION

"A leader's most important role in any organization is making good judgments – well-informed, wise decisions that produce the desired outcomes" (Tichy and Bennis, 2007, p. 94). Notwithstanding our heavy reliance on leaders to make judgment calls, we know relatively little about leadership judgments (Shotter and Tsoukas, 2014). Perhaps even less understood in the literature is the role of culture in the leadership judgment process – how the cultural context shapes the judgments and decisions leaders make.

We surmise that culture exerts an invisible yet imperative force on leaders' judgments because leaders necessarily draw on their value systems to make judgment calls. As Nonaka and Toyama (2007) noted, "the judgment of 'goodness' begins with individual values" (p. 380). In this chapter, we explore in greater depth the role of culture in leadership judgments. We present two complementary perspectives on how culture affects leadership judgments and decision making (LJDM): the cultural ethnology perspective and the cultural intelligence perspective.

The ethnological perspective examines how culture affects leadership judgments. This perspective offers a comparative view and explains why leaders make different judgments and decisions in the leadership process as a function of their cultural values. In essence, the ethnology perspective posits culture as a causal agent that shapes leaders' judgments.

The cultural intelligence perspective shifts from a cross-cultural to an intercultural space of inquiry. We examine how leaders' cultural intelligence (CQ), defined as one's capability to function effectively in intercultural contexts (Earley and Ang, 2003), affects their judgments and decisions in the context of a culturally diverse setting. We propose that in culturally diverse settings, leaders with high CQ are more likely to shape cultures, in addition to being shaped by culture.

Taken together, both the ethnology and the CQ perspectives of LJDM align with Patterson's (2014) observation that culture always acts in both "constraining and enabling human agency, in the process also facilitating structural and cultural changes" (p. 7). We frame our discussion of leadership judgments using a six-stage process of leadership (Locke, 1999). Below, we describe the leadership process framework, before discussing the ethnology and CQ perspectives of LJDM. We conclude with recommendations for future research directions to further advance our understanding of the role of culture in LJDM.

2.   A MODEL OF LEADERSHIP JUDGMENT AS A SIX-STAGE PROCESS

Theories of leadership abound in the management literature. Some theories focus on the qualities of an effective leader (Judge et al., 2002) whereas others emphasize leadership styles – the preferred behaviors through which leaders lead others (Bass et al., 2003). In this chapter, we consider leadership from a process perspective. We define leadership as *the process through which a person influences and inspires others to take action toward a desirable common vision, goal, or objective.* By viewing leadership through a process lens, we focus on leaders' judgments and actions, not their formalized position or status.

Drawing on Locke (1999) and Earley et al. (2006), we describe six stages of the leadership process. The first two stages, *formulating a vision* and *communicating the vision* refer to processes and judgments concerned with creating a vision. During these stages, the leader sets the organization's future direction and garners buy-in among employees to the vision.

Stages three to six focus on realizing that vision. They comprise *planning and budgeting* (i.e., developing an agenda and milestones for achieving the vision); *designing the organizational structure* (i.e., creating an appropriate organization structure and staffing it with the right people); *influencing and motivating* (i.e., delegating responsibilities and developing business processes to support activities to get work done); and *monitoring and controlling* (i.e., monitoring results and goal progress, and taking corrective and preventive actions with appropriate feedback).

Although the six stages form a generic leadership process, culture affects LJDM in each stage. That is, the judgments that leaders make in formulating, communicating, and achieving the vision are likely to differ according to cultural values. We elaborate on this ethnology perspective in the next section.

3.   ETHNOLOGY OF LEADERSHIP JUDGMENT

Hofstede (2001, p. 9) defined culture as "the collective programming of the mind that distinguishes the members of one group or category of people from another." A common way to theorize about the effects of culture is in terms of cultural values (Hofstede, 2001; House et al., 2004). Cultural values express what we like or desire to do; they are preferences for behavior that are shared by members of a group (Triandis, 1995).

Understanding the influence of cultural values on leadership behaviors is important because cultural values exert deep-seated, often unconscious influence at the neural and genetic level. Neuroscience evidence suggests that cultural values are represented in brain responses associated with critical mental functions (Shkurko, 2020). At the genetic level, Chiao and Blizinsky (2010) found that the effect of group-level collectivism on individual differences in risky decision making and learning is mediated by the short allele of the 5-HTTLPR polymorphism of the serotonine transporter gene. Many similar results (Christopoulos and Tobler, 2016) indicate that culture casts a strong shadow on human behavior, and thus any theorization of organizational behavior should take into account this essential driver.

Below, we describe how cultural values affect leadership judgments in each of the six stages of leadership. The cultural differences described here are by no means comprehensive, but they serve to illustrate how culture can influence judgments across the different stages of leadership.

Formulating a Vision

A corporate vision refers to an image of the future that clarifies the direction for the company, motivates and challenges people to take action in the right direction, and helps to coordinate the actions of different people (Kotter, 2012). In creating a vision, leaders focus on the future. A leadership judgment that leaders make (consciously or unconsciously) is: "How far into the future does one cast the vision?"

Cultural differences in short-term versus long-term orientation will affect how far into the future a leader's vision reaches. Cultures with a short-term orientation value proximate returns and efficiency and planning for the moment; cultures with a long-term orientation focus on and value the distal future (Hofstede, 2001). Asian countries, such as China, Korea, or Japan, tend to have greater long-term orientation than Western countries, such as the U.S. (Hofstede, 2001). Such differences in short-/long-term orientation may affect leaders' judgments and decisions about the time-horizons they consider in formulating a vision for their organization. Consistent with a greater long-term orientation, leaders of Asian companies tend to vision further into the future than many of their counterparts in Western companies. For example, Mosakowski and Earley (2000) observed this difference for many Japanese companies, "with strategic plans reflecting a company's history carried forward by planners for as much as a century" (p. 800).

Cultural differences in power distance may also affect vision formulation. Power distance describes the extent to which people accept social stratification and unequal distribution of power in society. Low power distance cultures emphasize equal status between people; high power distance cultures emphasize respect for authorities (Hofstede, 2001). In high power distance cultures, leaders may create visions in a top-down process. By contrast, leaders in low power distance cultures may be more likely to create visions with inputs from lower levels. Similarly, because greater power distance limits the contestability of a leader's power and position (Hofstede, 2001), leaders may feel less invested in the status quo and more empowered to adapt their vision as circumstances change (Geletkanycz, 1997).

Communicating the Vision

Once a vision is created, it has to be communicated. Here, leaders decide how to frame the communication to energize followers to achieve the vision. Cultures may differ in how favorably they respond to attributes that leaders communicate in their vision, such as brevity, clarity, abstractness, or stability (Baum et al., 1998). Uncertainty avoidance describes the extent to which risk is reduced or avoided through planning and creating clear structures and guidelines (Hofstede, 2001). For example, Germanic cultures tend to be higher in uncertainty avoidance than Anglo cultures (House et al., 2004). Due to their uncertainty avoidance, Germanic cultures may respond more favorably to visions that are brief, unambiguous, and highlight stability or predictability. Elenkov et al. (2005) indeed found that such vision attributes related stronger to administrative innovation in Germanic compared to Anglo cultures.

Leaders may also frame their communication based on the culture of the audience they address. For example, Ngai and Singh (2018) compared bilingual (Chinese and English) leader messages and addresses from 32 Chinese corporations. They found that English messages were more likely to be direct, concise, and results-oriented and downplay the leader's authority. By contrast, Chinese versions of the same messages emphasized the power, status, and authority of leaders. Chinese messages also reflected greater collectivism (i.e., the extent to which cultures view the self as interdependent with others and stress duties and obligations, Triandis, 1995) and warm regard of stakeholders through the use of words such as "社會" (society), "員工" (employee), and "責任" (responsible).

Planning and Budgeting

In the third stage of the leadership process, leaders develop specific organizational goals – tangible and intangible – that are aligned with the vision of the company. Leaders also decide on the allocation of resources, such as money, personnel, or equipment, to achieve these goals. Finally, leaders identify milestones and map specific deadlines for various projects to align followers' actions with organizational goals.

Research has documented cultural influences on resource allocation, especially with regard to risk-taking in financial decisions. For example, allocating resources to R&D could be riskier than allocating resources to process improvement, even though both may benefit the firm in the future. Across studies, uncertainty avoidance and power distance are negatively associated with risk-taking, while individualism is positively associated with risk-taking (for a review, see Kutan et al., 2020).

Cultural differences in clock-time versus event-time also affect the planning of milestones and specific deadlines (Levine, 1998). Clock-time versus event-time describes a culture's orientation toward tempo and punctuality (clock-time = value speed, efficiency, and punctuality; event-time = value social relationships and social obligations over fixed timelines). In event-time cultures, such as Egypt, there tends to be greater temporal flexibility and spontaneity than in clock-time cultures, such as Switzerland. As a consequence, leaders in clock-time cultures may plan, schedule, and budget work much more precisely and emphasize the keeping of timelines.

Designing the Organizational Structure

Designing the organizational structure requires leaders to make decisions related to two key dimensions (see Pugh et al., 1968): centralization (i.e., the locus of authority to make decisions affecting the organization) and formalization (i.e., the extent to which rules, procedures, instructions, and communications are written). Centralization and formalization are distinct dimensions of organizational structure (Kaufmann et al., 2019; Sandhu and Kulik, 2019), and thus may be differentially affected by culture.

Research suggests that power distance is positively associated with centralization. For instance, a recent study of Human Resources (HR) Directors-General responsible for public administration in the European Union and European Commission found that states with higher power distance values tend to have more centralized HR functions (Meyer and Hammerschmid, 2010). A study by Aycan et al. (2000) showed that leaders from high power distance cultures are less likely to decentralize their decision making because of their beliefs that employees are more reactive than proactive.

Whereas power distance influences the degree of centralization, uncertainty avoidance affects formalization. Research has found uncertainty avoidance to be positively associated with the number and clarity of procedures and rules (Newman and Nollen, 1996) and the degree of formalization in organizations (Harrison et al., 1994).

Influencing and Motivating

The influencing and motivating stage focuses on how leaders direct the energies of their followers toward achieving the organization's strategic objectives. Here, leaders decide on how best to motivate their followers to achieve organizational goals.

In general, research shows that leaders across different cultures rely on different bases of power to influence and motivate followers. For example, Rahim et al. (1994) found that American managers perceive their leaders to have greater position than personal power whereas Korean managers perceive their leaders to have greater personal than position power. Similarly, Bochner and Hesketh (1994) found that followers from countries with greater power distance tended to be more submissive, loyal, and obedient to their leaders.

Culture also influences reward allocation – an important motivational strategy that leaders use to influence followers. For instance, existing research shows that leaders from different cultures tend to apply different reward allocation rules. There are three major reward allocation rules: equity (outcome distribution based on productivity or other inputs), equality (equal distributions), or need (distribution based on the needs of the recipient). Early cross-cultural studies demonstrate that leaders from individualistic cultures tend to prefer the equity rule whereas collectivistic cultures prefer the equality rule (Hui et al., 1991) and need rule (Gomez-Meija and Welbourne, 1994).

Monitoring and Controlling

The final stage of the leadership process focuses on the systems and activities that ensure that the actions and performance of followers align with organizational rules, standards, and goals. Here, leaders decide on systems to monitor followers' behaviors and outputs.

A common example of a monitoring system is the performance appraisal (PA). Culture affects leaders' judgments about how to design PA practices and how to give and receive feedback. For example, Atwater et al. (2009) suggested that Korean executives may be less likely than their American counterparts to rely on subordinates as part of PA systems. More generally, Peretz and Fried (2012) documented cultural differences in PA practices, comparing 5,991 organizations across 21 countries. They found that power distance related negatively to using multiple rater-sources (i.e., assessments from superiors, peers, and subordinates) in PA; collectivism related positively to using PA for organizational purposes (such as HR planning) but negatively to using PA for personal purposes (such as merit-based compensation); and uncertainty avoidance related positively to formal implementation of PA systems.

Regarding feedback, several studies have demonstrated the influence of cultural values on leaders' rating biases and self–other agreement. For instance, Ng et al. (2011) found that cultural values in power distance and collectivism affect leniency and halo biases in multisource feedback ratings. Specifically, leaders who are more collectivistic tend to give more lenient peer ratings than those who are more individualistic. Conversely, Atwater et al. (2009) found that leaders from assertive cultures (i.e., willingness to express true thoughts and feelings) tend to achieve stronger self–other agreement in multisource feedback ratings. Cultural values also affect the nature of feedback that leaders pay attention to. Bailey et al. (1997) found that U.S. respondents were more likely to desire success feedback whereas Chinese and Japanese respondents were more likely to desire failure feedback.

Summary

Comparative cultural research has documented vast variability in leadership judgments across all stages of the leadership process. It is worth pointing out that, although we have discussed cultural influences on judgments in each stage, culture affects leaders' judgments across stages. One would expect this to be the case as judgments in the different leadership stages are related to each other and do not operate independently. For example, uncertainty avoidance affects the degree of formalization for both the broader organizational design and the specific implementation of PA systems. In sum, comparative cultural research enriches our understanding of the ethnology of LJDM and may foster a deeper level of appreciation for cultural differences in leaders when they work with followers from different cultures.

However, effective management of cultural differences requires more than their appreciation. We propose that expanding the focus from *cultural comparison* to *intercultural capabilities* can advance the science and practice of culture and LJDM. To this end, we introduce the cultural intelligence perspective.

4.   CULTURALLY INTELLIGENT LEADERSHIP JUDGMENT

Cultural Intelligence: Capabilities for Intercultural Effectiveness

Earley and Ang (2003) introduced the concept of cultural intelligence at a time when the world was experiencing unprecedented globalization and interconnectedness but also ideological clashes and cultural conflict such as the tragic events of 9-11. Amid the promises and pitfalls of globalization, CQ becomes an essential capability for global leaders. Defined as an individual's capability to function effectively across cultures (Earley and Ang, 2003), CQ marks a paradigm shift from a focus on detecting cultural differences to managing them.

Earley and Ang (2003) drew on Sternberg's (1986) "multiple loci" of intelligence argument to conceptualize CQ as a multidimensional construct. Sternberg argued that intelligence resides in different loci within a person – motivation, cognition, metacognition, and behavior – and that a more holistic view of intelligence must consider all loci. Thus, Ang and colleagues defined CQ as an aggregate multidimensional construct comprising four factors: (1) motivational CQ – the capability to direct and sustain effort toward functioning in intercultural situations; (2) cognitive CQ – knowledge about cultural similarities and differences; (3) metacognitive CQ – the mental capability to acquire and understand cultural knowledge; and

(4) behavioral CQ – the capability for behavioral flexibility in intercultural interactions (Ang and Van Dyne, 2008; Ang et al., 2007).

Empirical research on CQ attests to the potency of the construct in explaining differences in intercultural effectiveness (for a review, see Ang et al., 2020). Results from a recent meta-analysis based on 199 independent samples ($N = 44,155$) offer strong empirical support for positive relationships of both overall CQ and the four factors of CQ with various intercultural effectiveness outcomes (Rockstuhl and Van Dyne, 2018). In particular, research shows that CQ is positively related to both intercultural judgment and decision making (Ang et al., 2007) and leadership in cross-border contexts (Rockstuhl et al., 2011). Research also shows that cultural diversity is an important boundary condition of CQ effects (Groves and Feyerherm, 2011; Rockstuhl et al., 2011), highlighting that CQ is especially critical for leaders in culturally diverse organizations.

CQ and Culture-Making across the Six Stages of Leadership

The CQ perspective proposes that leadership judgments are not simply driven by leaders' cultural values. Rather, we proffer a more agentic approach and suggest that culturally intelligent leaders serve as norm-drivers who actively shape cultural norms to align with their desired outcomes for the organization (e.g., Dannals and Miller, 2017). They do so by first detecting existing cultural values that underlie organizational practices in the six stages of leadership. They then create new norms to achieve desired outcomes in each stage of the leadership process.

Norms differ from values in that the former refer to "shared rules that prescribe and proscribe what we ought to do in given situations" whereas the latter "express what we like or desire to do" (Patterson, 2014, p. 13). We focus on norms rather than values as leaders do not necessarily have to change the cultural values of organizational members.

Research on norm-interventions suggests that shaping norms, or culture-making, requires at least four steps (Dannals and Miller, 2017; Legros and Cislaghi, 2020; Patterson, 2014): (1) identifying current and desired norms; (2) creating behavioral indicators to reduce ambiguity about what ought to be done in what situation; (3) monitoring behavioral indicators; and (4) reinforcing and maintaining new norms through persuasion and sanctioning of norm violations.

Below, we describe why each of the four CQ factors is important in shaping new cultural norms that will help organizations thrive in culturally diverse settings. Although we discuss the four CQ factors in isolation, they are mutually interdependent and jointly influence a leader's effectiveness in shaping organizational norms across cultures.

Motivational CQ

Broadly, motivational CQ can be understood as approach versus avoidance motivation. Leaders with higher motivational CQ are more likely to approach cultural differences with curiosity, rather than avoiding them. Motivational CQ reflects the capability to direct attention and energy toward learning about and functioning in culturally diverse situations. Kanfer and Heggestad (1997, p. 39) argued that such motivational capacities "provide agentic control of affect, cognition, and behavior that facilitates goal accomplishment."

Leaders with high motivational CQ are more likely to invest in learning about cultural differences and new behaviors (Ang et al., 2007). They tend to be more curious about how cultures differ and direct more attention to detecting deep underlying cultural values. As Tichy and Bennis (2007) pointed out, the first phase for making good judgment calls is to pick up on signals in the environment. When operating in a culturally diverse environment, leaders need to be curious about the covert cultural values driving overt organizational practices.

Culturally curious leaders are more likely to spend time observing and interacting with their followers to understand what motivates them. For instance, a German CFO recounted his interaction with an Indian manager who appeared to have decided on a deadline almost without deliberation. A leader with low motivational CQ may immediately write this Indian manager off, thinking that the Indian manager is merely paying "lip service" and unlikely to deliver. However, someone with high motivational CQ may ask the Indian manager with curiosity how he can decide so quickly, to which the manager might respond, "Let's put down a date first and we can change as things unfold in the next two weeks."

By probing deeper rather than brushing aside the Indian manager's response, the German CFO will learn something new about his follower. The more curious a leader is, the more s/he can discover cultural values underlying existing practices. This in turn provides the leader with important insights on what new desired norms to make and the changes required to shift followers to the new norms.

Cognitive CQ

While motivational CQ addresses the level of interest in detecting and understanding cultural differences, cognitive CQ reflects a leader's level of knowledge of the cultural environment and knowledge of the self as embedded within a particular cultural context. Cognitive CQ includes culture-general knowledge (i.e., declarative knowledge of the universal elements that constitute a cultural environment) and culture-specific knowledge (i.e., declarative and procedural knowledge about cultural ethnologies in a specific domain, such as leadership) (Van Dyne et al., 2012). Having more elaborate knowledge structures helps leaders to appreciate why behaviors and interactions differ across cultures. This aids in making isomorphic attributions of behaviors, rather than misattributions of behaviors due to cultural differences.

Importantly, leaders with high cognitive CQ are likely to have a better understanding of the ethnology of leadership. That is, they are aware of the alternative cultural approaches in each of the six stages of leadership. For instance, leaders who understand concepts of individualism-collectivism, power distance, and uncertainty avoidance are more primed to look for cues in existing organizational practices to understand the culture of the organization. Going back to the example of the German CFO and his Indian manager, knowledge of the concept of clock-time versus event-time (Levine, 1998) will immediately help the German leader discern the cultural differences underlying his interaction with his staff.

Research suggests that cognitive CQ is most beneficial when coupled with high metacognitive CQ. For example, Chua and Ng (2017) showed that cultural knowledge increases the risk of cognitive overload and entrenchment when metacognitive CQ is low. Rockstuhl and Van Dyne (2018) extended this finding and suggested that cultural knowledge coupled with low metacognitive CQ may increase stereotyping. We thus discuss the important role of metacognitive CQ next.

Metacognitive CQ

Metacognitive CQ refers to the mental capability to acquire and understand cultural knowledge. This CQ factor involves higher-level cognitive strategies – strategies that allow leaders to reflect on how appropriate their own cultural norms are and to develop new heuristics and rules for leadership in novel cultural contexts.

We propose that metacognitive CQ promotes more effective culture-making. This is because leaders with high metacognitive CQ are likely to be more deliberate when creating new norms. They tend to take the perspective of diverse others and draw on their cultural knowledge to anticipate their actions and reactions in planning for norm-interventions. Instead of merely adhering to their plans, leaders with high metacognitive CQ monitor outcomes and pay attention to meaningful cultural cues. They suspend judgments until sufficient information is available for accurate sense-making, and adjust their assumptions when their experience disconfirms their expectations (Triandis, 2006). For example, Morris et al. (2019) showed that those with high metacognitive CQ monitor judgment errors in intercultural contexts and revise their mental models accordingly.

Importantly, we propose that leaders with high metacognitive CQ are likely to make better judgments to resolve cultural clashes. This is because they are more cognitively flexible to adjust their strategies on how to address cultural conflicts based on new information. In our ongoing research on situational judgments tests with C-suite executives, we identified multiple strategies that senior leaders used to resolve cultural conflicts (Barros et al., 2020). They include compromises – moves that involve "give and take"; "log-rolling" – drawing norms from different cultures in different stages; and "win–win" or integrative strategies.

We suggest that leaders with high metacognitive CQ are more likely to adopt a mix of compromises, log-rolling, and integrative strategies to effectively balance the myriad leadership dualities, such as individualistic and collectivistic; short-term and long-term; control and autonomy; structure and flexibility; and so on. For example, a leader may empower followers' individual decision making for decisions in which speed of decision making is crucial, but implement collective decision-making processes for strategic decisions that require greater buy-in from followers.

Behavioral CQ

Leaders are not only expected to make good judgment calls; they are expected to execute them well (Tichy and Bennis, 2007). Similarly, leaders not only decide on the new set of shared rules and practices, but they also need to execute and enforce the norms to ensure the organization thrives in culturally diverse environments. Behavioral CQ is important because it enables leaders to communicate, persuade, and reinforce the new norms in the organization.

Behavioral CQ reflects a leader's capability to enact a wide range of culturally relevant actions. These actions include verbal behavior (i.e., flexibility in vocalization, including accent, tone, etc.), non-verbal behavior (flexibility in communication via gestures, facial expressions, body language, etc.), and speech acts (flexibility in using words to communicate specific types of messages such as requests, invitations, apologies, gratitude, disagreement, etc.) (Van Dyne et al., 2012).

We propose that leaders with high behavioral CQ are likely to be more effective in priming the need to change and persuading people to change. This includes getting followers to listen to difficult messages, question their existing assumptions, and consider new ways of working (Garvin and Roberto, 2005). The elaboration likelihood model of persuasion suggests that besides the content of the message itself (i.e., the central route), factors affecting the general impression of the receivers (peripheral route) are important determinants of change in attitudes (Petty and Cacioppo, 1986). Hence, how leaders communicate the need for change is likely to affect followers' receptivity to change.

Given that culture affects norms of communication, leaders with a greater repertoire of speech acts, verbal behaviors, and non-verbal behaviors are more likely to use rhetorical devices effectively to resonate with followers. For instance, leaders may intentionally adapt their rhetorical leadership, such as the use of self-referential language (versus group-referential language), accomplishments (versus self-effacement), aggression (versus compassion), and certainty (versus ambivalence), to inspire their audience (e.g., Bligh and Kohles, 2008).

5.   FUTURE RESEARCH DIRECTIONS

We offer some ideas on how to advance our understanding of culture and LJDM based on the two perspectives discussed in this chapter. First, the cultural ethnology perspective forms the crucial foundation for understanding how culture affects LJDM in the leadership process. To expand our current understanding of cultural differences in LJDM, future research could examine alternative formulations of national culture beyond the value dimensions we have highlighted. Examples of such alternative formulations include tight versus loose cultures (Gelfand et al., 2011) or practical versus theoretical information-seeking cultures (Spina et al., 2020). A related direction would be to map the ethnology of LJDM not just across national cultures but also within national cultures. Doing so is critical because leaders need to deal with cultural differences in both domestic and global settings.

Second, the CQ perspective shifts from viewing LDJM as being driven by culture to a more agentic view where leaders are norm-drivers. This requires leaders to detect and bridge cultural norm differences. Future research could deepen our understanding of how leaders develop such capabilities. We suggest that one exciting direction is to examine the neurological activities of global leaders who effectively detect and bridge norms differences (Rockstuhl et al., 2010). This line of inquiry could contribute to new theories as well as revolutionize the way we select and develop global leaders (e.g., Waldman et al., 2017). For instance, future research could use the intercultural situational judgment test (iSJT; Rockstuhl et al., 2015) – a set of multimedia vignettes of intercultural conflicts, to investigate neurological processes underpinning the detection and bridging of cultural differences. For instance, studies could use the iSJT in a developmental context, providing leaders with repeated practice and feedback on the vignettes and examining changes in their neurological activities. With a deeper understanding of the neurological bases of norms detection and bridging, global leadership training programs could be more customized to suit the neurological profile of leaders.

6.   CONCLUSION

We began this chapter by noting the paucity of research on the role of culture in LJDM. Addressing this gap, we articulated two complementary views of how culture could affect LJDM: the ethnological and cultural intelligence perspectives. The ethnological perspective compares leadership across cultures. In doing so, the ethnological perspective can foster a deeper level of appreciation for cross-cultural judgment differences in leaders. The cultural intelligence perspective focuses on capabilities to exercise effective leadership judgments in culturally diverse contexts. Both perspectives work hand in hand, as leaders need to know and detect cultural differences as well as be able to bridge them. Ultimately, we believe that greater integration of the ethnological and cultural intelligence perspectives will advance our knowledge and practice to help leaders make better judgments in culturally diverse environments.

REFERENCES

Ang, S., Ng, K. Y., and Rockstuhl, T. (2020). Cultural intelligence. In R. J. Sternberg and S. B. Kaufman (Eds.), *The Cambridge handbook of intelligence* (2nd ed., pp. 820–845). Cambridge: Cambridge University Press.

Ang, S., and Van Dyne, L. (2008). Conceptualization of cultural intelligence: Definition, distinctiveness, and nomological network. In S. Ang and L. Van Dyne (Eds.), *Handbook of cultural intelligence* (pp. 3–15). New York: M. E. Sharpe.

Ang, S., Van Dyne, L., Koh, C., Ng, K. Y., Templer, K. J., Tay, C., and Chandrasekar, N. A. (2007). Cultural intelligence: Its measurement and effects on cultural judgment and decision making, cultural adaptation and task performance. *Management and Organization Review, 3*, 335–371.

Atwater, L., Wang, M., Smither, J. W., and Fleenor, J. W. (2009). Are culture characteristics associated with the relationship between self and others' ratings of leadership? *Journal of Applied Psychology, 94*, 876–886.

Aycan, Z., Kanungo, R. N., Mendonca, M., Yu, K., Deller, J., Stahl, G., and Kurshid, A. (2000). Impact of culture on human resource management practices: A 10-country comparison. *Applied Psychology: An International Review, 49*, 192–221.

Bailey, J. R., Chen, C. C., and Dou, S. G. (1997). Conceptions of self and performance-related feedback in the US, Japan and China. *Journal of International Business Studies, 28*, 605–625.

Barros, V., Rockstuhl, T., Ng, K.-Y., and Ang, S. (2020). *How global leaders resolve intercultural conflicts? Evidence using intercultural SJTs*. Paper presented at the Society for Industrial and Organizational Psychology Annual Meeting, Austin, TX.

Bass, B. M., Avolio, B. J., Jung, D. I., and Berson, Y. (2003). Predicting unit performance by assessing transformational and transactional leadership. *Journal of Applied Psychology, 88*, 207–218.

Baum, J. R., Locke, E. A., and Kirkpatrick, S. A. (1998). A longitudinal study of the relation of vision and vision communication to venture growth in entrepreneurial firms. *Journal of Applied Psychology, 83*, 43–54.

Bligh, M. C., and Kohles, J. C. (2008). Negotiating gender role expectations: Rhetorical leadership and women in the US Senate. *Leadership, 4*, 381–402.

Bochner, S., and Hesketh, B. (1994). Power distance, individualism/collectivism, and job-related attitudes in a culturally diverse work group. *Journal of Cross-Cultural Psychology, 25*, 233–257.

Chiao, J. Y., and Blizinsky, K. D. (2010). Culture-gene coevolution of individualism-collectivism and the serotonin transporter gene. *Proceedings of the Royal Society B – Biological Sciences, 277*(1681), 529–537.

Christopoulos, G. I., and Tobler, P. N. (2016). Culture as a response to uncertainty: Foundations of computational cultural neuroscience. In J. Y. Chiao, S.-C. Li, R. Seligman, and R. Turner (Eds.), *Oxford library of psychology. The Oxford handbook of cultural neuroscience* (pp. 81–104). Oxford: Oxford University Press.

Chua, R. Y., and Ng, K. Y. (2017). Not just how much you know: Interactional effect of cultural knowledge and metacognition on creativity in a global context. *Management and Organization Review*, *13*, 281–300.

Dannals, J. E., and Miller, D. T. (2017). Social norms in organizations. In *Oxford research encyclopedia of business and management*. Oxford: Oxford University Press.

Earley, P. C., and Ang, S. (2003). *Cultural intelligence: Individual interactions across cultures*. Palo Alto, CA: Stanford University Press.

Earley, P. C., Ang, S., and Tan, J.-S. (2006). *CQ: Developing cultural intelligence at work*. Stanford, CA: Stanford Business Books.

Elenkov, D. S., Judge, W., and Wright, P. (2005). Strategic leadership and executive innovation influence: An international multi-cluster comparative study. *Strategic Management Journal*, *26*, 665–682.

Garvin, D. A., and Roberto, M. A. (2005). Change through persuasion. *Harvard Business Review*, *83*(2), 26–33.

Geletkanycz, M. A. (1997). The salience of "culture's consequences": The effects of cultural values on top executive commitment to the status quo. *Strategic Management Journal*, *18*, 615–634.

Gelfand, M. J., Raver, J. L., Nishii, L., Leslie, L. M., Lun, J., Lim, B. C., … and Aycan, Z. (2011). Differences between tight and loose cultures: A 33-nation study. *Science*, *332*(6033), 1100–1104.

Gomez-Mejia, L. R., and Welbourne, T. (1994). Compensation strategies in a global context. In R. A. Noe, J. R. Hollenbeck, B. Gerhart, and P. M. Wright (Eds.), *Readings in human resource management* (pp. 561–562). Homewood, IL: Irwin.

Groves, K. S., and Feyerherm, A. E. (2011). Leader cultural intelligence in context: Testing the moderating effects of team cultural diversity on leader and team performance. *Group and Organization Management*, *36*, 535–566.

Harrison, G. L., McKinnon, J. L., Panchapakesan, S., and Leung, M. (1994). The influence of culture on organizational design and planning and control in Australia and the United States compared with Singapore and Hong Kong. *Journal of International Financial Management and Accounting*, *5*, 242–261.

Hofstede, G. (2001). *Culture's consequences: Comparing values, behaviors, institutions, and organizations across nations* (2nd ed.). London: Sage.

House, R. J., Hanges, P. J., Javidan, M., Dorfman, P. W., and Gupta, V. (2004). *Culture, leadership, and organizations: The GLOBE study of 62 societies*. Palo Alto, CA: Sage.

Hui, C. H., Triandis, H. C., and Yee, C. (1991). Cultural differences in reward allocation: Is collectivism the explanation? *British Journal of Social Psychology*, *30*, 145–157.

Judge, T. A., Bono, J. E., Ilies, R., and Gerhardt, M. W. (2002). Personality and leadership: A qualitative and quantitative review. *Journal of Applied Psychology*, *87*, 765–780.

Kanfer, R., and Heggestad, E. D. (1997). Motivational traits and skills: A person-centered approach to work motivation. *Research in Organizational Behavior*, *19*, 1–56.

Kaufmann, W., Borry, E. L., and DeHart-Davis, L. (2019). More than pathological formalization: Understanding organizational structure and red tape. *Public Administration Review*, *79*, 236–245.

Kotter, J. P. (2012). *Leading change*. Boston, MA: Harvard Business Review Press.

Kutan, A., Laique, U., Qureshi, F., Rehman, I. U., and Shahzad, F. (2020). A survey on national culture and corporate financial decisions: Current status and future research. *International Journal of Emerging Markets*. Advance online publication.

Legros, S., and Cislaghi, B. (2020). Mapping the social-norms literature: An overview of reviews. *Perspectives on Psychological Science*, *15*, 62–80.

Levine, R. (1998). *A geography of time: The temporal misadventures of a social psychologist, or how every culture keeps time just a little bit differently* (2nd ed.). New York: Basic Books.

Locke, E. A. (1999). *The essence of leadership: The four keys to leading successfully*. Lanham, MD: Lexington Books.

Meyer, R. E., and Hammerschmid, G. (2010). The degree of decentralization and individual decision making in central government human resource management: A European comparative perspective. *Public Administration*, *88*, 455–478.

Morris, M. W., Savani, K., and Fincher, K. (2019). Metacognition fosters cultural learning: Evidence from individual differences and situational prompts. *Journal of Personality and Social Psychology, 116*, 46–68.

Mosakowski, E., and Earley, P. C. (2000). A selective review of time assumptions in strategy research. *Academy of Management Review, 25*, 796–812.

Newman, K. L., and Nollen, S. D. (1996). Culture and congruence: The fit between management practices and national culture. *Journal of International Business Studies, 27*, 753–779.

Ng, K. Y., Koh, C., Ang, S., Kennedy, J. C., and Chan, K. Y. (2011). Rating leniency and halo in multi-source feedback ratings: Testing cultural assumptions of power distance and individualism-collectivism. *Journal of Applied Psychology, 96*, 1033–1044.

Ngai, C. S. B., and Singh, R. G. (2018). Reading beyond the lines: Themes and cultural values in corporate leaders' communication. *Journal of Communication Management, 22*, 212–232.

Nonaka, I., and Toyama, R. (2007). Strategic management as distributed practical wisdom (phronesis). *Industrial and Corporate Change, 16*, 371–394.

Patterson, O. (2014). Making sense of culture. *Annual Review of Sociology, 40*, 1–30.

Peretz, H., and Fried, Y. (2012). National cultures, performance appraisal practices, and organizational absenteeism and turnover: A study across 21 countries. *Journal of Applied Psychology, 97*, 448–459.

Petty, R. E., and Cacioppo, J. T. (1986). The elaboration likelihood model of persuasion. *Advances in Experimental Social Psychology, 19*, 123–205.

Pugh, D. S., Hickson, D. J., Hinings, C. R., and Turner, C. (1968). Dimensions of organization structure. *Administrative Science Quarterly, 13*, 65–105.

Rahim, M. A., Kim, N. H., and Kim, J. S. (1994). Bases of leader power, subordinate compliance, and satisfaction with supervision: A cross cultural study of managers in the U.S. and S. Korea. *International Journal of Organizational Analysis, 2*, 136–154.

Rockstuhl, T., Ang, S., Ng, K. Y., Lievens, F., and Van Dyne, L. (2015). Putting judging situations into situational judgment tests: Evidence from intercultural multimedia SJTs. *Journal of Applied Psychology, 100*, 464–480.

Rockstuhl, T., Hong, Y.-Y., Ng, K. Y., Ang, S., and Chiu, C.-Y. (2010). The culturally intelligent brain: From detecting to bridging cultural differences. *NeuroLeadership, 3*, 22–36.

Rockstuhl, T., Seiler, S., Ang, S., Van Dyne, L., and Annen, H. (2011). Beyond general intelligence (IQ) and emotional intelligence (EQ): The role of cultural intelligence (CQ) on cross-border leadership effectiveness in a globalized world. *Journal of Social Issues, 67*, 825–840.

Rockstuhl, T., and Van Dyne, L. (2018). A bi-factor theory of the four-factor model of cultural intelligence: Meta-analysis and theoretical extensions. *Organizational Behavior and Human Decision Processes, 148*, 124–144.

Sandhu, S., and Kulik, C. T. (2019). Shaping and being shaped: How organizational structure and managerial discretion co-evolve in new managerial roles. *Administrative Science Quarterly, 64*, 619–658.

Shkurko, A. (2020). Mapping cultural values onto the brain: The fragmented landscape. *Integrative Psychological and Behavioral Science*. Advance online publication.

Shotter, J., and Tsoukas, H. (2014). In search of phronesis: Leadership and the art of judgment. *Academy of Management Learning and Education, 13*, 224–243.

Spina, R., Ji, L. J., Guo, T., Li, Y., and Zhang, Z. (2020). Cultural differences in the tendency to seek practical versus theoretical information. *Journal of Cross-Cultural Psychology, 51*, 636–653.

Sternberg, R. J. (1986). A framework for understanding conceptions of intelligence. In R. J. Sternberg and D. K. Detterman (Eds.), *What is intelligence? Contemporary viewpoints on its nature and definition* (pp. 3–15). Norwood, NJ: Ablex.

Tichy, N. M., and Bennis, W. G. (2007). Making judgment calls. The ultimate act of leadership. *Harvard Business Review, 85*(10), 94–102.

Triandis, H. C. (1995). *Individualism and collectivism*. Boulder, CO: Westview Press.

Triandis, H. C. (2006). Cultural intelligence in organizations. *Group and Organization Management, 31*, 20–26.

Van Dyne, L., Ang, S., Ng, K. Y., Rockstuhl, T., Tan, M. L., and Koh, C. (2012). Sub-dimensions of the four factor model of cultural intelligence: Expanding the conceptualization and measurement of cultural intelligence. *Social and Personality Psychology Compass, 6*, 295–313.

Waldman, D., Ward, M. K., and Becker, W. J. (2017). Neuroscience in organizational behavior. *Annual Review of Organizational Psychology and Organizational Behavior*, *4*, 425–444.

13. Disjuncture and development: a learning theory approach to leadership judgement

Chris Saunders

INTRODUCTION[1]

Browse any train station or airport book shop, and you will find numerous texts by well-known business leaders outlining their approach to managing and leading. These are often reflective pieces of work in which the leader distils their personal wisdom into a set of guiding principles they claim helped to make them successful. For example, the former manager of Manchester United Football Club Sir Alex Ferguson cites listening, instilling discipline and proper preparation as the principles that guided him to become the most successful football manager in history (Ferguson, 2016).

It would appear that leaders in senior organizational roles operating in situations that are complex, uncertain and ambiguous develop a set of guiding principles to help make decisions and come to good judgements about what acts of leading they should carry out (Sternberg, 2003). It is possible that these principles have been learned from their direct experience, and they emerge as 'distilled wisdom' when subject to a process of reflection (Schön, 1991). As such, the existence of guiding principles may be linked to the idea of tacit knowledge (Polanyi, 1958), and the development of guiding principles may be similar to the ideas on how managers and leaders learn, and how wisdom is developed (Kempster, 2009; Marsick and Watkins, 1990, 2014; Sternberg, 2003; Yang, 2014; Shotter and Tsoukas, 2014a).

In this chapter the development of guiding principles will be explored using established learning theory. Guiding principles are defined as deep-seated ideas, understandings or truths learned over time by an individual leader. These truths prompt a person towards certain behaviours and/or certain patterns of thinking when faced with having to act or decide. The 'truth' that drives a principle is unlikely to be an objective one but is more likely to be subjective and perhaps context specific. Further, a principle may contain some idea or judgement that may be considered a virtue, being a belief in acts or behaviours that can be considered wise or morally correct (Sternberg, 2003; Yang, 2014). Academics and practitioners speculate that leaders need to employ wisdom to make good decisions when faced with complex problems (Korac-Kakabadse et al., 2001; McKenna et al., 2009; Sternberg, 2003; Davis, 2010), and may possess 'practical intelligence' which allows them to adapt their judgement to a given situation or problem (Sternberg, 2003, p388). It is proposed here that this practical intelligence may in fact be a set of tacit guiding principles used by leaders to decide how to act in any given situation.

The chapter will begin with a brief description of my research on acts of leading, and the development of guiding principles which influence a leader's action will be discussed. This will then be explored by discussing learning theory literature, before focusing in on how managers and leaders learn and how they may develop the tacit knowledge and wisdom needed for practical intelligence and good judgement.

One final clarification. When discussing leadership judgement I am referring to acts of leading. An act of leading can be anything someone in an organizational leadership position does that they would describe as leading. This might be, but is not restricted to, a decision involving themselves and others, a behaviour (e.g. role-modelling), or some form of written or verbal, official or unofficial, direct or informal communication. Acts of leading place the focus on what leaders actually do with colleagues in organizations on an everyday basis.

DECISION MAKING AND THE ROLE OF GUIDING PRINCIPLES

When faced with complex decisions, how do leaders decide? Are decisions involved in the act of leading instinctive, a form of 'non-deliberate practical coping' (Chia and Holt, 2006, p643), or are they influenced by a personal set of guiding principles.

My research on whether acts of leading are driven by guiding principles has endeavoured to explore these questions, and the initial results suggest that principles appear to be gained over time, both through everyday occurrences and through moments of disjuncture (Jarvis, 2009). It appears that disjuncture comes in many forms, including the influence of parents or managers, through the acquisition of knowledge which challenges pre-conceived ideas via books, films and social media, and through work and personal situations which have been difficult and challenging to the individual. The most common principles emerging are courage to make decisions, to stick to a plan or vision, and to be resilient; and integrity, especially the importance of acting in a way that builds trust from others.

Principles appear to only consciously emerge following a process of reflection. It seems that this reflection very rarely happens in the moment itself, but is most common after the event, either through some form of personal reflective practice or via a formal learning event.

Discovering that leaders can identify principles and reflect on their origin leads to the question as to whether guiding principles are actually used in practice. For this element of my research a group of individuals holding organizational positions of leadership have been keeping diaries of their personal acts of leading. What is emerging from this research is that organizational leaders are unconsciously or tacitly making decisions by following a set of personal guiding principles. They are practically coping, but not in a non-deliberate way. The leaders in the study are acting in an instinctive and deliberate manner, but they typically will only discover the principles used retrospectively, through a semi-structured reflective interview process.

This development and application of guiding principles reflects theories of adult, management and leadership learning, and ideas on the development of wisdom, theories which we will now consider.

LEARNING THEORY, DISJUNCTURE AND LEADERSHIP JUDGEMENT

How people learn has been a subject of investigation by professional educators for decades. Research on this subject has had many lenses, including psychological, sociological, experiential and pragmatic approaches.

Attempting to draw some of these perspectives together, Illeris (2009) creates a constructivist approach to learning, where the learner develops their own mental schemas or mental patterns which are drawn on when similar situations are encountered in the future. Learning comprises two main processes, 'namely an external interaction process between the learner and his or her social, cultural or material environment, and an internal psychological process of elaboration and acquisition' (Illeris, 2009, p8). These processes are integrated by the learner to achieve a state of learning.

The internal process divides into two internal dimensions, the content dimension and the incentive dimension. The content dimension is what is learned – knowledge, opinion, skill, insight, behaviour. In the context of leadership judgement this may be the bedrock from which judgements are made, the accumulation of and reflection on experience from which guiding principles are developed. The incentive dimension focuses on the motivation to learn, arguing that an individual must generate and utilize mental energy in order for learning to take place. Intrinsic motivation, emotional triggers, personal volition and feelings could all be sources of this energy. One could speculate that leaders possess intrinsic motivation to learn if they want to lead, but what they learn and what appears salient to them in terms of content may be driven by emotional experiences and encounters. Illeris is keen to point out that the cognitive and emotional elements always interact in order to generate learning.

The external process occurs between the learner and the environment in which learning is taking place. This process includes social interactions and the cultural and organizational influences which may aid or inhibit learning. It could be argued that the external process also provides much of the content of what can be learned. The idea that leadership is learned through an unconscious apprenticeship (Kempster, 2009) in which the aspiring leader gains knowledge of what leading actually is from key people and experiences, suggests that the external process may have a dominant impact on the process of learning to lead.

This emphasis on the social and environmental aspects of learning is core to the understanding of learning advocated by Jarvis (2009). He claims that learning always starts with an experience, and the experience is always social, not individual. But it is the individual who does the learning.

> Human learning is the combination of processes throughout a lifetime whereby the whole person – body (genetic, physical and biological) and mind (knowledge, skills, attitudes, values, emotions, beliefs and senses) – experiences social situations, the perceived content of which is then transformed cognitively, emotively or practically (or through any combination) and integrated into the individual person's biography resulting in a continually changing (or more experienced) person. (Jarvis, 2009, p25)

Jarvis believes that learning is both experiential and existential. Learners learn when they find something that triggers 'disjuncture' – a sense of not knowing what it is, or perhaps what to do. Disjuncture may cause the learner to question their world view and become suddenly aware of their own biases or assumptions. The learner then seeks meaning for the disjuncture, perhaps through understanding how their assumptions have developed and realizing their biases can be questioned or changed (Bateson, 1973; Burgoyne and Hodgson, 1983). The meaning given may not be objectively correct, but it satisfies the individual resolving the disjuncture, and thus learning has occurred. 'It is this disjuncture that is at the heart of conscious experience – because conscious experience arises when we do not know and when we cannot take our world for granted' (Jarvis, 2009, p27).

The resolution of a disjuncture is a social construct created by the individual to deal with the unknown. As such, Jarvis is agreeing with Illeris that learning happens within the social situation and culture in which it occurs, and it is interpreted and constructed in the mind of the individual.

Embedding this learning in guiding principles that inform everyday leadership judgement can be achieved through a process of practice, where what has been learned is repeated or practised in different circumstances. In this way the learning is not only memorized, but the learner also discovers what learning has salience across different scenarios. Practising happens in the social world; thus learners gain confirmation that their learning is correct or incorrect from the social situation in which learning is practised (Jarvis, 2009).

The theory of learning from experience and repeated practice has been empirically examined in management learning research. The majority of managers appear to learn in an iterative manner, where decisions, acts or behaviours that prove successful in one situation are learned or retained, and used again in future situations that appear similar (Burgoyne and Hodgson, 1983). Managers gain the most learning when faced with unpredictable circumstances (e.g. starting a new job) where new methods of working and new ways of coping are essential. Increased levels of responsibility for decision making, especially in 'non-routine' conditions (Marsick and Watkins, 1990, 2014), combined with a high level of motivation to learn, also contribute to high levels of learning (Davies and Easterby-Smith, 1984; Kolb et al., 1971; Mumford, 1980, 1981).

Illeris's and Jarvis's theories speak directly to the idea that guiding principles used during acts of leading may have been learned from a primary learning experience which may have a strong emotional element. The learner will be influenced by social and cultural aspects and is likely to have experienced some form of disjuncture. Jarvis goes on to suggest that this primary experience can be mediated by a secondary learning experience, although the primary and secondary may occur simultaneously. The secondary learning can come through reflection and discussion or via the written word (e.g. reflective writing or an interview) rather than through a new primary experience. This is learning from the experience itself, rather than from the social situation in which the experience occurred or from a sensation or emotion. Once learning has occurred, the person has changed, and the next social situation they enter will therefore also be changed.

This idea of secondary learning has the potential to allow the individual to reflect on and explore their formal and informal learning about leading. The learning of leadership typically aligns to ideas of formal and informal learning theories (Marsick and Watkins, 1990, 2014; Kempster, 2009). Formal leadership development occurs through deliberate interventions, training programmes, or organized mentoring or coaching opportunities. Informal development is about the experiences gained by individuals during their lifetimes which, on reflection, contribute to their understanding and enactment of leadership and leading. In this light, Jarvis's theories of experience and disjuncture could be seen as informal learning.

Studies on informal learning seek to understand how individuals and/or groups gain and interpret knowledge, information, and skills, creating meaning for themselves, which they might pass on or contribute to a wider group or organization (Marsick and Watkins, 1990). Marsick and Watkins make a distinction between informal learning and incidental learning. Informal learning has some element of planning attached to it. It is learning from experience, but in a very deliberate way. This might include self-directed learning – people gaining new knowledge from reading or perhaps TED talks, and applying it to their own situation. It could also include interactions with others, perhaps consciously seeking help in exploring experience from a mentor or a coach. Critical to informal learning is that the learner must be open to change and willing to engage with others' perspectives. This closely aligns with Illeris's (2009) ideas on motivation – if the learner is not constantly looking for learning opportunities, and not questioning their pre-suppositions, then they will hamper their own learning.

By contrast, incidental learning is unintentional, and is almost a by-product of a task or activity. It could stem from a difficult situation successfully or unsuccessfully resolved; from a reflection on mistakes or successes; or purely from a common everyday activity enacted in different circumstances. As such, learning due to disjuncture (Jarvis, 2009) can be considered as incidental learning. It may come from an interaction or relationship, be a product of immersion or socialization into an organizational culture, or even result from a training and development programme (Marsick and Watkins, 1990).

In both cases it is argued that the learner is in control of their learning, and they can enhance this through creativity (the ability to see problems differently); through proactivity (seeking out learning situations, journaling, creating space and time for reflection); and through critical reflection (deeply exploring personal beliefs, biases and assumptions that have been highlighted through close observation of one's actions) (Marsick and Watkins, 1990).

In summary, the literature on learning describes how individuals learn from routine and non-routine experiences, most powerfully when some form of disjuncture occurs. The motivation to learn, and the ability and willingness to reflect on these experiences, helps to focus in on what has been learned. These theories of experiential learning have been tested in numerous studies (McCall and Hollenbeck, 2002; DeRue and Wellman, 2009), giving more weight to the understanding that managers and leaders learn from various formal and informal personal experiences, some of which may be 'non-routine', and others of which will be repeatedly routine. Through this lens we can see that guiding principles can indeed develop over time and through experience, and that these principles may be further developed through deliberate reflective processes.

LEADERSHIP LEARNING, PRACTICAL INTELLIGENCE AND WISDOM

The importance of the experiential nature of learning is reflected in recent writings on leadership learning and development. Often in organizations a successful professional gains promotion and suddenly has to lead a group of people. If they are lucky the manager would have had some formal training, but this is not always the case. So the question arises, how do leaders learn to lead?

One contention is that leadership is learned in a similar way to an apprentice, over a long period of time, from many notable people, many experiences, and perhaps some hardships (McCall, 2004). This has prompted the notion that the learning of leadership is a never-ending process. The leader is always 'becoming' a leader through an ongoing process of experience and reflection, in which some experiences will have increased salience for learning over others, and in which leadership learning will be situated in the everyday context the leader encounters (Kempster, 2009; Edwards et al., 2013). Within this context, a leader will learn through observation of themselves and others, and through engaging with and acting in the situation. Their interpretation of and reflection on their action will be informed by their knowledge of leadership, perhaps of theories or skills and activities, which is both explicit and tacit (Nonaka, 1994; Kempster, 2009). It is this reflection that perhaps gives leaders the practical intelligence needed for good judgement (Sternberg, 2003, p388).

The development of practical intelligence is linked by Sternberg (2003) to Polanyi's ideas of tacit knowledge (Polanyi, 1958), which suggest that through gaining experience, leaders may have unconsciously developed some guiding principles that they employ to cope with complex problems and difficult situations. Sternberg argues that tacit knowledge is acquired through experience, and then deployed by a leader to achieve personally important goals. He claims that there is a link between gaining more experience and higher levels of tacit knowledge. The output of more tacit knowledge is wisdom, producing better or more effective leadership (Sternberg, 2003). If this is so, then perhaps guiding principles developed by leaders are in fact Sternberg's practical intelligence. As such, guiding principles would be co-created in the interactions leaders have with people, problems and situations throughout their career, and can be made explicit in the process of reflection and writing.

However, studies show that just because people are older, and thus more experienced, they are not necessarily any wiser (Yang, 2014). By gaining experience leaders may gain some guiding principles, but this does not necessarily mean they distil this into wisdom. It has been argued that wisdom is perhaps the most important quality possessed by a leader (Sternberg, 2003; Adair, 2005). It has also been identified as the rarest quality, making it a key area of work for leadership development professionals (Adair, 2005; Grint, 2007).

Adair defines phronesis as 'the wisdom of leaders relating to practice: what way to go, what to do next, when to do it, how to do it and with whom to do it' (Adair, 2005, p50). He proposes that practical wisdom is made up of intelligence, experience and goodness (Adair, 2005), whilst Grint suggests it is to do with moral knowledge or ethically practical action, it is context dependent, and it is focused on the collective not personal good (Grint, 2007, p237).

For Ardelt (2004) wisdom is aligned to the characteristics of one's personality, and is a combination of cognitive, reflective and affective traits. Yang (2014) sees wisdom as a process, an interaction between the individual and their environment. As such Yang's hypothesis is that wisdom is gained through a cognitive process, reflecting on and integrating one's experiences and ideas into something akin to a vision. This vision can only become wisdom if it influences the action of the individual; if it is embodied in their behaviour. In addition, like Adair and Grint, Yang argues that these actions can only be considered wise if they have a positive effect on the individual and others.

This concern for the common good is reflected in Sternberg's balanced theory of wisdom. He suggests a wise person will use their intelligence, creativity and experience to find a 'common good' by being able to balance the needs and desires of themselves and others, over the long and short term. Crucially the tacit knowledge used is moderated by the values of the individual to direct actions that result in some 'good' (Sternberg, 2003, p395).

These ideas, definitions and the subsequent research are mostly from a psychological perspective, where wisdom is the product of cognitive processes (Rooney and McKenna, 2008). Wisdom is something individuals derive from experience, their own experience, and as such appears to be treated as an entity in itself, divorced from the situations in which the experience was gained. The act of leading, making judgements and taking decisions are presented as rational acts, and the methods of research tend towards studying the judgement of the leader apart from the situation (Shotter and Tsoukas, 2014a).

However, practical wisdom is not something that can be divorced from the details of a specific situation, or from the emotional responses of the leader to that situation. Practical wisdom involves developing a 'discerning perception', the ability to understand the specifics of a given situation. This requires the leader to be fully in the situation, observing it rationally whilst also engaging with it on an intuitive level. The leader will be fully in the situation, acting in it, reflecting on it, understanding it, assessing a personal emotional response to it and so coming to a prudent judgement on it (Shotter and Tsoukas, 2014a; McKenna et al., 2009).

Shotter and Tsoukas go on to argue that this prudent judgement is influenced by a set of virtues which a leader has developed because these virtues lead to the 'good life'. These virtues, similar to guiding principles, are limited in number, and as a consequence leaders make decisions and judgements from a limited range of options informed by their guiding principles. In this sense, guiding principles act as ontological guides, meaning that they allow the leader to interpret a situation and to make what the leader believes to be appropriate decisions.

However, the act of leading cannot be reduced to a set of virtues, or sentences or verbs alone that describe some kind of generalized guiding principles. In the midst of taking action and making judgements, the specific situation encountered generates emotional and intuitive responses in the leader, which in turn influence the leader's response, and the responses of others (Shotter and Tsoukas, 2014b; McKenna et al., 2009). To fully understand this requires researchers to explore not just the decision itself and the guiding principles this may be based on, but also what the act of leading actually looked like, sounded like and felt like. In other words we need to dwell in the situation, or at least encourage the participants of our leadership programmes to learn to dwell in the leadership moment, to fully embrace the situation, and to try to learn from this rich tapestry of in-situ experience.

LEADERSHIP-AS-PRACTICE

There are similarities between the understanding of practical wisdom argued for by Shotter and Tsoukas above and the as-practice movements that have developed in the areas of strategy and leadership. Chia and Holt (2006) argue that traditional strategy theories have implicitly viewed the strategist as separate to the world in which they are working, detached from and acting on the world, rather similar to the research that has been done on wisdom (Sternberg, 2003; Yang, 2014). What is needed, they argue, is a different conceptualization of how strategy is created, one which understands that there exists a 'fundamental dwelling mode' where a symbiotic relationship is created between individuals and their strategies. A co-construction occurs in the very encounters individuals have with the world, in their actions, and in their relationships (Chia and Holt, 2006, p637).

This Heideggerian idea of 'dwelling' is useful when thinking about researching the act of leading with wisdom. Dwelling is described as being unintentional, unreflective action, which unfolds in response to moments encountered (Cunliffe and Hibbert, 2016). It is about dealing with the issues presented to you as a leader in an unheroic, unplanned way. Perhaps it is 'dwelling', or 'non-deliberate practical coping' (Chia and Holt, 2006, p643), that describes best how leaders deal with difficult problems and complex situations. It is from this complex set of relationships that guiding principles that produce wisdom and good judgements emerge.

WHAT DOES THIS MEAN FOR LEADERSHIP DEVELOPERS?

If the capacity for good leadership judgement develops over time by creating a tacit set of guiding principles, how can learning and development interventions help leaders to make these principles implicit? Learning theory would suggest that some form of deliberate, focused reflection could help (Schön, 1991; Jarvis, 2009). Learning theory would advocate for this as a secondary learning process (Jarvis, 2009), and my research findings suggest that reflecting on acts of leading and writing reflective documents can indeed help leaders to identify and question the guiding principles that inform their action.

For a leader to be consciously engaged in their acts of leading and to fully understand the leadership judgements they make requires them to have a process for reflection on their action (Schön, 1991). This will enable them to surface the guiding principles that guide their decision making. Only then can they engage in a conscious appraisal of whether these principles are suitable, desirable and acceptable to themselves, their colleagues and their organizational environments.

CONCLUSION

This chapter has explored the guiding principles that inform leadership judgement by focusing on adult, management and leadership learning theories. I have contended that learning leadership is a whole life discipline, where experience and especially moments of disjuncture can create tacit guiding principles which leaders use to decide how to act. Uncovering or making these principles conscious requires a process of deliberate reflection. I would argue that engaging in a process that allows a leader to better understand why they do what they do is crucial to aid the development of the practical wisdom, or practical judgement, that is so needed by leaders.

NOTE

1.   I would like to thank Dr Marian Iszatt-White and Professor Mike Reynolds for their wise help and advice in the construction of this chapter.

REFERENCES

Adair, J. E. (2005), *How to grow leaders: The seven key principles of effective leadership development*, London: Kogan Page.

Ardelt, M. (2004), Wisdom as expert knowledge system: A critical review of a contemporary operation-alization of an ancient concept, *Human Development*, *47*, 257–285.

Bateson, G. (1973), *Step to an ecology of mind*, New York: Ballantine Books.

Burgoyne, J. G. and Hodgson, V. E. (1983), Natural learning and managerial action: A phenomenologi-cal study in the field setting, *Journal of Management Studies*, *20*(3), 387–399.

Chia, R. and Holt, R. (2006), Strategy as practical coping: A Heideggerian perspective, *Organization Studies*, *27*(5), 635–655.

Cunliffe, A. L. and Hibbert, P. (2016), The philosophical basis of leadership-as-practice from a her-meneutical perspective, in Raelin, J. A. (ed.), *Leadership-as-practice: Theory and application*, New York: Routledge, Ch 3, pp50–69.

Davies, J. and Easterby-Smith, M. P. V. (1984), Learning and developing from managerial work experi-ences, *Journal of Management Studies*, *21*(2), 169–183.

Davis, R. D. (2010), *The intangibles of leadership*, San Francisco, CA: Jossey-Bass.

DeRue, D. S. and Wellman, N. (2009), Developing leaders via experience: The role of developmental change, learning orientation, and feedback availability, *Journal of Applied Psychology*, *94*, 859–875.

Edwards, G., Elliott, C., Iszatt-White, M. and Schedlitzki, D. (2013), Critical and alternative approaches to leadership learning and development, *Management Learning*, *44*(1), 3–10.

Ferguson, A. with Moritz, M. (2016), *Leading*, London: Hodder and Stoughton.

Grint, K. (2007), Learning to lead: Can Aristotle help us find the road to wisdom?, *Leadership*, *3*(2), 231–246.

Illeris, K. (2009), A comprehensive understanding of human learning, in Illeris, K. (ed.), *Contemporary theories of learning: Learning theorists ... in their own words*, London: Routledge, pp1–14.

Jarvis, P. (2009), Learning to be a person in society: Learning to be me, in Illeris, K. (ed.), *Contemporary theories of learning: Learning theorists ... in their own words*, London: Routledge, pp15–28.

Kempster, S. (2009), *How managers have learnt to lead*, Basingstoke: Palgrave Macmillan.

Kolb, D. A., Rubin, I. M. and McIntyre, J. M. (1971), *Organizational psychology: An experiential approach*, Englewood Cliffs, NJ: Prentice Hall.

Korac-Kakabadse, N., Korac-Kakabadse, A. and Kouzmin, A. (2001), Leadership renewal: Towards the philosophy of wisdom, *International Review of Administrative Sciences*, *67*, 207–227.

Marsick, V. J. and Watkins, K. E. (1990), *Informal and incidental learning in the workplace*, London: Routledge.

Marsick, V. J. and Watkins, K. E. (2014), Informal learning in learning organizations, in Poell, R. F., Rocco, T. S. and Roth, G. L. (ed.), *The Routledge companion to human resource development*, London: Routledge, pp236–248.

McCall, M. W. (2004), Leadership development through experience, *Academy of Management Executive*, *18*, 127–130.

McCall, M. W. and Hollenbeck, G. P. (2002), *Developing global executives: The lessons of international experience*, Boston, MA: Harvard Business School Press.

McKenna, B., Rooney, D. and Boal, K. B. (2009), Wisdom principles as a meta-theoretical basis for evaluating leadership, *The Leadership Quarterly*, *20*, 177–190.

Mumford, A. (1980), *Making experience pay*, London: McGraw-Hill.

Mumford, A. (1981), 'What did you learn today?', *Personnel Management*, *13*(8), 35–39.

Nonaka, I. (1994), A dynamic theory of organizational knowledge creation, *Organizational Science*, *5*(1), 14–37.

Polanyi, M. (1958), *Personal knowledge*, Chicago: University of Chicago Press.

Rooney, D. and McKenna, B. (2008), Wisdom in public administration: Looking for a sociology of wise practice, *Public Administration Review*, July/August, 709–721.

Schön, D. (1991), *The reflective practitioner: How professionals think in action*, Aldershot: Avebury.

Shotter, J. and Tsoukas, H. (2014a), In search of phronesis: Leadership and the art of judgment, *Academy of Management Learning and Education*, *13*(2), 224–243.

Shotter, J. and Tsoukas, H. (2014b), Performing phronesis: On the way to engaged judgment, *Management Learning*, *45*(4), 377–396.

Sternberg, R. J. (2003), WICS: A model of leadership in organizations, *Academy of Management Learning and Education*, *2*(4), 386–401.

Yang, S. (2014), Wisdom and learning from important and meaningful life experiences, *Journal of Adult Development*, *21*, 129–146.

14. On facilitating the development of leaders' ability to exercise good judgment

Matthew Eriksen

Leaders are operating in environments that are characterized as turbulent and rapidly changing (Anderson et al., 2018) and are experienced as disorienting (Shotter, 2016), unique, ill-defined, complex, and emotive (Cunliffe, 2002). Employed by the U.S. military as far back as the 1980s, the acronym VUCA describes a situation that is volatile, uncertain, complex, and ambiguous (Campbell, 2020). This certainly describes the world in which we find ourselves.

The news headlines on May 28, 2020, in the United States included coverage of the emerging COVID-19 pandemic, violent protests throughout the country against the killing of George Floyd, announcements by the United States of a slew of retaliatory measures against China, President Trump's announcement that the United States will be terminating relations with the World Health Organization, Congress's debate on a fourth aid bill to address the economic consequences of the COVID-19 pandemic, the commencement of the issuing of immunity passports by governments across the world, a study in the journal *Science* detailing how "[r]ising temperatures, deforestation, development and climate-induced disasters are transforming the very makeup of Earth's forests" (Rott, 2020), and, in retaliation for adding warning labels to his tweets that are inaccurate and threatening, President Trump signing an executive order to limit legal protections for social media companies (Alba et al., 2020).

In light of our turbulent times, the leadership crises and ethical lapses we seem to endlessly endure, and the recognition that practitioners are often driven by greed, gain, and glory (Schwartz and Sharpe, 2010), the ability to exercise good judgment is increasingly recognized as essential to being an effective leader (Cunliffe and Eriksen, 2011; Likierman, 2020; Nonaka and Takeuchi, 2011; Tichy and Bennis, 2007). Mumford and Higgs (2020) identify the essence of leadership as the exercise of discretion (Shotter and Tsoukas, 2014a, 2014b; Vickers, 1995) in deciding when and how to exercise social influence (Bass and Bass, 2009; Yukl, 2011) required to "solve complex, novel, ill-defined problems – problems arising in a distinctly social context (e.g., the team, the firm, the institution)" (3). While rules and regulation might be able to help leaders avoid disaster, they will not allow them to act wisely (Schwartz and Sharpe, 2010). Such bewildering circumstances in which a team or organization does not know how to go on (Shotter, 2016) call upon leaders to respond with the exercise of good judgment (Shotter and Tsoukas, 2014a), rather than the employment of abstract leadership theories or decontextualized techniques (Cunliffe and Eriksen, 2011).

> With a playing field that there were no rules, there were no coaches, there were not even referees, nothing when I came to this airport. Nothing. Stand up this organization. I went home and said how

am I going to do this? What am I going to do? How am I going to do it? [FSD 2] (Cunliffe and Eriksen, 2011)

Consistent with the above Federal Security Director's description, in our article "Relational Leadership" (2011), based on our study of Federal Security Directors (FSDs) in the newly created Transportation Security Administration (TSA) after 9/11, Ann Cunliffe and I put forth the concept of relational leadership as a way of being-in-relation-with-others that involves practical wisdom. FSDs are responsible for the leadership and coordination of TSA security activities at U.S. airports.

> FSDs working in the field who were dealing with ambiguous, evolving and stressful situations (1426) ... talked about the nature and quality of human relationships, to their own values and judgments: in other words, to the mundane imaginative work that goes on within the complexity of their everyday relationships ... and of their experiences of struggling with "small details" and making judgments in the present moment of their interactions. (1430)

For example, one FSD stated:

> ... women coming in with baby harnesses, and here we are asking mothers of two week-old babies to take that baby out of the harness so we could screen the harness separately. Now what is wrong with that picture? Mothers are often not real comfortable handling a two or three-week-old baby. Why are we doing this? Because Washington tell us to? Now come on! Let's come up with a better way ... [FSD 3] (1438)

FSD 3 exercised good judgment when encountering a situation within which a procedure did not serve the purpose of why the procedure was put in place or the aims of the organization. FSDs who were unsuccessful were "the ones that came in with their own management style that they thought would work in any environment [FSD 3]" (1426). In other words, they did not take into consideration the uniqueness of the aviation environment and each emerging situation within which they found themselves that is necessary to exercise good judgment.

Although there is widespread agreement that the exercise of good judgment is necessary to being an effective leader and evidence from psychology that it can be learned (Schwartz and Sharpe, 2010), there exists no agreement on what the exercise of good judgment *is* or how it can be effectively developed. In this chapter, taking a performative approach (Shotter and Tsoukas, 2014a) and relational-responsive social constructionism perspective (Cunliffe, 2016; Cunliffe and Eriksen, 2011; Shotter, 2016), I put forth and describe the exercise of good judgment as being consistent with Aristotle's notion of *phronesis* or practical wisdom (Cunliffe and Eriksen, 2011; Schwartz and Sharpe, 2010; Shotter and Tsoukas, 2014a, 2014b). *Phronesis* recognizes that exercising good judgment requires going beyond the employ-ment of decontextualized professional and tacit knowledge and is not a process made up of pre-identifiable components (Likierman, 2020). Exercising good judgment is envisioned as an ongoing practice of wisely relating and responding in the present moment within the unique emerging circumstances (Beckett and Hager, 2000) within which one is embodied and embed-ded. It recognizes that we are not separate from our emerging circumstances; we are *of* them. They influence us as much as we influence them, if not more (Crawford, 2015; Shotter, 2016).

As leaders are not concerned with understanding what good judgment *is*, but want to be able to exercise good judgment, I go on to articulate the first-person experience of exercising good judgment to shed light on its practice and, thus, what might be important to its development. Finally, based on my experience of attempting to facilitate the leadership development inside and outside the classroom, I will share activities that support and facilitate the development of the practice of exercising good judgment or practical wisdom. These are presented as an alternative to typical leadership development approaches that focus on the application of abstract knowledge (Ramsey, 2014) or routines of calculation and analysis that leave leaders unprepared for the dynamic and turbulent circumstance within which they increasingly find themselves (Van Buskirk et al., 2018).

EXERCISING GOOD JUDGMENT AS *PHRONESIS* OR PRACTICAL WISDOM

Aristotle believed that any fundamental social practice such as leadership demands making choices of what to do within concrete and unique circumstances, rather than through abstract deliberation (Aristotle, 2011). The exercise of good judgment demands *phronesis*, or practical wisdom, as we experience practical rather than theoretical challenges of how to fulfill the aim of a social practice. Practical wisdom depends "on our ability to *perceive* the situation, to have the appropriate *feelings* or desires about it, to *deliberate* about what [is] appropriate in these circumstances, and to *act*" (Schwartz and Sharpe, 2010, 5). It has to do with felt emotions and sensed bodily movements, as well as cognition (Shotter and Tsoukas, 2014a). This points to the fact that practical wisdom is an embodied and situated practice, not a purely cognitive and abstract activity. *Phronesis* is a way of being in which one draws on one's emotions and intuition, as well as reason and intellect, to explore, orient oneself, and respond within the particularities of the emerging situation in which one finds oneself to attempt to influence its trajectory in pursuit of the common good.

"*Phronesis* expresses the kind of person one *is* not the kind of knowledge one *has*" (Nonaka et al., 2014, 369). Thus, the exercise of practical wisdom is about exercising good judgment that draws on one's sense of self and values (Chia and Holt, 2009; Nonaka and Toyama, 2007), as well as a knowing-from-within one's emerging circumstances (Cunliffe and Eriksen, 2011; Shotter and Tsoukas, 2014b). When engaging in any social practice, acting wisely demands that one be guided by its proper aim or, as Aristotle called it, its *telos* (Aristotle, 2011). A good practitioner is motivated by the aim of one's practice and to do the right thing to achieve this aim. While a wise practitioner, as well as being good, is able to translate the aim of their practice into concrete action. Finally, determining what to do demands an understanding which one develops through experience (Shotter and Tsoukas, 2014b) that considers the particulars of the situation such as how others are thinking, feeling, and wanting; considers imagining the consequences of one's actions; and considers what is possible, not just ideal. Thus, practical wisdom requires skill, as well as a desire to achieve the proper aim of a practice (Schwartz and Sharpe, 2010).

As such, good judgment and practical wisdom are not taken to be concepts that reflect a person's mental state or a psychological trait. Nor are they achieved by developing certain rational, analytical, decontextualized, cognitive decision-making abilities (Nonaka and Takeuchi, 2011) or a decision-making process (Tichy and Bennis, 2007) that is a matter of making the best choice among a range of alternatives (Shotter and Tsoukas, 2014b). These approaches fail to take into consideration that we are embodied beings situated in unique emerging circumstances within which we must determine how to exercise good judgment (Shotter and Tsoukas, 2014a). Exercising good judgment requires that we engage our emotions and intuition, as well as our reason and intellect, and take into account the uniqueness of the emerging circumstances within which we find ourselves trying to fulfill our aim while acting consistently with our values.

FIRST-PERSON EXPERIENCE OF EXERCISING GOOD JUDGMENT

Practitioners are not concerned with *what* good judgment *is*. They want to be able to *exercise* good judgment within their experience of their day-to-day lives. As such, in this section, I will attempt to shed light on the emerging contours of our first-person experience of bewildering circumstances that disorient us in our everyday understandings, expectations, and assumptions, many of a pre-cognitive nature. Since our everyday understandings, expectations, and assumptions do not allow us to effectively go on, we are required to develop a wise course of action through the exploration of our unique emerging circumstances from within that will allow us to fulfill our aim while acting consistently with our values.

We become aware of circumstances that require the exercise of judgment by the arising of a felt bewilderment when we become disoriented and, at least at first, do not know our "way about" or how to go on (Shotter and Tsoukas, 2014a). Our embodied expectations and anticipations that usually effectively direct our attention to allow us to make sense of and spontaneously and effectively relate to the emerging circumstances within which we find ourselves, are inadequate to guide our actions to allow us to achieve our aim (Shotter, 2016; Shotter and Tsoukas, 2011). Such situations demand our explicit attention to determine how to effectively go on (Shotter and Tsoukas, 2014a). In such situations, we are not facing an intellectual problem to be cognitively, objectively, and analytically solved, as if from outside the circumstances within which we find ourselves. Rather, we are facing an orientational difficulty (Shotter, 2016) that has to do with how we relate ourselves as unique human beings to our emerging circumstances.

Much of our experience is taken for granted and unconscious but within which we possess a certain emotional attunement that communicates what matters to us and, thus, determines that to which we pay attention and how we respond within it. As such, our emotions can help us determine a wise line of action (Shotter and Tsoukas, 2014b). But we must not blindly respond based on our emotions. Exercising good judgment requires that we determine the appropriateness of our emotions about the situation for which we can draw on past experiences that possess similarities and differences to the present situation (Solomon, 2007). In doing so, we compare and contrast what it feels like within our present circumstances with what it has felt like in similar experiences in the past (Shotter and Tsoukas, 2014b). While drawing on our past experience, we also need to be present within the unfamiliar and indeterminant circumstance within which we find ourselves to explore its landscape in order to discern its salient features (Eriksen and Cooper, 2018; Ramsey, 2014) to create a hermeneutical whole (Shotter, 2016; Shotter and Tsoukas, 2014a, 2014b).

As part of our ongoing dialogue with our unfolding situation (Emirbayer and Mische, 1998), this requires taking some actions not to influence the situation but to have it "talk back" to us (Schön, 1983) to teach us to "see" it as *itself* in all its particular, uncategorizable detail

(Eriksen and Cooper, 2018; Shotter, 2016). This hermeneutical process of making sense of one's situation is about moving from one's initial "common sense" understanding of the situation to determine its relevant features and relationships among these features that influence the realization of one's aim to be able to reformulate a relational meaningful whole that allows one to determine how to effectively go on.

Shotter (2016) describes this imaginative exploration as follows:

> (1) We enter a new situation; (2) we are confused, bewildered, we don't know our way about; (3) however, as we "dwell in" it, as we "move around" within the confusion, a "something," an "it" begins to emerge; (4) it emerges in the "time contours" or "time shapes" that become apparent to us in the dynamic relations we can sense between our outgoing activities and their incoming results; (5) a *comparison* image or picture of what "it" is *like* comes to us, we find that we can express this "something" in terms of an image; (6) but not so fast, for we can find another, and another image, and yet another. (50)

Gradually, in this hermeneutical process, a particular meaningful whole composed of the connections among the existing internal relations begins to emerge, like achieving a visual fixation and focus. This allows us to think-with and develop action-guiding structures of anticipation to resolve on a wise course of action (Shotter, 2016). Exercising good judgment is about imagining possible steps forward, assessing their appropriateness, and narrowing in on a wise line of action.

> It involves moving around within a landscape of possibilities, and in so doing, being spontaneously responsive to the consequences of each move, and assessing which one (or combination of moves) seems best in resolving the initial tension aroused in one's initial confusion. Judgment is involved because we are operating here only in the realm of possibilities, not that of actualities that can be named and formalized. (Shotter and Tsoukas, 2014a, 388)

Although we must continue to keep an open mind, as hermeneutical inquiries are always open to further development, once we narrow in on a particular image of our circumstances, we can re-orient ourselves to engage in the deliberative thinking necessary to establish a wise line of action and then to act.

Practically, developing a knowing-from-within and possible lines of wise action afforded within one's emerging circumstance that allows the exercise of good judgment requires "going out and talking with people, getting many voices involved in dialogue, questioning, listening, coming to a kind of shared meaning" (Cunliffe and Eriksen, 2011, 1441). Rather than detached analytical thinking based on pre-existing meanings and structures, exercising good judgment is a dialogic-hermeneutical activity involving others and otherness in our surroundings (Cunliffe, 2016; Emirbayer and Mische, 1998) and the imaginative exploration with self, others, and the emerging situation and possible lines of wise action (Shotter and Tsoukas, 2014b).

In summary, the exercise of good judgment requires the development of an understanding within one's emerging circumstances, within which one is initially bewildered and does not know how to go on, that allows one to narrow in on a wise course of action to achieve one's aim while acting consistently with one's values and taking action. This requires that one go out and talk with people to explore the contours and landscape of one's emerging situation to develop a meaningful understanding. Exercising good judgment is not about acting *on* a situation to change it; it is about responding *within* a situation to influence its emergence towards the realization of one's aim. The exercise of good judgment does not take place at a singular moment in time (Tichy and Bennis, 2007) but is a process of engagement within one's emerging circumstances in which one gains a sense of the "invisible landscape of possibilities" (Shotter, 2016, 50). We never come to a final resolution, per se, as it is an open-ended process since our situation continuously emerges with future unpredictable twist and turns (Shotter and Tsoukas, 2014b).

FACILITATING THE ABILITY TO EXERCISE GOOD JUDGMENT

> How, then, are we to learn to be practically wise? There is no recipe, formula, or set of techniques. Skills are learned through experience, and so is the commitment to the aims of the practice … But not just any experience will do. Some experiences nurture and teach practical wisdom; others corrode it. (Schwartz and Sharpe, 2010, 8)

Based on my experience of attempting to facilitate leaders' development over the last 20 years in the classroom, military organizations, businesses, government, non-profits, and athletic departments, and the recognition that effective leading requires the exercise of good judgment (Cunliffe and Eriksen, 2011; Likierman, 2020; Nonaka and Takeuchi, 2011), I will put forth activities that contribute to the cultivation of leaders' *practice* of exercising good judgment (Antonacopoulou and Bento, 2010; Cunliffe and Wilson, 2017; Ramsey, 2014; Shotter, 2016). My approach can be contrasted with the common essentialist approach of business education of trying to *teach* the requisite knowledge, skills, and behaviors (Likierman, 2020; Mumford and Higgs, 2020; Tichy and Bennis, 2007) that are generalizable across individuals, contexts, and time and are believed to allow a person to exercise good judgment (Cunliffe and Wilson, 2017; Gosling, 2012; Schweiger et al., 2020; Shotter, 2016).

Cunliffe and Wilson (2017) describe facilitating the learning of leadership as creating "experiences within or outside the classroom where phronesis (or wisdom) may emerge" (532). It is about learning how to learn in situated experiential contexts (Antonacopoulou and Bento, 2010; Cunliffe and Wilson, 2017; Eriksen, 2012; Schwartz and Sharpe, 2010; Shotter and Tsoukas, 2014a). Such learning experiences date back to the Stoics (Case and Gosling, 2007). Below, I present a series of experiences and practices not as prescriptions for how to facilitate the learning of the ability to exercise good judgment but as "instructive experiences" (Shotter, 2016) that can contribute to leaders learning to exercise good judgment. What I share below are practices employed in my MBA Self-Leadership course.

I begin the semester by having students read my and Ann Cunliffe's "Relational Leadership" article (2011). During our first class we discuss the article, and I highlight that we realize our human and leadership potential by being practically wise – by developing the ability to continuously learn from our experience to realize our aim while acting consistently with our values within our emerging experiences. I also emphasize the notion of "relational integrity" that we introduce in the article. Exercising relational integrity is about being sensitive, attuned, and responsive to moments of difference, feeling responsible for working with those differences, and acting on them. It recognizes our inherent moral responsibility to act and relate to others in ethical ways.

I go on to introduce the notion that leadership is not about the application of theories or general concepts that apply to no particular situation, nor the employment of objective, rational, or abstract thinking. Rather it is about figuring out who to be and how to respond within the unique emerging circumstances within which we find ourselves embedded and embodied. We are not separate of our circumstances but of them. This requires a different way of knowing than is most often emphasized in business education. It requires a *knowing from within* one's emerging experience, rather than a *knowing about* our experience (Cunliffe and Eriksen, 2011; Eriksen and Cooper, 2018).

We talk about our basic human drive to survive and its social manifestations, many of which negatively impact our experience. We go on to discuss our human will to meaning and that we are endowed with consciousness that provides us the freedom to choose our response within our emerging circumstances to act on this meaning (Frankl, 2006). Students are assigned readings about these topics during the semester, as well as other readings that provide distinctions which students can employ to recognize salient features of their emerging circumstances that are important to effective leadership, including leaders' exercise of good judgment.

I share my belief that the essence of leadership is pursuing a purpose that transcends oneself to fulfill one's will to meaning. Students craft and share a story on the first day of class that articulates their purpose for taking the course. The story is to be based on an experience that motivated them to be here. I emphasize that the course is an elective, that they are making a choice by taking it and, as leaders, it is important to be conscious of and intentional about our choices. Ideally, as aspiring leaders, their choices should be consistent with their purpose.

In the first couple of weeks of classes, we collaboratively establish a shared purpose for the course and identify an enabling course context that consists of important ways of being, acting, and relating to one another to realize our shared purpose (Eriksen and Cooper, 2017). A number of times over the course of the semester, students and I self-reflexively and collectively explore how we are doing living out our shared purpose and enabling course context. At the end of the semester, through assignments that facilitate the exploration of their significant life experiences and relationships, students develop and share with one another a purpose-driven narrative that identifies their life purpose.

On a weekly basis, students engage in a structured assignment that facilitates their engagement in self-reflexivity (Eriksen, 2012; Eriksen and Cooper, 2018). Through the engagement of threshold concepts (Hibbert and Cunliffe, 2015; Yip and Raelin, 2011) in their assigned readings, students are prompted to identify and explore relevant lived experiences that they are asked to, writing in the first person, "articulate how you subjectively experienced the emerging experience from within. In other words, articulate what you were thinking, feeling/ emoting, and wanting during the experience and how these thoughts, feelings, emotions, and wants affected/determined your behavior, and how others responded to you within this unfolding experience." This helps them understand and become more aware of their subjective experience and how they are embodied and situated within their emerging circumstances in which they influence others and the emerging situation through their actions. In this process, they invariably begin to recognize the importance of this process and develop their ability to direct their attention to these aspects of their lived experience in the present moment of their day-to-day lives to positively influence their actions, relationships, and emerging circumstances to achieve their aims.

Students practice mindful meditation at the beginning of every class meeting and every day for one week as part of a course assignment and engage in seven additional mindfulness practice assignments over the course of the semester. These mindfulness practices develop students' ability to direct their attention to specific aspects of their emerging experience, within and outside their bodies (Gunaratana, 2011). There is empirical evidence supporting that mindfulness practices increase one's self-knowledge and choices (Carlson, 2013) which are necessary to exercise good judgment.

As acting consistently with one's values is an element of being practically wise (Chia and Holt, 2009; Nonaka and Toyama, 2007), students engage in a values-clarification exercise (Eriksen, 2009) and then in an assignment in which they practice living out their virtues, self-observation and reflexive questioning of their experience to learn from it and improve their practice during the following week (Eriksen et al., 2019).

Drawing from our shared purpose, the case-in-point methodology (Heifetz, 1994; Heifetz and Linsky, 2002) is employed throughout the semester to use the dynamics occurring within the classroom as a means to learn from our experiences of exercising or failing to exercise good judgment. Numerous unplanned opportunities arise to learn from the exercise of good judgment or its absence. Examples include a student consistently coming to class late, another student leaving the classroom for an extended period of time – multiple times during group work – with no "legitimate" reason, a student affirming another student after she was vulnerable, my shortness with a student because I became impatient with him, and when I was able catch myself from interacting with a student based on my frustration of him continuing to use social media in class after we had talked about its impact on his learning, as well as the learning of others, to be able to continue to act in a caring way rather than trying to control his behavior. We explore such experiences from within as they emerge among us and how our actions impact one another and our emerging circumstances to learn about exercising good judgment.

To practice exercising good judgment, students engage in a three-week assignment for which they asked to identify a relationship that they care about and that they wish was "better." They are then guided through a series of questions to explore how they perceive and experience its contours and landscape. This includes questions to help them identify what they have thought, felt, and wanted, as well as how they behaved and how they may be protecting themselves. Students identify how these aspects of their experience impacted their actions, the other person, and their emerging relationship. They are then asked to engage in empathetic thinking about the other person's experience of the relationship. Next, they are asked to reflexively question and challenge their present taken-for-granted ways of relating to the other person. After this, students are asked to identify the shared purpose or aim of the relationship, why they value the relationship, and who they would ideally like to be when relating with the other person and their imagined impact of this way of being. Students are then asked to explore lines of possible action that the relationship affords them and to narrow in on a wise course of action that they believe would be most likely to realize the relationship's aim. They then "experiment" with this wise line of action, learn from the experiment by being mindful when interacting with the other person and engaging in self-reflexivity a few times a week, and adjust their actions on an ongoing basis based on their developing knowing-from-within their emerging circumstances over a three-week period. At the end of the three weeks, they answer self-reflexive questions to capture their learning from this unique relationship.

In support of their personal development over the course of the semester, students receive training to engage in peer coaching (Eriksen et al., 2020) to support one another's development of their ability to learn from their experience and exercise good judgment within in-class and out-of-class experiential learning opportunities, including the above-mentioned assignments.

In addition, students provide one another developmental feedback on their coaching over the course of the semester.

Since exercise of good judgment demands vulnerability, provokes anxiety, and requires courage (Shotter and Tsoukas, 2014b; Srivastva and Cooperrider, 1998), I take students through presentations and experiential exercises that help them practice self-compassion and positively change their relationship with their anxiety. In addition, students explore their inner critic and engage in a saboteur assessment (Chamine, 2012) and an exercise in which they identify ways of thinking and feeling that were established to protect them when they were children but now impede their exercise of good judgment. They practice vulnerability by sharing their practical reflexivity posts with other students in discussion forums and other personal experiences during class discussions and in peer-coaching sessions.

In summary, the above activities are not presented as a formula for facilitating individuals' ability to exercise good judgment but in the hope that they will assist others in thinking through how they might facilitate aspiring leaders' ability to exercise good judgment.

CONCLUDING THOUGHTS

> Coming to judgment then, is not a matter simply of decision making – as if the possibilities from which we must choose can be clearly laid out before us – nor is it about providing "an interpretation" of an otherwise bewildering situation (for an uncountable number of interpretations is possible), but a matter of coming to, or resolving on, a clear perception of a circumstance and its performative meaning for us – what it calls upon us to do within it. (Shotter and Tsoukas, 2014a, 389–390)

Being a leader requires fulfilling a purpose. It requires caring enough about that purpose to be motivated to become practically wise to realize it. Wise leaders desire to realize their aim, *deliberate* about the appropriate actions they should take within their emerging circumstances to realize it, narrow in on a wise line of action, and *act*. Exercising good judgment is an ongoing process that requires practice and continuously learning from experience.

Rather than being simply about problem solving or decision-making events, leading is about exercising one's discretion to act wisely to influence the ongoing organizing among a group of individuals, within their emerging circumstances, towards fulfilling their shared purpose in ways consistent with their values. Although the exercise of good judgment can't be taught, we can create developmental activities that support and develop individuals' ability to act wisely. We can also facilitate and support individuals' development of their ability to exercise good judgment through the practice of trying to engage in wise action within their day-to-day lives.

I finish with the words of a past student's expression of the impact of engaging in the above outlined process in my MBA Self-Leadership course that I believe points to and is representative of students' developing their ability to exercise good judgment. It expresses the importance of who she wants to be, exercising discretion, learning from her experience, and taking actions to realize her purpose.

> I've also become better at listening to myself, of recognizing what I'm feeling and identifying why. I've been able to make life decisions – both small and significant – that would have once paralyzed me. I decided to leave my stable corporate job and join a non-profit that I cared for deeply. The work is demanding, meaningful and fulfilling. I participated in my first protest march. I stopped checking Instagram compulsively. I told someone how I really felt. I joined Crossfit. Then I left Crossfit when it no longer served me … Today, I am rooted in my purpose and act as my own guide.

REFERENCES

Alba, D., Conger, K., and Zhong, R. (2020, May 28). "Twitter adds warnings to Trump and White House tweets, fueling tensions." *New York Times*. https://www.nytimes.com/2020/05/29/technology/trump -twitter-minneapolis-george-floyd.html?action=click&module=Spotlight&pgtype=Homepage.

Anderson, L., Hibbert, P., Mason, K., and Rivers, C. (2018). "Management education in turbulent times." *Journal of Management Education*, *42*(4), 423–440.

Antonacopoulou, E. P., and Bento, R. F. (2010). "'Learning leadership' in practice." In J. Storey (Ed.), *Leadership and organization: Current issues and key trends*, 2nd edition, pp. 71–92. London: Routledge.

Aristotle. (2011). *Aristotle's Nicomachean ethics*. Translated by R. C. Bartlett and S. D. Collins. Chicago: University of Chicago Press.

Bass, B. M., and Bass, R. (2009). *The Bass handbook of leadership: Theory, research, and managerial applications*. New York: Simon & Schuster.

Beckett, D., and Hager, P. (2000). "Making judgments as the basis of workplace learning: Towards an epistemology of practice." *International Journal of Lifelong Education*, *19*(4), 300–311.

Campbell, H. (2020). "Vanquishing VUCA." *BizEd*, *19*(4), 38–41.

Carlson, E. N. (2013). "Overcoming barriers to self-knowledge: Mindfulness as a path to seeing yourself as you really are." *Perspectives on Psychological Science*, *8*(2), 173–186.

Case, P., and Gosling, J. (2007). "Wisdom of the moment: Pre-modern perspectives on organizational action." *Social Epistemology*, *21*(2), 87–111.

Chamine, S. (2012). *Positive intelligence: Why only 25% of team and individuals achieve their true potential and how you can achieve yours*. Austin, TX: Greenleaf Book Group Press.

Chia, R., and Holt, R. (2009). "Reflective judgment: Understanding entrepreneurship as ethical prac- tice." *Journal of Business Ethics*, *94*(3), 317–331.

Crawford, M. B. (2015). *The world beyond your head: On becoming an individual in an age of distrac- tion*. New York: Farrar, Straus and Giroux.

Cunliffe, A. (2002). "Reflexive dialogical practice in management learning." *Management Learning*, *33*(1), 35–61.

Cunliffe, A. (2016). "Twenty-one words that made a difference: Shifting paradigms." In T. Corcoran and J. Cromby (Eds.), *Joint action: Essays in honour of John Shotter*, pp. 173–190. New York: Routledge.

Cunliffe, A. L., and Eriksen, M. (2011). "Relational leadership." *Human Relations*, *64*(11), 1425–1449.

Cunliffe, A. L., and Wilson, J. (2017). "Can leadership be taught?" In J. Storey, J. Hartley, J. L. Denis, P. Hart, and D. Ulrich (Eds.), *The Routledge companion to leadership*, pp. 505–544. New York: Routledge.

Emirbayer, M., and Mische, A. (1998). "What is agency?" *American Journal of Sociology*, *103*(4), 962–1023.

Eriksen, M. (2009). "Authentic leadership: Practical reflexivity, self-awareness, and self-authorship." *Journal of Management Education*, *33*(6), 747–771.

Eriksen, M. (2012). "Facilitating authentic becoming." *Journal of Management Education*, *36*(5), 698–736.

Eriksen, M., Collins, S., Finocchio, B., and Oakley, J. (2020). "Developing students' coaching ability through peer coaching." *Journal of Management Education*, *44*(1), 9–38. https://doi.org/10.1177/ 1052562919858645.

Eriksen, M., and Cooper, K. (2017). "Shared-purpose process: Implications and possibilities for student learning, development, and self-transformation." *Journal of Management Education*, *41*(3), 385–414. https://doi.org/10.1177/1052562917689890.

Eriksen, M., and Cooper, K. (2018). "On developing responsible leaders." *Journal of Management Development*, *37*(6), 470–479.

Eriksen, M., Cooper, K., and Miccolis, A. (2019). "On becoming virtuous." *Journal of Management Education*, *43*(6), 630–650. https://doi.org/10.1177/1052562919866885.

Frankl, V. E. (2006). *Man's search for meaning*. Boston, MA: Beacon Press.

Gosling, J. (2012). "Management education as practice." In S. Kessler (Ed.), *Encyclopedia of manage- ment theory*, pp. 455–458. Thousand Oaks, CA: SAGE.

Gunaratana, B. H. (2011). *Mindfulness in plain English, 20th anniversary edition*, Boston, MA: Wisdom Publications.

Heifetz, R. A. (1994). *Leadership without easy answers*. Boston, MA: Harvard Business School Press.

Heifetz, R. A., and Linsky, M. (2002). *Leadership on the line: Staying alive through the dangers of leading*. Boston, MA: Harvard Business School Press.

Hibbert, P., and Cunliffe, A. (2015). "Responsible management: Engaging in moral reflexive practice through threshold concepts." *Journal of Business Ethics*, *127*, 177–188.

Likierman, A. (2020). "The elements of good judgment: How to improve your decision-making." *Harvard Business Review*, January–February, 103–111.

Mumford, M. D., and Higgs, C. A. (2020). "Leader thinking skills." In M. D. Mumford and C. A. Higgs (Eds.), *Leader thinking skills: Capacities for contemporary leadership*, pp. 1–13. New York: Routledge.

Nonaka, I., Chia, R., Holt, R., and Peltokorpi, V. (2014). "Wisdom, management and organization." *Management Learning*, *45*(4), 365–376.

Nonaka, I., and Takeuchi, H. (2011). "The wise leader." *Harvard Business Review*, May, 58–67.

Nonaka, I., and Toyama, R. (2007). "Strategic management as distributed practical wisdom (phronesis)." *Industrial Corporate Change*, *16*(3), 371–394.

Ramsey, C. (2014). "Management learning: A scholarship of practice centred on attention?" *Management Learning*, *45*(1), 6–20.

Rott, N. (2020, May 28). "Climate change and deforestation mean earth's trees are younger and shorter." National Public Radio. https://www.npr.org/2020/05/29/864151879/climate-change-and-deforestation-mean-earths-trees-are-younger-and-shorter.

Schwartz, B., and Sharpe, K. (2010). *Practical wisdom: The right way to do the right thing*. New York: Riverhead Books.

Schweiger, S., Müller, B., and Güttel, W. H. (2020). "Barriers to leadership development: Why is it so difficult to abandon the hero?" *Leadership*, *16*(4), 411–433. https://doi.org/10.1177/1742715020935742.

Schön, D. (1983). *The reflective practitioner*. London: Temple Smith.

Shotter, J. (2016). *Speaking actually: Towards a new "fluid" common-sense understanding of relational becoming*. Farnhill, UK: Everything is Connected Press.

Shotter, J., and Tsoukas, H. (2011). "Theory as therapy: Wittgensteinian reminders for reflective theorizing in organization and management theory." *Research in the Sociology of Organizations: Issue on Philosophy and Organizational Theory*, *32*, 311–342.

Shotter, J., and Tsoukas, H. (2014a). "Performing phronesis: On the way to engaged judgment." *Management Learning*, *45*(4), 377–396.

Shotter, J., and Tsoukas, H. (2014b). "In search of *phronesis*: Leadership and the art of judgment." *Academy of Management Learning and Education*, *13*(2), 224–243.

Solomon, R. C. (2007). *True to our feelings*. New York: Oxford University Press.

Srivastva, S., and Cooperrider, D. L. (1998). *Organizational wisdom and executive courage*. San Francisco, CA: The New Lexington Press.

Tichy, N. M., and Bennis, W. G. (2007). "Making judgment calls." *Harvard Business Review*, October, 94–102.

Van Buskirk, W., London, M., and Plump, C. (2018). "The poetic workspace." *Journal of Management Education*, *42*(3), 398–419.

Vickers, G. (1995). *The art of judgment: A study of policy making*. Thousand Oaks, CA: SAGE.

Yip, J., and Raelin, J. A. (2011). "Threshold concepts and modalities for teaching leadership practice." *Management Learning*, *43*(3), 333–354.

Yukl, G. (2011). "Contingency theories of effective leadership." In A. Bryman, D. Collinson, K. Grint, B. Jackson, and M. Uhl-Bien (Eds.), *The SAGE handbook of leadership*, pp. 286–298. London: SAGE.

15. Improving leader judgment through experiential learning

Anna B. Kayes and D. Christopher Kayes

INTRODUCTION

In this chapter, we show how experiential learning can serve as the basis for developing judgment in leaders. In particular, we focus on how discipline-specific as well as multidisciplinary knowledge can serve as the basis for learning judgment and leadership. Recent scholarly efforts have brought the study of judgment and leadership to the forefront of management studies (Shotter and Tsoukas, 2014a, 2014b). At the same time, there is growing interest in the practice of judgment, which is demonstrated in the trend among employers to hire students who can operate in more complex situations involving high levels of judgment (Johnson et al., 2005). Despite this interest, key questions remain.

We address two questions on how leaders learn judgment. First, how can leaders learn to exercise judgment in the face of ill-structured problems when formal academic and corporate training environments are designed around well-structured problems (King and Kitchener, 1994)? Second, how can leaders learn to move beyond memorization of discipline-specific concepts and learn to integrate their own experiences with abstract knowledge from multiple disciplines and the interests of various stakeholders and apply judgment in the context of real-world problems (Kolb, 1984; Mintzberg, 2004; Pfeffer and Fong, 2004; Trank and Rynes, 2003)?

To answer these questions, we begin with several considerations that serve as the basis for understanding the nature of learning judgment as experience-based processes associated with learning discipline-specific as well as multidisciplinary knowledge. We then enlist experiential learning theory and the learning cycle to propose a model for learning judgment in leadership that involves a four-phase process: (1) understanding context and problem structure; (2) acquiring knowledge from various sources including knowledge from different disciplines, evidence, experience, and expertise; (3) applying knowledge to solve problems; and (4) evaluating knowledge by establishing criteria for assessing the outcomes.

CONSIDERATIONS FOR LEARNING AND DEVELOPMENT OF JUDGMENT IN LEADERS

In this section, we outline four considerations for learning judgment and leadership. These considerations include understanding the role of problem structure, procedural knowledge, emotions, and use of evidence.

Context and Problem Structure

The first consideration is the structure of the problem that leaders are most likely to encounter when exercising judgment. In particular, we are concerned with the distinction between ill-structured and well-structured problems. Ill-structured problems are distinguished from well-structured problems based on four criteria. An ill-structured problem is defined as a problem where (1) there is low agreement on what constitutes success; (2) there is no clear path to solve the problem; (3) the problem itself is unclear; and (4) data are not objective, so interpreting data is necessary for reaching a judgment (Simon, 1973).

There is a divide between the structure of problems posed in formal settings, such as academic programs and training programs conducted in organizations, and the structure of problems faced by leaders when practicing judgment. Leaders are most likely to encounter ill-structured problems. Since a significant portion of leader development takes place in academic and training settings, and these settings tend to address well-structured problems, leaders may easily misunderstand the structure of the problem they are addressing. Further, ill-structured problems require different skills and approaches than do well-structured problems.

Several approaches can help leaders as they seek to form judgments in the face of ill-structured problems. One approach, reflective judgment, focuses on the epistemological assumptions that underlie judgment. Reflective judgment describes a multistage process that requires an understanding of the ambiguity and the subjectivity of knowledge associated with ill-structured problems. King and Kitchener (1994, 2004) described reflective judgment as a process founded on responding to ill-structured problems.

In the face of ill-structured problems, leadership requires formulating a response with clear knowledge and acceptance of ambiguity and the challenges that ambiguity creates. Judgment requires more complex thinking in the context of ill-structured problems. Solutions to ill-structured problems may require additional justification because there is less consensus on the "right" solution. Therefore, the need to build consensus, define problems, offer justification, and appeal to followers is greater in the face of ill-structured problems. In short, for leaders to learn how to exercise judgment, they not only need to be able to distinguish between ill- and well-structured problems, but also need to have the knowledge and skills associated with responding to ill-structured problems (Fernandes and Simon, 1999).

Approaches to addressing the nature of ill-structured problems have been developed in multiple disciplines. In information technology, Choi and Lee (2009) suggested that judgment should be viewed as a process and described three actions associated with learning to solve ill-structured problems: (1) asking questions, (2) seeking peer review and feedback, and (3) incorporating expert observation. Their model has been used to develop future educators, and they suggested that the defining elements that bring people to form a judgment include epistemological beliefs, metacognition, justification, and discipline-based knowledge. Choi and Lee (2009) outlined several evaluation criteria to assess judgment, including linking theory and evidence from the discipline, considering multiple perspectives, and providing and assessing clear reasoning. In occupational therapy, Mitchell (2013) provided a process-based approach for students to respond to ill-structured patient problems. In nursing education, Sarsfield (2014) emphasized the role of expertise as a form of knowledge important in solving ill-structured problems, pointing out that novices often present only superficial-level solutions to problems.

The distinction between ill- and well-structured problems is similar to the distinction between academic and practical problems. Sternberg (Sternberg et al., 2000; Sternberg and Hedlund, 2002), for example, described a divide between the structure of practical problems faced by leaders in organizations and the structure of academic problems faced by students in a classroom. For example, academic problems are well defined and formulated by others. In most academic situations, the necessary information for solving the problem is provided by the instructor, not the one who solves the problem (e.g., the leader in the role of learner), which results in a limited number of possible solutions. In contrast, the practical problems faced by leaders are ill-defined, unformulated, and require the leader to assess what additional information may be needed. Practical problems present leaders with a situation where there are multiple possible answers and multiple methods to resolve a problem.

In summary, problem structure is an important consideration for learning judgment in leadership. Two models that can help clarify this distinction are the ill-structured/well-structured distinction and the academic/practical distinction. Leaders need to be aware that developing judgment in practical settings requires a different set of processes and different types of solutions and need to focus on developing skills associated with solving ill-structured problems.

Procedural Knowledge

A second consideration for learning judgment comes from the literature on procedural knowledge. Procedural knowledge describes the types of knowledge needed to complete a task; such knowledge is stored as procedural memory and arises from experience (Willingham et al., 1989). In contrast, declarative knowledge, saved as declarative memory, is an assortment of facts. Many or most academic settings emphasize declarative knowledge (e.g., memorization of terms and concepts), but judgment requires moving beyond declarative knowledge acquisition to understanding the reasoning, consequences, and implications of actions. This is often difficult to achieve with the typical evaluation methods used in leadership development because they are discipline specific and related to the acquisition of specific knowledge (Brookfield, 2012). The exercise of judgment requires a much broader set of skills than is typically introduced in a standard management or leadership course.

Although the concepts rely on different underlying assumptions, procedural knowledge is similar to epistemic cognition (Greene et al., 2010), intuition (Klein, 2015), and practical intelligence (Sternberg et al., 2000). Each is associated with tacit or implicit knowledge, which is linked to learning through personal experience. Procedural knowledge is different from discipline-based knowledge because procedural knowledge mirrors the structure of the situation rather than the structure of codified knowledge (Groen and Patel, 1988). It is also helpful to acknowledge the literature on expertise, which is concerned with differences in the quality of decisions made by novices versus experts (Franklin, 2013). Experts hold a vast amount of discipline-specific knowledge as well as personal knowledge, and they can apply this knowledge in answering questions within their area of expertise.

Thus, the second consideration for learning judgment and leadership is to acknowledge that the type of learning and, therefore, the type of knowledge associated with learning is procedural knowledge and not strictly discipline-based, declarative knowledge. This means giving as much or more weight to experience as to declarative, discipline-based knowledge when learning judgment.

Emotions

A third consideration for learning judgment and leadership is associated with Shotter and Tsoukas's (2014a, 2014b) emphasis on emotions in judgment. They have reinvigorated interest in the role of emotions and intuition in judgment in management learning and education. Their postrationalist approach to judgment involves "sizing up a situation and the balancing of competing priorities." The postrationalist element emphasizes emotions, values, and moral agency. They argue that when analyzing judgment, the "language use, and, especially, the selective and integrative nature of perceptual processes, are far too easily ignored" (2014a, p. 224). Shotter and Tsoukas reaffirm a growing concern that leaders need to understand their own motives and the motives of others.

Emotions emphasize "the discretionary element" (Vickers, 1984, p. 244) of judgment by discerning the relevant contextual variables within a range of acceptable actions. This suggests that judgment must account for both the ambiguity of a situation and the need to present a clear path forward in light of the ambiguity. Understanding emotions, in summary, is important because they shed light on motives, play an important role in justification of judgment, and are a key element in interpretation of judgment, among other factors.

Use of Evidence

A fourth consideration is how leaders use evidence to justify their judgments. While learning procedural judgment reminds us of a type of on-the-job learning, evidence-based management highlights how research conclusions can help leaders in solving problems too. Evidence-based management describes the process by which practitioners utilize generalized knowledge to inform the unique context of an organization (Briner et al., 2009). Briner et al. (2009) described evidence-based management with five steps: (1) ask a question to understand the problem; (2) gather the right evidence to answer the question; (3) analyze the evidence; (4) apply the evidence; and (5) evaluate the decision (Jelley et al., 2012). Evidence-based management, like declarative knowledge, represents institutionally codified knowledge and is often used in classrooms as case studies (Gamble and Jelley, 2014) or even a type of textbook (Burke-Smalley, 2014). Evidence-based reasoning can be taught; in particular, it can be taught within the context of leadership and can be applied to respond to a variety of problems, including well-structured and ill-structured problems (Dietz et al., 2014). However, evidence-based knowledge is not the only form of knowledge necessary to learn judgment, especially when the problem structure is complex and context-specific information is required. Rather, it is important to consider a plurality of knowledge sources, including what is learned from experience, along with flexibility and openness to learning using multiple sources (Morrell and Learmonth, 2015).

The limits of evidence-based judgment are important to consider. Klein (1998) found that certain indicators that practitioners use to assess babies in neonatal care units were not found in the nursing and medical literature. The indicators were identified rather from the experience of nurses over time, what he called intuition (Klein, 2015). This implies that existing bodies of knowledge, primarily evidence-based learning from academic literature and discipline-based knowledge captured in textbooks, may be missing key concepts and indicators of making good judgments.

These four considerations form the basis of learning judgment and leadership. In the next section, we apply experiential learning theory and the learning cycle to describe how leaders learn judgment in various settings, including academic, formal training and on-the-job training.

AN EXPERIENTIAL LEARNING APPROACH TO JUDGMENT

Experiential learning provides the basis to address the four considerations of learning judgment described above. Experiential learning has several characteristics that support the kinds of learning necessary to develop judgment in leaders (Kayes and Kayes, 2021). First, it combines abstract (e.g., discipline-based) knowledge with personal (e.g., direct experience) knowledge. Second, experiential learning introduces an iterative process of learning judgment that facilitates responding to ill-structured problems. The experiential learning process helps developing leaders, as well as seasoned leaders, make connections between the problem they face and their own emotions, as well as the emotions of others. Finally, experiential learning helps leaders build procedural knowledge within and between disciplines. Thus, the model of experiential learning provides a strong basis for developing both declarative and procedural knowledge of leader judgment and can be applied in academic as well as practical settings (D. Kayes, 2007).

While experiential learning has been applied to judgment-related processes, notably problem-solving in general, we further develop the assumptions underlying experiential learning and the learning cycle to offer a detailed pedagogy of leadership judgment based on the learning cycle. The model describes a four-phase process that can aid in the design and implementation of a learning program based on the considerations listed above.

Experiential Learning as Learning Judgment

John Dewey's (1933, 1938) theory of learning from experience, which emphasizes learning as a process of practical problem-solving, provides a launching point for building an experiential learning approach to learning leader judgment. For Dewey and other pragmatists, learning is driven by engagement with problems; thus, experience with problems leads to learning. Memorization of terms and concepts alone supplies only an abstract understanding of a problem (Eriksen, 2007). Learning goes beyond abstract ideas and concepts to include an understanding of how these ideas and concepts could help solve the practical problems of everyday life.

A more contemporary view of Dewey's learning from experience can be found in Kolb's (1984) theory of experiential learning (Kolb and Kolb, 2005). Experiential learning describes a four-phase process of concrete experience, reflective observation, abstract conceptualization, and active experimentation. For Kolb, these four processes are associated with two overarching functions of learning—the gathering and the processing of knowledge—each involving tensions in choosing which learning procedure to use. For example, leaders are in constant flux in deciding if learning should occur through direct experience with a problem or through garnering abstract knowledge associated with the problem. The tensions between action and reflection impact how this knowledge is processed. The ultimate resolution of the tension occurs when a leader moves through all four modes of the learning cycle. In summary, Kolb's theory provides a concise summary of learning that integrates multiple learning processes. Because of this comprehensive approach (e.g., Fenwick, 2003; Jarvis, 1987, 2006), Kolb's model has been widely adopted across different areas of management education (e.g., Lewis and Grosser, 2012) and across multiple disciplines.

Experiential Learning as Judgment

From an experiential standpoint, exercising judgment occurs when a leader links direct experience with discipline-specific terms and concepts and engages this knowledge to guide action. The discipline-specific terms do have to be within a particular discipline but can come from a wider lexicon of concepts and ideas as well. Exercising judgment involves using experience to guide the application of this knowledge to specific cases or contexts. As a process of learning, judgment involves a fair degree of both inductive and deductive reasoning, as leaders learn to apply concepts in the context of specific organizational challenges. Over time, as leaders engage in the judgment process, evaluate and test their insights, and reengage new knowledge, the result is a new and better-developed skill.

This four-phase process of learning has also been linked to problem-solving in organizations (Kolb, 1984). For example, Carlsson et al. (1976) demonstrated how the learning model can be applied to innovation in research and development teams. Kolb's original model of problem-solving has seven processes within a cycle. Thus, problem-solving is seen not as a one-time effort, but as a process that is an iterative refinement of knowledge. By enlisting experiential learning, experience is interwoven with other forms of knowledge such as data, evidence (Burke-Smalley, 2014; Gamble and Jelley, 2014; Jelley et al., 2012), and expert opinion (Franklin, 2013; Groen and Patel, 1988; Klein, 1998; Sarsfield, 2014).

Here, the experiential learning serves as a cycle of learning judgment. This is important because learning judgment does not necessarily require stage optimization, where judgment is demonstrated only by climbing a predefined and progressive hierarchy (see King and Kitchener, 2004, for a discussion). Further, judgment can result from pursuing multiple judgment strategies simultaneously (see Siegler, 1996, for discussion), not just a single course of action. In this manner, the process of coming to a judgment is emphasized over the outcomes of the judgment (e.g., Kolb, 1984). From a process approach, the experiential learning model of judgment emphasizes four underlying values:

* Reviewing diverse perspectives and integrating and evaluating discipline-based knowledge, evidence, experience, and expert opinion;
* Responding to well- and ill-structured problems that require multiple evaluation criteria;
* Linking discipline-based knowledge to the situation that a leader faces;
* Evaluating responses by determining criteria.

The result is a four-phase process of judgment that corresponds to the four phases of the learning cycle, involving context, acquisition, application, and evaluation of knowledge (Figure 15.1).

Understanding the context. This process of learning requires defining and recognizing problems as either ill- or well-structured and determining the appropriate approach to take to

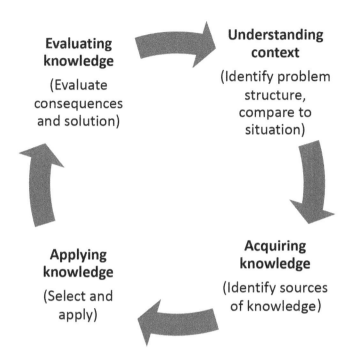

Figure 15.1   Integrated experiential model of learning and practicing judgment

solve the problem. This step involves gauging the complexity of the problem, understanding that there is lack of clear consensus as to the problem itself and its resolution, and accepting the perspectives of multiple stakeholders.

Acquiring knowledge. This process involves seeking out multiple sources of knowledge relevant to the problem. The types of knowledge acquired can include discipline-based knowledge, evidence, experience, and expert opinion. Critically evaluating one's own perspective, considering other perspectives (Wittmer and Fukami, 2017), and reframing one's initial individual perspective (A. Kayes, 2007) require attention. This involves planning and consideration of what knowledge is best to determine solutions (Brown, 1987).

Applying knowledge. This process involves taking knowledge and using it in pragmatic and useful ways (Dewey, 1933, 1938). Knowledge based on the discipline, evidence, experience, and expertise is integrated with experience in light of the particular situation faced by the leader.

Evaluating knowledge. This process emphasizes evaluating the response to the problem. For Tichy and Bennis (2007a, 2007b), when leaders come to a judgment, it is not an endpoint, but rather part of a larger process. The implementation of the judgment necessitates a review of the process to evaluate if the knowledge that was acted on was based on different sources and types and how the decision impacts various stakeholders. Justification involves comparing and reconciling differing understandings and solutions with well-reasoned arguments (Jonassen, 1997, 2004).

The processes of this model and their definitions are described in Table 15.1. Table 15.2 presents pedagogy-related issues such as learning goals, questions to guide learning, and examples. Further, Table 15.2 outlines the four processes associated with learning judgment and provides questions educators can employ to guide learning. We have found the model helps address two common problems in teaching judgment and leadership: when students jump to a solution without adequately understanding context, and when students are enamored with their solutions to problems without fully evaluating their solution. The examples provided in Table 15.2 give a sample of what students have written when responding to prompts using this framework.

The model serves as the basis for future development and application to leader development. Because the approach draws on the tools of experiential learning, it mirrors the reasoning associated with practice-based learning within the context and structure of management education (see Houde, 2007).

Widespread discussions around moving beyond declarative knowledge to deep knowledge and metacognition often fail to consider the developmental demands and cognitive challenges associated with these skills (see, e.g., Kegan, 1994; Kohlberg, 1969; Levinger, 1983; Vygotsky, 1978). The experiential learning approach that we present allows for capturing some of the desirable qualities of developmental learning theory, namely the higher-level thinking skills associated with considering multiple perspectives. At the same time, some of the more controversial aspects of developmental learning theory, such as its hierarchical nature and reliance on cognitive capacity, are eliminated.

The approach to judgment integrates diverse forms of knowledge into a single framework. Because an experiential learning-based approach focuses on the practical application of knowledge, it responds to calls for more applied and relevant management education without sacrificing discipline-based knowledge. The judgment model we present provides the basis for a course-embedded assessment of individual judgment and group knowledge as well as program-level examination for judgment within the specific context of management education (Moskal et al., 2008).

CONCLUSION

We began this chapter by posing questions about how to improve how leaders learn judgment within a learning environment. How do leaders learn judgment when they learn in one situation but make judgments in another? How can judgment be learned across disciplines? In response to these questions, we have argued for the importance of the continued development of an experiential learning agenda within the structure of academic and formal training settings. This approach to learning will provide emerging leaders, as well as seasoned leaders, a promising start to learning judgment. Exercising judgment to respond to a range of ill-structured and practical problems becomes a core skill to be learned and demonstrated. By providing a model for learning leadership judgment, we present the first step in a larger system of developing professional judgment in our students. This process model integrates and consolidates com-

Table 15.1   Processes of an integrated experiential model of learning and practicing judgment and related concepts

Judgment process	Definition	Related concepts	Representative sources
Understanding the context: Problem structure context	Understanding the context of the problem involves	Problem structure:	Fernandes and Simon, 1999; Jonassen, 1997, 2004; King and Kitchener, 1994; Kitchener, 1983; Simon, 1973; Sternberg and Hedlund, 2002; Sternberg et al., 2000
	• The ill-structured nature of the problem	• Academic and practical problems	
	• Complexity, the potential for multiple solutions or outcomes	• Ill-structured problems	
	• Perspectives that differ across stakeholders	• Complex problems	
Acquiring knowledge	Acquiring knowledge involves accessing	• Experiential learning	Briner et al., 2009; Brown, 1987; Dietz et al., 2014; Franklin, 2013; Gamble and Jelley, 2014; Greene et al., 2010; Kolb, 1984; Kolb and Kolb, 2005; Shotter and Tsoukas, 2014a, 2014b; Sternberg and Wagner, 1993; Sternberg et al., 2000; Willingham et al., 1989
• Theory	• Discipline-based knowledge	• Personal experience	
• Evidence	• Evidence	• Procedural knowledge	
• Experience	• Experience	• Epistemic cognition	
• Expert opinion	• Expert opinion	• Practical intelligence	
		• Evidence-based management	
		• Metacognition	
		• Expertise	

Judgment process	Definition	Related concepts	Representative sources
Applying knowledge to solve problem	Applying knowledge involves integrating discipline-based knowledge, evidence, experience, and expert opinion to make connections between course learning and workplace situations. This requires applying abstract concepts in pragmatic and useful ways.	• Practical problem-solving • Experiential learning • Action learning • Evidence-based management • Situational judgment	Brooks and Highhouse, 2006; Dewey, 1933, 1938; Franklin, 2013; Kolb, 1984; Salter and Highhouse, 2009; Schön, 1983
Evaluating knowledge • Applies multiple criteria for evaluation • Employs evidence, theory, experience, and expert opinion • Is reasonable and practical • Includes multiple and diverse perspectives	Evaluating the response to the problem includes applying criteria related to the reasonableness and practicality of suggested outcomes that consider multiple stakeholders and that are based on discipline-based knowledge, evidence, experience, and expert opinion.	• Multiple perspectives • Evaluation of argument • Justification • Reflective judgment	King and Kitchener, 1994; Kitchener, 1983; Tichy and Bennis, 2007a, 2007b

Table 15.2   *A pedagogy of leadership judgment using an integrated experiential model of learning and practicing judgment*

Process	Learning goals	Questions to guide learning	Examples of student demonstration of judgment process
Understanding the context	• Demonstrate the difference between ill-structured and well-structured problems. • Distinguish key variables. • Formulate the problem with regard to multiple stakeholders.	• Is the problem well-structured or ill-structured? What elements of the problem lead you to your conclusion? • What are the key variables that should be addressed? • How might different stakeholders see the problem?	• "The team needs to understand that we will never have perfect information about the acquisition. We cannot predict exact outcomes." • "We should acknowledge that politics will affect our decisions." • "Contextual criteria include any industry, market, or economic limitation" and "resources available." • "There is not enough time to realize all the complications." • "There are different approaches to decision-making, and different people … are inclined towards different approaches."
Acquiring knowledge	• Identify discipline-based knowledge. • Choose research evidence. • Recount personal experiences. • Summarize expert opinion.	• What specific course readings, theories, and concepts connect to this scenario? • What evidence from research explains what is occurring in this scenario? • What personal experience might help you assess and respond to the situation? • How would experts characterize this situation?	• "The Harvard Business Review article on culture would help establish a baseline …" • "We would consult an HR expert." • "Conduct a survey of employees or see if a study [on this topic] has been done." • "Look at prior companies who have faced this problem." • "I worked for a company that was similar to the one in the case … because employees were afraid. … It seemed to lead to lower productivity levels."

Process	Learning goals	Questions to guide learning	Examples of student demonstration of judgment process
Applying knowledge	• Connect discipline-based knowledge with evidence and experience. • Integrate expert application. • Plan a course of action and assess limitations and challenges that are faced during implementation.	• How do course concepts, evidence from research, or other sources influence your thinking about this problem? • How does your personal experience relate to the situation? • How would experts address this scenario? • What are alternative courses of action to take, and what are the limitations and challenges of each?	• Discipline-based knowledge: "There are four different approaches in the literature toward decision-making … rational, behavioral economic, organizational psychology, and naturalistic" (references course material). • Evidence: "An example of people's decision-making with stock markets—when people had positive emotions they were more likely to have confidence … and make risky decisions?" (cites specific study). • Experience: "Given that senior managers have dealt with similar situations in the past, know the target industry and market, and are used to making decisions under pressure and in a time-bound fashion, resorting to experience will be critical." "I faced a similar situation in my past work, and I chose to use the limited resources to make a decision." "Has the company been successful in previous risky acquisitions?" (emphasizes experience as important for decision criteria). • Expert opinion: "[Assigned reading] discusses the importance of … composition, communication, context, and control, and consensus." "One expert explained the need for 'red teams' in her critique of the fatal summit of Mt. Everest [and] would advise me of the potential pitfalls of pre-determined goals and temporary organization." "According to the decision shared by a decision-maker in the field …" (references readings and expert opinion).

Process	Learning goals	Questions to guide learning	Examples of student demonstration of judgment process
Evaluating knowledge	• Frame the solution in terms of the ill-structured nature of the problem. • Evaluate multiple stakeholder perspectives. • Anticipate a solution that is reasonable, practical, and based on discipline-based knowledge, evidence, experience, and expert opinion.	• Have you considered the ill-structured nature of the problem and assessed context-specific variables? • What different approaches to the problem might you take? Which is the best choice and why? • Have you offered clear criteria for evaluating your solution, and are those criteria practical, reasonable, and based on course concepts? • What would an expert say about your course of action?	• "Rational decision-making is appropriate in this context because an acquisition of a company involves a significant amount of due diligence, … financial research and modeling, involves a lot of data, determine probable outcomes." "Humans are inherently emotional and seldom have access to perfect information" (explains, justifies criteria). • "The main criteria is time … if we were told that we must make a decision in one day …. However, we can consider the outcomes and understand the politics embedded in the decision" (suggests limits of criteria). • "This is not a life or death situation" (establishes level of urgency). • "We don't have a time constraint; therefore we can systematically weigh all the options" (limitations of one approach). • "Maintaining dignity of the current culture" (establishes course-based criteria). • "There are many contextual criteria to consider individual traits and behaviors on the team, team dynamics, external environment and expectations, communication" (multiple criteria).

ponents of judgment, offering a comprehensive and yet practical way to engage leaders in the learning process.

REFERENCES

Briner, R. B., Denyer, D., and Rousseau, D. D. (2009). Evidence-based management: Concept clean-up time? *The Academy of Management Perspectives*, *23*(4), 19–32. https://doi.org/10.5465/amp.23.4.19.

Brookfield, S. D. (2012). *Teaching for critical thinking*. Jossey-Bass.

Brooks, M. E., and Highhouse, S. E. (2006). Can good judgment be measured? In J. A. Weekley and R. E. Ployhart (Eds.), *Situational judgment tests: Theory, measurement, and application* (pp. 39–55). Lawrence Erlbaum Associates.

Brown, A. L. (1987). Metacognition, executive control, self-regulation, and other more mysterious mechanisms. In F. E. Weinert and R. H. Kluwe (Eds.), *Metacognition, motivation, and understanding* (pp. 65–116). Lawrence Erlbaum Associates.

Burke-Smalley, L. A. (2014). Evidence-based management education. *Journal of Management Education*, *38*, 764–767. https://doi.org/10.1177/1052562914529418.

Carlsson, B., Keane, P., and Martin, J. B. (1976). R & D organizations as learning systems. *Sloan Management Review*, *17*, 1–15.

Choi, I., and Lee, K. (2009). Designing and implementing a case-based learning environment for enhancing ill-structured problem solving: Classroom management problems for prospective teachers. *Educational Technology Research and Development*, *57*(1), 99–129. https://doi.org/10.1007/s11423 -008-9089-2.

Dewey, J. (1933). *How we think: A restatement of the relations of reflective thinking to the educative process*. Heath.

Dewey, J. (1938). *Experience and education*. Collier.

Dietz, J., Antonakis, J., Hoffrage, U., Krings, F., Marewski, J. N., and Zehnder, C. (2014). Teaching evidence-based management with a focus on producing local evidence. *Academy of Management Learning and Education*, *13*, 397–414. https://doi.org/10.5465/amle.2013.0197.

Eriksen, M. (2007). Personal leadership conundrum. *Journal of Management Education*, *31*(2), 263–277. https://doi.org/10.1177/1052562906297142.

Fenwick, T. J. (2003). *Learning through experience: Troubling orthodoxies and intersecting questions*. Krieger.

Fernandes, R., and Simon, H. A. (1999). A study of how individuals solve complex and ill-structured problems. *Policy Sciences*, *32*, 225–245. https://doi.org/10.1023/A:1004668303848.

Franklin, C. L., II. (2013). Developing expertise in management decision-making. *Academy of Strategic Management Journal*, *12*(1), 21–37.

Gamble, E. N., and Jelley, R. B. (2014). The case for competition: Learning about evidence-based management through case competition. *Academy of Management Learning and Education*, *13*, 433–445. https://doi.org/10.5465/amle.2013.0187.

Greene, J. A., Torney-Purta, J., and Azevedo, R. (2010). Empirical evidence regarding relations among a model of epistemic and ontological cognition, academic performance, and educational level. *Journal of Educational Psychology*, *102*, 234–255. https://doi.org/10.1037/a0017998.

Groen, G. J., and Patel, V. L. (1988). The relationship between comprehension and reasoning in medical expertise. In M. T. H. Chi, R. Glaser, and M. Farr (Eds.), *The nature of expertise* (pp. 287–310). Lawrence Erlbaum Associates.

Houde, J. (2007). Analogically situated experiences: Creating insight through novel contexts. *Academy of Management Learning and Education*, *6*, 321–331. https://doi.org/10.5465/amle.2007.26361623.

Jarvis, P. (1987). *Adult learning in the social context*. Croom Helm.

Jarvis, P. (2006). *Toward a comprehensive theory of adult learning*. Routledge.

Jelley, R. B., Carroll, W. R., and Rousseau, D. M. (2012). Reflections on teaching evidence-based management. In D. M. Rousseau (Ed.), *The Oxford handbook of evidence-based management* (pp. 337–355). Oxford University Press.

Johnson, B. C., Manyika, J. M., and Yee, L. A. (2005, November). The next revolution in interactions. *McKinsey Quarterly*. http://www.mckinsey.com/business-functions/organization/our-insights/the-next-revolution-in-interactions.

Jonassen, D. H. (1997). Instructional design models for well-structured and ill-structured problem-solving learning outcomes. *Educational Technology Research and Development*, *45*, 65–94. https://doi.org/10.1007/BF02299613.

Jonassen, D. H. (2004). *Learning to solve problems: An instructional design guide*. Wiley.

Kayes, A. (2007). Power and experience: Emancipation through guided leadership narratives. In M. Reynolds and R. Vince (Eds.), *The handbook of experiential learning and management education* (pp. 363–375). Oxford University Press.

Kayes, D. C. (2007). Institutional barriers to experiential learning revisited. In M. Reynolds and R. Vince (Eds.), *The handbook of experiential learning and management education* (pp. 417–431). Oxford University Press.

Kayes, D., and Kayes, A. (2021). Experiential learning and education in management. In *Oxford research encyclopedia of business and management*. Oxford University Press. https://doi.org/10.1093/acrefore/9780190224851.013.294.

Kegan, R. (1994). *In over our heads: The mental demands of modern life*. Harvard University Press.

King, P. M., and Kitchener, K. S. (1994). *Developing reflective judgment: Understanding and promoting intellectual growth and critical thinking in adolescents and adults*. Jossey-Bass.

King, P. M., and Kitchener, K. S. (2004). Reflective judgment: Theory and research on the development of epistemic assumptions through adulthood. *Educational Psychologist*, *39*(10), 5–18. https://doi.org/10.1207/s15326985ep3901_2.

Kitchener, K. S. (1983). Cognition, metacognition, and epistemic cognition: A three-level model of cognitive processing. *Human Development*, *26*(4), 222–232. https://doi.org/10.1159/000272885.

Klein, G. (1998). *Sources of power: How people make decisions*. MIT Press.

Klein, G. (2015). A naturalistic decision making perspective on studying intuitive decision making. *Journal of Applied Research in Memory and Cognition*, *4*, 164–168. https://doi.org/10.1016/j.jarmac.2015.07.001.

Kohlberg, L. (1969). Stages and sequences: The cognitive-developmental approach to socialization. In D. A. Goslin (Ed.), *Handbook of socialization theory and research* (pp. 347–380). Rand McNally.

Kolb, A., and Kolb, D. (2005). Learning styles and learning spaces: Enhancing experiential learning in higher education. *Academy of Management Learning and Education*, *4*, 193–212. https://doi.org/10.5465/amle.2005.17268566.

Kolb, D. A. (1984). *Experiential learning: Experience as the source of learning and development*. Prentice Hall.

Levinger, G. (1983). Development and change. In H. H. Kelly, E. Berscheid, A. Christensen, J. H. Harvey, T. L. Huston, G. Levinger, E. McClintock, L. A. Peplau, and D. R. Peterson (Eds.), *Close relationships* (pp. 315–359). Freeman.

Lewis, A. C., and Grosser, M. (2012). The change game: An experiential exercise demonstrating barriers to change. *Journal of Management Education*, *36*(5), 669–697. https://doi.org/10.1177/1052562911435474.

Mintzberg, H. (2004). *Managers, not MBAs*. Pearson Education.

Mitchell, A. W. (2013). Teaching ill-structured problem solving using occupational therapy practice epistemology. *Occupational Therapy in Health Care*, *27*, 20–34. https://doi.org/10.3109/07380577.2012.757408.

Morrell, K., and Learmonth, M. (2015). Against evidence-based management, for management learning. *Academy of Management Learning and Education*, *14*, 520–533. https://doi.org/10.5465/amle.2014.0346.

Moskal, P., Ellis, T., and Keon, T. (2008). Summary of assessment in higher education and the management of student-learning data. *Academy of Management Learning and Education*, *7*, 269–278. https://doi.org/10.5465/amle.2008.32712624.

Pfeffer, J., and Fong, C. T. (2004). The business school "business": Some lessons from the US experience. *Journal of Management Studies*, *41*, 1501–1520. https://doi.org/10.1111/j.1467-6486.2004.00484.x.

Salter, N. P., and Highhouse, S. (2009). Assessing managers' common sense using situational judgment tests. *Management Decision, 47*, 392–398. https://doi.org/10.1108/00251740910946660.

Sarsfield, E. (2014). Differences between novices' and experts' solving ill-structured problems. *Public Health Nursing, 31*, 444–453. https://doi.org/10.1111/phn.12100.

Schön, D. A. (1983). *The reflective practitioner: How professionals think in action.* Basic Books.

Shotter, J., and Tsoukas, H. (2014a). In search of *phronesis*: Leadership and the art of judgment. *Academy of Management Learning and Education, 13*, 224–243. https://doi.org/10.5465/amle.2013.0201.

Shotter, J., and Tsoukas, H. (2014b). Performing *phronesis*: On the way to engaged judgment. *Management Learning, 45*(4), 377–396. https://doi.org/10.1177/1350507614541196.

Siegler, R. S. (1996). *Emerging minds: The process of change in children's thinking.* Oxford University Press. https://doi.org/10.1093/oso/9780195077872.001.0001.

Simon, H. (1973). The structure of ill-structured problems. *Artificial Intelligence, 4*, 181–201. https://doi .org/10.1016/0004-3702(73)90011-8.

Sternberg, R. J., Forsythe, G. B., Hedlund, J., Horvath, J. A., Wagner, R. K., and Williams, W. M. (2000). *Practical intelligence in everyday life.* Cambridge University Press.

Sternberg, R. J., and Hedlund, J. (2002). Practical intelligence, g, and work psychology. *Human Performance, 15*, 143–160. https://doi.org/10.1207/S15327043HUP1501&02_09.

Sternberg, R. J., and Wagner, R. K. (1993). The g-ocentric view of intelligence and job performance is wrong. *Current Directions in Psychological Science, 2*(1), 1–5.

Tichy, N. M., and Bennis, W. G. (2007a). *Judgment: How winning leaders make great calls.* Penguin.

Tichy, N. M., and Bennis, W. G. (2007b). Making judgment calls. The ultimate act of leadership. *Harvard Business Review, 85*(10), 94–102, 165.

Trank, C. Q., and Rynes, S. L. (2003). Who moved our cheese: Reclaiming professionalism in business education. *Academy of Management Learning and Education, 2*, 189–205. https://doi.org/10.5465/amle.2003.9901678.

Vickers, G. (1984). Judgment. In G. Vickers and The Open Systems Group (Eds.), *The Vickers papers* (pp. 230–245). Harper & Row.

Vygotsky, L. S. (1978). *Mind in society: The development of higher psychological processes.* Harvard University Press.

Willingham, D. B., Nissen, M. J., and Bullemer, P. (1989). On the development of procedural knowledge. *Journal of Experimental Psychology: Learning, Memory, and Cognition, 15*, 1047–1060. https://doi.org/10.1037/0278-7393.15.6.1047.

Wittmer, D. W., and Fukami, C. V. (2017). Educating future business leaders to be practically wise: Designing an MBA curriculum to strengthen good decision-making. In O. Gunnlaugson and W. Kupers (Eds.), *Wisdom learning: Perspectives on wising up in management education* (pp. 229–247). Routledge.

16. Conclusion: what the chapters tell us about leadership and judgment

Anna B. Kayes and D. Christopher Kayes

As editors, we have benefited immensely from working with this wonderful group of authors. While we hope this volume is seen as generative and not conclusive, we would like to offer a few key insights we gained from editing this volume. We hope that the contributions in this book can provide a range of possibilities that further our collective understanding of the relationship between judgment and leadership. We offer seven insights.

First, the *study of judgment spans a wide range of disciplines*. Rarely do these disciplines speak to one another. This volume showcases scholars who represent the multidisciplinary nature of judgment and leadership. Despite the breadth of this present multidisciplinary approach, there is still much to learn from fields that were not included. Examples of new insights in judgment and leadership can be found in information technology, occupational therapy, medical and nursing education, as well as other fields. In the study of leadership specifically, and in academics more generally, we often talk about multidisciplinary work but rarely have an opportunity to explore it. This volume serves as an example of how multidisciplinary work can be the first step in furthering a multidisciplinary model of the study of judgment specifically and leadership more generally.

Second, the book *clarifies the potential confusion between "making judgments about leadership" and exercising good judgment as a leader*. As a leadership process, judgment defines the processes by which leaders use knowledge, expertise, and experience in leadership practice. Judgment in leadership is about solving problems and taking actions that will have consequences for a group, organization, or society. At the same time, leaders need to be open to how judgments are interpreted and how followers justify the actions of leaders. We entered the project thinking there was a distinct line between judging and judgment, but we left thinking the line was thinner than when we started. In particular, Murugavel and Reiter-Palmon provide a way out of this limited thinking by suggesting that leaders judge and are judged. Leaders are judging when they make judgments, and these actions have consequences. Kornprobst shows that judgments are the basis of judgment as leaders seek to find justifications for ongoing events, some of which they have directly influenced and some of which they have not. Leaders are evaluators, exercising judgment about problems that have already presented themselves. They constantly revise their judgments. Justifications are always evolving.

Third, while judgment and leadership continue to be dominated by rationalist approaches, this book *provides the basis to consider the importance of both rationalist and intuitive approaches*. We advocate for an approach to judgment that balances these two aspects. In this book, the contributions overwhelmingly emphasize the qualitative, intuitive, and experience-based approaches to judgment. At the same time, one objective should be to develop leaders who learn to overcome bias and understand how heuristics influence judgments. Thus, the role of rationalist perspectives should not fall under a heading of "how can leaders be more rational" (e.g., using more probabilities to calculate their judgments). The role of rational approaches is to help us understand how patterns of bad judgment can be used to understand how leaders can form good judgments. Said another way, rational approaches may form the basis of a good judgment, but most leaders operate in a world of unspecified judgments. Sullivan provides a means to study this relationship as we consider the different brain functions associated with each approach. Leaders rely on data that are often neither generalizable nor predictable. Judgment lies somewhere beyond the narrow view of the rational mind. Sullivan provides us with a way forward, to understand the workings of the brain/body and its role in judgment in the context of complex systems.

Fourth, *judgment can serve as an integrating, higher-order construct associated with leadership that supersedes similar concepts such as critical thinking, problem-solving, and decision-making.* Although these terms are often used interchangeably, the term *judgment* captures what leaders do better than concepts such as decision-making, problem-solving, and critical thinking. Take each of these similar concepts in turn. Decision-making tends to focus on "rational" approaches embedded in probabilities and the quest for perfect information, but leaders work in more ambiguous worlds. Under most circumstances, leaders have neither the time nor the resources to compute probabilities when exercising judgment. Problem-solving, too, seems like a good candidate for describing what leaders do. Problem-solving tends to work like a puzzle, identifying all the pieces and making sure they fit, but leaders do not always have all the pieces. They need to make meaning when all the pieces are not objectively known. Problem-solving and judgment are interwoven concepts, as leaders form judgments when facing problems. Critical thinking may rely on cognitive aspects of leadership at the expense of emotions, affect, and experience. Decision-making, problem-solving, and critical thinking only tell part of the story of what leadership judgment is about.

Rather than rely on well-worn concepts such as these, it may be time for leadership studies to join other disciplines and embrace a dual-process approach to judgment that considers both known (explicit) and unknown (tacit) processes. The known-unknown mind works as two simultaneous processes. The notion of a known-unknown can be considered in different ways, but one approach to consider is that judgment involves a conscious and "preconscious" aspect. This means that building judgment in leaders requires making leaders aware of their unconscious decisions, including how they attend to self-interest in their judgments. Nguyen and Crossan explicitly state the need for dual-process thinking, but many or all of the authors hint at such an approach. For example, for Saunders, judgment is improved when leaders become more conscious of their guiding principles, which hints at a dual-process theory. For Pittarello and Foti, judgment is enhanced when leaders recognize their blind spots. Eriksen describes how this move to awareness (from preconscious to conscious) arises from a felt bewilderment. For Price, this sense of awareness can arise from something he calls "responsible-agent regret," an experience that happens "when [leaders] have good moral reasons to think that it can be separated from wrongdoing." Todd et al. hint at the idea of a dual process. Even though they emphasize cognitive skills, they conclude that leadership judgment must be conscious to be the most predictive of performance.

Fifth, *judgment is inseparable from the moral and ethical processes and outcomes associated with action.* Leaders need to be seen as moral agents, if not fallible ones. The very act of leadership is an inquiry into social, personal, organizational, and cultural standards. No form of judgment, nor the evaluation of judgments, can take place without at least some reference to ethical norms, ethics, and morality. At the same time that consequences must be considered, judgment entails that leaders remain attuned to the limits of their own judgment. Barriers and blind spots affect good judgment. When leaders lack awareness of their own guiding principles, their ability to make good judgments is limited. In the end, leaders may not be very good at judging the quality of their own actions.

Sixth, *judgment is a social process*. Judgment must be considered within a context and in step with the ultimate consequences the judgment has on followers. Followers play an important part in judgment. Leaders should show empathy towards followers by understanding their needs. Stated more emphatically, judgment cannot be exercised independently of followers, as leadership itself is an act defined by the consequences of a leader's actions on followers. Ang et al. place social understanding as a cornerstone of judgment. Leaders exercise judgment through their knowledge of culture and their understanding of differences.

Leaders do not make judgments in isolation. A leader's judgment is inseparable from the follower. The best judgments require knowledge of the positions of others and the consequences that those judgments have on others. Taken a step further, as O'Grady et al., Eriksen, and Gardiner & Fulfer imply, leaders do not form judgments as distant evaluators, but rather leaders are co-creators of solutions and problems.

Seventh, *judgment can be considered an ongoing enterprise that cannot exist without a full understanding of the process of learning from experience*. Judgment is developed over time through experience. Eriksen describes the development of judgment itself as a process of becoming. Nguyen and Crossan emphasize that character-based judgment is always cultivated. Judgment is never stable, but always changing and developing. Kornprobst offers a similar transitory interpretation of judgment, where judgment is expressed as the last relevant justification of an action that is subject to updating upon new information or pressures from followers. Kayes and Kayes provide a prescriptive approach to helping leaders learn to exercise judgment. Their interest is with developing leaders within the rules, traditions, and evidence of a specific discipline. But it is Saunders who may make the strongest point. Leaders learn to exercise judgment by taking note of the times when they do not know, the inevitable disjunctures that occur on the road to judgment.

But better judgment is not always the outcome of experience; sometimes leaders can learn negative things from experience. Hubris is one potential negative consequence that results when experience goes hand in hand with power. Power, as Sadler-Smith points out, can often lead to the wrong lessons. The wrong lessons are learned because leaders receive positive feedback in the form of early success or from others such as the media or admirers. The result is an overreliance on and overconfidence in a leader's own judgment. The overconfidence can be overcome by considering possibilities and how these can go wrong. Leadership itself may lead to excess, as leadership often requires "to push the boundaries of possibility," according to Sadler-Smith. Similarly, as Price points out, the very acceptance of leadership responsibilities may require leaders to assess the kinds of decisions they are going to make. Leaders are put in positions that require the acceptance of challenges and ill-structured situations that may require a different kind of judgment that those in less powerful positions will fail to understand.

Contempt for feedback from others further isolates leaders from the consequences of their decision. O'Grady et al. mention a similar caution. The heroic notion of leadership that so often preoccupies the perceptions of followers may result in more harm than good as leaders try to reinforce their own good judgments and justify their bad judgments with followers.

An integrating definition of leadership judgment remains elusive. However, a reading of judgment and leadership from a multidisciplinary perspective promises to enrich our understanding of the many different behaviors, thoughts, contexts, and mindsets that we associate with leadership. When we approach leadership as a multidimensional pursuit, we are likely to better grasp the intricacies of leadership and the complexities of making good judgments. Cultivating better judgment in our leaders seems a worthy and important pursuit in and of itself.

Index

abductive research epistemology 145
'aberrant behaviour' 105
Abulof, Uriel 68n4
accuracy
    of creative idea evaluations 79
    in decision making 94
    idea evaluation 80
'acquired personality change' 105
acquiring knowledge process 209
active procedural judgments 65, 68n5
Adair, J. E. 187
adult learning theory 8
"agent-regret" 122, 123
agreeableness 130
alternative cultural approaches 175
Amir, A. 139
amygdala 93
Andrews, F. M. 73
Anglo cultures 170, 171
Ang, Soon 7, 173, 221
ANS *see* autonomic nervous system (ANS)
Anscombe, G. E. M. 29
applying knowledge process 209
Ardelt, M. 187
Ardern, Jacinda 109
Arendt, H. 5, 51
    The Human Condition 49
    The Origins of Totalitarianism 49
Arendtian judgment
    biographical sketch 49
    examining leaders' messages around
        mask-wearing 55–6
    and leadership 50
    leadership, judgment, and practical wisdom
        51–2
    and leadership studies 56–8
    political judgments during covid-19
        pandemic 52–3
    testing 53–5
Aristotelian concept of practical wisdom 110
Aristotle 3, 29–30, 32, 35–6, 39–41, 51, 110–111,
    193–4
art-based methods of learning 40
Atwater, L. 172, 173

autonomic nervous system (ANS) 90, 94, 95
awareness or unawareness 134–5
Aycan, Z. 172

Bachmann, C. 110
Bailey, J. R. 173
balanced theory of wisdom 187
Basadur, M. 19, 75, 78
Bazerman, M. H. 131
behavioral cultural intelligence (CQ) 176–7
behavioral decision making 39
"behavioral ethics" 131, 134
behavioural decision theory 105
belief-bias reasoning 26
Benedek, M. 79
Bennis, W. G. 175, 209
Berg, J. M. 75
Bernstein, R. J. 68n2
Biden, Joe 109
Black Lives Matter 50
Blair, C. S. 80
Blair, Tony 62, 105
blind spots 139
    awareness or unawareness 134–5
    barriers and 221
    causes 137–8
    ethical 132
    frames and dishonesty 135–7
Blizinsky, K. D. 169
Blumer, H. 62
Bochner, S. 172
Bolsonaro, Jair 55, 109
Boltanski, L. 62
Borodai, Aleksandr 147
Bosnian Crisis 61, 64
Bottoms, Keisha Lance 55, 56
bounded-awareness approach 134
"bounded ethicality" 132
bounded rationality 31, 132
Bourdieu, P. 63
bracketed triggering events 150–151, 159
brain-first approach 6
brain-first interventions 94
"brain-first" system 96